The Birth of Missions in America

Other Books by the William Carey Library

General

Church Growth and Group Conversion by Donald A. McGavran $2.45p

Education of Missionaries' Children by D. Bruce Lockerbie $1.95p

Everything You Need to Know to Grow a Messianic Synagogue by Phillip E. Goble $2.45p

Growth and Life in the Local Church by H. Boone Porter $2.95p

Message and Mission: the Communication of the Christian Faith by Eugene Nida $3.95p

Reaching the Unreached: A Preliminary Strategy for World Evangelization by Edward Pentecost $5.95p

Verdict Theology in Missionary Theory by A. R. Tippett $4.95p

Area and Case Studies

Aspects of Pacific Ethnohistory by Alan R. Tippett $3.95p

The Baha'i Faith: Its History and Teachings by William Miller $8.95p

A Century of Growth: the Kachin Baptist Church of Burma by Herman Tegenfeldt $9.95c

Church Growth in Japan by Tetsunao Yamamori $4.95p

Circle of Harmony: A Case Study in Popular Japanese Buddhism with Implications for Christian Mission by Kenneth J. Dale $4.95p

A New Day in Madras by Amirtharaj Nelson $7.95p

People Movements in the Punjab by Margaret and Frederick Stock $8.95p

The Protestant Movement in Italy by Roger Hedlund $3.95p

Protestants in Modern Spain: the Struggle for Religious Pluralism by Dale G. Vought $3.45p

The Religious Dimension in Hispanic Los Angeles: A Protestant Case Study by Clifton Holland $9.95p

Solomon Islands Christianity: A Study in Growth and Obstruction by A. R. Tippett $5.95p

Taiwan: Mainline Versus Independent Church Growth by Allen J. Swanson $3.95p

Understanding Latin Americans by Eugene Nida $3.95p

Theological Education by Extension

Designing a Theological Education by Extension Program by Leslie D. Hill $2.95p

An Extension Seminary Primer by Ralph Covell and Peter Wagner $2.45p

Principles of Church Growth (programmed) by Weld and McGavran $4.95xp

Theological Education by Extension(revised edition) Ralph D. Winter $9.95p

The World Directory of Theological Education by Extension by Wayne C. Weld $5.95p

Writing for Theological Education by Extension by Lois McKinney $1.45xp

Applied Anthropology

Becoming Bilingual: A Guide to Language Learning by Donald Larson and William A. Smalley $5.95xp

Christopaganism or Indigenous Christianity? by Tetsunao Yamamori and Charles Taber $5.95p

Culture and Human Values: Writings of Jacob Loewen ed. by William A. Smalley $5.95p

Customs and Cultures: Anthropology for Christian Missions by Eugene A. Nida $3.95xp

God's Word in Man's Language by Eugene Nida $2.95p

Bibliography for Cross-Cultural Workers by A. R. Tippett $3.95p, $5.95c

Manual of Articulatory Phonetics by William Smalley $4.95xp

Readings in Missionary Anthropology ed. by William Smalley $4.95xp

The Birth of Missions in America

Charles L. Chaney

William Carey Library

533 HERMOSA STREET • SOUTH PASADENA, CALIF. 91030

In accord with some of the most recent thinking in the academic press, the William Carey Library is pleased to present
this scholarly book which has been prepared from an author-
edited and author-prepared camera-ready manuscript.

Library of Congress Cataloging in Publication Data

Chaney, Charles L   1934-
    The birth of missions in America.

    Bibliography: p.
    1. Missions, American. 2. Protestant churches--
Missions. I. Title.
BV2410.C48   266'.00973   75-26500
ISBN 0-87808-146-1

Published by the William Carey Library
533 Hermosa Street
South Pasadena, Calif. 91030
Telephone 213-799-4559

PRINTED IN THE UNITED STATES OF AMERICA

To First Baptist Church of Palatine, Illinois, who made years of study and research not only a possibility but also a joy, with whom I shared *koinonia* and *nikos* in Jesus Christ for a decade.

Contents

Abbreviations

ABS   American Bible Society

ABCFM   American Board of Commissioners for Foreign Missions

BMS   Particular Baptist Society for Propagating the Gospel Among the Heathen (Baptist Missionary Society)

CBM   *The Connecticut Evangelical Magazine*

GAMM   *The General Assembly's Missionary Magazine*

GAR   *Georgia Analytical Repository*

LMS   London Missionary Society

MBMM   *Massachusetts Baptist Missionary Magazine*

MBMS   Massachusetts Historical Society

MHSC   Massachusetts Historical Society, *Collections*

MMS   Massachusetts Missionary Society

MSC   Missionary Society of Connecticut

NMS   Northern Missionary Society

NYMM   *New York Missionary Magazine*

NYMS   New York Missionary Society

SPG   Society for the Propagation of the Gospel in Foreign Parts

SSPCK   Society in Scotland for Propagating Christian Knowledge

SPGNA   Society for Propagating the Gospel Among the Indians and Others in North America

UFMS   United Foreign Missionary Society

Foreword

The two earliest sources of the world mission of the Protestant churches are the evangelistic activities of the chaplains of the Dutch East Indies Company and the effort to evangelize the American Indians in the seventeenth and eighteenth centuries. It is the second which is the major font of Protestant mission action and which exerted the most influence in the calling of the Christians and churches of Great Britain, Europe and North America to their missionary obedience, and which provided principles and models for the great missionary movement of the nineteenth century.

European critics have often charged that American missions have been an expression of native activism, lacking theological foundation and motivation. This certainly was not true of the seventeenth and eighteenth century beginnings and of the initial stages of the overseas mission in the nineteenth century, although for eighty years after the passing of Henry Venn from the scene following the Civil War there was a period of some eighty years when theological thinking was meager. The root of the mission is in the eschatological orientation of the settlement of New England, and fresh theological thinking provided the dynamic for motivation, vocation and action during two hundred years.

Moreover, the myth is still current that Protestant missions began with William Carey and an assist by the London Missionary Society in the last decade of the eighteenth century, and that American missions are a reaction to the British movement and can be dated from the Haystack Prayer Meeting. Actually, a century and a half of American missionary action preceded that development and helped to inspire it.

Charles Chaney makes an important contribution to the understanding of the development of the American missionary movement from its beginning to the firm establishment of the overseas mission in the second decade of the nineteenth century. He demonstrates the unity and interaction of the Indian mission, the home mission, and the overseas mission in a single worldwide enterprise. Americans recognized a single world mission a century and a half before the concept was rediscovered in the middle of the twentieth century. He traces the continuing development of the underlying and motivating theology, and relates this to organization and action. Here is a wealth of knowledge, organized and interpreted for our illumination, which will give almost every reader an entirely new understanding of the mission of the American churches.

R. Pierce Beaver,
Professor emeritus of Missions,
The Divinity School of the
University of Chicago, and
Director of the Overseas
Ministries Study Center.

Preface

The radical expansion of Protestant missionary activity after 1790 is an integral part of what William H. McNeill has called "The Western Explosion," that period between the French and Russian Revolution.[1] However, Protestant missionary efforts were certainly no new thing on that October day, 1792, when the Baptist Missionary Society was organized in Kettering. A major section of William Carey's classical argument for English Baptists to undertake a mission, first read to a group of Baptist ministers in May, 1791, was founded upon his knowledge of eighteen centuries of missionary history and climaxed with a reference to the work of modern Protestants during the one hundred fifty years immediately prior.[2]

Sustained Protestant missionary activity began almost simultaneously on Formosa by the Dutch and in America by the English Colonists. The mission to the American Indians, however, has had most formal influence on the developing Protestant World Mission. Especially in America, the Puritan mission provided a significant contribution to the proliferation of missionary endeavor in the "Great Century." Missionary organization took place early in the life of the new nation. In 1787, the Society for Propagating the Gospel among the Indians and Others in North America was constituted. Beginning in 1796, with the New York Missionary Society and the Northern Missionary Society, a missionary progeny was spawned in the United States of America so prodigious and prolific that it has hardly slackened until this day.

About the time of the opening of the War of 1812, the American churches entered a new phase of involvement in the World Mission with the organization of the specifically overseas societies. The American churches' commitment to missionary expansion was briefly deterred through the Civil War Era, but, in 1886, the launching of the Student Volunteer Movement for Foreign Missions sent a new charge of missionary energy through the churches. Only the Great Depression and World War II significantly hampered American missionary involvement, and the War was hardly over when the third great wave of American missions began.[3]

The tidal wave of American missions that began in the 1790s was not without important theological foundations. The purpose of this book is to uncover the theological matrix from which American missionary organization came, to describe the erection of American missionary structures, and to delineate the missionary theology of the early National Period. William Bradford spoke more than he knew, in 1630, when at the beginning of his *History of Plimoth Plantation,* he wrote that one of the "weightie and solid reasons" that the Pilgrim Church removed to the "Northerne parts of Virginia" was

> a great hope, and inward zeall they had of laying some good
> foundation, or (at least to make some way thereunto) for the
> propagating, and advancing the gospell of the Kingdom of
> Christ in those remote parts of the world; yea, though they
> should be but even as steppingstones, unto others for the
> performing of so great a work.[4]

The research and writing of this book was done during the pursuit of a graduate degree at the University of Chicago. I wish to express my appreciation to R. Pierce Beaver who took a deep personal interest, not only in my work at the University, but also in my family, my ministry as a servant of Jesus Christ, and my career as a pastor, preacher and church planter. He was a constant encouragement to me throughout the graduate study and an indispensable guide during this research and writing project.

I also wish to acknowledge the contributions that Martin E. Marty and Jerald C. Brauer made to my understanding of the experience of the American churches. My entire experience with the Divinity School of the University of Chicago was a constant expansion of my intellectual horizons. I also recall with appreciation several long conversations with Joseph Haroutunian about the missionary dynamic in Calvinism and especially in New England Theology that have significantly shaped my own views.

I will not attempt to list all the libraries and library staffs that assisted me through this period of research. Harvey Arnold and his staff, however, at the Divinity School Library, showed extraordinary patience with me and have been incalculably helpful in every aspect of this study.

The book abounds with quotations. Spelling in these quotes has not been corrected, and only seldom, when original spelling could most easily be construed as a typographical error, has (sic) been used.

I need to say thank you to Gayle Balboa who typed the work in its dissertation form. That, of course, represented only part of the labor in completing this manuscript. My colleague, John Whitman, managing editor of *The Illinois Baptist,* made valuable suggestions that reduced the bulk and greatly improved the readability of this work. My friend, Tottie Carter, read most of the book twice, searching for technical errors. Elsie Taylor and Donna Kelly typed most of the revised copy. My secretary, Helen Williams, has been of invaluable assistance. A special word of appreciation goes to Carol McDowell who set the type for the final copy. She produced a beautiful copy in a short period of time. My family is always understanding. To all I am grateful.

At the suggestion of Ralph Winter, the address included in the *Appendix* has been added.

My parents, Mr. and Mrs. T. C. Chaney, have made the publication of this book possible. I am deeply grateful for their continuing interest in my work. Their contribution has been much more than monetary. Their character and commitment to Jesus Christ have marked my own life.

In reality, this book and the years spent in its research and preparation are an expression of my obedience to Jesus Christ as Lord. I testify with joy to his living presence in his Church. I pray that he may make this book useful, not only in helping to fill out our understanding of the past, but in helping to clarify and undergird the mission of the Church in the world today. Making disciples and multiplying churches is and always has been central to the Church's task. It will be till he comes.

Charles L. Chaney
Springfield, Illinois
July 4, 1975

FOOTNOTES TO PREFACE

1. William H. McNeill, *The Rise of the West* (A Mentor Book; New York: New American Library, 1965), first published Chicago Press, 1963, pp. 795-833.

2. William Carey, *An Enquiry into the Obligation of Christians to Use Means for the Conversion of the Heathen,* New facsimile ed. with intro. by Ernest A Payne (London: The Carey-Kingsgate Press Limited, 1961). Section II of this classic is entitled "Containing a short Review of former Undertakings for the Conversion of the Heathen." Sixteen pages deal with missions in the New Testament, five pages are given to that period from the second to the fifteenth century, and three pages deal with missions work in America from the time of Eliot to Kirkland and John Sergeant, Jr., of the Danes and Dutch in the East, of the Moravians, and the most recent activity of the Wesleyans in the West Indies.

3. See R. Pierce Beaver, *Ecumenical Beginnings in Protestant World Mission* (New York: Thomas Nelson and Son, 1962), pp. 294-295.

4. William Bradford, *History of Plymouth Plantation,* ed. with introduction by William T. Davis (New York: Charles Scribner's Sons, 1906), p. 46.

Part I
Missionary Matrix

The origin of missions is ultimately to be found in the heart of God. His are the redemptive purpose and plan. No thought of God is true to His revelation of Himself that does not rest on the fact that He "so loved the world that He gave His only begotten Son" that by believing in Him "the world should be saved through Him" . . . This attitude of God is eternal and is determinative in all His dealings with men. He is ever working towards the end that "they who have not heard" may have "the glad tidings preached unto them;" that "they who were no people may come to be a people of God's own possession."

W. O. Carver — 1909

The Spirit which impels to missionary labour is the Spirit of Christ. All missionary desire and effort proceed from the presence of Christ in the souls of His people. He is the only source. He also is the end. From Him proceeds the impulse; in Him it finds its fulfilment; to Him it moves. The Hope set before us in the manifestation of Christ, the unfolding of His nature, the demonstration of His power, the revelation of His glory. Our Hope is Jesus Christ.

Roland Allen — 1913

Introduction

*The work which we now have in hand will be as a pattern and
Copie before them. Great care lyeth upon me to set them right
at first, to lay a sure foundation for such a building, as I forsee
will be built upon it.*

John Eliot — 1651

No theme is more persistent in American missionary theology than
"wilderness and paradise." Studied against the backdrop of the vast continent, the Bible's frequent use of the wilderness/paradise figure stood in bold
relief. Alexander Whitaker, "apostle to Virginia," reminded his readers in 1613
that they were planting the Kingdom of God in the New World.[1] The Puritans came, voicing the same motif. The American experience underscored this
Biblical metaphor and made the concept more meaningful than it had been in
Western Europe.

New England churches, according to Puritan divines, were the garden of
God, planted in a howling wilderness. They were a beautiful pattern of the
Lord God's divine intention for the whole world. The Indian mission brought
more glorious prospects. Early success among the Indians brought hope, as
Thomas Mayhew wrote,

> that the Indians in this small beginning, being Gods husbandry,
> and Gods building, may be a fruitful glorious spreading Vine,
> builded together for an habitation of God through the Spirit.[2]

John Eliot's elaborate effort at civil and ecclesiastical organization
among the converted Indians expressed the passion that God would mold a
paradise out of the dry desert wilderness of Indian humanity.

In Pietism and the Evangelical Revival of the middle Eighteenth Century, the wilderness/paradise concept was interiorized. Cotton Mather led the
way. His early writings echoed the Puritan fathers. The American wilderness
was a place of refuge for the pure church and the battleground in the war
against Satan and for a more perfect Reformation. These thoughts recur
throughout his *Magnalia.* But Mather's later writings reflect the interiorization

3

of the wilderness concept. His concern was to discover healing waters for the "wilderness-condition" of the hearts of men.[3]

In the Great Awakening this latter idea is prominent, particularly in the theology of Jonathan Edwards. However, the American Revolution brought a new emphasis upon the conquest of the wilderness. David Avery expressed the opinion of many who preached up the Revolution that America, if God's conditions were met, would become

> IMMANUEL'S *land, a Mountain of Holiness, a Habitation of Righteousness! The* LORD'S *spiritual Empire of Love, Joy and Peace* will flourish gloriously in this *Western World!*

Samuel Sherwood had led the way to this new emphasis in the Revolutionary Era in his sermon, *The Church's Flight into the Wilderness.* He concluded that the twelfth chapter of *Revelation* contained "as full and absolute promise of this land, to the Christian Church as to the Jewish of the land of Canaan."[5] John Adams was encouraged when he heard the same type of sermon from George Duffield at the Pine Street Church of Philadelphia, in 1775. Adams wrote to his wife:

> His discourse was a kind of exposition of the Thirty-fifth chapter of Isaiah. America was the wilderness, and the solitary place, and he said it would be glad, 'rejoice and blossom as the rose.' . . . He applied the whole prophecy to this country. . . . He filled and swelled the bosom of every hearer.[6]

That this theme persisted can be readily illustrated. Sixty years later, on January 12, 1836, Z. N. Morrell, an itinerant Baptist preacher from Tennessee, stepped upon the foundation timbers of a new building in Nacogdoches, a thriving settlement in Mexico's eastern Texas, and delivered his first sermon in what was soon to become the new nation's twenty-eighth state. He followed his sermon with a long career of church planting in the Southwest. His text was identical to that of George Duffield, and his theme was essentially the same as that expressed two centuries before by Alexander Whitaker.[7]

The wilderness/paradise concept holds tremendous theological and eschatological implications. It also lends itself easily to historical and hortative considerations. It looks back to the divine plan of God, his purpose for the world, and forward to the end of all things, when he shall bring his plan to final consummation. It suggests the return of paradise, the hope for a new heaven and a new earth. The concept is useful in giving meaning to history. It explains the present age, i.e., wilderness, and it defines the goal sought after, i.e., paradise. In the hands of inspired men, it was most valuable in helping the Church understand its place and purpose in the world. Especially for the churches of Colonial America, scattered as they were along a narrow beach, and strung out before a vast, literal wilderness, this motif took on added significance. This theme will constitute a recurring refrain throughout the chapters that follow.

* * * * *

When the Maine Missionary Society met in Gorham on June 22, 1814, American missionary enthusiasm was white-hot. The American churches were galvanized by a "spirit of missions." Missionary societies had sprung up everywhere. Two national societies for "foreign missions were supporting missionaries in the Orient.[8] American nationalism was on the rise. The defeat of Napoleon, the restoration of the King of France, and the near end of the War of 1812 threw an eschatological shadow over the times. Speaking to the Maine Society, the Reverend Francis Brown (1784-1820) thought it exceedingly strange

> that Protestant Christians of the last two centuries did not make
> more vigorous and systematic efforts to evangelize the world.

Adequate means were available. Adversaries were not unconquerable. The Catholic missionaries even provided a provoking example. The conclusion was unavoidable: "Our fathers prayed, but they did not act."[9]

On May 11, 1670, Samuel Danforth (1626-1674) preached the election sermon in Boston. His sermon, entitled *A Brief Recognition of New England's Errand Into the Wilderness,* was an effort to restate the goals of the Great Migration and to stimulate attention to that "Errand."[10] Danforth had been reared by Thomas Shepard (1605-1649), an early propagandist of John Eliot's mission to the Indians. He had, since 1650, been the associate of Eliot in the church in Roxbury, and Eliot was his close friend. Danforth's son, Samuel, was currently learning the Indian language in preparation for becoming a missionary, and the Indian mission was then in its most flourishing state.[11] Yet when he spoke of New England's errand Danforth did not even mention the mission to the Indians or suggest that the preaching of the gospel among them might be a part of New England's *raison d'etre.* According to Danforth, they had come into those "wilde Woods and Deserts" for "the expectation of the pure and faithful Dispensation of the Gospel and Kingdome of God." [12]

These two widely separated sermons express and illustrate two current propositions of the historiography of American Christianity. The first is that the missionary motive in the colonial enterprise was, in the main, only alleged, a sort of "sanctimonious masquerade." [13] The corallary is that, in spite of these claims and as proof of their simulated character, there was in fact a general dearth of missionary activity.

Both propositions have been overstated. It was just the growth of the Indian mission during the years before King Phillip's War, and in the midst of the spiritual decline of the New England churches, that permitted it to go unmentioned in Danforth's sermon. The problem was with the *English* not the *Indian* churches. The Indian churches were held up as examples to chide the English churches in both old and New England. [14] Danforth, like Cotton

Mather, would have agreed that the Indian mission was one of New England's "peculiar Glories." [15] Francis Brown *may* have been ignorant of the missionary activity of early New England churches. However, it is more likely that his statement was prompted by his view of history. The "time" for missionary effort had not been right in the colonial era. He was sure, however, that during his own age the "time" for vigorous mission work had come. Neither example really supports these negative propositions. In fact, it is out of much speaking about missionary goals, the effort to set the whole colonial undertaking in the plan and providence of God, and the actual doing of mission work in America, that colonial mission thought developed.

The Colonial Period of American Christianity contributed much to the formation of the missionary character of the American churches in the National Period. The New England missionary efforts, especially, have had a marked influence in methodology, motivation and theology throughout the history of the Protestant World Mission. [16] These chapters will not be an effort, however, to explore all of those contributions. Nor will it be possible here to attempt a survey of all missionary activity in colonial America. The major contribution of colonial mission thought is twofold. The first, receiving its classical expression in the works of English and American Puritans, was structural. Reformed theology from all of its varied sources, molded the thought of those who returned to lead the English Church after the Marian Exile. Those ideas that related mission work to God and his Church, that dignified the mission by locating it in the fabric of history, and that provided missionary motive and zeal were generally common to all of English Protestantism in the Elizabethan period. [17] In reality, the English Reformation rather than distinctively Puritan thought provided the frame of colonial missionary theology. However, the ecclesiastical struggle that began with Elizabeth's settlement and intensified after the ascension of James I and the polarization of parties that culminated in the Civil Wars made Puritanism more particularly the reservoir of great missionary concepts. These ideas were more intensely held, more extensively expounded, and more dramatically put into practice by the Puritans. After 1630, these ideas received a distinctively Puritan emphasis in America.

The first chapter will, therefore, deal primarily with the missionary thought expressed in the writings of the American Puritans. Yet the bold lines that provided the framework of missionary theology were not the creation of the Puritans but were a part of the common heritage of the great portion of Elizabethan Protestantism with roots deep in the Continental Reformation.

The second major thrust of colonial mission thought arises out of the Great Awakening. While the first gives structure to missionary theology, the Great Awakening gives dynamic. The first chapter will deal with theological ribwork and be confined in the main to the generation of the Great Migration. The second will be devoted to the mission and the Great Awakening.

NOTES FOR INTRODUCTION

1. Alexander Whitaker, *Good Newes from Virginia,* in H. Shelton Smith, Robert T. Handy, and Lefferts A. Loetscher, eds., *American Christianity* (2 vols.; New York: Charles Scribner's Sons, 1960-63), I, 46.

2. Henry Whitfield, *The Light Appearing More and More towards the Perfect Day* (London: Printed by R. R. and E. M., 1651), Massachusetts Historical Society, *Collections,* Series three, IV, 1834, 118. Hereafter *MHSC.*

3. George H. Williarns has explored the significance of the wilderness/paradise theme in *Wilderness and Paradise in Christian Thought* (New York: Harper and Brothers, Publishers, 1962). He found it a theme with persistent ambiguity. *Wilderness* is often used by the same people to refer alternatively either to a state of bewilderment and struggle with the forces of evil or a place of refuge for God's elect people. *Paradise* or *garden* is that enclosure of God's people planted in the wilderness, which either maintains a precarious existence and is in constant danger of being invaded by the wilderness or is a sort of seed bed from which the wilderness can be made the garden of God. "The most interesting feature is the fact that generation after generation the Christian . . . applications of the garden and wilderness passages have with impressive frequency and inner cunning, despite all their variety and imprecision, faithfully reproduced the fascinatingly ambivalent character of the primordial desert motif in the Old Testament itself." p.7. The two sections of Williams' book trace the use of the theme through Christian history and relate it to the development of the concept of higher education in Western thought. Williams does, of necessity, speak of the relationship of this motif to the world mission of the Church. He could well have added a third section to this book to explore exclusively this significant area of relationship. A very recent study of this motif is found in Peter N. Carrol, *Puritanism and the Wilderness* (New York: Columbia University Press, 1969). This study emphasizes the influence of the literal wilderness on the intellectual development of the Puritans in the Seventeenth Century. Mark De Wolfe Howe, *The Garden and the Wilderness,* Phoenix Books (Chicago: University of Chicago Press, 1965) explores the theme in relationship to church and state in America.

4. David Avery, *The Lord is to be Praised for the Triumphs of His Power* (Norwich, Conn.: Printed by Green, 1778), pp. 45-46. Note the quote in Alan Heimert, *Religion and the American Mind* (Cambridge, Mass.: Harvard University Press, 1966), p. 396. Heimert has quoted this sentence so out of context that his reference is quite misleading. Avery (1746-1817), trained by Wheelock, served intermittently as missionary and pastor throughout his life.

5. Samuel Sherwood, *The Church's Flight into the Wilderness: An Address on the Times, Delivered on a Public Occasion, January 17, 1776* (New York: Printed by S. Louden, 1776), p. 23. Sherwood (1730-1783) was pastor at Northfield, Conn.

6. Quoted in Lefferts A. Leotscher, Maurice W. Armstrong, and Charles A. Anderson, eds., *The Presbyterian Enterprise* (Philadelphia: The Westminister Press, 1956), p. 85. Duffield (1732-1790) was an important Presbyterian leader and longtime pastor in Philadelphia.

7. Z. N. Morrell, *Flowers and Fruits in the Wilderness* (3rd ed. rev.; St. Louis: Commerical Printing Company, 1872), p. 48. Robert Baker, *The Blossoming Wilderness* (Waco, Texas: Word Books, 1970) continues the use of the theme in a recent history of Baptists in Texas.

8. The American Board of Commissioners for Foreign Missions was formed in 1810. The Baptists had just formed the General Missionary Convention of the Baptist Denomination in the United States of America for Foreign Mission, and Archibald Alexander and others were calling for the Presbyterians to form a "foreign" society. See Archibald Alexander, *A Missionary Sermon, Preached in the First Presbyterian Church in Philadelphia, on the Twenty-third of May, 1814* (Philadelphia: Printed by William Fry, 1814), p. 19.

9. Francis Brown, *A Sermon Delivered before the Maine Missionary Society at Their Annual Meeting*

in Gorham, June 22, 1814 (Hollowell, Me.: Printed by N. Cheever, 1814), pp. 12-13. The following year Brown was elected president of Dartmouth College, an institution which itself grew out of "vigourous and systematic" missionary effort.

10. Samuel Danforth, A Brief Recognition of New England's Errand Into the Wilderness; Made in the Audience of the General Assembly of the Massachusetts Colony, at Boston in N.E. on the 11th of the third Month, 1670, being the Day of Election There (Cambridge: Printed by S. G. and M. F., 1671), p. 5.

11. See Alden T. Vaughan, New England Frontier: Puritan and Indian, 1620-1675 (Boston: Little, Brown and Company, 1965), pp. 280-308.

12. Danforth, A Brief Recognition, p. 17.

13. This is Perry Miller's term for the judgment of modern historians. See "Religion and Society in the Early Literature of Virginia," in Errand into the Wilderness, Harper Torchbook (New York: Harper and Row, Publishers, 1964), p. 102. First published 1956.

14. The editors of one of the Eliot Tracts stated clearly: "Let these poor Indians stand up incentives to us. . . . This small Treatise is an Essay to that end, an Indian sermon, though you will not hear us, possibly when some rise from the dead you will hear them." Thomas Shepard, The Clear Sunshine of the Gospel (London: Printed by R. Cotes, 1648), p. 9.

15. Letter to Lt. Governor Drummer, March 29, 1724, in Diary of Cotton Mather (2 vols.; New York: Frederick Ungar Publishing Co., n.d.), II, 808.

16. Beaver, Ecumenical Beginnings, p. 18.

17. Several works have contributed to this view: R. Pierce Beaver, Church, State, and the American Indians (Saint Louis: Concordia Publishing House, 1966), pp. 5-13; Louis B. Wright, Religion and Empire (Chapel Hill: University of North Carolina Press, 1943); William Haller, The Rise of Puritanism, Harper Torchbook (New York: Harper and Brothers, Publishers, 1957) and Foxe's Book of Martyrs and the Elect Nation (London: J. Cope, 1963); M. M. Knappen, Tudor Puritanism (Chicago: University of Chicago Press, 1939): and Miller, Errand. The debt of the English Reformation to the leaders of the several centers of the Continental Reformation has been established. Puritan thought was significantly molded by the Rhinelanders and Zwinglians as well as John Calvin. Leonard Trinterud has shown conclusively that covenant theology has roots prior to Calvin's Institutes. See Leonard Trinterud, "The Origins of Puritanism," Church History, XX (March, 1951), 37-79.

Chapter 1

Puritan Ribwork

*We must not sit still and look for miracles; Up and be doing,
and the Lord will be with thee. Prayer and pains, through
faith in Christ Jesus will do anything.*

John Eliot — 1666

*I have laid together some Bones and Ribs preparatory at least
for such a work.*

John Eliot — 1666

The Puritans composed the bulk of the first massive transatlantic
movement — the Great Migration of 1630. From its most embryonic state,
they viewed this venture as a dual mission. While they were still on the high
seas, John Winthrop declared their twofold "errand into the wilderness." In
"A Modell of Christian Charity," he spoke primarily of the obvious. They
proposed, first, to set up a "due forme of Government both civill ecclesiasticall." But a second, larger and unspoken, undergirded the first:

> Winthrop and his colleagues believed . . . they could see in the
> pattern of history that their errand was not a mere scouting
> expedition: It was an essential maneuver in the drama of
> Christendom.[1]

Why did the Puritans see themselves as a people sent on a mission?
They believed they were participating in God's grand plot for the ages. What
pattern of thinking and what theological presuppositions caused them to consider an ocean-spanning errand? Was there something in their own self-image
in their understanding God, or their view of history that caused them to embark on such a mission?

The missionary leaders of the new American nation later saw themselves as partners with God in completing what God had purposed before the
foundation of the world. A basic theology in the Great Migration provided
the skeleton on which was formed the flesh-and-blood of missionary thought
and action in the early National Period.

The Puritan Doctrine of God

Many factors contributed to the actual launching of the Great Migra-

9

tion. A hurried perusal of John Winthrop's often revised "Reasons to be considered for iustifieinge the vndertakeres of the intended Plantation in New-England, and for incouringe such whose hartes God shall move to ioyne with them in it" reveals at least three different factors.[2] The socioeconomic situation is evident in three of Winthrop's reasons. Socioreligious dissatisfaction was the ground for two more of his statements. Predominantly religious sentiment made up the other considerations. John Cotton's reasons for removal in *God's Promise to His Plantation*[3] and John White's "Ground and Warrant" in *The Planters Plea*[4] include the same varied motivations.

The primary concern here is not with the particular immediate causes of this migration, but with the formal causes — influences, attitudes and broad concepts that gave structure to the great removal. This chapter seeks those ideas which fashioned this significant folk movement into an errand with purpose and goals.

Puritan religious commitment must be taken seriously.[5] To do otherwise is to fail to understand the Puritans. They were men with an authentic sense of God's terrible sovereignty. God was Wholly Other! They were men who submitted to his sovereign rule. This concept helped them fashion this great colonial adventure into a mission — an errand important in God's design in history.

By the time of John Eliot's death in 1690, quite a library of letters and other documents had been published concerning the mission to the Indians. The "Eliot Tracts," eleven in number, provide a wealth of material, with continuity in authorship and subject matter, that sets the mission in theological perspective. Written by many different men, both in England and America, these booklets also throw a great deal of light on a way of thinking that gave meaning to the entire colonial undertaking.

On November 11, 1646, when John Eliot and his friends went the second time to the "Wigwam of Waaubon" to preach to those Indians gathered there, he prefaced his sermon with these words:

> We are come to bring you good news from the great God
> Almighty maker of Heaven and Earth, and to tell you how
> evill and wicked men may come to bee good, so as while
> they live they may bee happy, and when they die they may
> go to God and live in Heaven.[6]

The Purpose and Providence of God

The Puritans were sure that the God who made the world also sustained the world and was bringing his creation to his own predetermined consummation. History was "the wisdom of Jehovah expressed in time."[7] The study of Biblical prophecy had convinced them that it was God's purpose to bring the whole world to submission to the Son of God. The Kingdom of Christ would include all nations. Through the mission to the Indians, it was said,

> the Kingdome of Christ is enlarged, and the promise made unto
> him in the Covenant between him and his Father accomplished,
> *his Dominion shall be from Sea to Sea, and from the floud unto
> the Worlds end,* therefore his design is upon all the Kingdomes
> of the Earth, that he may take possession of them for himselfe,
> they shall all *become the Kingdomes of the Lord and of his
> Christ.*[8]

The early success of the Indian missions under John Eliot and Thomas
Mayhew was construed as a sure sign that God was about to bring his "de-
signe" to completion.

In 1643, *New-Englands First Fruits,* published before the missionaries
began their work, reported that as the "ends of our Transplanting" in other
things had not been frustrated,

> so neither in the giving some light to these poore Indians, who
> have ever sate in hellish darknesse, adoring the Divell himself
> for their God.

The "first Fruits" God had gathered among them was "a sure pledge
of a greater *Harvest*" in God's own time.[9]

Thomas Shepard, commenting on Indian conversions, marvelled that
"such dry barren and long-accursed ground should yeeld" such sudden increase. He did not want to promise too much, and without a doubt the profession of many was but a "mere faint," yet he affirmed that

> God doth not usually send his Plough & Seedsman to a place but
> there is at least some little peece of good ground, . . . and me
> thinkes the Lord Jesus would never have made so fit a key for
> their locks, unless hee had intended to open some of their doores,
> and so to make way for his comming in.[10]

In 1647, John Eliot found two things that encouraged him to believe
that "the Lords time [had] come to make a preparative at least for the com-
ming of his grace, and Kingdome" among the Indians. First, God had "bowed"
their hearts. Second, he had raised a spirit of prayer in behalf of the Indians
in all the churches.[11]

The Indian mission was begun while the Civil War was raging in England. The conclusive victories of the New Model Army in 1649 and the reign
of the Saints that commenced soon after necessitated a new evaluation of the
purpose of the New England undertaking. The propagandists of the Indian
mission rose quickly to the occasion. It had been suggested that the experiment in New England was no longer needed. Laudian prelacy had been
crushed. The Church of England would now be purified and ordered accord-

ing to the primitive New Testament pattern. In 1648 the promoters in England explained how matters now stood.

> Indeed *a long time* it was before God let them see any *farther* end of their comming over, then to *preserve* their consciences, *cherish* their Graces, *provide* for their sustenance: But when *Providences* invited their return, he let them know it was for some farther Arrand that hee brought them thither, giving them some *bunches* of Grapes, some *clusters* of Figs in *earnest* of the prosperous *successe* of their endeavours upon those *poor out casts:* The *utmost* ends of the earth are *designed* and promised to be in time the possessions of Christ; And *hee sends his Ministers into every place where he himselfe intends to come,* and take possession. Where the *Ministry* is the *Harbinger* and goes before, Christ and *Grace* will certainly follow after. [12]

However, in 1648 the War was not over. The final overthrow and execution of Charles I was an earthshaking event, manifestly pregnant with eschatological implications. John Eliot saw it as a giant step toward the downfall of Antichrist. This latter event was one of the two most important episodes yet on the timetable of God. The other was the actual erection of the Kingdom of Christ in the world. According to Eliot, Cromwell had been raised up to begin the first and was in a strong position to help in the latter. [13] For Eliot, however, the erection of the Kingdom of Christ had actually begun in the work among the Indians. In characteristic frankness he wrote to Cromwell in 1652:

> Now as the design of Christ in these daies is double, namely, First, To overthrow Antichrist by the Wars of The Lamb; and Secondly, To raise up His own Kingdom in the room of all Earthly Powers. . . . And as the Lord hath raised and improved You, to accomplish (so far as the Work hath proceeded) the first part of His Design, so I trust the Lord will yet further improve You, to set upon the accomplishment of the second part of the design of Christ, not only by indeavoring to put Government in to the hands of Saints . . . but also by promoting Scripture Government and Laws, that so the Word of Christ might rule all. In which great Services . . . it will be some Comfort to Your heart to see the Kingdom of Christ rising up in these Western Parts of the World; and some confirmation it will be, that the Lords time is come to advance and spread His Blessed Kingdom, which shall (in his time) fill all the Earth: and some incouragement to your heart to prosecute that part of the Design of Christ, namely, That Christ might Reign. [14]

The death of Cromwell and the new decade brought a changed situation. Eliot was able to adjust even to the Restoration. God's design was still the same. The migration to New England was still an important errand in God's grand purpose. In 1663 Eliot dedicated his Algonquin New Testament to Charles II. He reminded the new king that, in the patent granted by James I, the evangelization of the Indians was declared to be the "principal aim." This second part, Eliot said, "Of our Errand hither, hath been attended with Endeavours and Blessing; many of the wilde *Indians* being taught . . . the doctrines of the Christian Religion."[15]

Through fair weather and foul the Puritan of the Great Migration was convinced that God was a God of purpose. He was assured that the Almighty would, in his own time and way, bring his plan to completion. The goal of God's work in the world he could comprehend. The Bible of Christ, a kingdom of righteousness, would be established throughout the earth. The time was not so clear. There were signs, however, for the discerning eye. The way that God would bring his plan to consummation was through his providence. The providence of God was his inscrutable method of achieving his own design for the ages.

Everything that happened, significant or insignificant, was in the providence of God. There was nothing, in fact, that was insignificant. Every event was consistent with God's ultimate purpose. The task of the Christian was to "learne to adore God in all his Providence, and wait to see his ends."[16]

Colonial success in New England constituted a series of "remarkable passages of his providence." The gathering of many churches among the English and the proclamation of the Gospel among the heathen especially were the consequence of God's providence.[17] They were "carried there by a sacred and sweet providence of Christ, to make known his name to those poor soules, who have been *Captives to Satan* these many ages."[18]

Looking back to the "Prelatical persecution" the Puritans were amazed how "Gods wisdome produceth glorious effects, from unlikely meanes." "The chasing away" of many ministers has "become a meane to spread the Gospel." The persecutors

> blew out their lights and they burn clearer: their silencing Ministers have opened their mouths so wide as to sound out his glorious praises to the uttermost parts of the earth. [19]

The persecution was compared to the crucifixion of Christ. It was a dastardly deed that God in his providence made an occasion of great blessing.

> God who doth often make mans *evill* of sin, serviceable to the *advancement* of the riches of his owne Grace . . . doth shew that hee had *mercifull* ends, in this their *malicious* purpose . . . so he suffer'd their way to be stopped up here, and their persons to be *banished* hence, that hee might open a passage for them in the Wildernesse, and make them *instruments* to draw soules to him, who had been so long *estranged* from him.
>   It was the end of the *adversary* to suppresse, but Gods to propagate the Gospel; theirs to smother and put out the light,

Gods to *communicate* and disperse it to the utmost corners of the Earth. [20]

The day by day events, the ups and downs of the Indian mission in particular, were interpreted as acts of God's providence and as steps on the way to the perfect fulfillment of his ultimate purpose. It was in the providence of God that rain harassed Eliot day and night on a missionary journey. It was God's providence that brought him home safe and well. The providential sickness of one member of the party searching for a suitable site for the first Indian town led them to the location of Natick. When expected tools did not arrive from England, it was God's providential message to trust him alone.[21] When the ship bringing the supplies did arrive and went aground along the coast, Eliot used it as an occasion to call the Indians to repentance. [22] The opposition of the Sachems to the establishment of the praying towns was God's loving means of keeping "the wicked off" from them, "who else might croud in among (them) and trouble (them). Eliot summed up this view of a purposeful and effective God:

> God is greatly to be adored in all his Providences, and hath
> evermore wise and holy ends to accomplish that which we
> are not aware of; and therefore although he may seem to
> crosse our ends with disappointments after all our pains and
> expectations, yet he hath farther and better thoughts then
> we can reach into, which will cause us to admire his love
> and wisdome, when we see them accomplished, and yet he
> is gracious to accept of our sincere labours for his name,
> though he disappoint them in our way, and frustrate our
> expectations in his way, and in his time, which shall finally
> appear to the eye of faith, a better way then ours, and a
> fitter time then ours; his wisdome is infinite.[23]

The Puritans came to America convinced that God not only gives being to the world "but, Himself the supreme intelligence, directs it to intelligible ends."[24] It is God's providence that orders everything to its right end. God's providence connects all the events in the long-range program man calls history.[25] Far from stifling effort, this understanding of God made the Puritans most active. It helped to form Eliot's philosophy of life:

> We must not sit still and look for miracles; Up, and be doing,
> and the Lord will be with thee. Prayer and pains, through faith
> in Christ Jesus will do any thing. [26]

It dictated involvement in God's design. It helped to fashion the migration to America into an errand. It located the New England saints in history.

The Wrath and Mercy of God

Another aspect of the Puritan doctrine of God that fashioned the mission structure of the Great Migration is the Puritan understanding of the wrath and mercy of God. The first reading of the Eliot Tracts impresses one with the severity of the wrath of the Puritan God against sin. A second reading notes the close association in presentation of both the wrath and mercy of God. A third reading brings an awareness of the tender mercy of God as a motivating factor in the entire mission.

Thomas Shepard's report of Eliot's first visit to preach in Indian language illustrates the Puritan message:

> For about an houre and a quarter the Sermon continued . . .
> through all the principall matter of religion, beginning first with
> a repetition of the ten Commandments, and a briefe explication
> of them, then shewing the curse and dreadful wrath of God
> against all those who brake them, or any one of them . . . and
> so applyed it unto the condition of the *Indians* present, with
> much sweet affection; and then preached Jesus Christ to them
> the onely meanes of recovery from sinne and wrath and eternall
> death, and what Christ was, and whither he was now gone, and
> how hee will one day come againe to judge the world in flaming
> fire; and of the blessed estate of all those that by faith believe
> in Christ, and know him feelingly: he spake to them also . . .
> about the joyes of heaven, and the terrours and horrours of
> wicked men in hell, perswading them to repentance for severall
> sins which they live in, and many things of like nature; not med-
> ling with any matters more difficult.

The Puritans offered no quarter in their attack on sin. Eliot's second sermon began at the same point:

> hee began first to set forth God unto them . . . and then set
> forth before them what his will was, and what hee required
> of all men even of the Indians themselves, in the ten com-
> mandments, and then told them the dreadfull torment and
> punishment of all such as breake any one of those holy com-
> mandments, . . . yet notwithstanding hee had sent Jesus Christ
> to die for their sinnes and to pacifie God by his sufferings in
> their stead and roome. [27]

There was a kind of logic that was used in presenting the Gospel of Jesus Christ to anyone, English or "wilde Indian." It was outlined in detail in one of the later tracts. "Heto whom service is due, should direct and prescribe the way whereby he will be served." [28] The way that the Almighty shall be served has been revealed in the Ten Commandments. Failing to meet God's requirement, men are sinners and come under the just condemnation of God's wrath. The published confessions of the Indians mirror the same concern. Totherswamp, one of the rulers of a hundred, testified:

> after I came to learn what sin was, by the Commandments of
> God, and then I saw all by sins, . . . then my heart feared greatly,

because God was angry for all my sins; . . . I see I deserve not
pardon . . . I can do no good, for I am like the Devil, nothing
but evil thoughts, and words, and works. I have lost all likeness
to God, and goodness, and therefore everyday I sin against God,
and I deserve death and damnation.[29]

The Puritans were very "painful" to deal with the matter of sin and
wrath. But they were just as faithful to present the mercy of God with much
care and "sweet affection." One of the first questions that Eliot directed to the
Indians was, "Doe you beleeve . . . that God is *musquantum, i.e.,* very angry for
the least sinne in your thoughts, or words, or workes?" When they answered
"Yes," Shepard explained:

hereupon wee set forth the terrour of God against sinners, and
mercy of God to the penitent, and to such as sought to know
Jesus Christ, and that as sinners should bee after death, *Che-
chainuppan, i.e.,* tormented alive, (for wee know no other word
in the tongue to expresse extreame torture by) so beleevers
should after death *Wowein wike Jehovah,* i.e., live in all blisse
with Jehovah the blessed God. [30]

On every occasion in the Eliot Tracts when the wrath of God on sin
and the sinner is discussed with the Indians, the great mercy of God in Jesus
Christ is also presented. Thus, Totherswamp would go on immediately in his
confession to add:

but Christ hath done for us all righteousness, and died for us
because of our sins, and Christ teacheth us, That if we cast
away our sins, and trust in Christ, then God will pardon all
our sins; . . . I can do no righteousness, but Christ hath done
it for me; this I beleeve, and therefore I do hope for pardon.

Another Indian confessor expressed the approach of the missionaries
best, however, when he began: "God in heaven is merciful, and I am sinful."[31]

In light of their views of the wrath and mercy of God, their insistence
that man must know God's mercy "feelingly," and the tenderness with which
they dealt with those Indians who came confessing their sin and guilt, the assertions of the missionaries that they were bringing God's mercy to "the ruines
of Mankind" takes on new meaning. When an old man asked if he were too old
for repentance, the missionaries were "affected . . . with compassion." Tenderly
the parable of the men hired at the eleventh hour was explained and the fa-
therly love and mercy of God illustrated. Then they told him that

now was the day of God risen upon them, and that now the
Lord was calling of them to repentance, and that he had sent
us for that end to preach repentance for the remission of sins,
and that therefore they might bee sure to finde favour though
they had lived many yeares in sinne.[32]

The Glory of God

The glory of God has been called the "taproot" of the mission of the Church.[33] God's glory was surely the most potent motive to missionary action in the first two centuries of the Protestant World Mission. When the Puritan of the Great Migration was at his best, God's glory was his all-consuming passion. The Puritan concept of the glory of God gathers up what has been said about God's sovereign purpose and great mercy and gives further understanding of the God who sent them to New England.

The glory of God is not one of God's attributes like "Wisedome, Holinesse, . . . Righteousnesse . . . Infinitenesse and Eternity.[34] The glory of God is the honor that is given to God by men or angels because of God's wisdom and power or his righteousness and grace. When something is brought to pass that magnifies God's omniscience or omnipotence or his holiness and love, that event brings glory to God. Fallen man is ignorant of who God is and how he is to be served. He worships the creature instead of the creator. Whenever anything happens that reveals God in all his power and grace, that stops the mouths of men, and exalts God for what he is and for what he does, that *thing* glorifies God. Since mankind, because of sin, is no longer aware of the glorious person of God, a part of the consequences of God's design for the ages is to recover that lost glory. So it was of great comfort and encouragement to John Eliot that the Scripture promised *"That all Languages shall see his Glory, and that all Nations and Kingdoms shall become the Kingdoms of the Lord Jesus."*[35] Thomas Shepard claimed no skill in prophesies, but he asserted:

> this is certain, God is at work among these [Indians] ; and it is not usual that the Sun is set as soon as it begins to rise, nor for the Lord Jesus to lose an inch of ground in the recovering times of his Churches peace and his own eclipsed and forgotten glory, . . . until hee hath won the whole field, and driven the Prince of darknesse out of it, who is but a bold usurper of the Lord Jesus inheritance, to whom are given the utmost ends of the earth.[36]

The vastness of the task, the extremity of the circumstances, or the meagerness of means but redounded to the greater glory of God. "I.D.," in his improvement on the letters from the missionaries in 1649, counselled:

> take heed of dispising the *day of small things.* It being Gods way to lay most glorious workes upon little and dispicable foundations: and to advance the Treasurey of the Gospel in earthen vessels, even to the ends of the Earth.[37]

John Eliot observed that

> the Lord delighteth to appear himself in the work, and will have us content our selves with little, low, poor things, that all the power and praise may be given to his great name.[38]

And William Leverich, discussing his own limited talents, said,

> I am resolved to bable to them as I may, considering that out
> of the mouths of babes God ordaines praise. . . . the beginnings
> of Gods great works are often in great obscurity, where he ap-
> points the end to be glorious.[39]

It is in events, the stuff of history, that the glory of God is seen. The
defeat of a great army, the sudden destruction of the profligate, the transformation of character in the conversion of a sinner, and the turning of a heathen
people to God are things in which the glory of God can be manifested, for
these things can be attributed only, or primarily, to the very work of God himself. Only the great power, wisdom or love of God can accomplish these things.

The final and complete triumph of Christ over all the nation, the planting of churches that will sing God's praises in every tongue, the kingdom of
righteousness that will ensue when God's mercy has pardoned men for Jesus
sake, these events can be brought to pass only by the power and grace of God.
They are, therefore, more particularly God's work and bring great glory to
him. The successes among the Indians in New England were thus seen as "the
visitation of the *most High* upon the *saddest* spectacles of degeneracy upon
earth." That the gospel was received by these people brought glory to God.

> The *distance* of place, . . . will be no lessening of the mercy, nor
> of our *thankefullnesse,* That *Christ* is glorified, that the *Gospel*
> doth any where find *footing;* and successe is a *mercy* as well worth
> the praise of the *Saints* on Earth, as the joy of the Angels in
> heaven.[40]

The mission to the Indians was commended again and again for support because it was a work "so much conducing to the glory of God."[41]

God is glorified when the Kingdom of God is advanced and the grace
of God is offered and received. This is just what God in his providence was
doing in the Great Migration and in the Indian mission. Edward Winslow insisted that to call the Indians to the "saving knowledge of Jesus Christ" was
"to advance the glory of God."[42] Richard Mather explained that the conversion of the Indians was a "thing wherein the Glory of God, and of Jesus
Christ" was not a little concerned. If a large nation honors a king,

> it must needs be the Honor of Christ Jesus the King of Sion
> when multitudes of People do submit unto Him as their King.[43]

Those human efforts, inspired by God's Spirit, and according to God's
plan, which bring about the advancement of the Kingdom of Christ or which
become means by which God's mercy is offered to mankind are then "glorious
workes." Redeemed man can enter into this work. "Lend us," some one wrote
from New England in 1643,

> we beseech you (all that love *Zion*) your prayers and helpe in
> heaven and earth for the furtherance of this great and glorious
> worke in our hands; great works need many hands, many prayers,

many teares. [44]

Thus the Puritan doctrine of God, a God of purpose and power, a God of mercy and grace, who was pleased to use his people as instruments of his glory, helped to fashion the Great Migration as a mission.

Puritan Anthropology

Before proceeding to the Puritan view of the Church and the goal of history, it will be worth while to digress briefly to examine some aspects of Puritan anthropology. The Puritan view of man did not make a direct contribution to shaping the Great Migration into God's errand. Rather, their understanding of man was a pervasive presupposition undergirding the entire enterprise. Their doctrine of man grows out of and is concommitant with their doctrine of God. Certain aspects of it are important facets of the developing missionary theology.

Children of Wrath

The sin of Adam, in the Puritan view, worked terrible and devastating consequences in the constitution of man. The Bible clearly demonstrated, so Thomas Shepard asserted, that God "made all mankind at first in a most glorious and happy estate, like unto himself." Fashioned in God's image, it was man's "perfection of holiness, resembling God's admirable holiness" that distinguished him from all of God's other creatures. In particular, God's image could be traced in man's understanding, affections, will and life. Adam's perfect understanding enabled him to see God in all of his infinite glory. With pure affections, he loved God more than himself or the world.

> As iron put into the fire seems to be nothing but fire, so Adam,
> being beloved of God, was turned into a lump of love, to love
> God again.

Adam, before the fall, willed nothing but good. God's will was his will. The image of God appeared in Adam's life because before his sin, he lived exactly as God would have lived had he assumed man's nature. Shepard put it succinctly: "Man, when he came first out of God's mint, shined most glorious."

The high estate for which man was made rendered his fall more terrible. Man's sin extended to every part of his nature. The temple of God is "burnt, the glory of God now vanished and lost." Because of sin, all mankind has fallen from that glorious estate in which it was created. [45]

> Every natural man and woman is born full of all sin, (Rom. i.29)
> as full as a toad is of poison, as full as ever his skin can hold; mind,
> will, eyes, mouth, every limb of his body, and every piece of his
> soul, is full of sin; their hearts are bundles of sin . . . look about
> thee and see, whatever sin is broached, and runs out of any man's
> heart into his life through thn whole world, all those sins are in
> thine heart; thy mind is a nest of all the foul opinions, heresies,

> that ever were vented by any man; thy heart is a foul sink of all
> atheism, sodomy, blasphemy, murder, whoredom, adultry, witch-
> craft, buggery; so that, if thou has any good thing in thee, it is
> but as a drop of rosewater in a bowl of poison; where fallen it is
> all corrupted. [46]

First hand observation convinced the American Puritans that the American Indians were the most salient examples of the total depravity of man. The
Indians had "ever sate in hellish darkness, adoring the *Divell* himselfe for their
God."[47] There was a great debate about how the Indians came to America;
there was no debate about their degeneracy.

> Certaine it is, that they are inheritors of a grevous and fearful
> curse living so long without Ephod or Teraphim, and in nearest
> alliance to the wilde beasts that perish. [48]

The Eliot Tracts describe the Indians as a "forlorne generation . . .
perishing . . . outcasts . . . the dregs of mankinde and the saddest spectacle
of misery of meere men upon earth,"[49] "the dregs and refuse of Adams lost
posterity,"[50] "as averse, and as farre off from God, as any heathen in the
world,"[51] "little better than the beasts that perish,"[52] and "the Ruines of
Mankinde."[53] The most popular theory, which was to be given classic expression by Cotton Mather,[54] was that Satan had led these people to America in
order to keep them from Christ. The land and people had belonged to Satan.
The Indian mission had set them free.

> Now Christ keeps the house, which Satan formerly kept; yea,
> they who were kept by Satan as his house, are now ready and
> earnestly desire to be built up as a house for Christ. [55]

> It was by the preaching of the Gospel to the Indians that the

> soules of men are rescued out of the snare of the Devill, in
> which they were before held captive at his will; The Lord hath
> manifested that there is a seed according to the Election of
> Grace, even amongst these also as well as other Gentiles.[56]

Even though the Indians had been "Captives to Satan these many Ages"[57]
with "chains of darkness ratling at their heels,"[58] not even the "deepest de-
generacies" could stop the "overflowing grace and bloud of Christ."[59]

Creatures of Reason

> In spite of human depravity, the Puritans made much of reason.

> The art of logic was a particular gift of God, bestowed upon
> fallen and hapless humanity, in order that they might not col-
> lapse in the ineptitude they had brought upon themselves. [60]

Though no Puritan believed that man could ever be redeemed by his reason,
the Gospel was always presented in a rational way. The Bible was not addressed to irrational creatures. The limits of man's natural ability were clearly
stated:

> No man naturally is able of his owne power to receive the spiri-
> tuall things of grace and salvation, no naturall man, that is, he
> that hath not the spirit of God working in him, no man that is
> in his naturall estate can receive the spirituall things of grace and
> salvation.[61]

But the limits of man's rational capacities were presented in a rational way.
Puritan sermons were models of logic.

The Indians too were approached in a rational manner and thus, as real
men. There were some suggestions that Indian depravity was such that they
were hardly human,[62] but this was mainly oratory. The whole approach to the
Indians was based upon the assumption that they could comprehend. Eliot's
presentation of the gospel was calculated to bring about understanding. He did
believe that civil and political organization should precede ecclesiastical organization. However, he certainly agreed with Thomas Shepard who ridiculed the
idea that "civility" of the Indians and a new Pentecost in the Church were
needed before evangelization could begin. Shepard further explained:

> mee thinkes now that it is with the Indians as it was with our
> New-English ground when we first came over, there was scarce
> any man that could believe that English graine would grow, or
> that the Plow could doe any good in this woody and rocky
> soile. And thus they continued in this supine unbeliefe for some
> yeares, till experience taught them otherwise . . .; so wee have
> thought of our Indians people and therefore have been discour-
> aged to put plow to such dry and rocky ground.[63]

By the time a decade had passed, the use of reason in presenting the
gospel to any pagan had been clearly stated in one of the Eliot Tracts. Edward
Reynolds spelled it out.

> The Lord was pleased at the first preaching of the Gospel to con-
> firme it with signs and wonders following, for the more speedy
> planting of it by only twelve . . . But certainly here may be much
> use made of naturall reason, to demonstrate unto Pagans the false-
> nesse of the way they are in, and so to prepare a way for entertain-
> ment of the Truth. Though the doctrine of the Gospel be superna-
> turall, and not investigable by human disquisitions, being made
> known to men and Angells onely by the impressions in the naturall
> conscience, will provoke men to attend & prepare them to enter-
> tain it, when it shall be preached unto them.

Rationality extended to all man. Reason could become the instrument
of God to prepare men for the coming of Christ.

Objects of Compassion

Compassion for souls is the most important missionary motive, except the glory of God, in the period of the Great Migration. It is one of the most important items in the missionary heritage which the Puritans give to the mission people of the National Period. Its roots are in Puritan anthropology.

John Eliot's references to the beginning of the Indian mission reflect his own compassion for men. His concluding lines in his *Indian grammar begun* deal with another subject but exhibit this motive.

> God first put into my heart a compassion over their poore Souls, and a desire to teach them to know Christ, and to bring them into his Kingdome. [65]

Twenty years earlier, speaking of the beginning of his mission work in a much different context the same motive shines through. Disturbed at the despair he could see among a group of the Indians when they tried to compete culturally and economically with the English and noting the difficulty with which they adjusted to the new kind of society brought in upon them by the New Englanders, he said:

> my heart moved within mee, abhoring that we should sit still and let that work alone, and hoping that this motion in them was of the Lord . . . I told them that they and wee were already all one save in two things . . . First, we know, serve, and pray unto God and they doe not: Secondly, we labour and work in building, planting, clothing ourselves, &c and they doe not . . . I told them that if they would learn to know God I would teach them. [66]

Eliot was to spend the rest of his life trying to help the Indians learn both.

In the Eliot Tracts the dual motives, glory to God and compassion for men, are often stated together. Edward Winslow saw the Indian mission as a "precious work" for "the glory of God, and the good of men." [67]   Thomas Mayhew reported in 1652 that "the Indians themselves do indeavor to propagate the knowledge of God, to the Glory of God and the good of others." [68] In 1655 Henry Whitfield urged the "Servants of God in England" to continue their prayers and contributions for the Indian mission. It was, he said, a glorious undertaking" for "the Glory of God" and "the Salvation of soules." [69]

The roots of compassion as a motive for mission are threefold. Compassion arose out of an encounter with need. The observable and reportable results of Indian depravity, moral, physical and spiritual, moved the Puritans to compassion. The immorality, the poverty and the religious darkness that they found in Indian culture was directly related to their ignorance of God in Jesus Christ. Turning to Christ was fundamental to the solution of all problems. Daniel Gookin expressed the idea in his *Historical Collections.*

> But this may upon sure grounds be asserted, that they are Adam's posterity, and consequently children of wrath; and hence are not

only objects of all christians' pity and compassion, but subjects
upon which our faith, prayers and best endeavours should be put
forth to reduce them from barbarism to civility; but especially to
rescue them out of the bondage of Satan, and bring them to salvation by our Lord Jesus Christ. [70]

Secondly, compassion developed in the midst of hope. In spite of depravity, those who ministered to the Indians discovered their capacity to understand. Thomas Mayhew wrote in 1647:

The encouragements I met withall touching the *Indians* conversion, next unto Gods glory, and his gracious promises was, the
notable reason, judgment and capacitie that God hath given unto
many of them; and also their zealous enquiring after true happiness. [71]

All of the men involved in the mission concluded that it was a lack of knowledge not a lack of capacity that hindered the work of the Holy Spirit among
the Indians. Thus Eliot replied, when asked how an Indian may come to know
Jesus Christ, that they could think and meditate on as much of the Bible as
had been taught them and pray God to reveal Jesus Christ to them. They
would then surely come to know Christ

because hee is such a God as will bee found of them that seeke
him with all their hearts, and hee is a God hearing the prayers of
all men both *Indian* as well as *English,* and that *English* men by
this meanes have come to the knowledge of Jesus Christ. [72]

It was compassion grounded in the knowledge that they could and would respond that drove Eliot in his translation work. It was a "heart of compassion"
that began and sustained him in all of his labors. [73]

Compassion also developed out of an evangelical concern for souls. Joseph Caryl wrote in 1651:

Surely 'tis cause of greater glorying that any of those Heathens
have found the way of life and salvation among our brethren,
then that our brethren have found place and safty . . . among
those Heathens. And how much doth it become Christians to let
Heathens see that they seek them more than *theirs*; That the gaining of them to Christ is more in their eye, then any worldly gain. [74]

Henry Whitfield, speaking of the Indian mission, related evangelical
compassion to God's own love.

The great Love of God, is Love to Soules, and our tenderest
compassion should be manifested in pittying of Soules, neither
know wee any other ordinary way that the Lord has appointed
by the preaching of the Gospel for the winning of Soules to

himselfe: *That being the Power of God to Salvation.*[75]

These three ideas, pity for man's misery in sin, the confidence that these "sons of Adam" could also respond to the Gospel, and the warm evangelical passion of men who were deliberate disciples of Jesus Christ, fashioned a missionary motive that was to be intensified and linger through the National Period of American Christianity.

The Puritan Concept of the Church

The instigators of the Great Migration were not only men with a great and mighty God, they were also all churchmen.[76] Cotton Mather's evaluation of John Eliot's purpose in New England could be applied to the whole movement: " 'twas *churchwork* that was his errand hither."[77] Their doctrine of the Church must therefore be examined. These were men with such a profound doctrine of the Church that it marked the character of their migration to the New World. It persisted to help form the missionary character of the American churches.

Volumes have been penned concerning the peculiar understanding of the Church held by New England Congregationalists, especially those of the Non-Separating variety who came out in the removal beginning in 1630. However, most that has been written has been primarily concerned with the church government of these congregations, with the theological presuppositions and assertions behind such views, and with how those particular views were related to the civil government and the Puritan society founded in New England.

Two closely related aspects of their understanding of the Church have been often neglected. The Puritan fathers continually preached that the Church was under the cross and sent into the world. Though in some ways these factors were modified by the civil organization of the churches once the Puritans arrived in New England, this commissioned-to-conflict attribute of the Church is almost omnipresent in the writings of such men as William Ames, William Perkins and John Preston. These aspects of their understanding of the church were potent factors in structuring the migration as an errand into the wilderness.

This section will therefore deal briefly with the concept of the gathered church as it related to the Indian mission and then explore th'' wayfaring and warfaring nature of the Church in Puritan theology.

The Church Gathered to Worship

The proposal of the men of the Great Migration to erect a "due forme of Government both civill and ecclesiasticall" was never more tenaciously upheld or assiduously attempted than with John Eliot in the Indian mission. Eliot said in November, 1648, that, all other things being acceptable, he would be willing to be a part of a church formed among the Indians, and "could finde out at least twenty men and women in some measure fitted of the Lord for it." [78] Nevertheless, the first church was not gathered until 1660. There were two primary reasons for this delay. The first was that the Indians had no "due forme" of civil government; at least they had none the Puritans would recognize. Eliot prefaced his willingness to enter into church-estate with them by explaining that

> were they but in a setled way of Civility and Government cohab-
> iting together, and I called (according to God) to live among them,
> I durst freely joyne into Church-fellowship amongst them.[79]

This was the problem for years. For Eliot, a due form of ecclesiastical government was not possible until a due form of civil government was established. They began to inquire, he reported the next year,

> after baptisme and Church Ordinances, and the way of worship-
> ping God as the Churches here do; but I shewing how uncapable
> they be to be trusted therewith, whilst they live so unfixed, con-
> fused and ungovernened a life, uncivilized and unsubdued to labor
> and order; they begin now to enquire after such things. And to
> that end, I have propounded to them that a fit place be found
> out for Cohabitation, wherewith they may subsist by labor, and
> settle themselves in such a way: And then they may have a Church,
> and all the Ordinances of Christ amongst them.[80]

For the next three years this was Eliot's goal. "The present work of God among them is to gather them together to bring them to Political life," he insisted in many letters to England.[81] The work of those years was to civilize them. Eliot had particular ideas about just what kind of government that should be. He went into detail in many of his letters, explaining his scheme.[82] It was a very "weighty consideration," and he consulted with John Cotton and others about it. He believed it would be the "patterne and Copie" for later mission work among the Indians. The general rule was that

> they shall be wholly governed by the Scriptures in all things
> both in Church and State; they shall have no other Law-giver;
> the Lord shall be their Law-giver, the Lord shall be their Judge,
> the Lord shall be their King.[83]

The pattern was the Pentateuch, with its rulers of hundreds, rulers of fifties, and rulers of tens.[84]

On June 6, 1651, at a great meeting at Natick, the Indian townspeople entered into a civil covenant with God. When rulers were elected according to the Biblical plan, Eliot was much moved:

> . . . it seemed unto me as if I had seen scattered bones goe, bone
> unto his bone, and so lived a civil political life, and the Lord was
> pleased to minister no small comfort unto my spirit, when I saw it.

The covenant, in a few short words, was "with God and each other, to be the Lords people, and to be governed by the word of the Lord." [85]

The conflict in mission philosophy between civilization-then-Christian-ization and Christianization-then-civilization (or perhaps just Christianization) among primitive peoples was present at the very beginning of the Protestant World Mission. The debate lingers into the Twentieth Century. In the context of the Great Migration the insistence on civilization first was based upon the Puritan commitment to a correctly ordered civil society as well as a correctly ordered church. Without close civil organization it was feared that sanctions against offending members of the disciplined church could not be enforced.

The debate was continued with gusto in the National Period. There the presuppositions of Puritanism mingled with those of revivalistic Pietism. Pietism was not nearly as concerned about a social compact as were the Puritans. In some cases the differing philosophies became factors in the organization for missions in this later period.

The second reason Eliot was so long in gathering a Church among the Indians had to do more specifically with the New England concept of a visible church. The Church is solely the creation of God. It could not be brought to birth by military power, legislative procedures, or intellectual effort. Thus, in rebuttal of a charge that the New England churches had done very little good on the hearts of the Indians, it was replied:

> 'tis as if they should reproach us for not making the windes to
> blow when wee list our selves, it must certainly be a spirit of
> life from God (not in mans power) which must put flesh and
> sinew unto these dry bones: if wee would force them to bap-
> tism . . . or if we would hire them to it . . . wee could have
> gathered many hundreds . . . into the name of Churches; but
> wee have not learnt as yet that art of coyning Christians or put-
> ting Christs name and Image upon copper mettle. [86]

But the Puritans also believed that when the Church became visible in local societies it should be after the same pattern. It should be constructed out of men upon whom "a spirit of life from God" had come, men whom God had "fitted" for a church-estate. A gospel church was thus composed of men who could give creditable confessions of saving faith and demonstrate the truth of them in the quality of life they lived. A church was gathered when a group of people, who could give a confession of faith, would bind themselves together in a covenant with God and each other to worship God in primitive simplicity, to maintain the ordinances of Christ, and to accept the discipline of the Word of God. Eliot could say after the Indians had entered into a civil covenant with God, that

> now our next work is to prepare them for Church-estate, in
> which end I doe instruct them, that the Visible Church of
> Christ is builded upon a lively confession of Christ, and Cov-

enanting to walk in all the Administrations of the publicue
worship of God, under the Government and Discipline of Jesus
Christ. [87]

For the Puritan to enter into church covenant was one of the most
exalted privileges and brought most sober responsibilities. When on August 13,
1652, the great day of Indian confessions at Natick, it became evident that it
would not be possible to form a church, Eliot was relieved. He knew that the

investing these young Babes in Christ, with the highest, and all
the external priviledges of the Church, the S pouse of Jesus
Christ on Earth, would have drawn upon me much more labor
and care, lest they should in any wise scandalize the same. [88]

The delay would give him more time to instruct them. It would give
them more time to train leadership for the church to be formed. The lack of
anyone to serve as yet as a pastor was, in fact, the primary reason, according
to Richard Mather, that the church was not then gathered.[89] Eliot worked
diligently to raise up an Indian ministry. He and those who worked with him
were largely successful. They were successful enough that in 1761, when a
number of Indian churches had been formed, he prepared a brief apology for
the practice of ordaining *"Indian Officers* unto the ministry of the Gospel."
It was his conclusion that an Englishman, "raw in that language," would be a
hindrance to an Indian Church. [90]

The Puritans, both in their goals for themselves and in the Indian mission, were interested not just in evangelism but in gathering those who responded into correctly ordered churches. In fact the planting of visible churches of
visible saints through all the world was a part of the ultimate design of Christ.[91]

The Church Under the Cross

The careful distinction between the Church visible and the Church invisible and between the Church triumphant and the Church militant is fundamental to the definition of the Church in Reformed theology. Zwingli delineated the usual distinction succinctly in 1531 when he prepared his *Exposition
of the Faith.* The invisible Church, the company of the elect, "knows . . . God
by the enlightenment of the Holy Spirit." Its members are hid from the eyes
of men and "known only to God and to themselves."[92] The visible Church is
the outward assembly of those who profess faith in Jesus Christ.

Heinrich Bullinger distinguished first between the Church triumphant,
"the great company of holy spirits in heaven," and the Church militant,

The Church militant is a congregation of men upon the earth,
professing the name and religion of Christ, and still fighting in
the world against the devil, sin, the flesh and the world, in the
camps and tents and under the banner of the Lord Christ.[93]

In the process of expanding the *Institutes*, John Calvin added a chapter entitled "On Bearing the Cross — One Branch of Self-Denial." Calvin found many reasons why the Church should expect to "live constantly under the cross." In the detailed exposition of this chapter, Calvin spoke of the Christians as "soldiers" and their activity as "warfare."[94]

These terms are related to the views of the Church militant held by other theologians of the Reformed tradition. They take on more importance in the literature of the English Puritans. It is impossible to argue that the Congregational Puritans built on Calvin's concept of the Church. At no point did Calvin define the Church as consisting of visible saints. But when the early Puritan fathers began to expound the view that the visible church was composed of visible saints, the concept of the Church under the cross became extremely significant. For these men, gathered congregations were real manifestations of the Church catholic.

William Ames develops his doctrine of the Church along these lines. Precisely, the Church is a "company of men that are called." But because the end of calling is faith and because faith brings union with Christ, it can be defined "a company of believers, . . . those who are in Christ and . . . have communion with Christ." Faith, then, is the "forme or constituting cause" of the Church. The Church is "catholique" because there is in it "something integrally universal . . . because it containes the faithful of all Nations of al (sic) places, and of all times." The Church is "Militant, or Triumphant" according to its degree of communion with Christ. It is the Church militant that does not yet have perfect communion with Christ and "so doth wrastle as yet with enemies in the field of the world." It is always both visible and invisible.

> But although the Church . . . may leave any part of the world,
> yet it hath never totally failed or shall faile from the beginning
> of the gathering it to the end of the World. For Christ must al-
> ways have his kingdome in the mids of his enemies, until hee
> shall make his enemies his footstolle.[95]

"The Church as it lives upon earth" can be visible in two ways; in the person of the individual member or in an organized society of believers.[96] Thus, when the Puritan preachers went into great detail describing the manner in which the Christian life should be lived, they were, indeed, outlining behavior for individual Christians, but they were also delineating what they understood to be the essential life of the Church. The visible churches, they stoutly affirmed, must be composed of visible saints. Therefore, in the Puritan context, when one speaks of the Christian life being lived under the cross and in constant warfare, he is also speaking of the warfaring or cross-bearing nature of the Church.

William Perkins was widely read by all the leaders of the Great Migration. His works abound with references to the warfare of the Church. Speaking through the Christian in his *Dialogue between the Christian and the Worldling*, he said:

> . . . the Church of God hath alwayes beene subject to the crosse
> and none must marvel if it be: how can the world love them that
> hate it, and have little acquaintance with it, and are on the earth
> as Pilgrims . . . experience teacheth, that as there is a perpetuall
> intercourse betweene day and night, so there is in the Church of
> God, not any perpetuall quietnesse, but trouble and quietnesse;
> affliction and ease do continually succeed one another.[97]

In his *Exposition of Christ's Sermon in the Mount*, Perkins alleged that
Christ voiced the beatitude concerning persecution because

> hereby hee would teach his Disciples, and us in them, that it is
> the will of God, his Church in this world should bee under the
> crosse.[98]

Perkins' works provide good illustrations of the fact that the early English Puritans were convinced that the Church was always to be under the cross.
Warfare was always to continue. The Church was the army of God.

John Cotton was expressing the same idea when he said

> the first day you came into the Church you were baptized, and
> God made account you should looke for Affliction from that
> day forward.

Baptism was, in Cotton's view, not only the sign of forgiveness and new life,
it also portended life under the cross.

> For the water doth not onely type the blood of Christ, to wash
> away the guilt of sinne, . . . but water in baptisme doth likewise
> figure to us all those afflictions wherewith wee shall not only be
> sprinkled . . . but sometimes drenched and dowsed all over, as
> was the old manner of baptizing. [99]

The Church was continually at war with the Antichrist and forces of
evil. The Kingdom of heaven is manifest in the visible church, Thomas Shepard asserted. When the Church lays aside its weapons, that kingdom can be
pulled down.

> No kingdom can be safe in an ordinary way, where all their
> weapons are taken from them, or not used by them when
> their enemies are upon their borders. When the churches
> hang by, and lay aside faith, the shield whereby we defend
> ourselves, and prayer, whereby we offend our enemies, what
> safety is to be expected now in churches.

The Lord's call to the Church is to "be strong" and go out in the
"great service of the Lord."[100]

Sent Through the World

William Haller, in *The Rise of Puritanism,* illustrated with multitudinous examples what he called the "Puritan legend of the wayfaring, warfaring Christian, of the Puritan epic of the fall and redemption of man."[101] The wayfaring Christian, as much as the warfaring Christian, is just the minute personal form of the wayfaring Church.

The Church was sent through the world. The Church was to "use" the world, to remain unattached in the world, only as pilgrims whose home and interests were in another country. In his *Commentarie upon the Eleventh Chapter of the Hebrewes,* William Perkins wrote:

> There is a third, a more spiritual . . . reason . . . that . . . God
> had in making Abraham live in Canaan as a stranger; namely to
> teach all Christian men their duty to the worlds end . . . we
> must live in this world as Pilgrims and Strangers, even in the
> middle of all our peace and prosperitie, of all our libertie,
> riches, land and possessions; yea, of all our worldly friends and
> acquaintances.[102]

Ames presented this same picture in his commentary on *First Peter*:

> All the faithfull are strangers and pilgrims in this world. Rea. 1.
> Because their Father, and their country is not here, but in hea-
> ven. 2. Because they doe not desire to stay long here. 3. Because
> their wealth and their friends are not in this world. 4. Because
> the world accounts them strangers.

A little later in the commentary Ames inferred that in going through the world the Christian had a distinct "duty to seeke" the conversion of the wicked. [103]

It is just this warfaring-wayfaring character of the Church that helped to structure the Great Migration into an errand into the wilderness. How this theological constellation of ideas about the Church helped to give form to the mission character of the Massachusetts Bay enterprise can be seen in a survey of the meaning of the metaphorical use of the word "wilderness."

Into the Wilderness

Alan Heimert, in a study of the meaning of the word "wilderness" for the New England divines, made a fundamental error. He asserted at the very beginning of his essay:

> Their concept of the American 'wilderness' we must conclude,
> was not, as it were carried to America on the Mayflower or
> Arbella, but came out of the wilderness itself. [104]

Quite the contrary, "wilderness" had a very profound and complex symbolic meaning to the Puritans who sailed for America in 1630. The Biblical roots of "wilderness" did not develop in the third generation of the New England Puritans, as Heimert has suggested, but had been long used in typological preaching to help explain the areas of conflict common to the Christian life. George H. Williams has traced the idea deep into medieval sectarianism and mysticism.[105]

For the Puritan preachers the source of this figure was the Bible. There were two Biblical epics that, in particular, were rich in "wilderness" meaning. The first was the wilderness wanderings of the Israelites. The second was the wilderness temptation of Jesus Christ. In the first, the Church was redeemed from the bondage of Egypt and sent through the wilderness to Canaan. This was very rich material for proclaiming the wayfaring nature of the Church. In the second, Christ was the great example for the Church by going into the wilderness to do battle with Satan. This story was extremely useful in explaining the Christian's warfare in the world.

All this is not to say that the Puritans' confrontation with the literal wilderness did not deepen and develop their understanding and use of the term. "Wilderness" was just the kind of arena that the Puritans expected in which to fulfill their "errand." William Perkins said that the "wilderness" was the "place of combat" that God had appointed between Christ and the devil.[106] It was in this way that the Puritans thought of "wilderness." Before they went to America and found themselves surrounded by the "thicke wood" the word alreadh had significant connotations to them.

These men did speak of New England as a Canaan. It is also true that "Canaan" was a figure of heaven. Yet these men understood clearly the Biblical use of the word. The Israelites did not go directly across the Red Sea into Canaan. They wandered for long years in the wilderness. When they did cross over the Jordan River, they went across to go to war. Canaan also was an arena of conflict. William Perkins went to great length to show that the children of Israel experienced the "intercourse between quietness and trouble" in Canaan as well as in the wilderness. [107]

"Wilderness" was an excellent word to describe the physical circumstances in which the Puritans found themselves. It was also most useful in describing their circumstances as they were related to their God. These men understood themselves to be the Church of Jesus Christ. They were sent through the world and commissioned to continual warfare with the elements of darkness. This was part of their essential character as the Church of Jesus Christ.

The wilderness was the most natural place for such wayfaring and warfaring to be waged. It is just at this point that the understanding of the church visible enters again. For the Church is not just to go through the wilderness or just to do battle in the wilderness. God has promised that the day will come when the wilderness will blossom and rivers will run in the desert. It is the proclamation of the Gospel by the church that God will eventually bless and,

thus, make the wilderness into a paradise. When this day comes, when the
Spirit of God is poured out, those who turn to God will be gathered into
churches. *It is in the gathering of churches that the wilderness becomes a
garden.* Henry Whitfield wrote to the Parliament in 1652:

> Wee hope your delight in the Worke of God will inforce a
> leasure, to view . . . that in the wilderness are waters broken
> out, and streames in the Desert, the parched ground is be-
> come a Poole, and the thirsty Landsprings of water in the
> Habitation of Dragons, where each lay, there is grasse with
> Reeds and Rushes, the Lord hath powred water upon him
> that is thirstie, and flouds upon the dry Heathen, & his
> blessing on their Off-spring, they spring up as among the
> grasse, as willowes by the water-courses: One sayes I am the
> Lords, and another calles himself by the name of *Jacob*, and
> another subscribes with his hand unto the Lord, and surnames
> himselfe by the name of Israel. The Lord hath done a new
> thing, and wee know it, he hath made a way in the Wilder-
> nesse, and Rivers in the Desert, the beast of the field doth
> honour him, the Dragons, and the Owles because he gives
> waters in the Wilderness, and Rivers in the Desert, to give
> drinke to his People his chosen, so that upon the Report
> heere read unto us, wee cannot but glorifie God with those
> Primitive beleevers of old, and say, then hath God also to
> the poore naked *Indians* granted Repentance unto life.[108]

This understanding of themselves as the Church of Jesus Christ is one
of the factors that helped the Puritans who came to New England to structure
their venture as a mission with meaning and goals. This has introduced one
other factor that made a significant contribution to the structuring of the Great
Migration. This factor has to do with their understanding of their place in history.

Puritan Eschatology

A fourth theological constellation that shaped the mission character of
the migration of the Non-Separating Congregationalists to America was Puritan
eschatology. There was a shift in Reformed theology between the time of the
reformers and the period of William Ames, Richard Sibbes and other Puritan
progenitors. But the roots of Puritan theology are in the Reformed rather than
the Lutheran branch of the Continental Reformation. The Puritan understanding of last things was very closely related to the fluctuations of Reformed theology, and, in particular at this point, to Genevan eschatology. For John Calvin, eschatology was written in the present rather than the aorist tense.[109] God
would work out his purposes in linear rather than punctiliar action. He reacted
violently to the chiliastic fanatics of his day. His exposition of the signs of the
time has been called a philosophy of church history rather than an eschatological interpretation of the End.[110] Calvin postulated a tri-epochal program of time

between the coming of the Holy Spirit and the second advent of Christ. The
first period was that of the Apostles, during which the Gospel was offered to
the whole world.[111] The second epoch was the period of the manifestation of
Antichrist. Calvin understood his own age to be that of the most effective work
of Antichrist.[112] This helps explain why all of Calvin's theology was written to
people in the throes of persecution. His theology was written to the Church
under-the-cross. The final period was that of the great expansion of the
Church.[113] During this epoch the fullness of the Gentiles would come in, the
ends of the earth would come to Christ, and the Antichrist would be defeated.

The Puritans of the early seventeenth century agreed with this scheme
of history.[114] However, they recognized that a century had passed since the
dawning of the Reformation. They argued that they were living at the very end
of the second period. They found evidence for this in the social, political and
religious situation of their own times. Thus they hoped to become the pure
remnant of the best of the Reformation, to provide a place of refuge from the
destruction at the end of the second eschatological period and to serve as an
example of the kind of churches that should prevail across the earth in the
third period. Thus Winthrop wrote:

> All other Churches of Europe are brought to desolation, and
> our sinnes . . . do threaten euill times to be comminge vpon
> vs, and whoe knowes, but that God hath provided this place
> to be a refuge for many whome he meanes to saue out of
> the generall callamity, and seeinge the Church hath noe place
> lefte to flie into but the wildernesse, what better worke can
> there be, then to goe and provide tabernacles and foode for
> her against she comes thether.[115]

The often quoted passage from Winthrop's sermon on shipboard reveals
the same concern: "For wee must Consider that wee shall be as a Citty upon a
Hill, the eies of all people are uppon us."[116]

However, with the first years of success in New England and the coming of the English Revolution, before 1660, some of the New England Puritans
dared to believe that they were living at the very beginning of the era of the
prosperity of the Church.

In light of this philosophy of history, even Winthrop's first "Reason"
for "iustifieinge" the "Plantation in New England," so often overlooked as
unimportant or disparaged as pious verbosity, is fraught with eschatological
implications. He averred:

> It will be a service to the Church of great consequence to carry
> the Gospell into those parts of the world, to helpe on the
> comminge of the fullnesse of the Gentiles, and to raise a Bul-
> worke against the kingdome of Ante-Christ which the Jesuites
> labour to reare up in those parts.[117]

A second factor in Calvin's theology, closely related to his eschatology, which influenced the Puritans' understanding of their own historical situation was an element of his doctrine of election. God's election was manifested not only in terms of personal selection or rejection of individuals to salvation but also in his providential choice of those nations who should hear the Gospel at certain periods of history.[118]   The Gospel is not offered equally to all at all times.[119] Calvin insisted that God would in time offer the Gospel to all the particular nations of the world.[120] God would, he asserted, in his own time and at his own pleasure, open doors so that the Gospel would be proclaimed and response would be forthcoming among the nations not yet made partakers of His salvation.[121]

The leaders of the Great Migration dared to hope that the day of the New England nations had arrived. Thus Winthrop could write:

It is the revealed will of God that the Gospell should be preached to all nations, and though we know not whether those Barbarians will receive it at first or noe, yet it is a good worke to serue Gods providence in offering it to them . . . for God shall haue glory by it though they refuse it, and there is a good hope that the Posterity shall by this meanes be gathered into Christes sheepefould.[122]

Also, John Cotton exhorted the Massachusetts Bay people on the day of their departure:

offend not the poore Natives, but as you partake in their land, so make them partakers of your precious faith: as you reape their temporalls, so feede them with your spiritualls: winne them to the love of Christ, for whom Christ died. They never yet refused the Gospell, and therefore more hope they will now receive it. Who knoweth whether God have reared this whole Plantation for such an end.[123]

Two books, one written at the very beginning of the Great Migration and the second published in the mid-1650s, reveal how this scheme of history molded the New England leaders' understanding of themselves and their undertaking as significant factors in fulfilling God's purpose in the world.

The Planters Plea

In 1630, shortly after the Arbella and her retinue had departed for New England, John White, one of the earliest and most important promoters of the Massachusetts Bay Company, published a booklet justifying the undertaking, explaining the developments that led to the enterprise, and intending to arouse interest and increase investments in the venture.

White was a Puritan of the Presbyterian strain. He certainly had no intention of founding a Congregational church-state in New England. However, he was amenable to the peculiar outlook the East Anglia element of the Company (the Independent group) had toward the venture. These men insisted that the undertaking be understood primarily as an enterprise for planting the Gospel in New England. Thus, his little book, *The Planters Plea,* is replete with the understanding these men had of themselves and their migration as a strategic move in God's plan of the ages.

It was White's contention that colonization had a warrant direct from God. Among his arguments was the assertion that colonization advanced God's honor.

> Gods honour must needs bee much advanced, when, together
> with mens persons, religion is conveyed into the severall parts
> of the world, and all quarters of the earth sound with his
> praise; and Christ Jesus taken in the Nations for his inheri-
> tance, and the ends of the earth for his possessions.

White listed several goals or purposes that had been pursued in establishing plantations. He insisted that the one supreme aim in colonization should be God's glory. Eschatological implications rise to the surface in his explanation of this apogee of all possible ends in colonization.

Colonization with this sort of goal "hath beene specially preserved for this later end of the world." Before Christ, God had shut up the Church in the Promised Land and had excluded men from active propagation. In the time of the Apostles He had used miracles and signs to win men to Him. Since that time, White was sure, God had been using colonies to bring men to his salvation.[124] Four considerations seemed to demand the proclamation of the Gospel of Christ in this way in White's age.

First, many men of note agree that the propagation of the Gospel in the last age is to be "upon the Westerne parts of the world."

Secondly, the Scripture leaves no doubt that the knowledge of Christ must be "manifested unto all quarters of the World." Since that has not taken place as yet, "it must follow, that worke of conveighing that knowledge to them, remaines to be undertaken and performed by this last age."

Thirdly, the discovery of the New World that had been possible because of the development of the use of the "Loadstone" must be viewed in the providence of God. God did not permit these discoveries just to "satisfy mens greedy appetites, that thirsted after the riches of the new found world." Rather, "hee who made all things, and consequently orders . . . them to his owne glory . . . aymed at (no) other thing but this . . . to cause at length the glorious Gospell of Jesus Christ to shine out unto them."

Finally, a fourth reason

> to prove that God hath left this great, and glorious worke to
> this age of the world, is the nearnesse of the Jewes conversion;

before which . . . the fulness of the Gentiles must come in . . .
let it bee granted that the Jewes conversion is neare, and that
the Gentiles, and consequently the Indians must needs be
gathered in before that day; and any man may make the conclusion, that this is the houre for the worke and . . . of our
duty to endeavour the effecting that which God hath determined.[125]

All of these lines of argument are in the context of Puritan eschatology.
To affirm this is not to deny the relevance of social and economic factors in
the motivation of the Great Migration. They understood the social and economic factors to be God's ordained means of sending them on such an errand. As
early as 1630 they were already answering the charge that the religious concern
was not sincere.[126] The eschatological way of thinking about themselves and
their undertaking gave meaning, courage and romance to their mission to New
England.

Wonder-working Providence

A most profound eschatological interpretation of the New England experiment before 1660 is Edward Johnson's *Wonder-working Providence of
Sion's Savior in New England.* Johnson came over in 1630. He returned to
England in 1636. The book was published in 1654 in London. Probably written over a period of several years, its primary thrust was directed against the
development of toleration in England. He agreed exactly with Nathaniel Ward's
statement that God does not "tolerate Christian States, to give Toleration" to
a varient sect if they have power to suppress it. [127]

His whole argument is in an eschatological framework. He said:

It hath been the longing expectation of many, to see that notable
and wonderfull worke of the Lord Christ, in casting down that
man of sin who hath held the whole world . . . under his Lordly
power, while the true professors of Christ have hardly had any
appearance to the eye of the world . . . take notice the Lord
hath an assured set time for the accomplishment of this work
. . . you that long so much for it, come forth and fight: who
can expect a victory without a battle?[128]

Johnson opposed the toleration because the day of the Lord was near.
He called the Puritan leaders to one great, last effort. In doing so he cast New
England history into a pervasive eschatological framework. Only the main lines
of his thought can be pointed out here.

Johnson was sure that the day of the fall of Antichrist was near. The
Puritan was "prest for the service of our Lord Christ, to re-build the most
glorious Edifice of Mount Sion in a Wilderness." He was called to prepare the
way for the coming of Christ, for he was coming again "to destroy Antichrist."
Defending the civil government of New England, Johnson insisted that it, and

any "Godly civill government," would have a "great share in that worke."[129]

The day of the fulness of the Gentiles was also at hand. The Lord had given the people of the Great Migration a great commission:

> Be sure you make choyce of the right, that all people, Nations and Languages, who are soonly to submit to Christs Kingdome, may be followers of you herein, as you follow the rule of Christ.[130]

Johnson predicted that the New England way would soon triumph throughout the entire world. The kind of fellowship that existed between churches in New England as much as one hundred miles apart could just as well exist between such churches throughout the world. The "Communion of Congregational Churches" was

> more universall then the Papall power, and assuredly the dayes are at hand, wherein both Jew and Gentile Churches shall exercise this old Modell of Church Government, and send their Church salutations and admonitions from one end of the World unto another, when the Kingdomes of the Earth are become our Lord Christs.[131]

Johnson joyously revealed that Congregational churches were coming into existence in other parts of the world. The New England churches were surely accomplishing more than the world was aware. They had an auspicious place in God's ultimate plan for the world.

> Let not man think these few weake Wormes would restraine the wonderfull Workes of Christ, as onely to themselves, but the quite contrary, these are but the Porch of his glorious building in hand, and if hee have shewed such admirable acts of his providence toward these, what will he doe when the whole Nation of English shall set upon like Reformation according to the direct Rule of his Word? Assured confidence there is also for all Nationa, from the undoubted promise of Christ himself.[132]

Both Johnson's *Wonder-working Providence* and White's *Planter's Plea* reveal that the leaders of the Great Migration felt they occupied a propitious place in history. These men understood that they had embarked on an errand that had significance for God's ultimate plan for the redemption of the world. The most profound statement of eschatological views, however, are to be found in the Eliot Tracts. A brief review of the eschatological dimension of these papers is necessary to complete this chapter.

The Eliot Tracts

There was in the early years of the Bay Colony, despite the powerful eschatological drive to mission, also an eschatological hindrance to active effort to convert the Indians. It concerned a minor disagreement among some of the Puritans concerning which should come first, the conversion of the Jews or the great ingathering of the Gentiles. Thomas Shepard attempted to deal with the problem in 1647. He found three commonly held views that discouraged attempts to evangelize the Indians. The first was the belief that until the Jews were brought into the kingdom of Christ that God had set a seal on the hearts of the Indians so that they would not believe. The second excuse was a widespread belief that little could be accomplished until the Indians had achieved civilization. The third view was that the work of converting such heathen was impossible until God should restore the miraculous and extraordinary gifts of tongues and spiritual power that he had granted the Church in the first century.

Shepard made no effort to refute the first two excuses, but he insisted that they should and could begin at once, even if the first two views were correct, to "lay the first stones of Christs Kingdome and Temple amongst them."[133]

The theorizing in the early years of the mission that the Indians were descendants of the lost ten tribes of Israel was an effort to gainsay this eschatological objection. Edward Winslow wrote in 1649 very positively that the Indians were in fact Israelites. He cited the opinion of a certain "Rabbi-ben-Israel" of Amsterdam and his own observation of Indian customs as proof. In the same work "I.D." listed six reasons that persuaded him that the Indians were Jews, or at least that

> there may be a remnant of the *Generation of Jacob* in America
> . . . And that those sometimes poor, now precious Indians . . .
> may be as the *first fruits* of the glorious harvest, of Israels redemption.[134]

Eliot never shared these views. He did feel, however, that there was as much evidence that the Indians were descendants of Shem as that the English were of Japhet. He thought specifically that the Indians were probably Hebrews, that is, descendants of Eber, "whose sonnes the Scripture sends farthest East."[135]

These theories slowly drop out of the Eliot Tracts. The early eschatological question was abandoned when it was seen that many Indians did in fact receive Christ. Henry Whitfield was also able to harmonize the two contrary views. The conversion of the Indians, he insisted, was the means by which the fullness of the Gentiles would draw near. This in turn would hasten the calling of the Jews. "The Scripture," he said,

> speaks of a double conversion of the Gentiles, the first being
> before the conversion of the Jewes, they being *Branches wilde
> by nature* grafted into the *True Olive Tree* . . . and till then
> *Blindnes hath hapned unto Israel.* The second, after the conversion of the Jewes, as appears (in) Acts 15,16,17.[136]

Eliot was not interested in speculation. His concern was to found his hope on "Scripture grounds only." As he considered the turmoil of civil wars in England, and the aftermath of the Thirty Years War on the Continent, and as he saw the progress among the English and Indians in New England, he concluded that "all signes preceding the glorious coming of Christ" were being accomplished. He judged that

> this glorious work of bringing in and setting up the glorious
> kingdome of Christ, hath the Lord of his free grace put into
> the hands of this renowned Parliment and Army.[137]

For Eliot the Kingdom of Christ was simply that dominion of Christ over men who were obedient to his Word. Whenever a people subjected themselves to no other law but the Scriptures, then the Kingdom of Christ had come in that place. This is exactly how the Millenial Kingdom would be brought in. God would bring nation after nation to subjection to his Word.

> When every thing both Civil & Spiritual are done by the direction
> of the word of Christ, then doth Christ reigne, and the great King-
> dome of Jesus Christ which we weight for, is even this that I do
> now mention; and by this means all Kingdomes and Nations shall
> become the Kingdomes of Christ, because he shall rule them in all
> things by his holy word.[138]

Eliot fervently hoped that the Parliament and then Cromwell would bring the government of England to the Scriptural standard. For eventually, he believed, God would bring every nation to that place.

> *Oh my heart yearneth over distressed perplexed England* . . . that
> (God) would . . . let them see their opportunity to let in Christ,
> and to advance his Kingdome over them; yea, my hope is, that he
> will not leave tampering with them untill he hath brought it to
> passe; O the blessed day in *England* when the Word of God shall
> be their *Magna Charta* and chief Law Book; and when all Lawyers
> must be Divines to study the Scriptures; and should the Gentile
> Nations take up Moses policie . . . make the Scriptures the founda-
> tion of all their Lawes, who knoweth what a door would be opened
> to the Jewes to come in to Christ.[139]

The purpose of God in all the war and turmoil in the world was just to bring the governments of the world to abandon their man-made governments and turn to the Scriptures.

> It is the very reason why the Lord in this houre of temptation
> will bring Nations into distresse and perplexity, that so they
> may be forced to the Scriptures; . . . all Governments are and will
> be shaken, that men may be forced to pitch upon th firme and
> unshaken foundation, *the Worde* of God; this is doubtless the
> great designe of Christ in these later dayes; Oh that mens eyes
> were open to see it, and when the world is brought into this
> frame, then Christ reigneth; and when this is, Government shall
> be in the hands of the Saints of the most high.[140]

It is just at this point that New England and the Indian mission are of such strategic importance. Other nations will only with difficulty give up their traditional forms to come into the Kingdom of Christ. They will have been

> adulterate with their Antichristian or humane wisdome; they
> well be loth to lay down their imperfect own Starlight of
> excellent Lawes, . . . for the perfect Sunlight of Scripture.[141]

With the Indians this is not true. They have very little of value to which to cling. Therefore there will be no such opposition to the "Rising Kingdome of Jesus Christ among them." Their churches and townes would become the patterns of what God would, through the world, shortly bring to pass.

The Puritans came to New England on God's errand. For that reason they came eagerly. Their God, who ruled in history, was bringing history to his own glorious consummation. They, as the Church of Jesus Christ, could participate in the erection of the great Kingdom he was raising up. The study of Scripture, the "passages of providence," and the signs of the times told them that the great day was drawing near. They believed the great adventure to New England was of major importance in God's ultimate plan. The whole enterprise was the work of God, the very mission of God.

This kind of God, this sort of understanding of the Church, and this view of history, which allows the church to join in the erection of the Kingdom of God, shaped the theology of the early missionary societies in America.

NOTES FOR CHAPTER 1

1. Miller, *Errand,* p. 11.

2. See Samuel E. Morison, ed., *Winthrop Papers,* (5 vols.; Boston: Massachusetts Historical Society, 1929), II, 106-148, for the different versions of this document.

3. John Cotton, *God's Promise to His Plantation* (London: Printed by William Jones, 1630), pp. 8ff.

4. John White, *The Planters Plea* (London: Printed by William Jones, 1630), pp. 1-9).

5. Perry Miller, *Orthodoxy in Massachusetts, 1630-1650* (Boston: Beacon Press, 1959), pp. xi-xii.

6. Thomas Shepard, *The Day-Breaking, if not the Sunrising of the Gospel with the Indians in New England* (London: Printed by Rich. Cotes, 1647), p. 8.

7. Miller, *Errand,* p. 11.

8. Henry Whitfield, *Strength Out of Weakness* (London: Printed by M. Simmons, 1652), in *MHSC* Series Three, IV (1834), 155.

9. *New Englands First Fruit* (London: Printed by R. O. and G. D., 1643), p. 1.

10. Shepard, *The Day Breaking,* p. 21.

11. Letter of John Eliot dated Sept. 24, 1647, in Shepard, *The Clear Sunshine,* p. 43.

12. *Ibid.,* "Dedicatory," n.p.

13. Eliot joined with Nathaniel Ward, *The Simple Cobler of Aggawam in America* (London: Printed by J. D. and R. I., 1647), as a critic of toleration that developed in the Commonwealth. He wrote on May 8, 1649: ". . . all those signes preceding the glorious coming of Christ are accomplishing, and a thick black cloud is gathered . . . and the thickest and most portentous black part of that cloud is the Toleration of the most grosse and convicted impieties under the pretence of conscience, which misapplication of the Word of Authority . . . cannot be innocent, and will undoubtedly prolong the storme and delay of the reigne of Christ." Whitfield, *Light Appearing,* p. 120.

14. John Eliot, *Tears of Repentance* (London: Printed by Peter Cole, 1653), in *MHSC,* Series Three, IV (1834), 211-213.

15. John Eliot, "Dedication of Algonquin New Testament," *MHSC,* Series One, VII (1801), 223.

16. *New Englands First Fruits,* p. 19.

17. Whitfield, *Light Appearing,* p. 45.

18. Edward Winslow, *The Glorious Progress of the Gospel amongst the Indians in New England* (London: Printed for Hannah Allen, 1649), in *MHSC,* Series Three, IV (1834), 95.

19. *New Englands First Fruits,* p. 19.

20. Shepard, *Clear Sunshine,* "Dedicatory," n.p.

21. Whitfield, *Light Appearing,* pp. 125, 138, 135.

22. Eliot, *Tears of Repentance,* p. 172.

23. Whitfield, *Light Appearing*, pp. 141, 135.

24. Perry Miller, *The New England Mind: The Seventeenth Century* (Boston: Beacon Press, 1961), p. 15.

25. Miller, *Errand*, p. 115.

26. John Eliot, *The Indian Grammar Begun* (Cambridge: Printed by Marmaduke Johnson, 1666) p. 15.

27. Shepard, *Day-Breaking*, pp. 2, 8.

28. Edward Reynolds, *A Further Accoumpt of the Progress of the Gospel Among the Indians in New England* (London: Printed by M. Simmons, 1659), n.p.

29. Eliot, *Tears of Repentance*, p. 229.

30. Shepard, *Day-Breaking*, p. 12.

31. Eliot, *Tears of Repentance*, pp. 229, 249.

32. Shepard, *Day-Breaking*, p. 9. The promoters in England and America were convinced that it was God's pleasure to offer his mercy to the Indians. The providence of God in the Great Migration was proof of this: "And you that are Christians indeed, rejoice to see the Curtaines of the Tabernacle inlarged, the bounds of the Sanctuary extended, Christ advanced, the Gospel propagated, and souls saved. And if ever the love of God did center in your hearts, if ever the sense of his goodness hath begot bowels of compassion in you, draw them forth towards them whom God hath singled out to be the objects of his grace and mercy." Shepard, *Clear Sunshine*, n.p.

33. R. Pierce Beaver, "Missionary Motivation through Three Centuries," in Jerald C. Brauer, ed., *Reinterpretation of American Church History* (Chicago: University of Chicago Press, 1968), p. 121.

34. This was the answer given to the second question on the day of the Indian examination, April 13, 1654. John Eliot, *A Late and Further Manifestation of the Progress of the Gospel Amongst the Indians in New England* (London: Printed by M.S., 1655), in *MHSC*, Series Three, IV (1834), 277.

35. Whitfield, *Light Appearing*, p. 120.

36. Shepard, *Clear Sunshine*, p. 44.

37. Winslow, *Glorious Progress*, p. 97.

38. Whitfield, *Light Appearing*, p. 143.

39. Whitfield, *Strength out of Weakness*, p. 183.

40. Shepard, *Clear Sunshine*, n.p.

41. Winslow, *Glorious Progress*, p. 89; Eliot, *Late and Further Manifestation*, p. 263; and Whitfield, *Strength out of Weakness*, p. 196.

42. Winslow, *Glorious Progress*, p. 79.

43. Eliot, *Tears of Repentance*, pp. 217-218.

44. *New Englands First Fruit*, p. 19.

45. Thomas Shepard, *The Sincere Convert: Discovering the Small Number of True Believers, and the Great Difficulty of Saving Conversion*, in *The Works of Thomas Shepard*, ed. by John A.

Alboro (3 vols.; New York: AMS Press, Inc., 1967), I, 18-20.

46. *Ibid.,* p. 28.

47. *New Englands First Fruits,* p. 1.

48. Shepard, *Day-Breaking,* p. 13.

49. *Ibid.,* pp. 1, 2, 13.

50. Whitfield, *Light Appearing,* p. 109.

51. Shepard, *Clear Sunshine,* p. 43.

52. Eliot, *Tears of Repentance,* p. 218.

53. Eliot, *Indian Grammar Begun,* p. 2.

54. Cotton Mather, *Magnalia Christi Americanna,* (2 vols., 1852 ed.; New York: Russell & Russell, 1967), I, 42,556.

55. Eliot, *Late and Further Manifestation,* p. 266.

56. Whitfield, *Strength out of Weakness,* p. 156.

57. Winslow, *Glorious Progress,* p. 95.

58. Whitfield, *Light Appearing,* p. 103.

59. Shepard, *Day-Breaking,* p. 14.

60. Miller, *New England Mind,* p. 111.

61. Thomas Hooker, *The Unbeleevers Preparing for Christ* (London: Printed by Tho. Cotes, 1638) in Everett H. Emerson, ed., *Redemption: Three Sermons 1637-1656* (Gainesville, Florida: Scholars' Facsimiles & Reprints, 1956), p. 39.

62. The English editor of Shepard, *Clear Sunshine,* suggested that the New England churchmen were "Dealing with such *whom* they are to make men, before they can make them Christians," n.p.

63. Shepard, *Day-Breaking,* pp. 14-15.

64. Reynolds, *A Further Accoumpt,* n.p.

65. Eliot, *Indian Grammar Begun,* p. 15.

66. Shepard, *Clear Sunshine,* p. 25.

67. Winslow, *Glorious Progress,* p. 89.

68. Eliot, *Tears of Repentance,* p. 210.

69. Eliot, *Late and Further Manifestation,* p. 263.

70. Daniel Gookin, *Historical Collections of the Indians in New England,* in *MHSC,* Series One, I (1792), 147.

71. Winslow, *Glorious Progress,* p. 77.

72. Shepard, *Day-Breaking*, p. 3.

73. Eliot, *Indian Grammar Begun,* p. 15.

74. Whitfield, *Light Appearing,* p. 100.

75. Whitfield, *Strength out of Weakness,* **p.** 156.

76. Miller, *New England Mind,* chapter XV, pp. 432-462, deals especially with their doctrine of the Church. In that chapter Miller says, "Except for some rather desultory efforts at converting a few Indians — to be cited in justifying the colonies at home — the New England brand of Christianity was not a missionary creed: it did not drive men into the trackless wilderness, but called them to their places within settled associations." p. 443. This is overstated, not in line with what Miller says in other places, and does not take seriously the commitment of the missionaries who worked among the Indians. His next sentence describes exactly what the missionaries were doing as well: "Its first aim was sorting out the elect from the mass, and its second providing a method whereby both could live stable concord under the rule of the elect." However, the thrust of this chapter is not necessarily to contradict Miller's statement here. It is rather to say that those ways of thinking about God which helped to structure the removal to America became important in structuring the missionary thought of the early National Period.

77. Mather, *Magnalia,* II, 531.

78. Winslow, *Glorious Progress,* p. 86.

79. *Ibid.*

80. *Ibid.,* pp. 89-90.

81. Whitfield, *Light Appearing,* pp. 127, 137, 142; Eliot, *A Late and Further Manifestation,* p. 269; Letter of Eliot to Jonathan Hanmer, July 19, 1652, in Wilberforce Eames, *John Eliot and the Indians, 1652-1657* (New York: Privately printed, 1915), pp. 7-8; and Whitfield, *Strength out of Weakness,* p. 171.

82. There is an eschatological dimension to Eliot's concept of Scriptural Government, and it will be discussed later in this chapter.

83. Whitfield, *Light Appearing,* p. 127.

84. Sidney H. Rooy, *The Theology of Missions in the Puritan Tradition* (Grand Rapids: William B. Eerdmans Publishing Co., 1965) gives one chapter to Eliot and discusses this at length, pp. 156-241.

85. Whitfield, *Strength out of Weakness,* p. 171.

86. Shepard, *Day-Breaking,* p. 14.

87. Whitfield, *Strength out of Weakness,* p. 172.

88. Eliot, *Tears of Repentance,* p. 244.

89. *Ibid.,* p. 223.

90. John Eliot, *A Brief Narrative of the Progress of the Gospel amongst the Indians in New England* (London: Printed for John Allen, 1671), p. 14.

91. John Eliot, *Communion of Churches* (Cambridge: Printed by Marmaduke Johnson, 1665) is Eliot's longest work and spells this out in detail. It is an enlargement of what he wrote in some of his letters. I have used the copy in *MHSC,* Series Three, IX (1846), 127-164.

92. Ulrich Zwingli, *Exposition of the Christian Faith,* in *Zwingli and Bullinger,* selected trans. with intro. and notes by G. W. Bromiley, Vol. XXIV of *The Library of Christian Classics,* ed. by John Baille, John T. McNeill and Henry P. Van Dusen (26 vols., Philadelphia: Westminster Press, 1953-1969), p. 265.

93. Heinrich Bullinger, *On the Holy Catholic Church, ibid.,* pp. 290-291.

94. John Calvin, *The Institutes of the Christian Religion,* trans. by Henry Beveridge (2 vols.; London: James Clarke and Co., Lmtd., n.d.) III, viii, 1ff. All citations of the *Institute* are by book, chapter and paragraph.

95. William Ames, *The Marrow of Sacred Divinity* (London: Printed by E. Griffen, 1638), pp. 135-137.

96. *Ibid.,* p. 139.

97. William Perkins, *The Works of that Famous and Worthy Minister of Christ, in the University of Cambridge, M. W. Perkins* (3 vols.; London: Printed by J. Legatt, 1609), III, 475.

98. *Ibid.,* p. 20. For a detailed outline of the Christian life in terms of warfare and cross-bearing see *ibid.,* I, 85-92.

99. John Cotton, *Gods Mercie Mixed with his Ivstice, or His Peoples Deliverance in times of danger* (London: Printed by G. M., 1641), pp. 38, 34-35.

100. Shepard, *The Parable of the Ten Virgins Opened and Applied,* in *Works,* III, 22.

101. Haller, *Rise of Puritanism,* p. 34. See also pp. 142, 147ff., 150, 154, 159, 189, 259, 330 and 367.

102. Perkins, *Works,* III, 73.

103. William Ames, *An Analyticall Exposition of Both the Epistles of the Apostle Peter* (London: Printed for E. G., 1641), pp. 53, 56.

104. Alan Heimert, "Puritanism, the Wilderness and the Frontier," *The New England Quarterly,* XXVI (September, 1953), 361.

105. Williams, *Wilderness and Paradise,* pp. 28-140.

106. Perkins, *Works,* III, 375.

107. *Ibid.,* p. 475.

108. Whitfield, *Strength out of Weakness,* pp. 152-153.

109. Books that have been most helpful in this brief analysis of Calvin's eschatology are T. F. Torrance, "The Eschatology of the Reformation," in *Eschatology,* Scottish Journal of Theology Occasional Papers No. 2 (Edinburgh: Oliver and Boyd Ltd., n.d.), pp. 36-52; T. F. Torrance, *Kingdom and Church* (Edinburgh: Oliver and Boyd, 1956); and Heinrich Quistorp, *Calvin's Doctrine of Last Things,* trans. by Harold Knight (London: Lutterworth Press, 1955).

110. Quistorp, *ibid.,* p. 144.

111. See for example John Calvin Commentary on Matthew 24:14, in *The Works of John Calvin,* (51 vols.; Edinburgh: The Calvin Translation Society, 1844-1856), XXXIII, 130.

112. Calvin, Commentary on 2nd Thessalonians 2:2-10, *Works,* XLII, 326-27, 333, 338 and *Institutes,* IV, vii, 25.

113. Calvin, Commentary on Matthew 24:30, *Works,* XXXIII, 146, 148.

114. Joy Bourne Gilsdorf, "The Puritan Apocalypse: New England Eschatology in the Seventeenth Century" (unpublished doctoral dissertation, Yale University, 1964), has traced the development of Puritan eschatology in detail from the Reformation to the Seventeenth Century. It was most helpful to me.

115. Morison, *Winthrop Papers,* II, 138-139.

116. Quoted in Miller, *Errand,* p. 11.

117. Morison, *Winthrop Papers,* II, 138.

118. Calvin, *Institutes,* III, xiii, 10. I discussed this more fully than I can do here in an article. See Charles Chaney, "The Missionary Dynamic in the Theology of John Calvin," *The Reformed Review,* XVII (March, 1964), 34-36.

119. John Calvin, *Sermons of M. John Caluin on the Epistles of S. Paule to Timothie and Titus* (London: Imprinted for G. Bishop and T. Woodcoke, 1579), p. 152.

120. Calvin, Commentary on 1st Timothy 2:4, *Works,* XLIII, 55.

121. Calvin, Commentary on 1st Corinthians 2:12, *ibid.,* XL, 155.

122. Morison, *Winthrop Papers,* II, 142.

123. Cotton, *God's Promise,* pp. 14-15.

124. See White, *The Planters Plea,* pp. 1-6.

125. *Ibid.,* pp. 7-9.

126. *Ibid.,* pp. 29-30.

127. Ward, *Simple Cobbler,* p. 6.

128. Edward Johnson, *Wonder-working Providence,* ed. by J. F. Jameson (New York: Charles Scribner's Sons, 1910), pp. 268-269.

129. *Ibid.,* pp. 52, 146.

130. *Ibid.,* p. 32.

131. *Ibid.,* pp. 137-138.

132. *Ibid.,* pp. 58-59.

133. Shepard, *Day-Breaking,* p. 15.

134. Winslow, *Glorious Progress,* pp. 72-93.

135. Whitfield, *Light Appearing,* p. 119.

136. Whitfield, *Strength out of Weakness,* p. 157.

137. Whitfield, *Light Appearing,* p. 121.

138. *Ibid.,* p. 136.

139. *Ibid.,* p. 131.

140. *Ibid.,* p. 127.

Chapter 2

The Evangelical Impulse

When I was 16, we heard a Strange Rumor that there were Extra-
ordinary Ministers Preaching from Place to Place. Some Time in
the Summer Some Ministers began to visit us and Preach the Word
of God; it pleased the Lord to Bless and accompany with Divine
Influences to the Conviction and Saving Conversion of a Number
of us.

Samson Occum

In 1802, Abraham Marshall wrote a sketch of his father, Daniel Marshall,
for the *Georgia Analytical Repository.* The elder Marshall, influential Separatist
Baptist preacher in the South, was a native of Windsor, Connecticut. He was converted in 1726. But, in 1741, his son reported,

> our worthy *parent* was one of the thousands . . . who heard that
> son of thunder, the Rev. *George Whitfield,* and caught his seraphic
> fire. Firmly believeing in the near approach of the *latter-day-glory,*
> when the jews, with the fulness of the gentiles, shall hail their
> REDEEMER, . . . a number of worthy characters ran to and fro,
> through the eastern states, warmly exhorting to the prompt adop-
> tion of every measure tending to hasten that blissful period. Oth-
> ers sold, gave away, or left their possessions, as the powerful im-
> pulse of the moment determined, and, without scrip, or purse
> rushed up to the head of the Susquehanna, to convert the heath-
> ens . . . One . . . of these pious missionaries was my venerable
> *father.*[1]

The French and Indian War soon made the continuation of Marshall's
mission impossible. Yet the "powerful impulse," persisted, and he spent the re-
mainder of his life in itinerate evangelism and gathering churches on the southern frontier.[2]

This chapter is concerned with this *evangelical impulse* and its influence
on missionary thought and activity. A revolution came and went. A decade of
struggle for national balance passed. Fifty years of decline in the established
churches and the ascendancy of a benign rationalism had its effect. But when
the churches stirred to life near the end of the Eighteenth Century, they gave
themselves to missionary organization and action as never before. The dynamic
of the renewed efforts was that "powerful impulse" let loose in America during

the Great Awakening.[3] "Pious missionaries" crossed the mountains, sought out the Indian tribes and invaded the southern frontier. They gathered churches in the cities, preached to the Blacks, and ultimately spread out to the islands and continents of the world. The categories that marked the boundaries of their theology came from the Puritans. The undergirding spirit that moved them to action and flavored their theology was that of the Evangelical Revival.

Robert Ellis Thompson's remark that "the Great Awakening . . . terminated the Puritan and inaugurated the Pietist or Methodist age of American church history," though not exact, is not far wrong.[4] It was the beginning of a new era both in the history of American Christianity and the "evolution of the American mind."[5] However, Continental Pietism and the religion of the Great Awakening are not synonymous. Neither is the exact reproduction of the other. Nor was the Great Awakening merely a restoration of primitive Puritanism or the triumph of any other type of English nonconformity.[6] Puritanism, Pietism and Evangelicalism are related but distinct.[7] Some roots of Pietism reach back to English Puritanism.[8] The Evangelical Revival, throughout the entire Atlantic Community, received much from Continental Pietism. But the Great Awakening, the American expression of the intercontinental spiritual renewal, in terms of religious background, was a mixture of Puritanism and Pietism ground together in the crucible of the American experience. The resulting religious form was different from those elements that went into its making. The new compound was an American piety that took its shape, at least through the first half of the National Period, from its Puritan parentage.

It is emphasis rather than exact definition which distinguishes the two periods. The major emphasis of the Puritan era was the sovereignty of God while that of the Evangelical period was the reign of Christ.[9] One underlined sovereignty; the other underlined grace. The Puritan age, while it did not negate emotion, demote Jesus Christ, or decry compassion for mankind, accentuated the role and will of the inscrutable God. The new age of American Christianity did not deny God's sovereign rule, but it emphasized the place of the affections in religion, the role of Jesus the Saviour, and his free grace to save. This difference in emphasis also marks the change in missionary theology.

Cotton Mather: Missionary Thought in the Interlude

In the era between Eliot and Edwards three men stand out in New England's ecclesiastical history, Increase Mather, Solomon Stoddard and Cotton Mather. Increase Mather did not belong to the generation which really spanned the period. He belonged to the age of those who planted the New England colonies. Solomon Stoddard is characteristic of this time of interlude. His innovations in the observance of the Lord's Supper were another step away from the classical sectarian stance of early congregational Puritanism. He expressed great interest in the evangelization of the Indians and his exposition of the Great Commission of Jesus in Matthew 28 is a forerunner of the work of William Carey.[10] His long ministry in the frontier town of Northampton was marked by a series of revivals that were the promises of the much greater things to come.

However, the Great Awakening was in many ways a return to the more primitive ecclesiology of early Independency and was often characterized by the renunciation of the Halfway Covenant and the view of the Lord's Supper as a converting ordinance.[11] Stoddard was typical and illustrative of the time between Eliot and Edwards, but he does not tie those two periods together.

Cotton Mather most adequately spans this *Age Between.* His ministry began before the death of Eliot, and he died a few months after Edwards began his ministry in Northampton. He exposed every innovation, real or supposed, as a departure from the "Old Pathes," his own excepted, of course.[12] He defended early New England Puritanism as the latterday manifestation of primitive Christianity. He introduced the thought and work of continental Pietism to New England and America. His descriptions of a coming reformation and outpouring of the Holy Spirit are prophetic of the Great Awakening. He is a forgotten apostle of Christian union from the same mold as the later Nicholas Ludwig von Zinzendorf, a rare verbal artist of the beauty of union. The period's most prolific writer on missionary subjects (indeed, on almost all subjects), his interest was world-wide. The missionary activities he promoted were of global proportions. All this was wrapped in a view of history that demanded action here and now. This partially explains his phenomenal literary output.[13]

Cotton Mather, the ugly toad of Colonial America, has been made the personification of all that Americans have found repulsive in Puritanism.[14] He was characterized as a man with "cosmic vanity," without a "grain of liberalism in his makeup" and basically unrelated to reality.[15] More recently efforts have been made to transform the toad into a prince. Rather, these revisionists claim, Mather was a man with a "strangely miscellaneous, observant and practical mind," and should be seen as "an early version of Benjamin Franklin."[16] One problem is simply to excavate his ideas from the verbal avalanche poured out in his published works.

Certain of his missionary insights and viewpoints are needed to introduce the Great Awakening.

The Time of Mission

Cotton Mather was a premillennialist. At this point he differed from those Puritan preachers whom he counted his mentors and with the majority of those men who would lead the way in missionary organization in the early National Period. As Mather studied his Bible and contemporary events, he found no time remaining for the gradual evangelization of the whole world and a thousand year reign of peace before the coming of Christ. Some spiritual victories would be won, but only in the midst of great earth-shaking events. Nations would fall. The Papacy would crumble. Peoples would be converted. The church would be spread through all the earth. This would be proceeded by a new and greater Reformation than had ever been experienced before. However, everything would take place suddenly. Then the Lord Jesus would come, and the great latterday reign of peace would arrive. Mather's calendar was *Revelation* 6-11.

Mather came to these views very early in his life, though he did continue to modify and develop his opinion. On December 19, 1689, in a thanksgiving sermon celebrating the cessation of hostilities with the Indians and the accession of William and Mary, he asserted that the Glorious Revolution was the beginning of God's "Resurrection of His Dead People." It was time to consider

> Whether the Blast of the Second Wo Trumpet, be not just
> expiring, . . . Yea, Whether the Gospel . . . will not quickly
> have Liberty with and Efficacy, not only in Popish Countreys
> . . . but also in Pagan Countreys.

> In a word, Whether the Day is not at Hand, when the King-
> doms of the World, shall be the Kingdoms of our Lord, and
> of his Christ?[17]

Three months later he spoke of the place that New England would occupy in God's purpose. If God intended Satan to continue to hold America
during the "Happy *Chiliad* which His Church" was about to enter, then they
would all soon be dead or returned to Europe. But, as Mather suspected,[18] if
God intended to "wrest America out of the hands of its old Land Lord" then
their present problems would quickly end and something better than a "Gold-
en Age" would speedily arrive, perhaps before all the founders had died.

Two other ideas are important in Mather's eschatology. He looked forward to a new and greater Reformation:

> I do conceive, That the *Antichrist,* having before passed his
> *Time,* and his *Times,* did enter his Last *Half Time* at the
> REFORMATION in the Last Century, commenced at the
> year 1517 . . . Wherefore, . . . about an Hundred and Four-
> score Years, from that REFORMATION, I do Firmly expect,
> a NEW REFORMATION to be begun; a REFORMATION
> more Glorious, more Heavenly, more Universal far away
> than what was in the former Century . . . Behold . . . we
> are got into the very *Dawn* of the Day, when God will
> vouchsafe a marvelous Effusion of His own *Spirit* upon
> many Nations, and REFORMATION, with all Piety, and
> Charity, shall gain the Ascendent.[20]

This theme occurred over and over again in his works throughout his life.[21]

The second important aspect of the eschatology, which Mather developed fully in later life, was his concept of a new Pentecost. It first appeared
in his *Diary* on August 11, 1716

> Our Encumbrances are insuperable; our Difficulties are infinite.
> If He would please, to fulfill the ancient Prophecy, of *pouring
> out the Spirit on all Flesh,* and revive the extraordinary and
> supernatural Operations with which He planted His Religion in
> the primitive Times of Christianity, and order a Descent of His
> holy *Angels* to enter and possess His Ministers, and cause them
> to speak . . . under the Energy of *Angels,* and fly thro' the
> World with the *everlasting Gospel* to preach unto the Nations,
> wonderful things would be done immediately; His Kingdome
> would make those Advances in a Day, which under our present
> and fruitless Labours, are scarce made in an Age.[22]

Mather's *Diary* illumines the maturing of this idea.[23] He prepared two books
that dealt with eschatology and with the new Pentecost particularly. The

largest was never published, and the manuscript has been lost.[24] The second, *Malachi,* further develops this idea.[25] He wrote just before its publication:

> The Perswasion grows upon me, . . . that the Kingdome of God
> will not come on without a Return of the prophetic Spirit, in
> such Operations as planted Christianity in the primitive Times;
> that the mighty Operations of the prophetic Spirit, are from
> Angels whom our ascended Lord . . . sends with their various
> Gifts to possess the Children of Men.[26]

Mather always attempted to read the signs of the time. He tried to find the "time of the day," in God's timetable, and then the "work of the day," exactly what the Church should be doing at that point in current history. His own day was precisely the time of mission. Whatever else the particular historical situation might warrant, the day was preeminently the time for proclaiming the Gospel to the nations and making ready for the new Reformation and the new Pentecost.

> The Planting of Churches is one of those Good Things that are
> now Required of us. The Vast improvement of Navigation since
> the late invention of the Load stone and the Compass, has, like
> the other Changes of the World, the Concerns of the Church is
> the Bottom of it; it makes us able to carry the Gospel unto such
> Corners of the Earth, as have hitherto sat in, The Region of the
> Shadow of Death.[27]

The Scope of Mission

The missionary expansion of the Church was an integral part of that constellation of events that would immediately precede the consummation of history. It was cosmic in scope. Mather never confined his interest or his activities to the American scene. God's purpose included the whole world. Mather had an insatiable interest in what God was doing throughout the world. He decoded current events and located them in the divine program of history.

Mather gave aggressive leadership to the work of the New England Company among the Indians in America. He was appointed a commissioner of Indian Affairs for the New England Company in 1689. His interest antedated that appointment and continued after he resigned. Earlier Mather had very little Christian compassion toward the Indians,[28] but his overall attitude mellowed. The evangelization of the Indians became a major concern of his life. His appointment to the Board of Commissioners on Indian Affairs, along with that of Samuel Sewall, marked the most vigorous period of labor for the Commissioners in New England.[29]

> Had we done as much, as the French have done, for the Prose-
> lyting of the Indians, in our *East,* we had not seen more than a
> whole province there Consumed by their Depredations; and God
> knows how far we may at some time or other be so Chastised,

for our like Omissions, in other Quarters: A Twentieth part of the Treasure spent in our Wars with the Savages, would have gone far towards the *Civilizing,* and the *Christianizing* of them all: and then we had been delivered from such Wars for ever.[30]

Mather's *Diary* reveals his continual preoccupation with the Indian Mission. He took offerings in his own Church and promoted that work throughout the colony.[31] In 1699 he prepared his first book especially for use with the Indians.[32] From that time he kept busy preparing books for the Indians, reporting on the progress of the Gospel among them, and writing books to help those who evangelized them.[33] He also agitated for active missionary work among the Indians on Long Island and in Connecticut.[34] In conjunction with Godefridus Dellius, a Dutch pastor in Albany, he published one book specifically designed for Christianizing the Iroquois in New York.[35]

This was only one aspect of Mather's missionary concern. He was also interested in the evangelization of Spanish America. He prepared a catechism of the Christian faith for the presentation of the Gospel among Spanish-speaking people.[36] He had an inordinate interest in France. He often reported on the condition of Reformed Christians in that land, predicted the fall of Catholic France, and prepared two evangelical books to hasten that day.[37] He was interested in the conversion of the Negroes of New England and throughout the Americas. He prepared books for use by the slaves and those who owned them to assist in their conversion.[38] He was concerned with planting of Churches on the frontier and converting Roman Catholics.[39] He wrote and sent to Maryland a number of books for Catholics there.[40] Throughout his life he was burdened for the conversion of the Jews and published several works designed especially to present the Christian faith to them.[41] He reported every incident of Indian conversion and actively witnessed to and prayed for those with whom he came in contact.[42] Mather continued his father's interest in the Danish mission in Tranquebar. He supported it with money. He corresponded with missionaries there and with August Hermann Francke and published reports of the progress of the mission from Halle.[43]

For Mather these efforts for evangelization were a part of the task of the Church in the world and particularly the work which the Church was to be engaged in at that time. This is illustrated in *India Christiana.* It contains not only his most celebrated sermon on the missionary task but other "Instruments relating to the Glorious Design of Propagating our Holy Religion, in the Eastern as well as the Western *Indies.*" Christ must be preached in every corner of the world. Every land would one day be his.

The Instrument of Mission

The agent of missionary advance was a reformed, renewed and unified Church. Mather watched for signs of the beginning of the New Reformation. He prayed diligently for the New Pentecost. Late in life, he became the great American advocate of Christian union.

Cotton Mather's interest in Christian union went back before the turn of the Eighteenth Century. While Increase Mather was in England during the struggle to recover the charter of the Bay Colony, he joined with John Howe and Matthew Mead in bringing the English Presbyterians and Independents together under a new name, the United Brethren. The instrument of union was a document called the "Heads of Agreement." As soon as news of this event arrived in New England, Cotton Mather preached a sermon and published it along with the "Heads of Agreement" in a little book called *Blessed Unions.* It celebrates and explains the union that had taken place in England. He boasted,

> the Christians in the American *Regions* . . . do now send back
> the loud and long Echo's of your UNION . . . Not only have
> those of the *Scotch* and the *French* Communions, been admit-
> ted unto a *Transient* Communion in these Churches, when they
> have come with due Testimonials for it; but also . . . the Name
> of PRESBYTERIAN and CONGREGATIONAL (Yea, and
> EPISCOPAL too when Piety is otherwise visible) and I may add
> . . . ANTIPEDOBAPTIST, is of no Consideration; both . . . do,
> as one man carry the Affairs of our Lords Ecclesiastical Kingdom.[44]

Mather's acquaintance and correspondence with the German Pietists and specifically his admiration of Francke led to his most mature thought on Christian union.[45] He knew of the work of Francke and other Pietists by 1710. On February 3, 1709/10, he sent two little books to the press, he alleged, were a statement of "true *American Pietism.*"[46] He introduced a Biblical figure that was to recur again and again in his works and on which Mather's views of eschatology, mission and union seem to converge.

> I considered that the People who are shortly to be the *Stone
> cut out of the Mountain,* will be a People of these Principles
> and Practices. And I was willing, to contribute unto the Shap-
> ing of that People; and furnish them with Instruments of Pi-
> ety, that may be of Use among them. I shall also endeavour
> to send these things unto Dr. *Franckius, in Saxony.*[47]

Mather discovered a kinship with the Pietists, that was astonishing. Like Spener, Mather was greatly moved by John Arndt's *True Christianity.* And, in typical Matherian fashion, he laid plans to make it and other pietistic books just as effective in his life as possible.[48] He believed *"American Puritanism* to be so much of a Peace with the Frederician Pietism" that Puritan books, his own specifically, could be of great service in "Lower Saxony."[49] Mather read Spener, Francke, and Anthony William Boehme himself, privately with his wife, and to his family and servants at meals.[50] He gave their books to Harvard "to correct the wretched Methods of Education there."[51] Many of his later books were inspired by the work of the Pietists and were expositions of the same themes.[52] He advertised the great charity works of the Pietists in Germany.[53]

This kinship with German Lutherans was the catalyst that stimulated Mather's mature thought on Christian union. He concluded that there were "Indisputable Maxims of the everlasting Gospel" that were common to all true Christians.[54]

> My expectation is, that God will raise up some . . . who from the . . . Sacred Spriptures, will dig . . . the Maxims of the everlasting Gospel; the glorious Maxims, wherein all the Children of God really are united . . . The children of God and of His Kingdome, under various professions will arrive to a declared and explicit union on these Maxims; and lesser points will be depressed into their due subordination . . . The Brethren thus becoming sensible that they are so, will associate for the Kingdome of God, in such methods, that the things to be consumed by the Stone cutt out of the mountain shall be all broke to peeces before them.[55]

Mather spent years defining, perfecting and promoting his "Maxims of Piety." He first developed these simple statements of the essence of the Christian faith for the education of his family. In 1713, he added "the *Maxims of the Kingdome*" to his book, *Things to be more thought upon,* and asked that they might be "much considered and entertained in the World." He expressed a wider interest and suggested a greater importance for these Christian axioms. The expanded purpose was couched in an eschatological context. He suggested that "Societies be formed on these maxims" because this would facilitate the "Formation of the People, who are quickly to become a great Mountain, and fill the whole Earth." The maxims should be presented in such a way that "People of the lowest Capacity and even little Children" could understand.[56] Later in 1713 he published a book that contained an exposition of the maxims,

> *offered as the only uniting Maxims, and the most unexceptionable TERMS OF UNION for that people, who from small Beginnings will certainly and speedily become a great Mountain.*[57]

His interest in Christian unity continued the rest of his life.[58]

Mather usually listed fourteen maxims.[59] However, in a letter to the Danish missionaries in Tranquabar, calling the Maxims the "most important articles of which true Christianity primarily exists," he discussed only three:

> First . . . how the one God who exists in three Persons who created the world, is to be accepted as our God . . . and how it should be the preeminent aim in our life (to) . . . obey Him . . . and . . . avoid everything which His light . . . condemns as sin against Him.
> Furthermore, how Christ, the eternal Son of God, who appeared in the flesh . . . is our only Redeemer who died for us . . . on whom our faith is based and who reconciles us to

God.
. . . .
Finally, that if we are filled wholly with the love of God . . . it
is our duty to love our neighbour . . . and to live continually
after the golden rule.[60]

These three points, drawn out a little more precisely, are for Mather the real substance of the Christian religion and Christian ethics.

The clearest and most succinct presentation of the maxims is found in *The Stone Cut out of the Mountain.* In this booklet Mather linked eschatology, unity and mission together in a great chain of meaning for the Church. Referring to warring bees that were pacified when all were sprayed with scented liquor, he said,

Most certainly, the *Maxims of the Everlasting Gospel* exhibit
such a *Sweet-scented Liquor,* which being poured, and cast
upon the Church-Militant . . . All the Faithful Servants of God,
of those *Union* the Blood of their Saviour is the Eternal Ce-
ment, will presently be sensible, that they all have the *same*
Scent . . . and they will without anymore ado, give over
wounding one another.[61]

The figure of the "stone" that became a "great mountain" is found in *Daniel 2.* The "Mountain that would fill the whole earth" is the Kingdom of God which will come with a new heaven and a new earth. The "stone," which will carry all worldly kingdoms before it and soon spread through the whole world, is the Church.[62]

There is a direct and essential relationship between Christian unity, the Church's mission, and the goal of God in history. The time had come, Mather asserted, for Christians to "beat their *Swords* into *Ploughshares,* and their *Spears* into *Pruninghooks,* to Till the Garden of God." The maxims of the Gospel were to be the *"Ploughshares* and *Pruninghooks* . . . employ'd for the Cultivation of the *New Earth"* which would bring about a "Restored PARA-DISE."[63]

Labor in the service of the "stone" would surely bring participation in the glory of the "Mountain." This was the mission of the Church and the task of the Christian. "May our Glorious Lord," he wrote,

keep us always united in Services to the *Kingdome of the*
Stone that we may have our share together in the *Kingdome*
of the Mountain.[64]

Mather's missionary thought continued the theological categories of the Puritans. However, he opened new vistas that would become increasingly important during the Great Awakening.

Jonathan Edwards: Mission Theology in the New Age

The Great Awakening gave "a new direction to the religious life of the country" and marks the dawn of "a new age for the churches of America."[65] Though American society did not undergo a great transformation, some even insist that the Great Awakening separated the medieval from the modern in American history.[66] Jonathan Edwards is of crucial importance to any discussion of the Great Awakening. His thought is the great intellectual and spiritual vein from which missionary theology in the period is mined. His theology is the most profound expression of the fresh and vigorous impulse that flavored missionary thought and activity through the next seventy-five years. His contributions to the development of the missionary enterprise in the American churches are extremely significant.

The Importance of the Personal

In the summer of 1751, Edwards, who had been the most prominent pastor in all of New England for two decades, moved with his family to Stockbridge in the Housatonic Valley on the remote frontier of the Berkshire Mountains. Historical interpretation of this event has been remarkably consistent. Edwards, it runs, had no other choice. Move he must, and only Stockbridge invited. He was innately unsuited for a missionary's role, being too much of a mystic and too intensely studious to deal with the myriad of practical problems that the missionary life demanded. He experienced little success. Stockbridge did, however, provide a quiet retreat where he was able to reap the harvest of thought that his mind had produced in thirty years of active ministry. The Stockbridge years became a useful exile.[67]

This interpretation will not withstand careful scrutiny. Edwards had an opportunity to move to at least three other places.[68] He went to Stockbridge only after careful investigation and at the advice of a council.[69] Stockbridge was no quiet retreat. It was more like a living hell. The village, and his home especially, was often crowded with refugees from the Indian wars and colonial soldiers. The village was contorted with a party strife as severe as the conflict that had driven Edwards from Northampton.[70] Instead of being unsuited for the mission, only a man of Edwards' stature and courage could have unraveled the intrigue that threatened completely to dispossess the Indians and have withstood the pressure that the family of Ephraim Williams was able to bring to bear on him.[71] As for success, no Indian mission was successful in the 1750's. The entire decade was characterized by Indian unrest that finally culminated in the Seven Years War, which ended after his death. There is evidence that Edwards spoke with deliberate clarity and simplicity when he addressed the Indians.[72]

Edwards often referred to his plans to become a missionary as a "new and important business."[73] It was new to him, however, only in terms of a new personal role in a new place. It illustrates something of the importance with which Edwards viewed the missionary calling. His interest in Stockbridge, or in Indian missions in general, did not begin when he became a candidate for that office or when he edited the Brainerd papers.[74] Solomon Stoddard had left his grandson a heritage of missionary interest. Stoddard had been one of those, along with Cotton Mather and Benjamin Coleman, who had helped to halt the deterioration of Indian missions in the decades after the King Phillip's War.[75]

Moreover, the Stockbridge mission had been brought to birth in Northampton. John Stoddard, Edwards' uncle and closest friend, was the most powerful man in western Massachusetts. He was also more informed about Indian affairs than any man in New England.[76] Stoddard advised that the Housatonic Indians, uninfluenced by the French, were the best prospects for the mission. The decisive meeting for organizing the mission took place in Stoddard's house in March, 1734, the year of the first awakening in Northampton under Edwards' ministry.

Edwards was in close contact with the Stockbridge mission through all of its history. He often sent reports of it to his correspondents in Scotland. He passed on all the information that he could discover about any mission anywhere in the world to other ministers in New England, but with the Stockbridge enterprise he maintained direct ties. When Benjamin Coleman published John Sergeant's letter proposing the foundation of a boarding school for boys at Stockbridge, Edwards was named as one of those who accepted responsibility to "receive and disburse Monies."[77]

Moreover, Edwards' interest was not confined to the mission at Stockbridge. In the 1740s, when, under the impulse and fervor of the Revival, missionary work among the Indians was intensified, Edwards became one of the fathers of the whole movement. His interest and encouragement of David Brainerd is well known. His published letters contain in many references to John Brainerd and his work, and record several visits of John to Edwards' home. David Brainerd recommended two young men to the Correspondents of the Society in Scotland for Promoting Christian Knowledge shortly before his death. They were Elihu Spencer of Haddam (Brainerd's birthplace) and Job Strong of Northampton. In the summer of 1748 both were sent to Northampton to study under Edwards. Strong was prohibited from performing his mission because of ill health. Spencer did go to the Iroquois, and the church in Northampton contributed significantly to his mission.[78]

Stockbridge was not a forced exile for Edwards. The seven years he spent as a missionary to the Indians came after many years of interest in evangelizing the Indians. He did not look upon his ministry there as insignificant. Missionary work was an important strategy in God's plan for the ages. His practice was consistent with his expressed thought about the importance of the missionary task. However, the contribution of his missionary career to the forming of the missionary character of the American churches is not nearly as significant as the contribution of his theology. His own mission among the Indians takes its significance not from what he did to evangelize pagan peoples but from who he was as the theologian of God's great work of redemption.

A Theology of Evangelism

Edwards' first great contribution to missionary thought is what might be called his theology of evangelism. He held tenaciously to God's sovereignty and at the same time proclaimed the gospel boldly to all men. He defended God's decrees, but insisted that a man did not believe in Christ because he would not believe in Christ. He declared God's righteousness and justice in saving sinful man against the backdrop of God's sovereignty and the eschatological outpouring of God's Spirit in the latter days.

On July 8, 1731, in his first Boston lecture, Edwards drew the battle lines against the incipient Arminianism of New England's covenant theology.[79] The "nature and contrivance" of man's redemption was just such that

the redeemed are in every thing directly, immediately, and entirely dependent on God: they are dependent on him for all, and are dependent on him in every way.

God was the absolute and only source of all the good that the redeemed had. He was the agent, the "medium," through which all good came to the believer. He was himself the good that the believer had in redemption.[80]

The grace of God is absolutely free. God is under no obligation to bestow it. He could with justice reject fallen man just as he did fallen angels. Nothing good and excellent in man, nor any divine hope of repayment, attracted God's love to man. "He is sovereign, and hath mercy on whom he will have mercy." The whole work of redemption is completely dependent on God.

God has given us the Redeemer, and it is by him that our good is purchased. So God is the Redeemer and the price; and he also is the good purchased. So that all that we have is of God, and through him, and in him.[81]

No flesh shall glory in His presence!

The place of faith in this entire scheme is of interest here. It is Edwards' understanding of faith as it relates to God's sovereignty which is most important in his theology of evangelism. For Edwards faith, too, was a gift of God's grace. "It is of God that we receive faith to close with him, that we may have an interest in him. We are dependent on the power of God to convert us, and give faith in Jesus Christ, and the new nature." The doctrine that God was glorified in man's utter dependence on him in redemption revealed at least one reason "why faith is that by which we come to have an interest in this redemption." The nature of faith includes

a sensible acknowledgment of *absolute dependence* on God in this affair . . . Faith is a sensibleness of what is real in the work of redemption; and the soul that believes doth entirely depend on God for all salvation, in its own sense and act. Faith abases

> men, and exalts God; it gives all the glory of redemption to him
> alone . . . Humility is a great ingredient of true faith.[82]

Faith should properly be required of all who are redeemed, since this innately includes an awareness of man's absolute dependence on God. Faith is God's means of glorifying himself in redemption. It is the soul's *act* of entire dependence on God for salvation.

Awakening came to Northampton in 1734. Edwards later asserted that it was a fresh investigation of the doctrine of justification by faith alone that launched the revival and served as the point of departure through its duration.[8] In 1738, largely because he and the people in Northampton hoped that it would be instrumental in reviving that earlier awakening, Edwards published his lectures on justification by faith and four other sermons from that period. This provided a kind of evangelistic handbook for revivalistic Calvinists during the Great Awakening. The essay on justification explicitly states the doctrine. The remaining sermons show how the doctrine was put into practice.

Justification was far more than merely the forgiveness of sins or deliverance from wrath. It was also "an admittance of a title to that glory which is the reward of righteousness." A person is justified when

> he is approved of God as free from the guilt of sin and its
> deserved punishment, and as having that righteousness be-
> longing to him that entitles to the reward of life.

The crucial problem had to do with the import of the little word "by" in the phrase "justification by faith." Faith was *a* condition of justification, and, in a manner of speaking, *the* condition of justification. But because of the ambiguity of the word "condition," this was not the significance of the word "by." Properly speaking,

> there are many other things besides faith, which are directly
> proposed to us, to be pursued or performed by us, in order
> to eternal life, which if not done, or not obtained, we shall
> surely perish.

It is not this "inseparable connexion with justification" that is meant by the word "by." It is rather "some particular influence that faith has in the affair.[84]

Neither is faith the "instrument" of justification and salvation. Since faith is the act by which justification is received, how could it be both the instrument and the act? It was much more simple than this. According to Edwards, justification *by* faith was simply

> that (there being a mediator that has purchased justification)
> faith in this mediator is that which renders it a meet and
> suitable thing, in the sight of God, that the believer rather
> than others should have this purchased benefit assigned to him.

Christ purchased justification for infinitely unworthy creatures. God has declared that the qualification by which this benefit could be assigned to one person rather than another is faith. Faith is that which, in the sight of God, makes it a "meet and condecent thing," for a sinner to receive the justification that Christ has secured. This arrangement is consistent with God's nature, is dictated by God's wisdom, and results in God's glory alone.

Faith alone, rather than any virtue or goodness in man, qualifies him for justification. Even though faith is properly a Christian virtue, it is not

> on account of any excellency or value that there is in faith, that
> it appears in the sight of God a meet thing, that he who believes
> should have this benefit of Christ assigned to him, but purely from
> the relation faith has to the person in whom this benefit is to be
> had, or as it inites to that mediator, in and by whom we are
> justified.[85]

Between Christ and the true disciple, there is a new relationship. Christians are said to be in Christ and members of Christ. "This *relation* or *union* to Christ . . . is the ground of their right to his benefit." It is a real relationship that implies that the one is accepted, in God's sight, for the other. What properly belongs to Christ also belongs to the Christian. This is how faith is *the* qualification in a person that makes it acceptable for God to assign Christ's righteousness to him. "It is that in him which, *on his part,* makes up this union between him and Christ."

The believer is not given an "interest" in Christ as a reward of faith. Faith is an act, the very "act of unition" on the part of the believer. It is fit and proper, if two "intelligent active beings" are to be looked upon as one, that they be united by a mutual act of both. Faith is man's part in this union.

> God, in requiring this in order to an union with Christ as one of
> his people, treats men as reasonable creatures, capable of act and
> choice; and hence sees it fit that they only who are with Christ
> by their own act, should be looked upon as one in *law.*

Therefore, the real union between Christ and the believer becomes the foundation for the legal view that God has of that man, that his sins are forgiven, his punishment removed, and his reward deserved. In this manner faith alone justifies. "It makes Christ and the believer *one* in the acceptance of the Supreme Judge."[86]

This view of faith as the act of coming into a new relationship to Christ, a real union with Christ, and as that which "reasonable creatures, capable of act and choice" have as their part, provided a basis for evangelistic and missionary activities well into the National Period. This view in no way derogated God's sovereign and effectual call to the elect. Rather, Edwards found evidence in the Bible and experience that at certain times God poured out his Spirit in an extraordinary manner for the effectual calling of many to his Son. As the dawn of the millenial age approached there would be more and more of these times of harvest, until the whole world would be brought to the feet of Christ. In this *milieu* the sermons he published in 1738 were preached. An event like this called for celebration.

> Now if such things are enthusiasm, and the fruits of a distem-
> pered brain, let my brain be evermore possessed of that happy
> distemper! If this be distraction, I pray God that the world of
> mankind may be all seized with this benign, meek, beneficent,
> beautifical, glorious distraction!
> . . . .
> As there is the clearest evidence . . . that this is the work of
> God; so it is evident that it is a very great and wonderful and
> exceeding glorious work.[87]

Edwards' evangel was offered from two vantage points: (1) God's own nature as a God of grace and salvation and (2) the evidence that the present time was one of God's extraordinary times. "God bestows mercy" at the dictate of "his sovereign pleasure." Yet men should persevere, continue to press and even with violence, enter the Kingdom of God. Just because God was a god of mercy there was great hope.

> If you sit still, you die; if you go backward, behold you shall
> surely die; if you go forward, you may live. And though God
> has not bound himself to any thing that a person does while
> destitute of faith, and out of Christ, yet there is great probabil-
> ity, that in a way of hearkening to this counsel you will live;
> and that by pressing onward, and persevering, you will at last,
> as it were by violence, take the kingdom of heaven.[88]

He sometimes based his plea on Christ's tender compassion.

> And if you come, you need not fear but that you shall be accepted;
> for he is like a Lamb to all that come to Him, and receives them
> with infinite grace and tenderness . . . You need not hesitate one
> moment; but may run to him, and cast yourself upon him. You
> will certainly be graciously and meekly received by him.[89]

The awakening, however, provided the major note of urgency and hope for inviting men to Christ. God has his appointed times for exercising both judgment and mercy. Just as there are remarkable days of vengeance, God has "laid out in his sovereign counsels seasons of remarkable mercy." The revival of 1734 and the much greater explosion of the 1740s were those times of God's visitation.

> It is indeed a day of grace with us as long as we live in this
> world, in the enjoyment of the means of grace; but such a
> time as this is especially, and in a distinguishing manner, a
> day of grace. There is a door of mercy always standing open

for sinners; but at such a day as this, God opens an extraordinary door.[90]

In his famous Enfield sermon of 1741 he declared,

now you have an extraordinary opportunity, a day wherein Christ has thrown the door of mercy wide open, and stands in calling, and crying with a loud voice to poor sinners; a day wherein many are flocking to him, and pressing into the kingdom of God.[91]

Men were stupid and unreasonable not to act under this sort of encouragement.

At this point, at least one aspect of the relationship between revivalism and missions can be seen. In the eighteenth and early nineteenth centuries both have an eschatological dimension. Revivals, extraordinary outpourings of the Holy S pirit in the conviction, calling and conversion of sinners, are characteristic of this last age. Most of the evangelistic enterprises and missionary efforts of the late Colonial and early National Periods were undertaken in the confident expectation of these promised periods of the Spirit's outpouring. Seed could be sown, the ground cultivated, with the quiet assurance that God would have his harvest among all nations.

Knowing God's willingness to save and the empirical evidence that God was gathering his elect, Edwards called men to come to Christ. He invited them by faith to make Christ and everything belonging to Christ their own. He was merciless in his denunciation of those who excused themselves on grounds of their own inability and the decrees of God. Unconverted sinners "have rejected, and do wilfully reject, Jesus Christ." Christ does not seek a forced compliance. "He seeks a free and willing acceptance." He does not want men to "receive him *against* their will, but with a *free* will."

No man should object that he cannot make himself willing to have Christ as his saviour. Inability is no excuse if the defect also reaches the will. If a man *would* not accept Christ, if he *could,* his inability is no excuse. The fact that a man is not willing to have Christ is proof that he is not willing to be willing. The will always "necessarily approves" what it really wills.

Say what you will about your inability, the seat of your blame lies in your perverse *will,* that is an enemy to the Saviour. It is vain for you to tell of your want of power, as long as your will is found defective.[92]

For those who hid behind the decrees of God, Edwards said:

Let the decrees of God be what they will, that alters not the case as to your liberty, anymore than if God had only foreknown. And why is God to blame for decreeing things? Especially since he decrees nothing but *good.* . . . And what is that to you, how God has

fore-ordered things, as long as your constant experience teaches
you, that it does not hinder you from doing what you choose
to do.[93]

Edwards conducted a lifelong war with Arminianism. *God glorified in
Man's Dependence* constitutes one attack; certain sections of his *Five Discourses*
set off a second barrage. His *Careful and Strict Enquiry into the Modern Prevail-
ing Notions of the Freedom of Will* was calculated totally to destroy the enemy.
In this work he made his classical distinction between natural and moral inability. The concept was largely misunderstood by his theological descendants.[94]
But misunderstood or not, it became a very important distinction in the forming of an evangelical theology. Edwards related this distinction to evangelism
long before he used it in his grand attack on Arminianism.

Man is free, Edwards said in 1754, when he can *"do as he pleases."* This
defines the freedom of man. It consists in "his being free from hindrance or
impediment in the way of doing, or conducting in any respect, as he wills."
Edwards' distinction between *natural* and *moral* inability to do something even
if one wills to do that thing. Man is not free to fly, no matter how intensely he
may will to fly. But moral inability consists "in the opposition or want of inclination to do a thing." Moral inability is not, therefore, a real inability, because "the thing wanting is not a being *able,* but a being *willing.*"[95] A man who
cannot obey God because of a natural inability cannot be held responsible and
is not worthy of blame. A man who claims a want of inclination, or a lack of
desire, or some undefined inward opposition to obey God or love God, which
may be a real moral inability, is accountable, because the will is always exactly
identical with that which is most preferred by the mind. There is, properly
speaking, no such thing as a faculty of the will. It is the mind that wills, or
rather that chooses what is the most apparent good, which is the same thing.[96]
Moral inability is, therefore, without excuse.[97]

Edwards' choicest illustration of this distinction is the stubborn rebel
who, though the prison doors are open and his chains unlocked, will not come
out of his dungeon, ask forgiveness of his compassionate king and go free.

'Tis true, a man's evil dispositions may be as strong and immov-
able as the bars of a castle. But . . . it may properly be said to be
in the rebel's power to come out of prison, seeing he can easily
do it if he pleases.[98]

On the basis of this distinction, years before he wrote *Freedom of the
Will,* Edwards charged those outside of Christ with willful rejection of Jesus
Christ, the sin of unbelief.

Salvation is ready brought to your door; and the Saviour stands
. . . and calls that you would open to him, that he might bring it
in to you. There remains nothing but your consent. All the difficulty now remaining is with your own heart. If you perish now
. . . it must be because you would not come to Christ . . . All that

is now required of you, is that your heart should close with
Christ.[99]

These things form the theological foundation of Edwards' evangelism.
He postulated a new and lively view of faith that united the sinner with Christ
himself. He insisted that man was morally responsible to believe in Christ. Only
man's perverse will, his own choice, kept him from Christ. He boldly offered
salvation on the authority of the God of grace himself and in the context of
God's promise of latter day outpourings of the Holy Spirit. This kind of evangelism became the legacy of the missionary enterprise in the early National
Period.

Sign of the New Age

Jonathan Edwards also gave a new direction to eschatology in America.
In the Matherian Age, a period of almost constant war in Europe and America,
and of a declining vitality in Christian piety, the Christian hope had focused on
some cataclysmic and catastrophic invasion of history. With the breath of revival, Edwards moved back to the optimism of the Puritan fathers. The arrival
of the millenium would be progressive and gradual, rather than with one sudden
explosive denouement. The missionary activity of the churches had a significant
place in this schema for the new age. Edwardsean eschatology was to be significant in American missionary thought into the Twentieth Century. This constitutes Edwards' second great contribution to the development of American missionary theology.

In 1739, Edwards preached a series of sermons in Northampton which
he called *A History of the Work of Redemption.* They became the nucleus for
a project that he worked on for the rest of his life.[100] In these sermons Edwards announced the near and certain advent of the millenium. Though the
sermons were not published in his lifetime, he shared his millenial ideas through
several other publications.[101] When these sermons were finally issued in 1786,
they helped to fashion the eschatology of the new nation.

This eschatology was more a philosophy of history than an interruption
of history. He divided the time between the fall of man and the end of the
world into three periods. In the first, from the fall of man to the incarnation,
it was God's work to make preparation for Christ's purchase of redemption.
The second period, from Christ's incarnation to his resurrection, though the
briefest of times, was the most important period of history. In this period it
was God's work in the death of Christ actually to purchase man's redemption.
The last period, between Christ's crucifixion and the end of the world, was
"taken up in bringing about the great effect or success of Christ's purchase."
God's work of redemption in this period was uniquely to offer the redemption
Christ had secured to men throughout the entire world.

Edwards made his greatest contribution to missionary activity and
thought in his exposition of this third period. This period is the "time for ob-
taining the end, the glorious effect" of Christ's redemptive work. This goal gives

meaning to current history, that time between the resurrection of Christ and
his final coming in his Kingdom.

> The end of God's creating the world, was to prepare a kingdom
> for his Son . . . which would remain to all eternity. So far as the
> *Kingdom of Christ is set up* in the world, so far is the world
> brought to its end, and the eternal state of things set up — *so far*
> are all the great changes and revolutions of the world brought to
> their everlasting issue, and all things come to their ultimate period
> — *so far* are the waters of the long channel of divine providence,
> which has so many branches, and so many windings, emptied
> into their proper ocean.[102]

The events in this period of current history will attain the erection of
the kingdom of heaven. This *"kingdom of heaven* is that evangelical state of
things in the church, and in the world, wherein consists the success of Christ's
redemption." Setting up this kingdom is the work of redemption in the present
time. But it is to be accomplished in "various steps" beginning at the resurrection and continuing to the world's end.

God is, therefore, still performing his wonderful works in this present
age. History is progressively moving to its glorious consummation. The implications of Edwards' view are somewhat similar to those views expressed by the
late Jesuit missiologist, Jean Danielou. Danielou insisted that the "purport and
import of current history" is the Christian mission. The church's mission

> is what gives substance and consistency to the history of our era.
> It is the intrinsic reality underlying the phenomena of secular his-
> tory. It means the progressive building-up in love of the incorrupt-
> ible body of Christ which shall go through the fire of judgment.
> Being the work of the Holy Ghost, the mission continues the
> mighty works, the *mirabilia Dei,* recorded in the two Testaments.[103]

For Edwards, the "various steps" in setting up this kingdom consist
chiefly in "four successive great events, each of which is in Scripture called
Christ's coming in his kingdom."[104] The first was the wonderful works of
God in the days of the apostles that ended at the fall of Jerusalem. The second
great event in this third era of the work of redemption was the destruction of
the old pagan empire and the advance of the Church in the time of Constantine.
The third great advance would be marked by the destruction of Antichrist, and
the fourth would be ended with the literal appearance of Jesus Christ, the last
judgment, and the glorification of the Church.

Each successive step would constitute a new "coming" of Jesus Christ
and would be marked by a great deliverance of the Church, each deliverance
more glorious than the one before. The fall of Antichrist would be such a wonderful deliverance that the age of the latter day glory of the Church would be
ushered in. The gospel would be preached and believed, and churches gathered
throughout the world.

Edwards found himself in the midst of this third epoch, moving toward that great event that would mark a new and glorious day for the Church, the destruction of Antichrist. This third epoch was divided by the Reformation. The first half marked the darkest period of Christian history, the time of the rise of Antichrist. The power of Antichrist reached its zenith just before the Reformation. The Reformation marked the beginning of his fall. Things will be dark again for the Church, but the Antichrist will never regain his former strength.[105] The work of redemption since the Reformation had known victories and defeats. More recently its success had been marked by new reformations in doctrine, specifically in Russia with the work of Peter the Great, by the propagation of the gospel among the heathen, and by revivals of religion. Missionary work in America and Malabar and the awakenings among German pietists and in America were particular illustrations of this new success.[106]

Edwards found little remaining to be done before God should begin pulling down Satan's visible kingdom and the destruction of Antichrist. "There are but few things, if any at all, foretold to be accomplished before the *beginning* of that glorious work of God." It could be expected to begin in *"a very dark time* with respect to the interests of religion in the world." Though the progress of the kingdom might be relatively swift, there was no reason to think that "this great work of God" would occur other than *"gradually."* It would be a *time of means, not of miracle.*

> This work will be accomplished by *means*, by the preaching of
> the gospel, and the use of the ordinary means of grace . . . Some
> shall be converted, and be the means of others conversion. God's
> Spirit shall be poured out first to raise up instruments, and then
> those instruments shall be used with success.

The day of "Zion's prosperity" will be accomplished *via* three events.

> The Spirit of God shall be gloriously poured out for the won-
> derful *revival* and *propagation* of religion. This great work shall
> be accomplished, not by the authority of princes, nor by the
> wisdom of learned men, but by God's Holy Spirit.
> . . . .
> God, by pouring out his Holy Spirit, will furnish men to be
> glorious instruments of carrying on this work; will fill them
> with knowledge and wisdom, and fervent zeal for the promot-
> ing of the kingdom of Christ, and the salvation of souls, and
> propagating the gospel in the world.[107]

Revivals and missions are the signs of the New Age. They mark the third great spiritual "coming of Christ in his kingdom." The outpourings of the Spirit that constitute this renewal of the Church will bring about the work of conversion "in a wonderful manner." They will result in the calling of new laborers who will be zealous to carry the gospel to the nations of the world.

And as the gospel shall be preached to every tongue, the kindred, and nation, and people, before the fall of Antichrist; so we may suppose, that it will be gloriously successful to bring in multitudes from every nation: and shall spread more and more with wonderful swiftness.

The missionary action of the churches is the instrument for the destruction of Antichrist and the means by which the great day of the Church's prosperity is introduced.

Secondly, there will be a great reaction. Satan will see the crumbling of his kingdom and will fight back violently. Wars will result; nations will be shaken. When Satan "sees such multitudes flocking to Christ in one nation and another . . . all hell will be greatly alarmed." All the forces of Satan's visible kingdom shall be mounted against the Church.

Finally, the Church will "obtain a complete and *entire victory*." This complete victory will be over heresy and infidelity, the papal kingdom, Islam, Jewish unbelief and Paganism. When this happens,

> then the heathen nations shall be enlightened with the glorious
> gospel. There will be a wonderful spirit of pity towards them,
> and zeal for their instrument and conversion put into multitudes
> and many shall go forth and carry the gospel unto them.[108]

With this interpretation of history Edwards set the stage for the proliferation of missionary organizations and activity after the Revolution. He directly related missions to God's great work of redemption. The work would begin in the midst of struggle with infidelity and be occasioned by great revivals. It would witness the destruction of the papacy, the conversion of the Jews, and earth-shaking wars between nations. When the children of the Great Awakening read Edwards in the 1790s, they could only conclude that the end of the age had come upon them.

Co-laborers with God

In 1744, some ministers in Scotland issued a call to the churches of Scotland to join in a united effort of public prayer for the coming of the millenial age of the Church. After two years, the response was such that twelve ministers printed a memorial that was sent throughout Scotland and England and to America. This memorial, called *A Concert For Prayer, To Be Continued For Seven Years*, struck a spark in the imagination of Jonathan Edwards.[109]

To further the aims of this call to prayer Edwards prepared *An Humble Attempt to Promote Explicit Agreement and Visible Union Among God's People, In Extraordinary Prayer for the Revival of Religion, and the Advancement of Christ's Kingdom on Earth*. This book had a fantastic influence in stimulating missionary interest, organization and support in the early National Period and throughout the nineteenth century.[110]

This work is a penetrating argument for united prayer by Christians throughout the world on a vast scale and through an intriguing scheme. An exposition of *Zechariah* 8:20-22, this entire proposal is cast in an eschatological framework. It is second only to the *Work of Redemption* as a thorough and profound presentation of Edwards' eschatological views. It is a clearer presentation than the *Work of Redemption* of those views as a motive for missionary action.

> Nor is there any one thing whatsoever, if we viewed things aright, for which a regard to the glory of God, a concern for the kingdom and honour of our Redeemer, a love to his people, pity to perishing sinners — love to our fellow-creatures in general, compassion to mankind under their various and sore calamities and miseries, a desire of their temporal and spiritual prosperity, love to our country, our neighbours, and friends, yea, and to our own souls — would dispose us to be so much in prayer, as for the dawning of this happy day, and the accomplishment of this glorious event.[111]

However, the great contribution of the *Humble Attempt* is not in its interpretation of history. Its importance lies rather in its insistence that the glorious age of the Church's prosperity would be initiated by the common action of ordinary Christians. He asserted that the participation of God's people was not just desirable but essential, in God's order of things, to the glorious expansion and advancement of the Church throughout the world.

This text explained, "*how* this future glorious advancement of the church of God should be introduced." It would be accomplished by many people from many different places

> taking up a *joint resolution,* and coming into an express and *visible agreement,* that they will, by united and extraordinary *prayer,* seek to God, that he would come and manifest himself, and grant the tokens and fruits of his gracious presence.[112]

The duty called for was not just common, ordinary worship but special and extraordinary prayer. The goal sought in prayer was God himself. In a day of religious decline, it was through prayer that God would return to his Church and grant such manifestations of himself to his Church that the great day would come. The program of united prayer was an integral part of God's pattern for victory and success.

> There shall be given much of a spirit of prayer to God's people, in many places, disposing them to come into an express agreement, unitedly to pray to God in an extraordinary manner, that he would appear for the help of his church, and in mercy to mankind, and *pour out his Spirit, revive his work,* and advance his spiritual *kingdom* in the world, as he has promised.

Edwards, like Mather, joined union among Christians with the hope for the universal spread and triumph of the Church of Christ throughout the world. The responsibility was great for Christians to get together for this best of all reasons. The prophesy, he insisted, demanded visible and public union by explicit agreement with fervent and constant performance. Such a union in prayer would be a *"becoming* and *happy* thing, . . . acceptable to God, and attended with glorious success."[113]

    "Prayerfulness for the coming of Christ's kingdom" was a very great Christian duty. The spiritual renewal that would bring on the evangelization of the world, consistent with God's determined order, was contingent upon Christian union and prayer. He concluded from his exposition of the text that

> it is a very *suitable* thing, and *well-pleasing to God* for many
> people, in different parts of the world, by express *agreement,*
> to come into a *visible union* in extraordinary, speedy, fervent
> and constant *prayer,* for those great effusions of the *Holy Spirit,*
> which shall bring on that *advancement* of Christ's church and
> kingdom, that God has so often promised shall be in the *latter
> ages* of the world.[114]

    The great significance of the *Humble Attempt* was that it laid down a firm footing for the participation of the Church in the work of redemption. It made the age-old assertion that men could be co-laborers with God a vivid and practical reality. Entering into God's work was not just something that God invited his people to do, as if it were optional. Participation with God in bringing the world to that end for which he created it was essential. While his people waited on God, in a sense, God also waited on his people. Being a co-laborer with God in the work of redemption became an exciting and meaningful possibility.

    Nor did this participation stop with unity and prayer. God's people would be the instruments for spreading the spiritual awakening from nation to nation. Long ago he had observed that one person telling another was the most effective means by which a revival penetrated a community.[115] Another development that he expected at the very "beginning of that glorious work of God's Spirit" was that "the streams of wealth" would be turned toward God's people. Then they would "devote to the service of God the silver and gold" that came their way.[116] A deep conviction of the omnipotent power of God's sovereign government over all the world did not prevent Edwards and those who followed him from becoming "effort" Calvinists.

Creating a New Missionary Image

    When the Evangelical Revival came to Europe and America in the Eighteenth Century, Protestants had no attractive image of the missionary vocation. Two hundred years of confronting the farflung and astoundingly successful missions of the Roman Catholic Church had left the word with a bad taste in the mouths of most Protestants. By 1740, the missionary efforts of some Protestants had made the word somewhat more palatable. The New England Company had been supporting missionaries among the Indians for a hundred years. Over that century a considerable number of men had served as missionaries. However, it is difficult today, even for a church historian, to recall any of those men except John Eliot and, perhaps, the Mayhews.

None of the Mayhews was able, in spite of their remarkable record, to create a captivating image as missionaries to the Indians. Their isolation on Martha's Vineyard and the fact that the work of one fades into the work of another probably has contributed to this. Thomas Mayhew certainly was destined to make a singular contribution to Indian evangelization but for his untimely death. His father rendered yeoman's service to the growth of the Indian Church on Martha's Vineyard, but he was both missionary and helpful magistrate. Though Eliot was known as the "apostle to the Indians" long before 1740, he, nevertheless, lived and died as the pastor of the church in Roxbury. Even Cotton Mather, in his famous biography of Eliot, only devotes one section to him as an "evangelist." Eliot's career *almost* provided a Protestant missionary idea. But the formation did not quite take place. He was widely honored and extolled, but few were moved to imitate him.

The missionary impulse of Quakers had dispersed them almost all over the western world by 1740, but they were still not in the main stream of Protestantism. The work of the Society for the Propagation of the Gospel in Foreign Parts is important, but one looks in vain for a missionary among them whose character and career captures the imagination of the Christian world. In fact, their reputation among English dissenters, especially in New England, further soured the minds of many devout Christians to the idea of a missionary calling. This tinge of disgust grew out of the observation that the SPG missionaries spent most of their time attempting to proselyte dissenters to the Church of England and expended little energy to converting the heathen.[117]

The Danish mission to India certainly sent out capable men, but the missionaries always stood in the shadows of Francke. The great missionary movement from Herrnhut had just begun by 1740, and is, generally, a part of the overall Evangelical Revival. Missionary efforts intensified among Protestants in the century between 1650 and 1750, but until 1748, there was, with the possible exception of John Eliot, and perhaps, among some in Northern Europe, Bartholomaus Ziegenbalg, no great Protestant missionary saint. There was no firm image, as Ziegenbalg's career illustrates, of what a missionary was supposed to be and do. There was no single, great missionary example for inspiration and emulation. Protestants had only the apostle Paul.

On October 9, 1747, in the Edwards' home in Northampton, David Brainerd died. He put most of his papers in Edwards' hands to be disposed of in the way most likely to bring God glory.[118] The following year Edwards issued his *Account of the Life of the Late Reverend Mr. David Brainerd.* In this biographical work Edwards addressed himself to the same problem with which he dealt in *The Distinguishing Marks of the Work of the Spirit God* and *The Treatise Concerning Religious Affections.* He was trying to distinguish true from false religion. This time it was his intention to present "instance and example" rather than "doctrine and precept."

How far Edwards was successful is debatable. There can be no debate about the contribution that this book has made to Protestant missionary zeal and practice. Edwards exhibited a modern apostle, a flesh-and-blood illustration, who gave some substance to the character of the missionary vocation. Whatever Brainerd was in truth, he emerged from Edwards' *Account* as the "instance and example" of the missionary ideal. The long sought for missionary image for evangelical Protestants had been found. Brainerd provided an ideal with which later missionaries could identify and by which they could be challenged and inspired.

Brainerd was not a very likely candidate for the incarnation of the missionary ideal. Though a favorite of many of the leaders of the Revival party, his early association with Separatism was difficult for him to overcome, especially in Connecticut. His missionary career spanned less than five years. Edwards himself had a longer career as missionary to the Indians than did Brainerd. Gideon Hawley, Samuel Kirkland, Azariah Horton, John Brainerd and the two John Sergeants had much longer and more significant ministries during the same general era. But there were some things about Brainerd's life, or at least about that life as it was drawn by Edwards, that captured the imagination of those young and old who would give themselves to the missionary enterprise in the century that followed. The inspiration of Brainerd was especially important among those first young men and women who went to foreign fields from the American churches. However, the influence of Brainerd's image has continued even into the Twentieth Century.[119]

What were the distinctive marks of this Protestant missionary image? In this biography of Brainerd they do receive profuse and intriguing illustration. The missionary's one great concern is to glorify God. Love for Christ, compassion for souls in darkness, and pity for the pagan in his misery are secondary motives to the glory of God. Since that which gives God the greatest glory is "the enlargement of Christ's kingdom by the conversion of the heathen," the missionary is one who is engaged, without any reservation, in this great work. A few months after his ordination and his final decision not to accept the invitation to become a settled pastor, Brainerd wrote:

> last year I longed to be prepared for a world of glory, and speedily to depart out of this world; but of late all my concern almost is for the conversion of the heathen; and for that end I long to live . . . I long and love to be a pilgrim; and want grace to imitate the life, labours, and sufferings of St. Paul among the heathen. And when I long for holiness now, it is not so much for myself as formerly; but rather that thereby I may become an 'able minister of the New Testament,' especially to the heathen.

"All my desire was the conversion of the heathen."[120]

Self-sacrifice is the primary virtue of the missionary. He has given up all to follow Christ. Brainerd was never very far from a settlement of whites. He regularly, especially in the early part of his ministry, spent the Sabbath in an English-speaking settlement. He was close enough in the most difficult time of his ministry with the Indians often to join in family prayers in an English home. He also made regular trips back to the seacoast. Yet the total impact of this biographical work is that he was completely alone and separated from the civilized world in order to reach the pagans.

Several things contributed to this. First, Brainerd's diary, and his *Journals*. which were published before his death,[121] are primarily documents of his inner soul, not the events of his life. It is difficult to read these documents and really know what he was doing. Second, Edwards' purpose gives emphasis to the workings of the mind and emotions. But primarily, the accent on self-sacrifice seems to have been an integral part of Brainerd's own concept of the missionary calling.

> I . . . could think of undergoing the greatest sufferings, in the cause of Christ, with pleasur e; and found myself willing, if God should so order it, to suffer banishment from my native land, among the heathen, that I might do something for their salvation, in distresses and deaths of any kind.[122]

He linked his vocation as a missionary directly with self-denial and self-sacrifice:

> my heart rejoiced in my particular work as a *missionary;* rejoiced in my necessity of self-denial in many respects; and still continued to give up myself to God.

Later he reported, "I . . . did give up myself afresh to God, for life or death, for all hardships he should call me to among the heathen."[123]

The consequence of the missionary's work was progress in the work of redemption. The missionary was the instrument through whom God chose to do his work. The sudden and sovereign outpourings of God's spirit which brought success to Brainerd's mission exactly fit the pattern that Edwards had asserted God would use in converting the Gentiles and bring in the day of the Church's prosperity. Brainerd laboured for almost four years without a single conversion. Then, without warning, some began to respond to his message. This came when Brainerd had almost lost hope, when he was considering resigning his commission, and when he was physically weak. Brainerd asserted that it was just because God was concerned with his glory that "*this* was the very season that God saw fittest to begin this glorious work in." Edwards emphasized the pattern of success. It was interesting to note

> how great and long-continued his desires for the spiritual good of this sort of people were; how he prayed, laboured, and wrestled, and how much he denied himself, and suffered, to this end.[124]

The missionary could do his work with confidence. For God would sooner or later do his work. "Special" success would come. For God had designed, in bringing the latter day glory of the Church, to pour out his Spirit on all flesh.

These four areas mark Edwards' major contribution to the developing missionary character of the American churches. All four relate the mission of the Church to God's great work of redemption. Edwards' thought is the most important theological pillar upon which the churches of the new American nation were to erect their missionary organizations. It was upon Edwardsean principles that much of the missionary labour in the early National Period was undertaken.

Samuel Hopkins: Missionary Theology Through the Revolution

Frank Hugh Foster, in *A Genetic History of New England Theology,* contrasted the influence and importance of Joseph Bellamy and Samuel Hopkins. He asserted that, when Hopkins moved from the frontier to Newport

> he became involved in larger attempts, and performed a larger service . . . His theological service was larger, for he gathered his theology into the first New England 'system,' but he was also a reformer . . . (and) gave the impulse which finally brought into existence the American Board of Commissioners for Foreign Missions.[125]

Many have concurred in this estimate of Hopkins' importance to the beginning of extensive missionary activity in America. William Warren Sweet averred that Samuel Hopkins should be called the "Father of American Missions."[126] The principle spokesman for this view is Oliver Wendell Elsbree. In the only work that has attempted to tell the story of the early developmnnt of the American missionary enterprise, *The Rise of the Missionary Spirit in America,* 1790-1815, he affirms that "it is Hopkinsian Calvinism . . . that made the most effective contributions to the cause of disinterested benevolence in that it furnished men and missionary machinery for carrying the gospel" to the world.[127]

However, more careful study of Hopkins' thought and influence modifies this claim. Elsbree's thesis can be qualified at several points. Hopkins' influence is not direct and intensive, but indirect and restricted.[128] The role of Hopkins' theology has been overestimated.

The school that grew up around Edwards' writings developed along two lines.[129] That branch which historians have alleged most directly related to the developing American missionary movement was headed by Hopkins.[130] However, Samuel Hopkins' thought was not the only theological fabric of which the missionary enterprise of the American churches was constructed. His distinctive ideas were not even the only theological element in mission work in New England. Rather on principles common to all Edwardseans, and, as a result of a series of cooperative efforts, the great missionary organizations in New England were created. Those views that set Samuel Hopkins' theology apart are not the central tenets of this missionary theology.

Ezra Stiles listed those tenets that were popularly held to be uniquely Hopkinsian. These points were

> that an unconverted man had better be killing his father than
> praying for converting grace; that true repentance implies a
> willingness and desire to be damned for the glory of God; that
> we are to give God thanks that he has caused Adam to sin and
> involve all his posterity in total depravity, that Judas betrayed
> and the Jews crucified Christ, &c.; that the children of none
> but the communicants are to be baptized, &c.; that the churches
> and ministers are so corrupt and Laodicean, and have so inter-
> mixed with the world, that the New Divinity churches and
> ministers cannot hold communion . . . (with) them.[131]

When one strips the satire from this caricature, some of these points were generally common to all Edwardseans. Edwards, Hopkins and Bellamy all refused to admit that the faithful use of the means of grace laid any obligation on God.[132] All three insisted that God permits sin and orders sinful acts so that they result in good.[133] All three would have insisted that only the children of communicants are to be baptized.

Leonard Woods insisted that only five main points separated the Hop-kinsians from the others "attached to the theology of Edwards:" 1) a willing-ness to endure the just penalty of the law and to sacrifice ones own eternal life if the glory of God required it; 2) that God is the direct efficient cause of sinful acts in the same manner as of holy deeds; 3) that man is fully able to render perfect obedience to the divine law; 4) that "imputation" does not im-ply a literal transfer of personal attributes and personal acts; and 5) that all sin is actual sin, since original sin is not a corruption o the moral nature. "But," Woods concluded,

> in reality Hopkinsians were not more distinguished by their
> efforts to defend the peculiar opinions above specified, than
> by the prominence they gave to the grand principles which
> they held in common with other Calvinists, and by the zeal
> and fidelity with which they taught them.[134]

On these "grand principles." reaching back to Edwards, the missionary organization and activity of the American churches arose.

This is not to suggest that Samuel Hopkins' thought did not play an important part and make a distinct contribution to the developing missionary character of the churches. Samuel Hopkins spanned the era of the Revolution. His system became a sort of theological conductor from colony to nation. But it is as he stood in the lineage of Edwards that his theology is most important for laying the ground work of mission. Only one of his leading ideas — disin-terested benevolence — made a distinct contribution to later missionary theol-ogy. However, this concept was so significant that it became one of the slogans for the great missionary advance of the Nineteenth Century.

Continuing a Syndrome

Hopkins, like Edwards, was a fervent advocate of missionary endeavor. Edwards was a pastor, theologian and missionary statesman. Hopkins followed in his train. Both men were not only great theologians but also personally involved in efforts to extend the Gospel of Christ to all peoples.

At Great Barrington, Hopkins spent almost a quarter century as a neighbor of the Stockbridge mission. The settlement around the Indian mission was only seven miles from the farm where Hopkins lived. In 1750, after John Sergeant's death, he was invited by the Commissioners in Boston, the English church in Stockbridge, and the Indian congregation to become their pastor and missionary. He declined but recommended Jonathan Edwards to them. When Edwards left Stockbridge, Hopkins preached for some time for the Indian church.[135]

On July 23, 1769, Hopkins began preaching for the First Congregational Church of Newport, Rhode Island. There he reached his maturity as a theologian and became one of the pioneer advocates of the abolition of slavery in America. In these efforts he became the close friend and colleague of Moses Brown, the Quaker philanthropist and abolitionist in Providence, and established lasting friendship with Granville Sharp in England and other leaders of the movement for manumission. Hopkins' antislavery ideas were couched in his concern for the extension of the church and his conviction that all nations would eventually turn to Christ.

Sometime in 1770, Hopkins attacked slavery and the slave trade from his pulpit. Because Newport was an important center of slave trade, his open opposition to slavery and its supporting trades created unrest in his church and the community. In 1784, he asserted that Newport was the most guilty city on the American continent "respecting the slave trade" and had been in a "great measure, built up by the blood of the poor African."[136]

The sting of this early attack may have been eased somewhat by his growing interest in another plan. In April, 1773, Hopkins approached Ezra Stiles of the Second Congregational Church with a novel idea. He suggested that they unite in raising funds to send Negro ministers as missionaries to Guinea in Western Africa. Stiles did not at first favour the idea. He suspected Hopkins' motives. If successful, he expected that the movement would undergo secularization as he judged Eleazar Wheelock's Indian School had done. He anticipated opposition from the Anglicans already in Africa.[137] Also he was perhaps somewhat sympathetic with Charles Chauncy's suggestion that a white missionary, not of Hopkinsian principles, be sent with the Negro brethren. Chauncy thought the Africans had "better continue in paganism than embrace Mr. H. scheme."[138]

Hopkins suggested two possible candidates, Bristol Yamma and John Quamine, both members of his own church. Yamma was still a slave. After Stiles had met and interviewed the two men and discovered that Hopkins was willing for them to be trained under Witherspoon at Princeton, he changed his mind.

They issued two broadsides that described their plan and called for funds. The appeal addressed especially those who were "convinced of the iniquity of the *slave trade*" and suggested that such a missionary effort was the "best compensation" available for atrocities inflicted on the Africans because of slavery. It called on all who prayed *"Thy kingdom come"* to "forward this attempt to send the glorious gospel of the blessed God to the nations."[139]

The first appeal was dated August 31, 1773. The interest was significant but not overwhelming. On November 21, 1774, the two Negroes sailed for Princeton. A second circular was published in April, 1776. It reported on the progress of the two men under Dr. Witherspoon, reported favorable correspondence with the Black SPG missionary, Philip Quaque, already working in Guinea, and appealed again for funds actually to launch the mission. The Society in Scotland for Promoting Christian Knowledge had contributed thirty pounds. Two more candidates had come on the scene, Alsmos Nubia and Newport Gardner. So had hostilities with England. The mission failed because of war and the lack of general support.

After the Revolution, Hopkins continued his efforts. Three of the candidates were still available for the mission. He also proposed, in 1784, a colonization plan to go hand in hand with the evangelization program. His plan called for the outfitting of a trading ship for western Africa manned by free Blacks with instructions not only to trade but to find and secure suitable land for a colony. Then the colony would be outfitted and established. Such a plan would not only provide a place of refuge for slaves who had secured their freedom but would also be a means of Christianizing Africa, of discouraging slave traffic, and providing a much needed outpost for American trade.[140]

This plan, too, was unsuccessful, though he advocated it until his death. When the first group of colonists left for Liberia on January 4, 1826, Salmos Nubia and Newport Gardner were aboard. They were deacons in the Church constituted among the immigrants one week before. All of the first group of colonists were from Rhode Island. Hopkins' personal efforts, at this point, come into direct relationship with early Nineteenth Century attempts at African evangelization and colonization.

Slavery and Missions

Hopkins published three short pieces on the slavery question. His opposition to slavery was grounded in his understanding of the Christian faith. It was the natural and inevitable consequences of his understanding of disinterested benevolence. His optimism that slavery would be finally overcome was grounded in his theological understanding of history. Slavery's demise was part and parcel of the triumph of Christ over all nations. The defeat of slavery and the planting of the church of Christ throughout the world were both a part of the great and glorious work that God was doing in the world.

In 1776, *Dialogue Concerning the Slavery of the Africans* was a bold and devastating attack on both the slave trade and slavery. Systematically the arguments in defense of slavery are demolished. The pamphlet was dedicated to the Continental Congress, and an appeal was made for the Congress to make slavery illegal on the basis of the same logic that led that Congress to resist the tyranny of King George. Hopkins' case, like that of Isaac Backus for the dissenters in New England, in spite of its reasonableness, went unheeded.

One of the arguments in favor of the slave trade was the assertion that in reality the slavers were ships of mercy, for they brought the Negro from "a heathen land to places of gospel light, and . . . put them under special advantages to be saved."[141] The West Indies and the plantations of the southern colonies were not places of gospel light, Hopkins alleged. The fact that they were held in bondage by men claiming in some fashion to be Christians, instead of helping, only served "to prejudice them in the highest degree against the Christian religion." Nor could this hypocritical evangelical justification of slavery or the fact that some few slaves were converted be construed as obedience to the missionary command of Christ. To adopt slavery as a missionary method was a disobedience to the stated program of Christ for his Church.

> To take this method to Christianize them would be a direct and
> gross violation of the laws of Christ. He commands us to go and
> preach the gospel to all nations, to carry the gospel to them, and
> not to go and with violence bring them from their native country
> without saying a word to them, or to the nations from whom they
> are taken, about the gospel or anything that relates to it.[142]

Hopkins' second publication on slavery was issued under the pseudonym *Crito.* It was designed especially for the Constitutional Convention then meeting in Philadelphia. It took the Declaration of Independence for its text. Slavery and the slave trade formed a modern Achan, who brought trouble and defeat to the new American Israel. Hopkins' list of American troubles is a contemporary expose' of the failures of the Confederation. He judged them all to be consequences of the "frown of Heaven" because of slavery.[143]

Hopkins' third publication against slavery was published in 1793. It is one of the great missionary sermons of the Eighteenth Century and has been almost completely overlooked as such. Delivered before the Providence Society for Abolishing the Slave Trade, May 17, 1793, its text was Mark 16:15, "Go ye into all the world and preach the gospel to every creature." Along with William Carey's *Enquiry*, published a few months before, it is one of the early modern interpretations of the last commission of Christ as a great missionary command to be obeyed by the modern church.[144] "This command of Christ," he said,

> respect not only the apostles and disciples who then heard him
> speak, and the ministers of the gospel in general who have since
> been, . . . appointed to that work, but is extended to all Christians, in every age of the church, requireing them in all proper
> ways, according to their ability, stations, and opportunities, to
> promote this benevolent design, and exert themselves for the

furtherance of the gospel, that, if possible, all may hear and
share in the happy effects of it.

This command was an expression of the greatest divine benevolence to
man. When Christ had finished his redemptive work, which delivered man from
sin and death,

> he ordered that this good news should be published through the
> whole world, and the offer of this salvation be made to all man-
> kind, of whatever nation or complexion, whether Jews or Gentiles,
> the more civilized or barbarians, rich or poor, white or black; this
> being the only remedy for lost man, suited to recover him from
> that state of darkness, sin and misery in which the world of man-
> kind lay.[145]

The gospel of Jesus Christ was God's greatest kindness to man. It not
only delivered him from death and hell and fitted him for heaven and eternal
life, it made the best kind of life on earth a possibility. It forms men into "intelligent and good members of society." It "raises the mind" to the contempla-
tion of the most sublime objects and thus makes men "truely wise" and dutiful.
It makes men into creatures of righteousness and universal benevolence who love
their neighbors and live in harmony with them. It banishes the evils of mankind
and institutes kindness and love. To be engaged in this enterprise is therefore an
act of the greatest benevolence and the natural consequence of the proper understanding of God's great benevolent act in Christ.

> Every true disciple of Christ who understands the gospel, and
> prizes it above silver and gold, and whose heart is expanded
> with love to Christ and benevolence to his fellow-man, must
> not only wish and pray that all nations may enjoy the bless-
> ings of it, and come to the knowledge of this saving truth, but
> consider it as an unspeakable privilege to be in any way, and
> in the least degree, an instrument of promoting this design,
> whatever labor and expense it may require.

The gospel is "suited" to root out the evils of the world and to "wholly
abolish slavery," where that gospel is "fully and faithfully preached, and cordial-
ly received and obeyed." This will surely come to pass because God has assured
that "the time is hastening on, when all the people shall be righteous and benevolent." Therefore, it is the Church fulfilling its mission that is the greatest instrument for good in the world. It is through the gospel proclaimed and believed
that victory over evil shall be won.[146]

Hopkins believed not only that God had determined to bring slavery to
an end in the world but also that God would make this great evil an instrument
of good to the world. Perhaps it was "designed by the Most High to be the
means of introducing the gospel among the nations in Africa." In this way the
evil that the Africans had suffered through slavery might be the occasion of an
"overbalancing good. It might hereafter appear," he asserted hopefully,

> as in the case of Joseph . . . that though the slave traders have
> really meant and done that which is evil, yet God has designed
> it all for good, the good which all this evil shall be the occasion.[147]

Because God characteristically overruled man's evil with good, His people should give their best prayer and exertions to promoting this "happy
event." Whatever happened, Hopkins assured his hearers,

> we are engaged in a cause which will finally prosper. The slave
> trade, and all slavery, shall be totally abolished, and the gospel
> shall be preached to all nations; good shall be brought out of
> all the evil which takes place, and all men shall be united into
> one family and kingdom under Christ the Savior . . . In the
> prospect of this we may rejoice in the midst of the darkness and
> evils which now surround us, and think ourselves happy if we
> may be, in any way, the active instruments of hastening on this
> desirable predicted event.[148]

Disinterested Benevolence

This sermon introduces us to the other aspect of Hopkins' thought that
must be mentioned. His greatest contribution to the development of missionary
theology in America was his concept of disinterested benevolence.

Hopkins was not a theologian of note until after the death of Edwards.
His first published work was in preparation during the time that Edwards was
deciding to move to Princeton. It was not published until after Edwards' death.
At Edwards' death, Mrs. Edwards put her husband's papers in Hopkins' hands
and asked him to prepare a memoir. Hopkins studied Edwards' manuscripts for
several years. His confidence as a theologian was born during that time.[149]

Disinterested benevolence reached back to Edwards. In 1765 Hopkins
was the editor of a volume containing Edwards' *Nature of True Virtue.* Hopkins contended that this little volume could be improved and that, if Edwards
had lived, he would have made "some changes" before publication.[150] In 1773,
when *The Nature of True Virtue* had come under attack by William Hart, Hopkins published *An Inquiry into the Nature of True Holiness.* In this book he
first made extensive use of the term "disinterested benevolence." He denied
that he had departed from Edwards. His was the "same account of holiness for
substance, though under a different name. All I can pretend to," he continued,

> as an improvement on (Edwards), is to have explained some things
> more fully than he did, and more particularly stated the opposition
> of holiness to self-love, and shown that this representation of holi-
> ness is agreeable to the Scripture: and to have answered some ob-
> jections he had not mentioned, and made a number of inferences.[151]

Hopkins does not base his presentation on the profound philosophical
ground that characterizes thn work of Edwards. Hopkins "lacked the intellectual

grasp of his master, and therefor e could not but modify his teaching at every turn."[152] Nevertheless, it was Hopkins' "disinterested benevolence" and not Edwards' "benevolence to being in general" that became the slogan of America's missionary movement in the early Nineteenth Century.

For Hopkins, holiness consisted of conformity to the law of God. This conformity, expressed in one word, is love.[153] Yet, he insisted, all love is not holiness. That love specifically of which holiness consists is

> love to God and our neighbor, including ourselves, and is universal benevolence, or friendly affection to all intelligent beings. This universal benevolence . . . is the whole of true holiness.[154]

Sin is the opposite of true holiness. Properly speaking it can be defined as self-love, which is "wholly an interested, selfish affection."[155] On the other hand, true holiness, or "universal benevolence of love to being in general," is a completely disinterested benevolence which has as its object universal being and the highest good of the whole.[156] Disinterested benevolence, thus, actually describes the moral character of God. Divine love and disinterested benevolence are exactly the same. "Disinterested benevolence is the love in which God's holiness consists."[157] God's requirement for man, or the holiness that the law of God demands, is nothing less than conformity to this kind of love, or disinterested benevolence.

Disinterested benevolence is, therefore, the sign of true religion. It is the one essential mark of the work of the Spirit of God on a man's heart. The great concrete expression of one's election by God was this desire to serve God and mankind without any self-interest. In his *System of Doctrines,* Hopkins explained:

> Men are no further converted than they are conformed in the exercise and affection of their hearts to the law of God, which requires disinterested love, and nothing else, and excludes and forbids all selfishness, or self-love, which is the same. Therefore, the new heart and all truly Christian exercises, consist in *disinterested affection.*[158]

This natural and spontaneous character of disinterested benevolence makes it important to the missionary enterprise. The "highest and most remarkable exercise" of God's holy love, which consists in disinterested benevolence.

> appears in redemption, in giving his Son to die for sinners . . ., and that the holiness of men consists in imitating this benevolent love.

The missionary task is thus the highest, noblest and most disinterested task in which a Christian could become involved. Missionary activity was the finest expression of disinterested benevolence, or of real and vital religion.

Hopkins strengthened the ties between disinterested benevolence and missionary themes by relating it to the kingdom of God. Disinterested benevolence in no way conflicted with the command of Christ to seek the kingdom of God and

his righteousness. In fact, it was in no manner distinct from, but rather completely consistent with, seeking God's kingdom. For, he explained,

> in seeking the glory of God, and interest of his kingdom, we
> necessarily seek the greatest good of mankind; and, so far as we
> are devoted to their best interest, we act as friends to God, and
> seek his honor and the interest of his kingdom. The whole, there-
> fore, is summed up in *seeking first the kingdom of God,* or mak-
> ing this our supreme and ultimate end, so as to be willing to do or
> suffer anything that shall be necessary or proper to promote this.
> In this the love of God and our neighbor centre (sic) in one point,
> so that they cannot be divided; and this affection, in which all
> holiness consists, really has but one object viz., *the kingdom of
> God.*

The kingdom of God that is to be sought is nothing less than the "glorious work of redemption, including the salvation of the redeemed and the overthrow of all (God's) enemies. The holiness of men consists wholly in seeking this
kingdom which is love to God and their neighbor, or universal benevolence."[159]

In the concept of disinterested benevolence the two great missionary motives, the glory of God and the salvation of man, become one. "Christ," Hopkins
asserted,

> was devoted to the greatest general good, the glory of God in the
> salvation of sinners; or that kingdom of God in which God is glori-
> fied in the highest degree, and all the good of the creature is com-
> prised. So that his being wholly devoted to the glory of God . . .
> was not in the least inconsistent with his benevolence to man, nor
> did in any degree exclude it; but the latter is implied in the former,
> and the more benevolence he exercised towards God in seeking his
> glory, the more love did he exercise and discover to man. So that
> Christ did not only seek the glory of God and the salvation of men,
> and express his love to God and man in the same actions, but his
> was one and the same thing, the greatest happiness and glory of
> God's kingdom, or the greatest good of the whole; so that he really
> sought but one thing, which is all comprised in the glory of God.[160]

This confounding of the two great missionary motives, led, by the 1820s,
not to the greatest emphasis on the glory of God but to the gradual disappearance
of this primary missionary motive. "The glory of God," Hopkins said, "and the
salvation of men by Christ are not to be distinguished as different objects of pursuit." When you seek one, you necessarily seek the other. This identification was
a surrender to the spirit of the Age of Revolution. "Calvinism had unconsciously
adopted the ideals of its humanitarian rivals, appropriated their philosophy and
their social moralism."[161] Disinterested benevolence provided a great impetus in
the missionary movement for improving mankind's physical and social conditions.
It also thereby became the primary defense for the missionary enterprise. Yet disinterested benevolence contributed not only to the waning glory of God in theol-

ogy but also to the decline of the glory of God as the great driving force of the missionary enterprise.

Disinterested benevolence by definition is concerned with the social and physical condition of man. Hopkins' peculiar eschatological slant helped to foster and direct this concern and to fashion the missionary character of the American churches as one concerned both with changing religious commitment and transforming human conditions.

In 1793, Hopkins published *A Treatise on the Millennium.* The book is no significant advance or addition to Edwards. While Edwards paints with bold, clear strokes, Hopkins pencils in with minute detail. This utopian minutia is almost completely concerned with the social, educational, and physical prosperity of man in the millennium. It will be a time of eminent holiness, which is disinterested benevolence, and all evils will be banished from the world. There will be a great increase in knowledge. There will be universal peace and friendship. Sadness will vanish, and joy will prevail. Prosperity and plenty will reach into every home. The art of husbandry will be greatly advanced, and great improvements will be made in the mechanical arts. The world will be well populated, with full employment. One language will be used in every nation. Churches will be regulated in the "most beautiful and pleasing order."[162]

The millennium dawns gradually, though in the midst of earth-shaking events. It arises through the regenerating work of the Spirit of God and the progressive extension of the kingdom of God. When the Spirit of God works a "renovation of the hearts of men," those men belong "to the new creation."

This new creation of the new heaven and new earth goes on and makes advances as the church is enlarged and rises to a state of greater prosperity, and proceeds towards perfection.[163]

This new heaven and new earth is nothing less than God's glorious work of redemption.

Disinterested benevolence, pregnant with social implications and concern, set in the context of this view of the end of history, gave birth to a passion to minister to the physical needs of people. It fashioned the missionary thrust of the American churches not only into a bearer of culture but also into an agent of mercy. It provided the youth of the American churches with a high calling to completely unselfish and disinterested service. Regrettably, his chronological speculations about the millennium contributed to the distortion of true eschatological motivation by providing a rationale for a sentimental stress on "plucking the brands from the burning" while there was yet time. Nevertheless, this was Hopkins' major legacy to the missionary enterprise of the American churches.

Mather, Edwards and Hopkins completely span the Eighteenth Century. Mather was the prognosticator. His missionary theology presages the religion of the New Age. Edwards is *the* theologian of the Great Awakening. It is his thought that provides the dynamic for the missionary theology of the early National Period.

He, too, was a theologican of the evangelical religion of the Great Awakening. It was this sort of missionary and evangelistic faith that was to give rise to the most important early missionary efforts in the new nation. In 1800, near the end of his life, Hopkins took cognizance of the increased missionary efforts in the new nation. In 1800, near the end of his life, Hopkins took cognizance of the increased missionary interest of the previous decade and pronounced words that augured the future. His words could have just as well come from Edwards or Mather. They express something of the relationship that exists between the evangelical theology of the Eighteenth Century and the missionary organization and activity of the Nineteenth Century. "Within a few years past," Hopkins said,

> a great and extraordinary zeal and engagedness to propagate the gospel among the heathen and others who have it not preached to them has appeared, and been uncommonly exerted, both in Europe and America . . . This is an important and commendable design and work, and worthy to be pursued with increasing zeal and steady perseverance by all Christians, whatever difficulties, disappointments, and apparent discouragements may occur . . . In this view, I rejoice, and heartily wish success and Godspeed to all who are, and the many more who hereafter shall be, engaged in this happy, glorious work.[165]

NOTES FOR CHAPTER 2

1. *The Georgia Analytical Repository*, I (July and August, 1802), 3. Hereafter *GAR*.

2. William L. Lumpkin, *Baptist Foundations in the South* (Nashville: Broadman Press, 1961) is an exciting account of the Separate Baptist movement on the southern frontier, with a rather full account of the labors of Daniel Marshall.

3. A good case can be made for the proposition that the Great Awakening continued right through the Revolution and into the National Period. Though the leaders of the standing order churches tended to get bogged down in theological, legal and political debates, C. C. Goen, in *Revivalism and Separatism in New England* (New Haven: Yale University Press, 1962), has shown that in a measure the Separatists were able to perpetuate the expansion and growth of the Great Awakening through the Revolution and into the National Period. Wesley M. Gewehr's classic, *The Great Awakening in Virginia, 1740-1790* (Durham, N.C.: Duke University Press, 1930), presents the continuing influence of the Great Awakening among the Baptists, Presbyterians and Methodists to the first stirring of the second great revival. Heimert's major theme in *Religion and American Mind* is that " 'evangelical' religion, which had as its most notable formal expression the 'Calvinism' of Jonathan Edwards . . . provided pre-Revolutionary America with a radical, even a democratic, social and political ideology, and . . . embodied, and inspired, a thrust toward American nationalism," p. viii. If Heimert's thesis is correct, that the Revolution was, to the evangelical Calvinists, a part of the Work of Redemption, and thus God's work, then there was a second transference during the decade after the French Revolution. The work of redemption became the work of world evangelization.

4. Robert Ellis Thompson, *A History of the Presbyterian Churches in the United States*, Vol. 6 of *American Church History*, ed. by Philip Schaff, et al., (13 vols.; New York: Charles Scribner's Sons, 1894-1923), p. 34. Sidney E. Mead, *The Lively Experiment* (New York: Harper and Row, Publishers, 1963), quotes Thompson twice at this point, pp. 55, 127.

5. Alan Heimert and Perry Miller, eds., *The Great Awakening* (New York: The Bobbs-Merrill Company, Inc., 1967), p. xiv.

6. George Whitfield quoted Nehemiah Walter, Eliot's last colleague and successor at Roxbury, in the 1756 edition of his *Journal* as referring to the developments of 1740 as *"Puritanismus redivivus."* George Whitfield, *Journals* (London: The Banner of Truth Trust, 1960), p. 461.

7. John T. McNeill, *Modern Christian Movements*, Harper Torchbooks (New York: Harper and Row, Publishers, 1968), pp. 15-103.

8. *Ibid.*, pp. 53, 71ff. This statement is true even though a distinction be made between Dutch and German Pietism. See James Tanis, *Dutch Calvinistic Pietism in the Middle Colonies* (The Hague: Martin Nijhoff, 1967), p. 1ff.; Theodore G. Tappert, "Introduction" in Philip Jacob Spener, *Pia Desideria*, trans. by Theodore G. Tappert (Philadelphia: Fortress Press, 1964), p. 9. See also Paulus Scharpff, *History of Evangelism*, trans. by Helga B. Henry (Grand Rapids: William B. Eerdmans Publishing Co., 1966), p. 23; and Earnst Troeltch, *The Social Teaching of the Christian Churches*, trans. by Olive Wyon, Harper Torchbook (2 vols.; New York: Harper and Brothers, 1960), II, 678.

9. H. Richard Niebuhr, *The Kingdom of God in America*, Harper Torchbook (New York: Harper and Brothers, 1959), pp. 45-126.

10. Solomon Stoddard, *Question Whether God is not Angry with the Country for Doing So Little Towards the Conversion of the Indians* (Boston: Printed by B. Green, 1723).

11. Edwin Scott Gaustad, *The Great Awakening in New England* (New York: Harper and Brothers, 1957), p. 106.

12. John Wise attacked the Mathers and others between 1710 and 1717 for "presbyterianizing too much" in their effort to develop the consociation system in Massachusetts. See Mather's letter to Robert Wodrow, Sept. 17, 1715, *Diary*, II, 327, and Williston Walker, *A History of the Congregational Churches in the United States* (Fifth edition: New York: Charles Scribner's Sons, 1900), p. 207ff.

13. Mather had 444 works that reached publication, plus many others that never saw the light of day. Many still exist in manuscript. See Thomas James Holmes, *Cotton Mather: A Bibliography of His Works* (3 vols.; Cambridge, Mass.: Harvard University Press, 1940).

14. Alan Heimert, "Introduction" in Barrett Wendell, *Cotton Mather: The Puritan Priest* (New York: Harcourt, Brace & World, Inc., 1963) says that Mather's ignoble image was first successfully fashioned by William Douglass in 1747 in his *General History of America*, p. xiv.

15. Vernon L. Parrington, *The Colonial Mind*, Vol. 1 of *Main Currents in American Thought* (New York: Harcourt, Brace & World, Inc., 1927), pp. 107-118.

16. Daniel J. Boorstin, *The Americans: The Colonial Experience* (New York: Vintage Books, 1958), p. 221.

17. Cotton Mather, *The Wonderful Works of God Commemorated* (Boston: Printed by S. Green, 1690), p. 41.

18. Cotton Mather, *Theopolis Americana* (Boston: Printed by B. Green, 1710) spells out Mather's faith that America would play an important part in God's ultimate plan for the world.

19. Cotton Mather, *The Present State of New-England* (Boston: Printed by Samuel Green, 1690), p. 35.

20. Cotton Mather, *A Midnight Cry* (Boston: Printed by John Allen, 1692), p. 63.

21. See *Things to be Look'd for* (Cambridge, Mass.: Printed by Samuel Green & Barth. Green, 1691); *The Day, and the Work of the Day* (Boston: Printed and Sold by B. Harris, 1693); *Things for a Distress'd People to think upon* (Boston, Mass.: Printed by B. Green and F. Allen, 1699), Section xxx; his most expanded work on the New Reformation idea is *Eleutheria: Or, An Idea of the Reformation in England* (London: Printed for J.R., 1698) which was prepared in 1696, the year before he expected that the new reformation could possibly begin; and *Theopolis Americana*. See other citations below. There are two major eschatological works that were never published that are preserved in the American Antiquarian Society in Worchester, Massachusetts: "Problema Theologicum. An Essay, Concerning the Happy State Expected for the Church upon Earth; Endeavouring to Demonstrate that the Second Coming . . . will be at the Beginning of that Happy State" prepared in January, 1703/04 and "Essays on Triparadisus," prepared sometime shortly before 1720.

22. Mather, *Diary*, II, 366.

23. *Ibid.*, 376, 387, 396, 453, 462.

24. It was entitled "Boanerges: The Work of the Day" and was sent to London, October 31, 1716, *ibid.*, 381.

25. *Malachi. Or, The Everlasting Gospel, Preached unto the Nations* (Boston: Printed by T. C. for Robert Starke, 1717).

26. Mather, *Diary*, II (May 18, 1717), 453.

27. Mather, *Things to be Looked For*, p. 62.

28. Cotton Mather, *Souldiers Counselled and Comforted* (Boston: Printed by Samuel Green, 1689), pp. 28-29.

29. William Kellaway, *The New England Company 1649-1776* (New York: Barnes & Noble, Inc., 1961), p. 203.

30. Mather, *The Day and the Work of the Day*, pp. 63-64.

31. Mather, *Diary*, I, 217.

32. This was the *Indian Primer*, published in 1699, of which no copy has been found. It was probably

based on the Savoy-Confession of Faith. See Mather, *Diary,* I, 328, and Holmes, *Mather: A Bibliography,* II, 505.

33. He prepared several books specifically for the Indians including: *Epistle to the Christian Indians* (Boston: Printed by Bartholomew Green and John Allen, 1700), and *Hatchets to Hew Down the Tree of Sin* (Boston: Printed by B. Green, 1705). Several of his other books were translated into the Indian language: *The Day Which the Lord hath made* (Boston, N. E.: Reprinted by B. Green, 1707); *Family Religion Excited and Assisted* (Boston: Printed by B. Green, 1714); and *Monitor for Communicants* (Boston: Printed by B. Green, 1714). The Indian edition was issued in 1716 but no copy of it has been found. See *Diary,* II, 355.

   His reports took varied forms. He translated Increase Mather's *De Successu Evangelii,* with voluminous notes, in his biography of John Eliot, *The Triumphs of the Reformed Religion, in America* (Boston: Printed by Benjamin Harris and John Allen, 1691) and included this in *Magnalia,* I, 552-565. He included Matthew Mayhew's *Triumphs of Grace,* a detailed report on the Indian mission on Martha's Vineyard, *Magnalia,* II, 422-446. He wrote *Letter about the Present State of Christianity among the Christianized Indians* (Boston, in N. E.: Printed by Timothy Green, 1705), added "A brief Account of the Evangelical Work among the Christianized Indians of New-England" in *Just Commemorations* (Boston, in N.E.: Printed by B. Green, n. d.) and another report in *India Christiana* (Boston in New-England: Printed by B. Green, 1721). He also wrote numerous personal letters reporting on the progress of the work among them. See Mather, *Diary,* II, 512, 802, 807. Mather also wrote a series of circular letters to the missionaries and Indian pastors, Kellaway, *New England Company,* p. 209.

34. Mather, *Diary,* I, 571; II, 133, 210, 512, 531.

35. Cotton Mather, *Another Tongue Brought in to Confess the Great Saviour of the World* (Boston: Printed by B. Green, 1707). See Holmes, *Mather: A Bibliography,* I, 47-52, for the relationship between Mather and Dellius.

36. Mather, *Diary,* I, 206, 284-5, 402. His book was *La Fe del Christiano* (Boston: n. p., 1699).

37. See *Wonderful Works of God Commemorated,* pp. 46-48 (1690); *Things to be Look'd for* (1691), p. 16; *A Letter Concerning the Terrible Sufferings of our Protestant Brethren* (1701); *Perswasions from the Terror of the Lord* (Boston in New England: Printed and Sold by Timothy Green, 1711); *Shaking Dispensations* (Boston: Printed by B. Green, 1715); and *Suspiria Vinctorum* (Boston: Printed and Sold by T. Fleet, 1726). All these contain reports on the Reformed Churches of France. His predictions of the collapse of Catholic France are in his *Diary,* I, 263, 301, 207-208, 222, 226. Mather's two evangelical facts for France were *Une Grand Voix du Ciel a La France* (1725); and *Le Vrai Parton des Saines Paroles.* There is little bibliographical information on either of these tracts. The latter was first published in 1704, for use with French captives, Holmes, *Mather: A Bibliography,* III, 1194.

38. Cotton Mather, *The Negro Christianized* (Boston: Printed by B. Green, 1706).

39. See Cotton Mather, *A Letter to Ungospellized Plantations* (Boston: n. p., 1702); *Frontiers Well Defended* (Boston in N. E.: Printed by T. Green, 1707); and *A Proposal for an Evangelical Treasury* (Boston: n. p., n.d.). The latter was probably printed in 1725, but the idea had been suggested in 1710. See *Bonifacius: an Essay upon the Good,* ed. with an intro. by David Levin (Cambridge: Harvard University Press, 1966), pp. 115-116. See also Cotton Mather, *Old Paths Restored* (Boston: Printed and Sold by T. Green, 1711) which was prepared to strengthen churches in the southern colonies. Numerous copies were sent to South Carolina.

40. Cotton Mather, *The Fall of Babylon* (Boston: Printed by B. Green, 1707).

41. Cotton Mather, *Faith of the Fathers* (Boston: Printed by J. Allen, 1718) was for Jewish people and copies of it were sent to Jews he knew in Europe and America; *Things to be more thought upon* (Boston: Printed by Thomas Fleet, 1713) contains an "Address to the Jewish Nation," pp. 10-27. He also included the same material in a little book to report on the conversion of several Jewish children in Berlin, Cotton Mather, *Faith Encouraged* (Boston: Printed by J. Allen, 1718), pp. 17-32.

42. Mather, *Diary,* I, 459.

43. See "An Appendix, Giving a more particular Account of the Glorious and Wonderful Success which the Gospel hath had in the East-Indies," in Cotton Mather, *Pillar of Gratitude* (Boston: Printed by B. Green and J. Allen, 1700), pp. 45-58, and *India Christiana.*

44. Cotton Mather, *Blessed Unions* (Boston: Printed by B. Green, 1692), in "Preface," n.p.

45. See Ernst Benz, "Pietist and Puritan Sources of Early Protestant World Missions," *Church History,* XX (June, 1951), 28-55. This is an introduction of the correspondence between Cotton Mather and August Hermann Francke. It very adequately introduces the leading missionary ideas of Mather, but it suffers from a lack of familiarity with Mather's works besides the *Diary* and the *Magnalia.*

46. *Dust and Ashes* (Boston in N. E.: Printed by B. Green, 1710); *The Heavenly Conversation* (Boston in N. E.: Printed by Barth Green, 1710). In the "Preface" to the latter Mather says that the booklet might be entitled "American Pietism."

47. *Diary,* II, 23.

48. *Ibid.,* II, 193.

49. Letter to A. W. Boehme, August 6, 1716, *ibid.,* p. 411.

50. *Ibid.,* pp. 348, 376, 378, 406, 497.

51. *Ibid.,* p. 348.

52. Besides *Dust and Ashes* and *The Heavenly Conversation,* see *Christianity to the Life* (Boston in N. E.: Printed by T. Green, 1702), *Christianus per Ignem* (Boston: Printed by B. Green and J. Allen, 1702), *The High Attainment* (Boston: Printed by B. Green and J. Allen, 1703), *The Spirit of Life entering into the Spiritually Dead* (Boston in N. E.: Printed by Timothy Green, 1707), *Pia Desideria* (Boston: Printed by S. Kneeland, 1722), *Deus Nobiscum* (Boston: Printed for S. Gerrish, 1725), and *Vital Christianity* (Charlestown in New England: Printed by Samuel Keimer, 1725).

53. Cotton Mather, *Menachem* (Boston: Printed for Benjamin Gray, 1716), and, his one book devoted solely to the work of Pietists in Europe, *Nuncia Bona e Terra Longinqua* (Boston in New-England: Printed by B. Green, 1715).

54. Mather, *Diary,* II, 465.

55. Letter to Robert Wodrow, September 17, 1715, *ibid.,* 329.

56. See *ibid.* 16, 200-202, 215. He published his first effort as *The A,B,C, of religion* (Boston: Printed & Sold by Timothy Green, 1713).

57. Mather, *Diary,* II, 220.

58. In no less than seven books he pleaded for union based on these "Maxims." Besides those mentioned in the text see Cotton Mather, *The Stone Cut out of the Mountain* (Boston: n. p., 1716); *Malachi; Three Letters from New England, Relating to the Controversy of the Present Time* (London: Printed by Eman. Matthews, 1721); and *Brethren dwelling together in Unity* (Boston: Printed for S. Gerrish, 1718). The participation of both Increase and Cotton Mather in the ordination of the pastor of the Baptist Church in Boston comes as a complete surprise to one familiar only with the Mather image. The *Diary,* II, 530, 531, 535, 536 and 537, makes it clear that he decided to do this out of his growing concern for Christian unity.

59. In Mather, *Stone Cut out of the Mountain,* they are:
  "I. There is ONE Infinite and Eternal GOD, who is in Three Persons . . . and for me to Know, and Love, and Serve, and Enjoy GOD must be my chosen Blessedness.
  "II. The Eternal SON of GOD is *Incarnate*, and *Enthroned* in the Glorious Jesus . . .

"III. I must . . . embrace the Sacred Scriptures of the Bible . . .

"IV. Whatever the *Light of GOD* in me pronounces to be a *Sinful Thing*, I must heartily abhor it . . .

"V. I must, by . . . Purifying Changes Produced by the Spirit of God, become a New Creature . . .

"VI. I must endeavour to fill my life with *Acknowledgements* of the Great GOD . . . I must . . . do my best, that I may bring as many others as may be, in like Manner to *Acknowledge* Him . . .

"VII. I must continually have the Example of the Holy and Lovely JESUS before my Eyes . . .

"VIII. I must have an heart full of *Benignity* unto Mankind.

"IX. My *Dealings in the World* must be regulated by that Golden Rule of Equity . . .

"X. I must not frowardly Refuse the *Blessings* of God . . . in this Life, which I am to seek with the Industry of a Lawful Business . . .

"XI. My high Value for the unquestionable *Institutions* of the Gospel must be for ever inviolable . . .

"XII. With a Pure, and Peaceable Spirit . . . I must abhor all Approaches towards the Persecuting of any man.

"XIII. If ever I am . . . in any Office . . . I must labour to discharge the Works . . . with all possible Fidelity, and Integrity . . .

"XIV. I must . . . have my eye fixed with Faith, and Hope, and Joy on the great Things of that Heavenly World."pp. 2-4.

60. Letter to Bartholemew Ziegenbalg, Dec. 31, 1717, in Latin and English, Mather, *India Christiana*, p. 67ff. These three are quoted in Benz, "Pietist and Puritan Sources," pp. 44-45. Benz bases most of his expositions of Mather's position on this very important letter. He does not seem to be aware that it was published in *India Christiana*. Also in *India Christiana*, in English and Indian, is a document called "The Religion, which All Good Men are United In," in which he lists these same three maxims as "THREE Grand MAXIMS of PIETY," pp. 53-54.

61. Mather alleged that in these "MAXIMS of PIETY we have the Highest, and the most Reasonable, and Unquestionable Marks of Truth," *The Stone Cut out of the Mountain*, pp. 6, 9.

62. *Ibid.*, p. 12.

63. *Ibid.*, p. 7.

64. Letter to Thomas Prince, Jan. 13, 1726-27, *Diary*, II, 816.

65. Thompson, *History of the Presbyterian Churches*, pp. 28, 95.

66. Perry Miller, "The Great Awakening from 1740 to 1750," *Encounter*, March, 1956, p. 5, quoted in Heimert and Miller, *The Great Awakening*, p. xiv.

67. See Alexander V.G. Allen, *Jonathan Edwards* (Boston: Houghton Mifflin and Company, 1890), who divides Edwards' life into three periods and calls 1750-1758 "Philosophical Theologian," almost completely ignoring his work in Stockbridge; Henry Bradford Parks, *Jonathan Edwards, the Fiery Puritan* (New York: Minton, Balch and Company, 1930), entitled his third section "The Exile" and said that Edwards went to Stockbridge "out of want," p. 213; Ola Elizabeth Winslow, *Jonathan Edwards 1703-1758* (New York: Collier Books, 1961), p. 248, and Perry Miller, *Jonathan Edwards* (New York: Meridian Books, 1959), p. 129. The source of almost every one of these misconceptions about Edwards' ministry in Stockbridge is no other than Samuel Hopkins, *The Life of the Late Reverend, Learned and Pious Mr. Jonathan Edwards* (Boston: S. Kneeland, 1765), pp. 49, 64-65, 74. Of all people Hopkins knew that Stockbridge was no quiet retreat. Rather there is evidence that Hopkins wanted his biography to be a sequel to Edwards' own biographical work on David Brainerd. He wanted in the life of Edwards to show "pure and undefiled religion, in distinction from all counterfeits," "Preface."

68. He received inquiry from Scotland, Hopkins, *Life of Edwards*, p. 65, and Letter to John Erskine, July 5, 1750, in Jonathan Edwards, *The Works of Jonathan Edwards, A.M.*, with an Essay on his Genius and Writings by Henry Rogers and a Memoir by Sereno E. Dwight, revised and corrected by Edward Hickman (2 vols., 10th ed.; London: Henry G. Bohn, 1865), I, clxi. He evidently could have gone to Canaan, Conn., Ezra Stiles, *Extract from the Itineraries and Other Miscellanies 1775-1794*

with a Selection from his Correspondence, Franklin B. Dexter, ed., (New Haven: Yale University Press, 1914), pp. 181, 182. The most tempting option was a second church in Northampton, which was just why the second ecclesiastical council met on May 15, 1751, Hopkins, *Life of Edwards,* p. 65. He also got an invitation from Samuel Davies and a portion of his church in Luenenburg, Virginia, to settle there, but this was already after he had settled at Stockbridge, Letter from Samuel Davies to Joseph Bellamy, July 4, 1751, in William Henry Foote, *Sketches of Virginia,* Second series (2nd ed., rev.; Philadelphia: J. B. Lippincott & Co., 1856), p. 41, and Letter of Edwards to John Erskine, July 7, 1752, in *Works,* I, clxxxviii.

69. Hopkins, *Life of Edwards,* p. 65.

70. See Miller, *Jonathan Edwards,* p. 248ff, and Winslow, *Jonathan Edwards,* p. 247ff.

71. See Letter to the Commissioners in Boston concerning the problems at Stockbridge, Edwards, *Works,* I, clxxvi.

72. Letter of Gideon Hawley, *MHSC,* Series One, III (1794), 213.

73. Letter to John Erskine, June 28, 1751, Edwards, *Works,* I, clxxiii.

74. This is Winslow's theory, *Jonathan Edwards,* p. 243.

75. See Kellaway, *New England Company,* p. 162, for a discussion of Stoddard's contribution.

76. See Samuel Hopkins, *Historical Memoirs, Relating to the Housatonic Indians* (Boston: S. Kneeland, 1752) and Edwards, *God's Awful Judgment in the Breaking and Withering of the Strong Rods of a Community, Works,* II, 39.

77. John Sergeant, *A Letter from the Revd. Mr. Sergeant of Stockbridge to Dr. Colman of Boston; Containing Mr. Sergeant's Proposal of a more effectual Method for the Education of Indian Children* (Boston: Rogers and Fowle, 1743), p. 9.

78. Letter to John Erskine, Oct. 14, 1748, Edwards, *Works,* I, cxlv.

79. Miller, *Jonathan Edwards,* p. 30ff.

80. Edwards, *God Glorified in Man's Dependence, Works,* II, 3, 4.

81. *Ibid.,* pp. 4, 6.

82. *Ibid.,* pp. 3-7.

83. Edwards, *Five Discourses on Important Subjects, Nearly Concerning the Great Affair of the Soul's Eternal Salvation, Works,* I, 620.

84. *Ibid.,* p. 623.

85. *Ibid.,* pp. 624, 626.

86. *Ibid.,* p. 626.

87. Edwards, *Some Thoughts Concerning the Present Revival of Religion in New England, Works,* I, 378-379.

88. Edwards, *Five Discourses, ibid.,* p. 658.

89. *Ibid.,* p. 686.

90. *Ibid.,* p. 659.

91. Edwards, *Sinners in the Hands of an Angry God, Works,* II, 11.

92. Edwards, *Five Discourses, Works,* I, 675-676.

93. *Ibid.,* p. 679.

94. I am indebted to Joseph Haroutunian, *Piety Versus Moralism* (Hamden, Conn.: Archon Books, 1964), pp. 220-228, for help in understanding of Edwards' views of freedom and responsibility.

95. Edwards, *Freedom of the Will, Works,* I, 11.

96. *Ibid.,* pp. 4, 6, 7.

97. *Ibid.,* p. 51.

98. *Ibid.,* p. 66.

99. *Ibid.,* p. 156.

100. *Ibid.,* p. ccxvi.

101. See Edwards, *Thoughts on Revival, Works,* I, 381ff.; *The Church's Marriage to Her Sons and to Her God,* II, 25; *True Saints, When Absent from the Body, Are Present with the Lord,* I, 34ff.; and *An Humble Attempt to Promote Explicit Agreement with Visible of God's People in Extraordinary Prayer,* II, 280ff., which will be discussed in some detail below.

102. Edwards, *History of the Work of Redemption, Work,* I, 536-584.

103. Jean Danielou, *The Lord of History,* Meridian Books (Cleveland and New York: The World Publishing Company, 1968), pp. 11-12.

104. See Ernest Lee Tuveson, *Redeemer Nation* (Chicago: University of Chicago Press, 1968), p. 26ff, for a most helpful study of Edwardsean eschatology as it relates to America's millennial role and Manifest Destiny. However, he implies that Edwards suggests no real end to history or literal appearing of Christ. This is not correct.

105. Edwards, *Work of Redemption, Works,* I, 597.

106. *Ibid.,* pp. 599-600.

107. *Ibid.,* p. 605.

108. *Ibid.,* pp. 606-608.

109. *Ibid.,* p. cxxxiii.

110. See R. Pierce Beaver, "The Concert for Prayer for Foreign Missions, An Early Ventury in Ecumenical Action," *The Ecumenical Review,* July, 1948, pp. 420-427 for an estimate of the influence of this book during the last two centuries.

111. Edwards, *Humble Attempt, Works,* II, 288.

112. *Ibid.,* p. 381.

113. *Ibid.,* pp. 281-282.

114. *Ibid.*

115. Edwards, *A Faithful Narrative of the Surprising Work of God, Works,* II, 355.

116. Edwards, *Humble Attempt, Works,* II, 309.

117. Cotton Mather noted in his *Diary,* January 3, 1712/13, that he had been writing to ministers encouraging them to work at raising money for the "Support of Missions, for which they have reason to express the greatest aversion." *Diary,* II, 148.

118. Edwards, *The Life and Diary of the Rev. David Brainerd, Works,* II, 313-315.

119. For an example of Brainerd's influence on early missionaries see Rufus Babcock, ed., *Memoir of John Mason Peck, D.D.* (Carbondale, Illinois: Southern Illinois University Press, 1965), p. 52. Conservative evangelical and missionary groups still read about Brainerd. See David Synbeck, *David Brainerd: Beloved Yankee* (Grand Rapids: Wm. B. Eerdmans Publishing Company, 1961) and the most recent edition of Edwards, *The Life and Diary of David Brainerd,* newly edited by Philip E. Howard, Jr. (Chicago: Moody Press, 1957).

120. Edwards, *Life and Diary, Works,* II, 348-350.

121. Two journals published in the same book with different titles: David Brainerd, *Mirabilia Dei inter Indicos, Or the Rise and Progress of a Remarkable Work of Grace amongst a Number of the Indians in the Province of New-Jersey and Pennsylvania* and *Divine Grace display'd Or the Continuance and Progress of a Remarkable Work of Grace amongst some of the Indians* (Philadelphia: Printed by William Bradford, 1746). These journals were put through the press by the Correspondents in New York and New Jersey of the Society in Scotland for Propagating Christian Knowledge. The journals were not included in Edwards' first edition of the Account of the Life in 1749, but were included with the Edinburgh edition of 1765, and the later editions issued in America in 1793 and 1811.

122. Edwards, *Life and Diary, Works,* II, 322.

123. *Ibid.,* pp. 348-349.

124. *Ibid.,* pp. 359, 399.

125. Frank Hugh Foster, *A Genetic History of the New England Theology* (Chicago: The University of Chicago Press, 1907), p. 129.

126. William Warren Sweet, *Religion in the Development of American Culture 1765-1840* (New York: Charles Scribner's Sons, 1952), p. 235.

127. Oliver Wendell Elsbree, *The Rise of the Missionary Spirit in America, 1790-1815* (Williamsport, Pa.: Williamsport Printing and Binding Co., 1928), p. 147. See also Williston Walker, *Ten New England Leaders* (Boston: Silver, Burdett and Company, 1901), p. 355, and Kenneth Scott Latourette, *The Great Century in Europe and the United States of America,* Vol. IV of *A History of the Expansion of Christianity* (6 vols.; New York: Harper and Brothers, Publishers, 1937-45), 77-79, which follow Elsbree's estimate.

128. See Dick Lucas Van Halzema, "Samuel Hopkins — 1721-1803, New England Calvinist" (unpublished doctoral thesis, Union Theological Seminary, New York, N.Y., 1956), pp. 350-356.

129. Foster, *Genetic History,* p. 189, suggests that Hopkins and Bellamy began the subschools; Walker, *History of the Congregational Churches,* p. 299, suggests that the division comes later with Emmons and Dwight; and Sydney E. Ahlstrom, "Theology in America: a Historical Survey," in *The Shaping of American Religion,* vol. 1: *Religion in American Life,* ed. by James Ward Smith and Leland Jamison (Princeton, N.J.: Princeton University Press, 1961), p. 255, hints that the division came much later in conjunction with the establishment of literal schools, and developed three branches instead of two, headed by Leonard Woods at Andover, N. W. Taylor at Yale and Bennet Tyler at Hartford.

130. Edward A. Park did much to contribute to this in his biographical works on Samuel Hopkins and Nathanael Emmons. See Edward A. Park, "Memoir" in Vol. I of *The Works of Samuel Hopkins, D.D., First Pastor of the Church in Great Barrington, Mass., afterwards Pastor of the First Congregational Church in Newport, R.I., with a Memoir of His Life and Character* (3 vols.; Boston: Doctrinal Tract and Book Society, 1854), pp. 129-156; and *Memoir of Nathanael Emmons: with Sketches of his Friends and Pupils,* Vol. I of *The Works of Nathanael Emmons,* ed. by Jacob Ide (6 vols.; Boston: Congregational Board of Publication, 1861), pp. 176-200.

131. Quoted in Park, "Memoir," Hopkins, *Works,* I, 108.

132. See Edwards, *Misrepresentations Corrected, and Truth Vindicated, in A Reply to the Rev. Mr. Solomon Williams' Book, The True State of the Question Concerning the Qualifications Necessary to Lawful Communion in the Christian Sacraments, Works,* I, p. 530; Joseph Bellamy, *True Religion Delineated, The Works of the Rev. Joseph Bellamy, D.D.* (3 vols.; New York: Published by Stephen Dodge, 1811), I, 222; and Hopkins, *An Inquirey Concerning the Promises of the Gospel and The True State and Character of the Unregenerate,* in *Works,* III, 185ff and 279ff.

133. See Edwards, *Freedom of the Will, Works,* I, 76; Bellamy, *The Wisdom of God in the Permission of Sin, Works,* II, 7ff; and Hopkins, *Sin Through Divine Interposition an Advantage to the Universe, Works,* II, 493ff.

134. Leonard Woods, *History of the Andover Theological Seminary* (Boston: James R. Osgood and Company, 1885), pp. 35-39.

135. Samuel Hopkins, *Sketches of the Life of the Late, Rev. Samuel Hopkins, D.D., Pastor of the First Congregational Church in Newport,* ed. by Stephen West (Hartford: Printed by Hudson and Goodwin, 1805), p. 54, and Park, "Memoir," in Hopkins, *Works,* I, 45ff.

136. Letter to Moses Brown, April 29, 1784, Hopkins, *Works,* I, 119. In "The Slave Trade and Slavery," published first in the *Providence Gazette and Country Journal,* October 13, 1787, he said of Newport, "This trade in the human species has been the first wheel of commerce in Newport, on which every other movement in business has chiefly depended. That town has been built up, and flourished . . . at the expense of the blood, the liberty, and happiness of the poor African; and the inhabitants have lived on this, and by it have gotten most of their wealth and riches." *Works,* II, 615.

137. Ezra Stiles, *The Literary Diary of Ezra Stiles, D.D., LL.D.* (2 vols.; New York: Charles Scribner's Sons, 1901), I, 346.

138. *Ibid.,* p. 414.

139. Hopkins, *Works,* I, 132.

140. *Ibid.,* p. 139.

141. Hopkins, *Dialogue Concerning the Slavery of the Africans, Works,* II, 556.

142. *Ibid.,* p. 457.

143. Hopkins, "The Slave Trade and Slavery," *Works,* II, 619.

144. Carey's exposition of Matthew 28:19-20 was included in *Enquiry* and was first published in 1792. Before Carey most Protestant expositions of Christ's commission related it only to the Apostles.

145. Hopkins, *A Discourse upon the Slave Trade and the Slavery of the Africans, Works,* II, 598-599.

146. *Ibid.,* pp. 599-605.

147. *Ibid.,* p. 607.

148. *Ibid.,* p. 609.

149. Hopkins, *Sketches,* p. 58.

150. Letter of Hopkins to Thomas Foxecroft, December 5, 1759, in Park, "Memoir," Hopkins, *Works,* I, 265.

151. Hopkins, *An Inquiry into the Nature of True Holiness, Works,* III, 7.

152. Haroutunian, *Piety versus Moralism,* p. 82.

153. Hopkins, *Works,* III, 14.

154.   *Ibid.,* p. 116.

155.   *Ibid.,* p. 23.

156.   *Ibid.,* pp. 16-17.

157.   *Ibid.,* pp. 40-41. See also Hopkins, *System of Doctrines, Works,* I, 237.

158.   *Ibid.,* p. 385.

159.   Hopkins, *Works,* III, 38-41.

160.   *Ibid.,* pp. 46-47.

161.   Haroutunian, *Piety Versus Moralism,* p. 87.

162.   Hopkins, *A Treatise on the Millennium, Works,* II, 271-296.

163.   *Ibid.,* p. 265.

164.   Between 1780 and 1800 Edwards' works were published far more extensively in America than in
the twenty years following his death. *The Great Christian Doctrine of Original Sin Defended* was
reissued and two previously unpublished revival sermons published in a volume entitled *Sermons
on the Following Subjects: The Manner in which Salvation is to be Sought and The Unreasonable-
ness of Indetermination in Religion* in 1780, at Hartford. *The History of the Work of Redemption*
was first published in America in 1782 and was reissued in 1786, 1792 and 1793. *Sinners in the
Hands of an Angry God* was reissued in 1786, 1796 and 1797. Some other works of Edwards and
their dates of reissue are as follows: *Some Thoughts on Revival,* 1784; *Religious Affections,* 1784,
1787 and 1794; *Freedom of the Will,* 1786 and 1790; *A Faithful Narrative of the Surprising Work
of God,* 1790; *True Grace Distinguished from the Experience of Devils,* 1790, two editions in 1791
and 1799; *The Humble Attempt,* 1789 and 1794; *A Divine and Supernatural Light,* 1795; and *The
Justice of God in the Damnation of Sinners,* 1799. Separate editions of some of Edwards' works
were also issued no less than 29 times from 1800 to 1819.

165.   Hopkins, *Two Sermons, Works,* III, 748-749.

Part II

Missionary Structure

It often happens, that the stirring up and agitation of men's minds . . . though fearful at the time, is the providential preparation for spiritual reformation, intellectual progress, and great social improvement. It was so in the early part of the present century. An impulse was given to the human mind that has been greatly felt in all the departments of science and art, in all the forms and conditions of social life, and perhaps most of all in the Christian church. Is it not remarkable what an influence this has had in stimulating and organizing the churches for religious effort? At all events, it is certain that a great change has come over the spirit and habits of God's people as a body. Practical piety is now a very different thing from what it once was — more comprehensive in its views and feelings, more active, more benevolent and aggressive, more alive to its individual and social responsibilities, and a thousand times more influential, in the aggregate, than it was fifty years ago. Somehow, the denominational and social conscience can no longer sleep amid the groans of a perishing world. Somehow, the churches have been led into extensive systematic organizations for propagating the gospel at home and abroad, and these are gaining strength and momentum in every free Protestant community; and somehow, the missionary institutions have been planted over a large portion of the heathen world, with the declared purpose of taking possession of the whole for Christ.

Rufus Anderson — 1851

Introduction

The missionary cause combines within itself the elements of all that is sublime in human purpose, nay, combines them in a loftier perfection than any other enterprise, which was ever linked with the destinies of man.

Francis Wayland — 1823

Missionaries of the cross go into the very heart of the wilderness, and clear the soil, and sow the seed on ground which had been unbroken for ages, and so speedily reap as rich harvest, as is gathered by the majority of laborers, who cultivate the fields which have been tilled and fertilized for many generations.

Warren Fay — 1825

Samuel Adams wrote to Thomas Paine in 1802, urging him to cancel plans to publish further on the principles of his *Age of Reason.* Adams opposed new controversy while the nation moved toward unity and peace. "The people of New England," he said, "if you will allow me to use a Scriptural phrase, are fast returning to their first love."[1]

Did Adams speak of the calm that had begun to settle over New England after the election of 1800?[2] Political defeat stunned the Federalists in the months after Thomas Jefferson's inauguration. Did he refer to the steady growth of trade and commerce that had continued since the Crises of 1794 and the ratification of Jay's Treaty? Neither are probabilities. Adams spoke more pervasive and subtle than either. He referred to the renewed vigor of the churches which was evident in almost every congregation and manifest in the proliferation of new institutions.[3] That movement, readily perceptible by 1802, is now called the Second Great Awakening.

The churches of the religious establishments reached their nadir in the revolutionary generation.[4] This situation was true among some sectarians also. The Baptists and Presbyterians experienced significant growth on the southern frontiers.[5] The Methodists, arriving at the beginning of the Revolutionary Epoch, enjoyed slow steady expansion.[6] In general, rationalism had invaded the colonial schools and colleges, and slipped quietly into many of the churches.[7] An unobtrusive Deism describes the religious commitment of the most influential men of the period, who were almost all politicians. The overarching interests of Americans had changed since the Great Awakening. The Enlightenment had come to the new American nation.[8]

The last quarter of the Eighteenth Century saw a marriage, to use Sidney Mead's analogy, of rationalism and pietism in America (sectarian pietism primarily). The house the two built was religious freedom. This union and struggle continued in parts of New England until 1833. But during the Second Great Awakening pietism arranged a "hasty divorce in order to remarry traditional orthodoxy."[9] After this second union and in the climate created by the first, American Christianity took shape.

The first great wave of American missionary organization and activity took place during this new revival.[10] Missionary action was both a consequence of and one stimulus of the total movement. Missionary labor had been underway for 150 years. Missionary organization began even before the Revolution, and intensified at the fir st tremor of revival in the 1780s. At the turn of the century, missionary organizations exploded on every side. They gathered strength as the churches stirred with life. Those men who were sent to the "Indians of the wilderness, to the depressed African, to the remote settler on the frontier, and to the poor in many other parts," almost invariably had been converted and called in revivalistic churches. Wherever they went, they were messengers of revival.[11]

A third factor is a significant part of the *milieu* of American missionary activity in the years immediately following the Revolution. Along with the new spiritual life and social situation that made the voluntary principle normative for all religious groups, the massive western movement determined the major thrust of American missionary endeavor. The churches gave themselves to winning these transients to Christ and gathering them into churches. This alone would transform the wilderness.

The next three chapters explore the strategies used as American churches addressed themselves to the literal wilderness that was becoming the United States. This investigation concerns one of those potent factors that shaped American Christianity.

> The Christianity which developed in the United States was unique. It displayed features which marked it as distinct from previous Christianity in any other land.[12]

One determinative factor was the place of mission in the churches.[13]

Commitment to mission and efforts to organize for mission were stimulated by many different forces and shaped by experiences past and present. Primarily they were the response to the task of evangelizing and churching the wilderness. In the context of planting churches in the wilderness the churches turned their attention to "the whole world," and, in this entire process, the missionary character of the American churches developed.

NOTES FOR INTRODUCTION

1. Samuel Adams, Letter to Thomas Paine, November 30, 1802, in *The Life and Works of Thomas Paine,* ed. by William M. Van Der Wyde, (Patriots ed., 10 vols.; New Rochelle, New York: Thomas Paine National Historical Association, 1925), VIII, 297 or William V. Wells, *The Life and Public Service of Samuel Adams* (3 vols.; Boston: Little, Brown & Company, 1865), III, 372. Paine published the letter with his answer early in 1803, and it has been reprinted often in historical collections.

2. John C. Miller, *The Federalist Era: 1789-1801,* New American Nation Series (New York: Harper and Row, 1960), p. 176ff. The peace between England and France, 1801-1803, had caused trade to boom in New England. See Reginal Horsman, *The Cause of the War of 1812,* Perpetua Books (New York: A. S. Barnes & Company, 1962), p. 19ff.

3. Both Thomas Thacher, who preached Samuel Adams' funeral and Adams' first major biographer, William V. Wells, interpreted the letter in religious terms. See Wells, *Life of Samuel Adams,* pp. 373, 397.

4. Robert Baird, *Religion in America* (New York: Harper & Brothers, 1856), p. 207, calls the twenty years after the Revolution "a long period of prostration." Leonard W. Bacon, *A History of American Christianity,* Vol. XIII of *American Church History,* p. 219, describes the same period as "the lowest ebb-tide of vitality in the history of American Christianity."

5. Goen, *Revivalism and Separatism* has shown that the Separatists were able to perpetuate the expansion and growth of the Great Awakening through the Revolution and into the National Period, but points out that the "most phenomenal story of Separate Baptist expansion was written not in New England but in the South," p. 296. Lumpkin, *Baptist Foundations* has told the Baptist story in an enchanting way, and Gewher, *Great Awakening in Virginia* presents the influence of the Great Awakening among all groups in Virginia down through the first stirrings of the Second Great Awakening. Heimert, *Religion and the American Mind* has documented evangelical successes throughout the period of the Revolution.

6. Wade Crawford Barclay, *Early American Methodism, 1769-1844,* Vol. I, *History of Methodist Missions* (3 vols.; New York: The Board of Missions and Church Extension of the Methodist Church, 1949), p. 1, suggests that Wesley could not have chosen a more "inopportune time for planting Methodism in the New World" than the Revolutionary Era. However, the lack of vitality in the established churches may indeed have created the kind of need that Methodism could most adequately have filled.

7. Adolf Koch, *Republican Religion,* Studies in Religion and Culture: American Religion Series VIII (New York: Henry Holt and Company, 1933), Vernon Stauffer, *New England and the Bavarian Illuminati,* Studies in History, Economics and Public Law, Vol. LXXXII, No. 1 (New York: The Columbia University Press, 1918), and Martin E. Marty, *The Infidel,* Living Age Books (New York: World Publishing Company, 1961), all present this development from various viewpoints. Koch's explanation that the "American liberal, while a republican in politics, was unable to accept republican religion Deism," (p. xii) does not tell the complete story.

8. I am aware of Daniel J. Boorstin's asseveration that the idea of an American Enlightenment is "one of the most respectable stereotypes which gets in the way of our seeing the American experience." See "The Myth of an American Enlightenment," in *America and the Image of Europe,* Meridian Books (New York: World Publishing Company, 1960), pp. 65-78. One must agree with the major themes of Professor Boorstin in this essay and with his general emphasis that the American environment was as much or more the source of American intellectual development as were European ideas. It has been too simple to explain American intellectual history as European philosophical systems camouflaged in American homespun. Boorstin's *The Lost World of Thomas Jefferson* (Boston: Beacon Press, 1960) is an attempt to relate Jefferson's thought to the American environment instead of the Enlightenment. However, vital commitment to traditional, orthodox Protestantism, especially the established variety, had waned considerably since the Great Awakening. Sentiments strangely like English Deism, French Enlightenment thought, and/or German idealism were to be found at most levels of American society. See Marty, *The Infidel,* p. 21. It is this presence that I refer to with

"Enlightenment." For an effort to combine both American experience and European thought as the source of American intellectual development see Russel Blaine Nye, *The Cultural Life of the New Nation,* New American Nation Series (New York: Harper and Row, 1960), p. 4ff.

9.   Mead, *Lively Experiment,* p. 38. The value of Professor Mead's parable is only suggestive. If pietistic elements of rightwing Protestantism were wed to leftwing sectarian Protestantism, it was at best a stormy marriage. Perhaps it was a marriage like that of Jacob to Leah: the whole thing was a great surprise. The Baptists, Methodists and Quakers were constantly being attacked by and attacking the rightwing Protestant groups and, at the same time, attacking one another, even in the earliest period of their nuptials. Perhaps this marital instability is what shaped American Protestants.

10. Beaver, *Ecumenical Beginnings,* p. 294, refers to the great proliferation of independent faith mission societies since World War II as a "second wave of 'Protestant' missionary activity." In terms of American missionary effort one could speak of three waves: 1800ff., 1886ff., and post-World War II.

11. *The General Assembly's Missionary Magazine,* 1805, p. ii. Hereafter *GAMM.* The letters and journals of the missionaries are filled with reports of "revivals of religion." They lament when no revival was underway, rejoice when one is, and were hopeful when it looked as if one might begin. See a letter from Joseph Cornell to the trustees of the Massachusetts Baptist Missionary Society, April 6, 1803, in *Massachusetts Baptist Missionary Magazine,* 1803, pp. 11-15, hereafter *MBMM; Glad Tidings, Or an Account of the State of Religion, within the Bounds of the General Assembly of the Presbyterian Church in the United States of America and Other Parts of the World* (Philadelphia: Printed by Jane Aitken, 1804), the first printed report of the Standing Committee of Missions of the General Assembly plus information that had been gathered from many other societies, which sees the frontier revival and the "missionary business" as one and the same thing; and Samuel Miller, *A Sermon, Delivered before the New-York Missionary Society at their Annual Meeting, April 6th, 1802* (New York: T. & J. Swords, 1802), p. 46, where he cites revivals, missionary enterprises and progress against infidelity and vice as a "pledge from God of his presence with his Church." The report of the Connecticut Missionary Society in 1803 is completely about revivals. See *The Connecticut Evangelical Magazine,* 1803, pp. 303-326. Hereafter *CEM.*

12. Latourette, *History of the Expansion of Christianity,* IV, 484.

13. Mead, *Lively Experiment,* p. 115ff.

Chapter 3

The Mission Takes Shape

*The light begins to break forth a little among us in yonder
wilderness toward the setting sun.*

Chief Onondego — 1792

The Protestant World Mission had its rise in the first half of the Seventeenth Century. The first efforts at evangelism were conducted by chaplains of the Dutch East Indies Company in the Malay Archipelago.[1] The colonial enterprise of the Virginia Company was launched with profound theological and missionary presuppositions.[2] The Massacre of 1622 destroyed the limited efforts at Indian evangelism by the earliest colonists, and extinguished the motive of that missionary undertaking. The New England Mission to the Indians, begun in the 1640s, provided the greatest stimulus and continuity to the World Mission of Protestant Christianity.[3] However, not just New England Christians labored to bring the American aborigines to Christ. Before the Revolution, there were efforts at Indian evangelization up and down the British colonies.

Summary of Indian Missions Before the Revolution

It will be useful to describe the centers of Indian mission during the Colonial Period and delineate the major thrust of missionary activity before the Revolution.

New England

Sporadic personal efforts to convert individual Indians describes the missionary activity of New England Puritans before 1640. A determined, public effort to evangelize entire villages began soon after Thomas Mayhew established a colony on Martha's Vineyard in 1642. Thomas, Jr., moved with concern for the plight of the Indians and for the glory of God, set himself to learning the language and began teaching at every opportunity. The mission was most successful. The Mayhews provided remarkable missionary leadership throughout the Colonial Period.[4]

John Eliot launched a larger mission to the Indians on the mainland in 1646. In five years he established an extensive preaching circuit. During the next

101

fifteen years numerical growth continued and the translation enterprise began. The decade before the King Phillip's War of 1675 was a time of extensive growth. But the war almost destroyed the Indian mission.

Eliot did not work alone. Abraham Pierson began working with the Connecticut Indians in 1651. William Leveritch preached to the Indians in Plymouth during the same period. Richard Bourn, appointed in 1756, was the most persistent missionary in Plymouth. James Fitch also worked in Connecticut but had little success. John Cotton, son of the famous Boston preacher, began his missionary career in 1663. Others, including Eliot's own sons, labored for shorter periods. Daniel Gookin, magistrate for the Indians, was probably Eliot's most effective helper in the two decades before Eliot's death in 1682.[6]

Even Eliot could not get the mission going again after the war. Others labored in maritime New England between the King Phillip's War and the American Revolution, but the Indians in that area were a defeated and dying race. So, Indian evangelization shifted further west.

A second missionary effort in New England began after 1730. Cotton Mather, Benjamin Coleman and Solomon Stoddard had called for a vigorous renewal of Indian evangelization after the turn of the century. The northern and western frontier was a constant menace. French and Indian conspiracy had its own terrible mystique in New England. Several unsuccessful efforts were made to establish a mission. The eventual establishment and funding of the Stockbridge mission best represents this phase of Indian evangelization in New England.

The Great Awakening was a mighty stimulus to missionary endeavor among the Indians. Daniel Marshall was not the only New Light who was moved to leave his home and begin a ministry among the heathen. David Brainerd was the most famous Indian missionary produced by the Great Awakening in New England. His ministry, however, was in the Middle Colonies. Though his association with New Light sectarians hindered Brainerd's ministry in New England, he was not without influence there also. Edwards described Brainerd's last visit to Boston as a "triumphal entry." He not only testified to true religion in that metropolis, but also stimulated liberal gifts for Indian missions and the formation of an embryo organization that holds the distinction, though it did not continue, of being the first effort toward an American society for missionary purposes.[7]

The most visionary Indian mission of the Colonial Period had its roots in the Great Awakening. Eleazar Wheelock founded his Charity School in 1754 as an integral part of a plan to evangelize the American wilderness. This mission, along with the attempt to form a Boston model of the Society for Propagating Christian Knowledge, demands considerable space in this chapter. These two endeavors reach into the National Period and play significant roles in developments after the Revolution.

The Middle Colonies

Efforts at Indian evangelization in the Middle Colonies before the Revolution developed along four separate lines. The founding of Pennsylvania brought Quakers to the Middle Colonies in great numbers. They came to America with a distinct charge to preach to the Indians. However, from the visit of Josiah Coale to Martha's Vineyard in 1658 to the journey of Zebulon Heston and John Parrish to preach to the Delaware Tribe in 1773, the pattern was the same. The mission was not the burden of the Weekly, Quarterly or Yearly Meetings. Indian evangelization was attempted by individual Quakers under a particular "concern." There was no general missionary policy, organization or program to call Quakers to a concerted Indian mission before the Revolution.[9]

The second line of Indian missions in the Middle Colonies was that conducted by the Church of England among the Mohawks in Upper New York. The Earl of Bellamont called for the mission to begin in 1700.[10] The first missionary arrived in 1704, but every effort ended in failure.[11] A second phase began in 1727 when John Miln arrived in Albany. In two decades, through the ministry of Miln and Henry Barclay, there was considerable success in Anglicanizing Indians near Albany.[12]

The third phase of the Mohawk mission began in 1749. That year William Johnson, Superintendent of Indian Affairs, began twenty-five years of active involvement to christianize the Six Nations. A full-time missionary was not actually sent to the Indians until 1770. But Johnson was so effective that, with the aid of Chief Joseph Brant, the Mohawks became a Christian nation.[13] They were so devoted to England and England's Church that they moved into Canada after the Revolution. The Mohawk mission is, from several points of view, the most successful of all the pre-revolutionary missions to the Indians.

The Moravian Mission to the American Indians began in the Middle Colonies in 1740. That year Christian Heinrich Rauch attached himself to the village of Shekomeki in Dutchess County, New York. His mission was not unsuccessful, but by 1745 antagonism from the white settlers and persecution by legal authorities had forced the abandonment of this mission.[14] In the meantime the groundwork for a much more significant mission to the Iroquois and the Delawares had been laid. While Count Zinzendorf was in America, 1741 to 1743, a definite missionary strategy had been adopted by the Moravians. The settlements of Bethlehem and Nazareth became beehives of missionary activity. The entire colony engaged in a semi-communal enterprise in which a few served as "fishers" while the rest labored to support them.

The most prominent missionary of the period was David Zeisberger. He began the mission among the Six Nations in Pennsylvania. When the Unitas Fratum was recognized as an ancient episcopal church by the Parliament in 1749, missionary endeavor switched to the Indians around Lake Onondaga. The work was disrupted by the Seven Years War in 1755. The mission among the Delawares began in 1765. It was the most important mission of the Moravians before the

Revolution. Near the end of the war, the American militia mercilessly destroyed the major centers of the Christian Indians, by then located in Ohio. Most of the Indians moved to Canada under English protection.

The fourth missionary thrust in the Middle Colonies came from the New Light Presbyterians. Azariah Horton was their first missionary. He settled down among the Indians on Long Island in 1742. David Brainerd was their most renowned missionary. It was John Brainerd, however, who continued David's work and labored longest among the New Jersey Indians. His activity is an integral part of this chapter.

The South

Missionary labor among the Indians in the southern colonies was sparse. Such men as Alexander Whitaker certainly had a missionary concern in the first years of the colony in Virginia.[15] The Massacre of 1622 destroyed both missionary plans and enthusiasm. However, the missionary motive in colonization resurfaced in Georgia. James Oglethorpe was a member of Thomas Bray's Associates, a group formed to do something for the imprisoned poor of England and for Negro slaves in the colonies. This interest eventually led to the founding of Georgia. John and Charles Wesley and Benjamin Ingham were invited to go to Georgia in 1735 as chaplains. Ingham was charged to evangelize the Indians.

The Moravians were already on the scene when Ingham arrived. He joined Peter Rose and wife at Irene, a mile upriver from Savannah.[16] The mission of the Holy Club failed in two years.[17] The Moravians lost favor because they would not bear arms against the Spanish. Their mission was abandoned in 1740. The Moravians returned to the South in 1753 to a large land tract in North Carolina. Their intention was to make it a center of missionary activity among the Creeks and Cherokees. Aggressive mission work was not begun, however, until after the Revolution.[18]

New Light Presbyterians were briefly involved in a mission to the Indians in the South. Samuel Davies and Gilbert Tennet returned from England in 1755 with two hundred pounds for Indian missions. Davies became the secretary of the Society for Managing the Missions and Schools among the Indians organized in the Hanover Presbytery.[19] At least two missionaries worked among the southern Indians until wars brought the mission to a close.

Organization For and Support of Indian Missions
Before the Revolution

Response to missionary efforts among the American aborigines led to the first organizations for missionary recruitment and support. Before the Revolution, missionary organization among the American churches was limited to two sorts. Both influenced organization for missions in the early National Period.

European Missionary Societies

Five principle missionary societies functioned in the Colonies before the

Revolution. Three are not materially germane to this chapter. Each played an insignificant part in the shaping of missionary thought and organizational structure among the American churches. However, a brief characterization of the origin and work of these societies is needed before the more important societies are discussed in detail.

Three Missionary Societies

The Society for Propagating the Gospel in Foreign Parts (SPG), was organized in London in 1701. It was largely the result of the enthusiasm of Thomas Bray who had just returned from his brief visit to Maryland as Commissary of the Bishop of London.[20] Unlike the Society for Promoting Christian Knowledge (SPCK) that Bray had founded in March, 1699, it was a chartered body designed to collect and hold funds and maintain missionaries in the colonies.

The SPG became the missionary arm of the Church of England in the Colonial Period. Its purpose was the support of the clergy in the British colonies and the evangelization of the aborigines and Negro slaves in these same plantations.[21] This society provided most of the pastors for the Anglican establishment in North and South Carolina and Georgia. It strengthened the Anglican Church in Virginia and Maryland. The SPG provided missionaries for planting the Church of England in Pennsylvania and New York. It fostered the mission to the Mohawks rather reluctantly. None of its missionaries can be credited with winning these Indians to the Christian faith.[22] SPG missionaries were largely responsible for founding the Anglican churches in New England and joined with Quakers, Baptists and Methodists in attempts to gain religious liberty in New England.

The influence of the SPG on the development of the missionary character of the American churches is mainly indirect and often negative. This indirect influence will be mentioned below. The Society ceased its activities in the United States at the end of the Revolution. The Protestant Episcopal Church, engaged in a struggle for its life in the years after the War of Independence, did not send missionaries to the frontier until 1819. It organized its Domestic and Foreign Missionary Society two years later.

The summer of 1742 was a crucial time for the mission of the Moravian Church to American settlers and Indians. Zinzendorf was bringing his stint in America to a close. Bethlehem was molded into a nerve center for evangelistic outreach and missionary expansion. The entire Moravian Brotherhood in America was organized into two companies.[23] One group, the House Congregation, occupied Bethlehem and supported those who itinerated among the white settlers or lived among th "Indians. This second group, the Pilgrim Congregation, occupied the missionary outposts. Zinzendorf's Indian missionary tours suggested the direction the mission to the Indians would take.[24]

Zinzendorf left for Europe in 1743. Peter Bohler and David Nitschmann were left in charge. Augustus Gotlieb Spangenberg returned to America in 1744. He in reality made the "Economy," as the plan was called, function.[25] In December, 1745, at a meeting of the Pennsylvania Synod, largely a Moravian gathering, Spangenberg organized a society for the Propagating of the Gospel.[26] This society disintegrated after Spangenberg was called back to Europe in 1762. John Ettwein resurrected this agency in 1787 when he incorporated the Society of the United Brethren for Propagating the Gospel among the Heathen, for the purpose of holding title to property and raising monies.[27] Missions and missionaries were directed and, in main, recruited from Herrnhut. The Moravian Church in America did not become an independent missionary-sending church until later. Its significance and growing influence on the American churches came primarily through the later English societies. The contributions of the Unitas Fratrum to the missionary character of the American churches was essentially that of example, not theology or structure.[28]

In January, 1723, Thomas Bray, dangerously ill at the time, organized a small body of Associates to handle the disbursement of income from 900 pounds that had been left to him to use in the conversion and education of Negroes in the British Plantations. Bray lived on for another six years and became interested in prison reform and in aiding those thousands of Englishmen then in prison for indebtedness. The Associates were increased in number in 1729. The new body guided the humanitarian aspect of the founding of Georgia. Bray's Associates primarily funded schools and provided libraries for the use of educating American Blacks.[29] The mission to the slaves and the work of this society made little impact on the missionary character of the American churches. Most Negro evangelism before and after the Revolution came in the Great Awakening and the revivals that followed. Before the Revolution the force in missions to the African slaves was a partnership of Bray's Associates, the SPCK and the SPG.

Two organizations in the British Isles supported extensive mission work in the colonies. Both were also policymaking bodies. Each appointed representatives in the colonies who determined missionary needs, recruited and appointed missionaries and disbursed mission money provided by the parent society. Both organizations influenced the missionary organization in American churches. American churchmen learned a method of conducting "missionary business" from these societies.

The New England Company

Extensive reference has already been made to the work of the New England Company in America. John Eliot and Cotton Mather were key figures in the ministry of this society. The Act for the promoting and propagating the Gospel of Jesus Christ in New England" was passed by the Long Parliament on July 27, 1649. The bill created a corporation called "The President and Society for Propagation of the Gospel in New England." When Charles II was returned to the English throne in 1660, the Society had to secure a new charter. Early in 1661 the new charter was approved, renaming the corporation "the Company for Propagacion of the Gospell in New England, and the parts adjacent in America."[30] As "Society" and "Company" this earliest of all Protestant missionary organizations functioned in what was to become the United States for over 125 years.

In 1643, the General Courts of the colonies of Massachusetts Bay, Plymouth, New Haven and Connecticut, after six years of consideration, got together in a *confederation.* Continuing Indian unrest, threats from the Dutch and French, and trouble in England combined to make the confederation a reality. Each General Court appointed two *commissioners,* who usually met each September. In 1649, when the people in London who were lobbying for the constitution of a missionary society looked for someone to assume responsibility in New England, the Commissioners of the United Colonies were their choice. Edward Winslow was the agent of the Massachusetts Bay Colony in England in 1649. He was the moving force behind the chartering of the Society. He had been governor of Connecticut and a Commissioner of the United Colonies. The Commissioners were the most representative and imposing group in New England. Most of their time was already spent trying to find solutions to Indian problems. They proved an excellent choice which was also acceptable to the Parliament.

> The naming of the Commissioners in the act constituted the only occasion on which they were officially recognized by the English government, and the only authority exercised by them in their own right was that given them under the act.[31]

The fifty-eight men who served as Commissioners of the United Colonies[32] were all politicians and members of the General Courts of the Colonies. Not one was a minister. This left the enterprise open to criticism. However, it set a precedent that continued in American missionary efforts toward the Indians until the end of the Nineteenth Century. The mission to the Indians was closely aligned with the powers of state.[33]

In September, 1684, the Commissioners of the United Colonies met for the last time. The New England Company appointed others to assume the responsibilities of the Indian mission. Five Commissioners for Indian Affairs were named the following year. All were prominent men from the Boston area. Simon Bradstreet was governor of Massachusetts Bay. Thomas Hincley was governor of Plymouth Colony. Joseph Dudley was still a loyal New Englander in 1685 and destined the next year to become the first president of the Dominion of New England. William Stoughton had held almost every public office, in 1685, except that of Governor of Massachusetts Bay. Peter Buckeley, the least prominent of the five, served many years as Deputy and Assistant in the Bay Colony. All had previously served as Commissioners of the United Colonies.

In 1690, Increase Mather was appointed a Commissioner on Indian Affairs. He was the first clergyman appointed, the first of a long line of prominent New England clergymen to serve. The list includes Cotton Mather, Benjamin Coleman, Epheriam Williams, Johnthan Mayhew and Charles Chauncy. Eighty-five men served the Company between 1685 and 1775. They were, whether politicians, educators, ministers or merchants, among the most important men of their time. This became characteristic of American mission boards and societies, especially in New England. Some of the most prominent men in the community were involved, at least in name, in the missionary enterprise.

The Company's exertions in the Seventeenth Century were dominated by the work of John Eliot and, to a lesser degree, the Mayhew family. The mission to the Indians had reached its acme when the King Philip's War erupted in June, 1675. Daniel Gookin wrote *Historical Collections of the Indians in New England* in 1674. There were then fourteen praying towns in the Bay Colony with 1,100 inhabitants. Over 2,500 Christian Indians lived on Martha's Vineyard and Nantucket and in Plymouth Colony.[34] When the war was over only four towns remained. The Christian Indians were scattered, and the New England Indians were a diminishing people.

For forty years after Eliot's death, in spite of the efforts of men like Cotton Mather, Samuel Sewall and Solomon Stoddard, the Indian mission was at best a holding action. Between John Eliot and John Sergeant, almost half a century, only Experience Mayhew stands out as a missionary of significance and effectiveness.

The most important project of the Company in the Eighteenth Century was the Stockbridge mission. In 1773, Isaac Hollis, an eccentric English Baptist, read of the triple ordination of Stephen Parker, Ebenezer Hinsdell and Joseph Seccombe as missionaries for the Society in Scotland for Propagating Christian Knowledge. He wrote to Benjamin Coleman in Boston and offered "twenty Pounds Sterling per Anum, for Ever, for the Support of a fourth Missionary."[35] Coleman could not at that time direct Hollis' funds toward another missionary. While the correspondence was passing, plans were being made in western Massachusetts for a more permanent Indian mission to which the Hollis money and the New England Company funds were to be significantly related.

Samuel Hopkins and Stephen Williams, both pastors in Springfield, conceived of a mission, probably in conjunction with John Stoddard of Stockbridge and William Williams of Hatfield, addressed to the "westward Indians."[36] A proposal was sent to the Commissioners of Indian Affairs. Governor Jonathan Belcher was chairman of the Commissioners. Approval was secured. Stephen Williams and Nehemiah Bull of Westfield contacted the Indians and found them willing to have a teacher. Land was secured on the Housatonic River and John Sergeant, a tutor at Yale College, was enlisted as missionary.

Sergeant served effectively until his death in 1749. He was succeeded by Jonathan Edwards, Stephen West and finally his son, John Sergeant Jr., who continued the Stockbridge school into the Nineteenth Century.

The Great Awakening brought an intensification of missionary activity to the Indians. The New England Company supported many missionaries in the period between the Great Revival and the Revolution. It discontinued its financial support to New England in May, 1779.

The SSPCK

The Society in Scotland for Propagating Christian Knowledge was chartered in Edinburgh by proclamation of Queen Anne and an act of the Lords of

Council and Session on July 9, 1709. It had its rise in 1701, when a small Society for the Reformation of Manners had been formed in that city to combat ignorance and Catholicism in the Highlands and Islands of Scotland. Finding that a much broader-based organization was needed, a request was made to the General Assembly of the Church of Scotland in 1706 to lend its support to the project. After study, in 1708, the National Church recommended the enterprise to the presbyteries and churches.

The purpose of the SSPCK, according to its charter, was to increase "Piety and Virtue in Scotland, especially in the Highlands, Islands and remote Corners thereof, . . . and for propagating the same in Popish and Infidel Parts of the World." [37] During its first thirty years, the Society was content to direct its resources and efforts only toward Scotland.

In 1716, Daniel Williams, wealthy London clergyman and philanthropist, died leaving an estate to the SSPCK to be used to evangelize pagans in some undesignated foreign country. The bequest was not without strings. It could only be received after the SSPCK had supported three missionaries "in foreign and infidel countries" for one year, and then only so long as the proceeds were to be used "for the conversion of infidel countries, and the members of the . . . Society" were freely elected. [38] For ten years leaders of the SSPCK did their best to acquire the estates promised without meeting the prescribed conditions. They insisted that

> the smallness of their stock and the Great Ignorance . . . of the
> Highlands and Islands . . . requires a greater number of schools
> than they have been . . . able to support upon their yearly revenue. [39]

To take on the added responsibility of three missionaries in a foreign land was not practicable.

The SSPCK undertook to meet the conditions of Williams will on April 9, 1731. The officers of the Society wrote to Governor Belcher of Massachusetts Bay asking him and several others including Benjamin Coleman and Joseph Sewall, to serve as a Board of Correspondents for the Society. The Correspondents were granted power "to chuse persons qualified . . . as missionaries, and not employed by any other society, to fix the salary which should be given to each . . . and to specify the particular places where they should serve." [40] These men complied and, with the assistance of the General Court of the Province, sent Stephen Parker, Ebenezer Hinsdell and Joseph Seccombe to posts on the frontier. [41] The mission failed. In 1737, the three missionaries were dismissed.

After the failure of the mission, the Correspondents in Boston ceased to function. But the SSPCK was ?busy on other fronts. In 1735, it began to support Gaelic-speaking John Macleod as the minister of the Highlander's colony in Georgia and missionary to nearby Indians. This support continued until 1740. [42] In 1741, the SSPCK established a Board of Correspondents in the New York-Newark area. Jonathan Dickinson, Ebenezer Pemberton and Aaron Burr petitioned the Society to sponsor work among the Indians on Long Island and in New Jersey. These three, with other members of the New York Presbytery, were appointed as Correspondents in 1741.[43] Azariah Horton and David and John Brainerd are the best known missionaries commissioned by this group of men. In 1761, when David Bostwick served as president of the Correspondents, Samson Occum was briefly under the direction of this Board.

Samuel Davies and Gilbert Tennent toured Scotland and England on behalf of the College of New Jersey in 1753-55. In Edinburgh, on May 30, 1754, Davies met with the SSPCK and gave them his "advice about the best method of conducting the mission among the Indians."[44] When he returned to Virginia he engrossed himself in securing missionaries for the Indians. A "Society in Virginia for managing the Indian Mission" was set up.[45] John Martin and William Richardson preached to the Cherokees in 1757, and in 1758. Both these young men had entered the ministry under the tutelage of Samuel Davies. Davies attempted to enlist both Gideon Hawley and Samson Occum as a permanent missionary to the Cherokees.[46] The New England Company joined with the SSPCK in this enterprise. Because of the Indian War, the mission was completely abandoned in 1763.[47] This, however, was the first American missionary society actually to deploy missionaries among the Indians.

In 1760, the SSPCK re-established its Board of Correspondents in Boston. Thomas Hutchinson, then Lieutenant Governor of the province of Massachusetts Bay, was the most prominent person named as correspondent. This second Board of Correspondents sponsored a number of missions throughout the Revolutionary Era. In 1773, the SSPCK began to support Samuel Kirkland, and remunerations continued until 1777. After the war, Kirkland tried to recover his salary for missionary labor during the Revolution. The SSPCK allowed less than half of his claim, but in the process, the Board of Correspondents in Boston was reassembled. The SSPCK continued to support the evangelization of the American Indians through the first half of the Nineteenth Century.

A third Board of Correspondents of the SSPCK was commissioned in Connecticut in 1764. Eleazar Wheelock requested the formation of such a Board to lend stature and support to his school and the missionary enterprise that he conducted. The Connecticut Correspondents were all men in the Association around Lebanon, where the school was located. All members were nominated by Wheelock.[48] Because of conflict with Wheelock, the SSPCK withdrew support in 1774, and this Board of Correspondents ceased to exist.

American cooperation and involvement in the Indian missions of the Colonial Period became a guide to earliest organizational efforts in the new nation. Policy, methodology and patterns of cooperation were the heritage bequeathed to the American churches by the New England Company and the SSPCK. The results of these years of missionary effort were still visible in 1787. The example of the missionaries was still in the memory of the American churches. When American churchmen began missionary organizations in the early National Period, first they had to make provisions for the missions begun in the Colonial Period. These two societies were most influential in shaping the new missionary endeavors.

American Missionary Organizations

Indian evangelization was undertaken from the outset by American colonists. Neither the Company nor the SSPCK engaged in sending missionaries. Those involved in the Puritan mission called the churchmen in Great Britain to do the work. These efforts to involve others led to the formation of the New England Company. The Indian mission conducted by these two societies was a partnership in which the Colonies furnished men and Britain provided the funds.

It is difficult to document the extent of local support for the Indian mission. The colonial legislatures, with some consistency, committed financial resources to Indian Christianization.[49] The magnitude of other local support remains a puzzling question. Eliot was unwilling to give a full report to the Company of what he received in New England. Mather gives evidence of support for the Indian mission, even in the period of the mission's recession. The New York Presbyterians undergirded one of Samson Occum's missionary journeys in a significant way.[50] Though the full range of local support cannot be documented, it was never enough. English Christians remained primarily responsible for funding the mission.

The mission was directed by Colonials who served by commission from the societies in the British Isles. One attempt was made to create a society fashioned after the British pattern in the colonies before the Revolution. Another significant missionary undertaking was launched in Connecticut on an entirely different plan. The first proved abortive and the second became the most impressive missionary enterprise in America in the Eighteenth Century. Both were dependent on the support and encouragement of Christians in Great Britain. These organizations were expressions of American missionary initiative but were intentionally related to the funding societies in England and Scotland. These projects demand attention.

Wheelock's Indian Charity School

By 1743, the Great Awakening had begun to wane in New England. Connecticut was rent with dissension. Eleazar Wheelock had almost stopped his itinerant preaching. He had settled down in Lebanon and opened a school to supplement his income. Samson Occum, converted in 1740 under the ministry of James Davenport, had been diligently learning to read and write.

Perhaps Davenport told Occum of Wheelock's school. In December, 1743, the twenty-year-old Occum went to Lebanon to study with Wheelock for a fortnight and "Spent 4 years with him."[51] Occum insinuated that it was his presence in Wheelock's home and school that first gave Wheelock the idea of a school designed to train both Indian and English boys for missionary careers on the frontier. Twenty years later, when Wheelock published his first account of the rise of the Charity School, he described his experience with Occum as a "trial" that had proved eminently successful. The Commissioners of Indian Affairs in Boston had subsidized the education of Occum.

By 1754, Wheelock had formulated a distinctive plan that was carefully engineered to avoid the pitfalls which so often thwarted Indian missions. The Indians could be brought to Christ

> by the Mission of their own Sons in Conjunction with the *English*;
> and that a Number of Girls should also be instructed in whatever
> should be necessary to render them fit, to perform . . . as house-
> wives, School-mistresses, Tayloresses . . . And prevent a Necessity
> of their turning savage in their Manner of Living . . . and also rec-
> ommend to the Savages a more rational and decent Manner of Liv-
> ing . . . And thereby, in Time, remedy . . . (the) Difficulty, so con-
> stantly complained of . . . as the great Impediment in the Way to
> . . . Success, . . . their continual rambling about.[52]

This kind of mission could become a reality, Wheelock reasoned, by the creation of an Indian school. Whites and Indians could be trained together in the fundamentals of a liberal education, in the "Divine Skill in Things spiritual, (and) pure and fervent Zeal for the Salvation of Souls." These were the "most necessary Qualifications in a Missionary."[53] In such a school the English lads could absorb Indian culture and master the Indian languages. The Indian boys could learn the technology of agriculture and the trades. The Charity School was to be fashioned after the extensive enterprises of charity founded by August Hermann Francke. "It was begun," wrote some of Wheelock's friends in 1766,

> in the same Spirit with which the late Reverend and Eminent
> Professor *Francke* founded the present famous Orphan-House
> at *Hall* in *Germany*.[54]

Wheelock was never able to get his school chartered in Connecticut. He did produce a number of students who rendered significant service to the evangelization of the Indians and churching of the wilderness. The missionary aspect of the School was at its peak in the decade between 1761 and 1769.

For a time, Wheelock had the encouragement of Sir William Johnson, the financial assistance of the New England Company through their Commissioners in Boston, and the monetary assistance of the Correspondents of the SSPCK in Boston. The Commissioners of the Company had an anti-revivalist mentality in the 1750s and 1760s. Wheelock was suspect and often subject to criticism, not always without warrant. An open break came in the middle sixties when Wheelock and George Whitfield carried out their plan of raising money in England and Scotland for the Charity School and the Indian mission. Since there was close association and some interlocking of membership between the Commissioners and the Boston Correspondents of the SSPCK, Wheelock had more and more trouble maintaining a working relationship with that group.

In 1764, he was successful in getting himself and some close associates recognized as Connecticut Commissioners of the SSPCK. This Board became the primary sponsor of his mission work. The missionaries that went out from Wheelock's school after 1764 were commissioned by the Connecticut Correspondents. But they were, in fact, Wheelock's missionaries. They looked to him for support, directions, encouragement and the assignment of fields.[55]

Wheelock was an able propagandist. He and his friends produced a series of booklets, on the order of the Eliot tracts, that kept the public informed, in England and America, with the progress of his mission.[56] The tour of Samson Occum and Nathaniel Whitaker in England and Scotland was a public relations coup of considerable proportions.[57] Even though he did not realize at once all of the proceeds, the money collected and retained in Great Britain enabled his missionaries to continue with some support until 1774. Wheelock had a unique capacity to inspire men. But, the young men he sent out were never adequately supported. His break with Samuel Kirkland in 1770 was a rancorous affair. Yet, in the main, these men remained his loyal friends and staunch supporters.

By 1770, Wheelock was discouraged with some aspects of his plan. He doubted the Indians could ever be evangelized with Indian missionaries. Of the forty he trained in sixteen years, only twenty continued to conduct themselves as Christians. Wheelock became

> fully convinced, by many weighty reasons, that a greater proportion of English youth must be prepared for missionaries to take entirely the lead of the affairs in the wilderness.[58]

This conviction helped him reach the decision to move from Lebanon to Hanover, New Hampshire, and establishing Dartmouth College. More's Indian Charity School, as it was called, was moved also and conducted in conjunction with the college in the wilderness. The Charity School continued to exist until 1829.

Wheelock's primary contribution was his training of future leaders and the depth of dedication to the missionary task that he was able to instill in them. Samson Occum and Samuel Kirkland were the best known of Wheelock's students who became missionaries to the Indians. However, David McClure, David Avery, Levi Frisbie and John Lanthrop continued an interest in Indian evangelization throughout their lives. Wheelock's missionary plan was the most creative produced in America in the Colonial Period. It was also the most extensive missionary undertaking in America in the Eighteenth Century.

Wheelock was not temperamentally fitted to manage such a mission. He found it difficult to work with those who did not share his views. He had nothing but contempt for Indian culture and was never able to bring himself fully to trust his Indian missionaries. Yet such was his motivation and commitment that for nearly two decades he sent missionaries to the American Indians and established an institution that has stood now two hundred years.

Aborted Society of 1762

The outcome of the French and Indian War was certain long before the Peace of Paris. Canada had been won on November 8, 1760, with the fall of Montreal. The Boston newspapers in 1762 are filled with optimism as they recount in detail the news from different battlefields. The defeat of the French in Canada was really good news for New England. New lands opened in the north and west. Fear of a conspiracy of Indians and French evaporated. For some it heralded the end of Jesuit influence among the Indians and the hope that at last New England missionaries might go among them with success.[59] This optimism was first expressed by several exploratory mission tours sent out in 1761. Gideon Hawley, who had served among the Six Nations before the war reached its height, accompanied Eli Forbes and Amos Toppan to Onohoquaga to introduce them to those Indians with whom he had worked. Samson Occum went to the same area during the same year. There seemed to be, Samuel Buell said in 1761, "a glorious door . . . opening for their being evangelized."[60]

Another war began in New England, a struggle between the Society for the Propagation of the Gospel in Foreign Parts and the Congregational Standing Order in New England. This war got into the papers also.[61] The SPG, congregational ministers said, was not interested in evangelizing the heathen but in proselytizing the New England dissenters. Its goal was to build the Church of England where churches of the New England Way had long since been gathered. This, Jonathan Mayhew argued a year later, was a violation of the SPG's royal charter and a perversion in the use of its funds.[62] The entire situation was further complicated because it was all tied together with the threat, from the New Englander's point of view, of an Anglican bishop being consecrated for the American colonies. Amid optimism about the future of Indian missions and distress and fear about the work and intentions of the SPG missionaries, the first chartered missionary society in America was formed.

On May 6, 1762, the Society for Propagating Christian Knowledge among the Indians of North America was organized.[63] The Massachusetts General Court incorporated the society, but royal approval was required. Two thousand pounds had been subscribed to its fund.[64] James Bowdoin was elected president and Joseph Sewall vice president. The remaining members were mostly people already serving as Commissioners of the New England Company or Correspondents of the SSPCK.

The new society received a pledge of support from the New England Company and from the Corporation of Harvard College which had funds to be expended for the education of Indians. A concerted effort was made to enlist the cooperation of the SSPCK. Joseph Bowman was ordained by the Boston Correspondents to join Forbes' mission among the Six Nations.[65]

This society discontinued when George III refused to grant the charter. The New England men were correct in charging that intervention by the SPG, through the Archbishop of Canterbury, was responsible for the refusal.

The denial of the charter was not soon forgotten. The Peace of Paris, in February, 1763, brought a new government to Great Britain. George Grenville, as Chancellor of the Exchequer, formulated a new and harshnr colonial policy. When the colonists began to rebel against the laws of 1764, they counted the refusal of this charter as one of a long list of unacceptable measures.[66] A quarter century later, some men still living who helped to form this aborted society, joined others in forming the earliest continuing American missionary society.

In 1772, Samuel Hopkins and Ezra Stiles formed a fourth American society. Its purpose was an overseas mission, and its story is best told in a later chapter.

Missionary Expansion by Colonial Ecclesiastical Bodies

New Kind of Wilderness: Mission and Church Planting

In addition to efforts to evangelize the Red Indians of the American wilderness and to gather them into churches, American Christians developed a new concept of mission in the Eighteenth Century. This new concept led to a second way of doing mission work, a way other than through special societies organized for missionary purposes. This second missionary method, church planting through the agency of larger ecclesiastical bodies, is a new thing in the history of Christianity. This new notion properly marks the beginning of "Home Missions" for American churches, a most significant event in the shaping of American Christianity.

A new concept, of course, is never completely new. The work of the great English missionary, Boniface, among the disordered churches and semi-Christianized populations of the southern Germanic tribes in the Eighth Century is a possible parallel. The first generation of the New England Puritans conceived both the planting of English churches and the gathering of churches among the Indians as a part of its errand into the wilderness.[67] By the time of the adoption of the Half-Way Covenant in 1662, however, the dynamic of the revolutionary ideas of New England Congregationalism had begun to fade. The radical assertion that visible churches should be composed of visible saints and their children was abandoned. Churches were no longer gathered from the ranks of men who could testify of their conversion. By means of "Half-Way Measures," the chur ches embraced those who could not give an account of saving grace.

Twenty years after the Great Migration, responsible spokesmen of the city upon a hill were already reconciling it to perpetuation by a succession of formal and possibly hypocritical generations.[68]

The *missionary* errand of the New England Puritans focused almost entirely on the Red Indians. Evangelism, ?winning to Christ from the world, was confined to the indigenous people.

"To reduce the Quakers to the Christian faith" was one of the early goals Thomas Bray designed for the SPCK.[69] By "Christian faith" Bray always meant Anglicanism. The SPG, by its efforts to found churches in Maryland, Pennsylvania, New York and New England, identified "mission" with the planting of congregations of a particular persuasion. Indeed, Puritans themselves, especially the separating variety, gathered churches from adherents of the Church of England in the early Seventeenth Century. It is somewhat ironical that the New England Establishment would take such offense at the work of SPG missionaries in New England after 1760.

Nevertheless, a new understanding of missions arose in the mid-Eighteenth Century among many Am'rican Christians. The emphasis on the *new birth*, which is central to the entire Evangelical Revival, essentially constituted a new definition of the word "Christian." George Whitfield's famous sermon on regeneration preceded him to America. In it he clearly distinguished between the two ways that one may be "in Christ." One way was by outward profession, i.e., to be "baptized into Christ's church" or be "called a Christian." The second way, and "undoubtedly the proper meaning," is to be in Christ "not only by an outward profession, but by an inward change and purity of heart, and cohabitation of his holy Spirit . . . The sum of the matter" was that if "we are not inwardly wrought upon, and changed by the powerful operations of the holy Spirit . . . however we may call ourselves christians, we shall be found naked at the great day."[70] Samuel Davies called the new birth the "grand constituent of a Christian, and prerequisite to our admission into the kingdom of heaven."[71]

This essential attention in the meaning of "Christian" represented a radical interiorization and individualization of the wilderness concept.[72] Jonathan Edwards described the true Christian's life as a journey toward heaven. It begins with conversion but is a continuing trek through "wilderness." The deliverance of Israel from Egypt, the wilderness wanderings and the entrance into Canaan are an epic illustration of what God does for his people in Christ. God's way for those intended for mercy is "to bring them into a wilderness."[73]

The theology of the Great Awakening underline man's depravity and the absolute necessity of an experience of new birth. "Natural man," no matter what his nation, exposure to the means of grace, or relationship to the visible church, is in a "dreadful condition."[74] The English nation, including America, "in all its light and learning," is composed of men further from Christ than "Mahometans."[75]

> The savages who live in the remote parts of this continent . . . as
> well as the inhabitants of Africa, are naturally in exactly similar
> circumstances towards God with us in this land. They are no more
> alienated or estranged from God in their nature than we.[76]

The only advantage Englishmen had was the means of grace. When settlers moved to the frontiers where there was no regular preaching of the gospel, even that distinction disappeared. Frontier settlements along with Indian villages thus became the proper sphere of missions. Indeed, those who could not testify of the "birth from above," especially for the Separate Congregationalists, the New Light Presbyterians and the Baptists, became proper subjects of the evangelical invitation. Place of residence and accessibility to a parish church were not matters of consideration.

This new concept of "missions," or of what constitutes "heathen" and "Christian," enabled the ecclesiastical bodies of the Colonies to view church planting among European emigrants as an integral part of missions. The young, expanding ecclesiastical bodies, shaped by the Great Awakening and local revivals that followed, placed Indian evangelization and church planting among white settlers in the same missionary basket, often to the neglect of the Indians.

The Rise of the Larger Ecclesiastical Bodies

The representatives of the New England Company and the SSPCK in the Colonies were men of varied motivation. Some, like Mather, Sewall or Wheelock, had complex and intense motives for becoming involved in Christianizing the Indians. Others were involved simply because they were appointed to do so. They considered Indian evangelization and civilization a project closely related to the peace and good government of the colonies. These representatives were mostly Standing Order Congregationalists and Presbyterians. Some Church of England laymen served with distinction as commissioners of the Company. Whatever their motivation, these men served separately from their churches, in a more or less private capacity. The action of the commissioners and correspondents did not commit the churches to missionary support or involvement.

While these missions to the Indians were being conducted, the number of churches in the Colonies was increasing. The Great Awakening led to a great proliferation of churches. In the South and Middle Colonies, this growth continued until the Revolution. Added to the effect of the Revival, immigrants continued to pour into the country and move into the valleys of the eastern mountains.

The churches began forming larger ecclesiastical fellowships with one another very early in the Eighteenth Century. Cotton Mather led efforts to centralize church control in Massachusetts Bay that climaxed in the Proposals of 1705. These Proposals were rejected in that Province, but they were adopted by the Synod at Saybrook in 1708 for the Connecticut churches. Consociations of churches and associations of ministers became the structure of church establishment throughout Connecticut. The first General Association met in 1709.

The Presbytery of Philadelphia was organized in 1706. It was enlarged to a general synod in 1717. The Philadelphia Baptist Association was constituted in 1707. Because of their close supervision and subjection to the Reformed Church in Holland, the Reformed churches in New York and Pennsylvania did not organize until after 1740.

The need to strengthen existing churches and to assist in securing proper ministerial leadership were important factors in the rise of these larger bodies. Church extension also became an early concern of each larger body. At the meeting of the Philadelphia Presbytery in 1707, the ministers were instructed to "supply neighbouring desolated places where a minister is wanting." The poverty of the people and the churches hindered extensive work in the early years. The Synod of Philadelphia, at its first meeting, established its "fund for Pious uses" to address this problem. The Synod wrote the Presbytery of Dublin and the "Dissenting Ministers in London." It told them of the "earnest breathings of many small and poor places" which could not support a minister and entreated help.[77]

The Baptists were so poor and indisposed to help groups wishing to form into churches that for thirty-five years, the Philadelphia Association advised those sending requests for ministerial help to pray more and to encourage laymen to "exercise their gifts."[78] Only after the Great Awakening did the Association send representatives to assist in the constitution of churches. However, except for the Reformed groups, each ecclesiastical organization was involved in sending missionaries by the beginning of the American Revolution.

The Presbyterians

The most extensive missionary efforts of an American larger-church body in the Colonial Period were by the Presbyterians. Francis McKamie, himself a missionary of sorts, imbued the early Presbytery with a missionary spirit. In fact, in 1718, the Presbyterians considered their newly-organized Synod as an instrument "for spreading and propagating the gospel of Christ in these dark parts of the world." In 1722 they sent Hugh Conn, John Orme and William Stewart, their first three missionaries, to Virginia. The following year, the same men and Jonathan Dickinson itinerated in that colony. From that time, Presbyterians were actively involved in gathering churches on the Virginia frontier. Before the Great Awakening, most Presbyterian advance was in the great Shenandoah Valley. The Synod established a significant correspondence with William Gooch, Governor of Virginia, in securing toleration for the new congregations.[79]

The Philadelphia Synod excluded its New Brunswick Presbytery in 1741. Division had been growing for five years. The split was certain by 1738. That year those who opposed the revivalistic methods of Gilbert Tennent and the other Log College men pushed an overture through the Synod that restricted the preaching of itinerants outside their own presbyteries. This, said the Log Cabin men, hindered much needed help to unsupplied churches.[80]

The departure of the Revivalistic party in 1741 and the group that had opposed strict subscriptionism, led by Jonathan Dickinson, in 1745, left the Synod of Philadelphia with little dynamic. It had few strong leaders. Many of its ministers were plagued with moral problems. Discipline was usually lax. Ministers unpopular at home because of moral irregularities were often sent to supply the vacant churches in western Virginia. The Synod did not send out any additional missionaries until 1748. In the decade before reunion, the Old Side Synod did not organize a single church in Virginia.[81]

The story of the Synod of New York is vastly different. From the very beginning its people were fiercely evangelistic and committed to church extension.

> Intensely missionary-minded, they, by their unparalleled zeal and efforts, far outstripped the Old World Presbyterianism that had been transplanted into the colonies, and gave birth to a new order of Presbyterianism, an American Church.[82]

In 1743, the New Brunswick Presbytery sent William Robinson as an evangelist to Virginia and the Carolinas. He stopped in Hanover County, in southeastern Virginia.

There, without benefit of clergy, the Great Awakening was making its mark. He spent four days there; *"Days of the Son of Man,"* one eye-witness called them. Before he left, he formed the group into Presbyterian church order.[83] His ministry was followed by that of John Blair, John Roan, Gilbert Tennent and Samuel Blair. In 1747, Samuel Davies settled at Hanover. Presbyterian churches sprouted all through middle Virginia.[84] Missionaries were sent to North and South Carolina and to western Pennsylvania during the thirteen years the Synod of New York had a separate existence.

This Synod also was actively involved in Indian missions. Members of the Presbytery of New York had been appointed Correspondents of the SSPCK in 1741. Azariah Horton, ordained in 1742, settled among the Indians on Long Island, supported by the SSPCK. He was one of the members of the Synod of Philadelphia who withdrew in 1745 to form the Synod of New York. David Brainerd was ordained in 1743. His brother, John, succeeded him after his death. The New Side Synod soon joined in support of this Indian mission. In 1751, it ordered an annual collection in the churches to be used to "promote so important and valuable design." When Gilbert Tennent and Samuel Davies returned from England in 1755 they brought with them two hundred pounds "for the propagation of the gospel among the Indians." A committee was appointed by the Synod to draw up a plan for the use of the money. Their plan placed the money in the hands of the trustees of the College of New Jersey. The interest from it was to be used

> towards the support of a pious . . . missionary . . . among the Indians . . . or the supporting of a pious . . . schoolmaster in teaching the Indians . . . or for maintaining a pious . . . Indian youth in the College of New Jersey (for preparation for missionary service) . . . or for maintaining a pious . . . youth of English or Scotch extract, at that college, during his preparatory studies for . . . preaching the gospel among the Indians.[85]

The Synod was prepared to give this money to John Brainerd's work in 1757, "in case the correspondents shall continue him in the mission." However, because of the Indian wars and general unrest, the SSPCK support of this mission was dropped that year. Brainerd took a charge in Newark and continued there until 1759, when he again, on the advice of the Synod now re-united with the Old Side group, took up the Indian mission.[86]

The Synod addressed a long letter to the General Assembly of the Church of Scotland in 1754. It described the College of New Jersey as an institution designed to make the conversion of the Indians and the churching of the frontier a reality. The letter is typical of the missionary spirit and commitment to church extension that characterized this revivalistic branch of the Presbyterian Church.

> In the colonies of New York, New Jersey, Pennsylvania, Maryland, Virginia and Carolina, a great number of congregations have been formed upon the Presbyterian plan, which have put themselves under the synodical care of your petitioners . . . There are also large settlements lately planted in various parts, particularly in North

and South Carolina, where multitudes are extremely desirous of
the ministrations of the gospel; but they are not yet formed into
congregations, and regularly organized for want of ministers.

. . . .

The young daughter of the Church of Scotland, helpless and exposed
in this foreign land, cries to her tender and powerful mother for relief. The cries of ministers oppressed with labours and of congregations famishing for want of the sincere milk of the word, implore
assistance. And were the poor Indian savages sensible of their own
case, they would join in the cry, and beg for more missionaries to
be sent to propagate the religion of Jesus among them![87]

When reunion came in 1758, the flourishing missionary endeavors of the
New Side were continued. The Indian mission of John Brainerd was much enlarged in the 1760s. New Jersey's government purchased land in its southern area
as a home for the scattered Indians in the province. John Brainerd was appointed
"Superintendent and Guardian" of these Indians in 1762 by Governor Josiah
Hardy.[88] The Synod applied the interest of the Indian fund and of the annual
collections to Brainerd's mission and to the Indian school he established. Support
continued through the remaining years before the Revolution.

The SSPCK entered the picture again in 1760, but it never gave adequate
support to Brainerd. There were great hopes of a new mission led by Samson Occum among the Oneidas at the beginning of the decade. William Kirkpatrick returned from his stint as chaplain to the New Jersey troops on the frontier with
great enthusiasm for the possibilities of opening up a new mission. However, the
Synod refused to commit itself to that mission, citing the need of greater support
of the Brainerd mission as their reason. When the SSPCK failed adequately to fund
Occum's mission tour, the Synod underwrote the additional cost.[89]

The synodical missions to the "southward" continued in the re-united
Synod of New York and Philadelphia. The western parts of the Carolinas became
the principle area of missionary exertions. The Synod also turned to the western
and northern frontiers. Missionaries were regularly sent to upper New York and
across the mountains of western Pennsylvania. The most important missionary
venture of the sixties was the visit of George Duffield and Charles Beatty to the
Ohio country in 1767. The mission did not accomplish a great deal, but it kindled
missionary concern that lasted through the Revolution.[90]

The mission was first proposed in 1762. The Synod of Philadelphia had
authorized the formation of a "Corporation for ye Relief of poor & distressed
Presbyterian Ministers & their Widows & children" in 1757. This corporation was
a combination insurance company, relief organization, and missionary society.
When the wars were nearing an end on the frontier, this Corporation proposed that
the Synod join with it in sending two missionaries to the frontier to

preach to the distressed frontier inhabitants, and to report their
distresses, and to let us know where new congregations are a form-

ing, and what is necessary to be done to promote the spread of the gospel among them, and . . . what opportunities there may be of preaching the gospel to the Indian nations in their neighbourhood.[91]

The Synod took the request "much at heart" and appointed Charles Beatty and John Brainerd to go. But the Indian war broke out with great intensity again in 1763. The mission was not accomplished. However, in 1766, Beatty and George Duffield were sent according to the instructions of 1763. The missionaries travelled into the Ohio Country, beyond Pittsburgh. Their report called the entire Church to concerted missionary action. The reaction of the Synod expresses the views of the Presbyterians in the years just before the Revolution on the dual task involved in churching the wilderness.

The Synod laying to heart the unhappy lot of many people in various parts of our land, who at present are brought up in ignorance, and . . . are perishing for lack of knowledge, . . . are unable without some assistance to support the gospel . . . among them; considering, also that it is their duty to send missionaries to their frontier families, who may preach . . . and form them into societies for the public worship of God, and being moved with compassion towards the Indians . . . have resolved to attempt their relief, and to instruct such as may be willing to hear the gospel.[92]

A plan for extensive collections for missionary purposes was set up. The following year John Brainerd and Robert Cooper were sent to the Ohio Indians. Many missionaries travelled to frontier settlements. Nothing significant came of this effort. In 1768, an attempt was made to form a plan for Indian evangelization. The committee judged that the time had not come for putting such a plan into practice.

By the beginning of the Revolution the Presbyterians were very adept at gathering churches on the American frontier. They had learned to cooperate together in supporting a mission to the Indians. They clearly perceived that the future of the Church was on the frontier. When the Synod met, in 1779, in the midst of War, the great opportunity on the frontier was punctuated. Missionaries of "genious, prudence, and address," who could form the people into regular congregations were the need of the hour. All presbyteries were charged to give "their attention to this object, as peculiarly . . . important."[93] The Presbyterians entered the National Period with over half a century of missionary success behind them.

The Baptists

The Baptist development around Philadelphia before the Great Awakening was largely a Welch immigrant movement.[94] Consequently, a lack of ministerial leadership plagued the churches for a generation. Those churches in existence in 1740 were not usually directly affected by the revival, but the Awakening was so general that the movement invariably left its mark.[95] Though the associational minutes never mention the revival, there are tacit comments that suggest its influence. In 1740, the Association had "great ground of rejoicing" because "the

powers of hell hath not been able to blow" the churches away or "hinder . . .
growth and numbers." There was hope that God was dwelling "among his little
tabernacles . . . in this wilderness." Near the end of the decade, the minutes
note the steady growth of the last ten years. "The Lord has been watering his
garden with the increase of God, which we pray may abound more and more."[96]
In the 1750s, the Philadelphia Association became significantly more involved in
missionary pursuits. The little cluster of churches was actually perched on the
northern boundary of a vast unchurched wilderness.

The back parts of the southern colonies were filling up rapidly, but the
Church of England had difficulty providing pastors for its maritime churches. In
1750, there were 102 Anglican churches in Virginia, almost all within fifty miles
of the seacoast, only nine in all of North Carolina, and only nineteen in South
Carolina. The number of clergy was much smaller.

Oliver Hart, one of the most promising young men in the Association,
went to Charleston in 1749 to assist the aging pastor of the Baptist Church. The
pastor was buried the day he arrived, and Hart remained in Charleston thirty
years. He led in forming the Charleston Baptist Association in 1751, modeled
after Philadelphia. The same year, preachers from Philadelphia visited the Opeckon
Church, just west of the Blue Ridge, in Virginia. These men helped to order that
Church along the lines of the churches in the Association.[97] Indian unrest forced
some of the members back east of the mountains to Ketocton Creek where a new
church was formed. In 1754, both the Opeckon and Ketocton churches were received into the Association.[98]

The reception of these two new Virginia churches and a request from the
Charleston Association in 1755 was the occasion of much more extensive efforts
at church planting by the Association. Another of the Association's young preachers, John Gano, was sent out in 1754 on a preaching and survey mission through
the Carolinas. Like Hart, he had been converted during the Awakening and was a
close friend of Gilbert Tennent. He returned to urge the Association to continue
its practice of sending itinerates through the southern colonies.[99] In 1755, the
Charleston Association began missionary efforts on its own. The churches were
asked to make contributions for the support of a missionary to itinerate in North
Carolina.[100] Hart carried a request for such a preacher to Philadelphia in 1755.
John Gano was persuaded to become that missionary. He became the most active
missionary and evangelist that the Philadelphia Association produced in the Eighteenth Century.

Churches continued to be organized in the northern parts of Virginia.[101]
In 1765, several churches were dismissed from the Philadelphia Association to
join with others in forming the Ketocton Association.[102] "Before 1770, the Regular Baptists were spread over the whole countrh, in the Northern Neck above Fred-
ericksburg."[103] In 1770, the Association began choosing one of their number as an
"evangelist." His task was essentially the same as the missionaries sent out by the
Presbyterians. He itinerated, principally toward the South, assisted in gathering
churches, and preached in congregations not having the regular ministry of the
word. In 1774, the "Quekulky" (Keehukee) Association in North Carolina wrote

their appreciation to the Philadelphia body for "sending messengers among them" and solicited "the continuance of correspondence and MISSIONS."[104]

In 1772, the Philadelphia Association almost became involved in a mission to the Indians. David Jones, one of its pastors, decided to go on a mission to the Indians in Ohio. Jones' motivation grew out of the surge of revival that was stirring among Baptists in some parts of New England and throughout the South and the dearth of spiritual life that had overtaken some of the more established churches in the Middle Colonies. "By reading of the Scriptures," he said,

> it appeared, that the gospel is to be preached to all nations, and
> that some out of all shall join in the praises of the Lamb of GOD:
> seeing but little signs of the kingdom of CHRIST among us, it
> was thought that it might be the day of GOD'S mercy and visita-
> tion of these neglected savage nations.[105]

He hoped to settle on the Ohio and support himself. His missionary journey was to determine if the Indians would receive him as a missionary. The mission was divided into two trips of six months duration. On the second visit, 1772-1773, he received some support from the Association. His hope to be welcomed among the Indians did not materialize. He returned to continue his pastorate in New Jersey and serve as chaplain in the Revolutionary War.

A third thrust of the Philadelphia Association must be mentioned. Agents of the Association became active in the gathering of churches in already nominally churched areas. The move to Separatism from Standing Order Churches was well underway in New England by 1745. Devotees of the Great Awakening, dissatisfied with lethargic churches and pastors who did not preach in an "affecting" manner nor overly emphasize the doctrine of new birth, soon began to defect and form their own strict congregations. Oppression by civil authority followed, especially in Connecticut. After 1749, there was a pronounced turning of Separatists, or Strict Congregationalists, to Baptist ranks.[106]

In 1757, Benjamin Miller and William Marsh constituted a church in Duchess County, New York, on the borders of Connecticut. John Gano, returned from the South, became the pastor of a revivalistic church in the city of New York in 1762. Churches continued to be formed with assistance from Philadelphia in Long Island and into Connecticut. In 1766, the Association raised a fund from which the proceeds were to be "laid out every year in support of ministers travelling on the errand of the churches."[107]

The most important contribution that the Philadelphia Association made to Baptist development in New England was the sending of James Manning and Hezekiah Smith to Rhode Island in 1764. Manning became the president of Rhode Island College the next year and pastor of the newly organized church in Warren. Hezekiah Smith, who had previously itinerated as far south as Georgia, had a very successful ministry as an evangelist in both Baptist and Paedobaptist Churches in New England. In 1764, he was invited to supply one of the Standing Order Churches in Haverhill, and in 1765 a Baptist church was organized. Smith remained as pastor and became a great founder of Baptist churches in Massachusetts, Maine and New Hampshire.[108]

In 1766, Manning convinced some of the New England Baptist leaders they needed an association. Representatives from ten churches met in September, 1767, and formed the Warren Association. Gano and two other Philadelphia representatives were present.[109] This body gave leadership to the fight for religious liberty in New England. It soon began to send missionaries to the eastern, northern and western frontiers of New England. They were exceedingly effective in forming into Baptist churches those Strict Congregationalists who fled to the frontiers because of the oppression of civil authorities. These men aggressively evangelized the uncommitted and dispossessed who also moved to the wilderness. By the end of the Revolution there were three more associations in New England and others ready to be formed.

Is this properly called "evangelizing the wilderness"? Or is it denominational invasion of already fully churched territory? Is this an illustration of equating denominational expansion in competition with others as "missions"? First, the frontier was not fully churched. Very often the sectarians were years ahead of the Standing Order in gathering churches in frontier communities of New England. Further, in all parts of New England, for the Strict Congregationalists and Separate Baptists, who were imprisoned and fined for preaching and whose property was taken and sold to support the parish ministers, the struggle was a battle for social justice. But the soul was for social justice with an evangelical and eschatological dimension. The wilderness theme was evident. The fight was with the *Beast of Revelation.* "If that Beast which hath two Horns like a Lamb, and speaks as a Dragon, has not rule in this Land, . . . Whence it is that the Saints of God have been so Imprisoned?" Ebenezer Frothingham asked in 1750.[110] A few years later Henry Fisk wrote a report of the distraining of goods from people who would not pay their ministerial rates which he called "The Testimony of a People Inhabiting the Wilderness."[111] Isaac Backus consistently alleged that the Separatists, not the Standing Order churches, were the true descendants of the Puritan fathers.[112] The goal of the Strict Congregationalists and of their descendants, the Separate Baptists, was to restore true Gospel Church Order in the wilderness of oppressive, magisterial establishment.

The most exciting Baptist story of church planting before the Revolution is the labors and success of the Separate Baptists on the southern frontier after 1754.[113] Shubal Stearns and Daniel Marshall arrived at Sandy Creek, in central North Carolina, in 1755, with fourteen other New England Separatists-become-Baptists. Both men had a missionary calling. Marshall had already spent a few years trying to evangelize the Indians in the Susquehanna Valley. Stearns left New England with a conviction that he was to travel to the West where the Lord would use him to carry on a great work.

While spending some months in the Opeckon area in northern Virginia, Stearns heard that in North Carolina

the work of God was great, in preaching to an ignorant people, with little or no preaching for a hundred miles, and no established meeting.[114]

The group moved into a religious vacuum. In 1750, there were only nine Anglican churches, no Presbyterian, and one Lutheran church in the colony. Only one Anglican minister was at work in North Carolina in 1754. The largest group were the Quakers, who had twenty-four meetings scattered along the rivers. The Moravians began the settlement of Wachovia in 1753, when Bethabara was founded. Bethania was not established until 1759, and Salem in 1766.

The sixteen New Englanders formed themselves into a church and began to evangelize the frontier. Revival began. Evangelistic journeys were made in all directions. In three years the church of sixteen had become six hundred. In 1758, representatives from six churches met at Sandy Creek to form the Sandy Creek Association.

The primary achievement of the first four years of labor by Stearns and Marshall was the raising up of many preachers who literally traveled the length and breadth of the southern frontier evangelizing, exhorting, baptizing and gathering churches. The movement spread eastward to New Bern and the mouth of Cape Fear River. Before 1762, Daniel Marshall had carried the torch to Virginia. By 1767 the revival had reached as far north as Orange County where it met the Regular Baptist movement. There, as John Leland put it, "the fires from the northern preachers, and those in the south, met, like . . . two seas."[115] One leader wrote the Philadelphia Association in 1771 that

> there are four Associations now in Carolina, and two in Virginia, that he hath planted seventeen churches lately; that two of our ministers are in Chesterfield gaol; that there is an unusual outpouring of the Spirit on all ranks of men in those parts; that many negroes endure scourgings for religion's sake; that two clergymen of the Church of England, preach Jesus Christ with unusual warmth.[116]

After 1762, there was new expansion toward the South. Phillip Mulkey and Daniel Marshall were sent into South Carolina. In 1771, Marshall moved on into Georgia where he gathered the first Baptist Church on Kiokee Creek in 1772. In 1771, the Sandy Creek Association divided into three associations: Congaree in South Carolina, General Association of Separate Baptists in Virginia, Sandy Creek in North Carolina. In the seventeen years that the Separates had been at work in the South they had grown from one church with sixteen members to forty-two churches with one hundred twenty-five licensed or ordained ministers.

> The details of the missionary strategy devised by the Sandy Creek leaders remains a secret, but a careful plan for overspreading the entire surrounding country with gospel preaching evidently was set in motion . . . The neighboring Moravians noted and praised the zeal of the Separates, recording that 'the Baptists are the only ones in the country who go far and wide preaching and caring for souls.'[117]

Revival continued in Virginia, in the midst of determined persecution, right up to the beginning of the Revolution. Deterioration and dispersion began in North Carolina in the late 1760s. Opposition to the Regulator Movement finally degenerated into an open harrassment of Baptists. When the Revolution was over, the churches were in decline.

There is a significant difference between the Baptist and Presbyterian approach to evangelizing the frontier. William Warren Sweet is correct when he speaks of the Baptist "farmer-preacher."[118] Most of the associations did send out missionaries before the Revolution. In the main, however, the Baptist mission work on the frontier was done by men who made their own living. They settled on their own farms, itinerated on the frontier from a sense of inward call, and gathered those who responded into churches. The question is, can these men correctly be called, as Jesse Mercer named them in 1838, "devoted heralds — Missionaries of the Cross?"[119]

If one means by "missionary" only those sent out and supported by organizations distinctly formed for missionary purposes, the majority of these men can not properly be called missionaries. However, from their own Biblical perspective, these men considered themselves missionaries in exactly the same way that Paul was a missionary. They were men with a divine call and inward compulsion to preach the gospel of Christ. They were sent by God himself. While Paul made tents, they cleared the wilderness and planted corn. They were men, as John Leland described the Baptists in "Berkshire and the borders of New York" a generation later, who believed that "a missionary spirit and missionary practice is apostolical."[120]

The Congregationalists

The larger ecclesiastical bodies of the Standing Order Churches in New England did not become involved in missionary enterprises in the same manner as those of the Baptists and Presbyterians. There are several obvious reasons for this. The New England churchmen were already most active in the support of Indian missions through extra-church organizations. The SSPCK had two Boards of Correspondents in New England during the decade before the Revolution. The New England Company's activity was almost totally Boston based.[121]

Further, since these Congregational Churches were established by law in the several New England provinces, except Rhode Island, little was done in church extension without the assistance and approval of civil government. This was true even in reference to the Indian missions. The Stockbridge mission was launched with all the civil and military fanfare that Governor Belcher could muster for the occasion.[122] Because of this close association between church and state, the settlements in New England tended to be created in a much more orderly manner than was often the case in the middle or southern colonies. In addition, the New England provinces were much more restricted in space than the larger colonies to the south and west.

The law required certain provisions for school and church. Little was left to missionary enthusiasm until New Englanders began to move outside the boundaries of New England. Finally, the pronounced congregational character of the New England churches hindered the formations of strong associations and synods and, thus, favored the society method of missionary work. John Wise and his friends were able to defeat the move toward a stronger connectionalism envisioned in the Proposals of 1705 in Massachusetts. Even in Connecticut, where the plan was adopted in the Saybrook Synod of 1708, the idea was not universally welcomed.[123] As late as 1741, the General Association of Connecticut had to charge the local associations to

> take it into their serious Consideration whether there ought not to be more weight laid upon the matters transmitted to them from the General Association than has been usually done.[124]

Nevertheless, the involvement of larger ecclesiastical bodies in missionary enterprises began before the new nation had won its independence. In Connecticut, concrete action was first taken by the General Association in 1774. On June 21, that body agreed that

> taking into Consideration the State of ye Settlements now forming in the Wilderness to the Westward & North-Westward . . . who are mostly destitute of a preached Gospel, many of which are of our Brethren Emigrants from this Colony, . . . it is advisable that an attempt should be made to send missionaries among them.[125]

The General Association met again on September 15, 1774. They had found such encouragement in this missionary plan that they thought it advisable to appoint "2 Missionaries to go upon this business" the next Spring. They also laid plans for the raising of support in every county of the colony, and appointed a committee to receive the monies and to give direction to the missionaries.[126]

When the General Association met on June 20, 1775, Elizur Goodrich reported that, because of the "perplexed & Melancholly State of public Affairs," the mission was not fulfilled. However, the Association, "being of Opinion that great and good Ends . . . may be answered by sending Missionaries" and "being unwilling that the Design should fail," instructed the Committee to continue to receive the monies and hold them until it could "carry the Plan into the Execution."[127] In 1778, the missionary fund in "Continental Bills" was put out to loan. The silver was put in the hands of Benjamin Trumbull for safe keeping. Not until 1786 did the General Association again turn itself to churching the wilderness.

The situation in Massachusetts was different. In spite of the fact that no general association was organized among the standing order churches there during the Eighteenth Century, local associations of ministers continued to form. Church extension was steady throughout the period before the Revolution. During the forty years before the Great Awakening, one hundred thirty-five churches were gathered in the province. In the second forty years, which includes the French and Indian Wars and the War for Independence, one hundred fourteen churches were planted.[128]

There was no formal connectionalism between these churches. The pastors were usually organized in local associations. These small, informal bodies assisted in the ordination and installation of pastors and officiated over church disputes. There was a yearly convention of ministers that met in Boston at the time of election. Its influence was only moral and advisory. Neither the larger body nor the smaller associations undertook missionary projects before the Revolution.

On the border of New Hampshire and Maine, however, there was one ministerial association that actually participated in sending out a missionary to the frontier. The Eastern Association of Ministers was founded before 1750. It was the eastern-most ministerial fellowship in New England, literally on the edge of the wilderness. In 1772, "Trustees of an Eastern Mission" were appointed, and Daniel Little, of Wells, member of the Piscataqua Association, visited the most eastern parts of Maine that summer. He returned in 1774, but political unrest and war prevented him from continuing the preaching tours until after the Revolution.[129]

By the end of the Revolution, the American missionary enterprise was in a generally deplorable condition. The Christian Indians were scattered and highly suspect. Their villages had been overrun, and their missionaries, who were mostly supported from Great Britain, were unpaid and poverty stricken. War had dispersed and destroyed many of the English churches, and many frontier settlements were completely abandoned. Inflation was rampant. Continental currency was almost worthless, and "hard money" was scarce. The fledgling country, and the various states, faced the great task of building a nation. In addition, the War had a general adverse effect on the spiritual life of the nation. Deism had never had such influential advocates. The future was dark.

Adverse circumstances notwithstanding, four generations of missionary activity had left its mark. Not only Indian evangelization, but the mobilization of the churches for that task had begun. Also, hundreds of churches had been gathered between the seacoast and the frontier. In the process, the distinctive shape of the mission of the American churches had formed. The missionary burden was two-fold. Not just the evangelization of the heathen, but also the bringing of gospel order to the young nation was the missionary goal. The wilderness, whether literal forests or unregenerate hearts, must become the garden of God. The planting of churches in the vast wilderness that had become the United States of America was one of the primary tasks that faced the Christians of the new nation.

NOTES FOR CHAPTER 3

1. Latourette, *History of Expansion of Christianity,* III, 303ff.

2. See the collection of materials in Alexander Brown, *The Genesis of the United States* (2 vols.; Boston: Houghton, Mifflin and Company, 1891) for illustration of these theological roots and Miller, "Religion and Society in the Early Literature of Virginia," *Errand,* pp. 99-140, for a sparkling discussion of the theological foundations of the colonial enterprise of the Virginia company.

3. Beaver, *Ecumenical Beginnings,* p. 18.

4. The only attempt to study the Mayhew Mission, of which I know, is Lloyd C.M. Hare, *Thomas Mayhew, Patriarch to the Indians* (1593-1682) (New York: D. Appleton and Company, 1932).

5. Vaughan, *New England Frontier,* pp. 235-308, has an excellent historical study of the Eliot mission.

6. Kellaway, *New England Company,* contains a useful account of the long list of missionaries who served the Indian mission before the Revolution, pp. 81-121, 228-276.

7. Edwards, *Life and Diary of the Rev. David Brainerd,* in *Works,* II, 457.

8. See Norman Penney, ed., *The Journal of George Fox* (2 vols.; Cambridge: The University Press, 1911), II, 236, 337, and George Fox, *A Collection of Many Select and Christian Epistles, Letters, and Testimonies* (2 vols.; Philadelphia: Marcus T. C. Gould, 1831), II, 160, 218.

9. See Frederick B. Tolles, *Meeting House and Counting House* (New York: W. W. Norton & Company, Inc., 1963), p. 34; Rayner W. Kelsey, *Friends and Indians, 1655-1917* (Philadelphia: Associated Executive Committee of Friends on Indian Affairs, 1917), pp. 19-59; and Rufus M. Jones, *The Quakers in the American Colonies* (New York: W. W. Norton & Company, Inc., 1966), p. 498.

10. Ernest Hawkins, *Historical Notices of the Missions of the Church of England in the North American Colonies, Previous to the Independence of the United States* (London: B. Fellowes, 1845), p. 264.

11. David Humphreys, *An Historical Account of the Incorporated Society for the Propagation of the Gospel in Foreign Parts* (London: Printed by Joseph Downing, 1730), p. 117.

12. Hawkins, *Historical Notices,* pp. 83-86.

13. See letter of John Stuart in John W. Lydekker, *The Faithful Mohawks* (New York: The Macmillan Company, 1938), p. 135. The same idea can be discovered in "Memoir of the Rev. John Stuart," in E. B. O'Callaghan, ed., *The Documentary History of the State of New-York,* (4 vols.; Albany: Charles Van Benthuysen, Public Printer, 1849-1851), IV, 505-520.

14. See J. E. Hutton, *A History of Moravian Missions* (London: Moravian Publication Office, 1922), pp. 85-90 for an interesting popularized version of this mission.

15. Francis L. Hawks, *Contributions to the Ecclesiastical History of the United States of America,* (2 vols.; New York: Published by Harper and Brothers, 1836), I, 28ff.

16. See Edmund Schwarze, *History of the Moravian Missions among Southern Indian Tribes in the United States* (Bethlehem, Pa.: Times Publishing Co., Printers, 1923), pp. 7-13, for an excellent account of this early mission.

17. Francis J. McConnell, *John Wesley* (Nashville: Abingdon Press, 1939), deals in some detail with the relationship between the members of the Holy Club and Oglethorpe and with the general lack of success in Georgia. See pp. 41-54.

18. Schwarze, *Moravian Missions,* is the principle history of the missionary thrust of the Moravians among the southern Indians from the headquarters in Salem, North Carolina.

19. George Bost, "Samuel Davies: Colonial Revivalist and Champion of Religious Toleration" (unpublished doctoral dissertation, University of Chicago, 1942), pp. 228-230, contains a brief account of this mission and the society formed. See also, George William Pilcher, ed., *The Reverend Samuel Davies Abroad: The Diary of a Journey to England and Scotland,* 1753-55 (Urbana, Illinois: University of Illinois Press, 1967), p. 103.

20. See C. F. Pascoe and H. W. Tucker, eds. *Classified Digest of the Records of the Society for the Propagation of the Gospel in Foreign Parts, 1701-1892* (Fifth edition; London: Published at the Society's Office, 1895), pp. 1-9; C. F. Pascoe, *Two Hundred Years of the S.P.G. An Historical Account of the Society for the Propagation of the Gospel in Foreign Parts, 1701-1900* (London: Published at the Society's Office, 1901); and H. P. Thompson, *Into All Lands: The History of the Society for the Propagation of the Gospel in Foreign Parts, 1701-1950* (London: Society for Promoting Christian Knowledge, 1951).

21. This is not clearly spelled out in the charter of the Society, but its members very early "perceived" that its work "consisted of three great branches, the care of our own . . . settled in the colonies; the conversion of the Indian savages, and the conversion of the negroes." Humphreys, *Historical Account,* p. 16.

22. The success of the SPG among the Mohawks was not due primarily to the mission conducted there, but to the influence and labor of Sir William Johnson and Joseph Brant, Mohawk Chief. There are many biographical studies of both men. The most recent are J. T. Flexner, *Mohawk Baronett: Sir William Johnson of New York* (New York: Harper and Brothers Publishers, 1959) and Harvey Chalmers, *Joseph Brant: Mohawk* (East Lansing, Mich.: Michigan State University Press, 1955). A fair account of the mission can be found in John W. Lydekker, *Faithful Mohawks.* A fine account of the mission and an effort to give the theological foundations of the SPG enterprise in New York can be found in Frank J. Klingberg, *Anglican Humanitarianism in Colonial New York* (Philadelphia: The Church Historical Society, 1940). The primary sources of the work of Johnson are preserved in O'Callaghan, *Documentary History,* IV, 289-520.

23. J. Taylor Hamilton and Kenneth G. Hamilton, *History of the Moravian Church: The Renewed Unitas Fratrum 1722-1957* (Bethlehem, Pa.: Interprovincial Board of Christian Education, Moravian Church in America, 1976), p. 86.

24. See John R. Weinlick, *Count Zinzendorf* (Nashville: Abingdon Press, 1956), p. 170ff.

25. John Heckewelder, *A Narrative of the Mission of the United Brethren among the Delaware and Mohegan Indians, from Its Commencement, in the Year 1740, to the Year 1808* (Philadelphia: Published by McCarty and Davis, 1820) is an early account of the Indian mission during the time of the Economy. A recent account is Elma E. Gray, *Wilderness Christians: The Moravian Mission to the Delaware Indians* (Ithaca, N.Y.: Cornell University Press, 1956).

26. J. Taylor Hamilton, *A History of the Unitas Fratrum, or Moravian Church in the United States of America,* Vol. 8: *American Church History,* p. 456.

27. Kenneth G. Hamilton, *John Ettwein and the Moravian Church During the Revolutionary Period* (Bethlehem, Pa.: Times Publishing Co., 1940), p. 115ff, gives some details of this organization and documentation that it was never the intention of the Society to usurp the Church in the sending of missionaries or the management of the missions. See also, Hamilton, *History of the Unitas Fratrum,* pp. 464-465.

28. R. Pierce Beaver, ed., *Pioneers in Mission* (Grand Rapids: William B. Eerdmans Publishing Company, 1966), p. 14.

29. H. P. Thompson, *Thomas Bray* (London: S.P.C.K., 1954), p. 98. An excellent account of the Associates work in New York can be found in Klingberg, *Humanitarianism,* pp. 121-186.

30. Kellaway, *New England Company,* pp. 17-61 tells the story of the development of the Society and Company. This is the most comprehensive and most recent history of the New England Company.

See also Frederick L. Weis, "The New England Company of 1649 and its Missionary Enterprises" in Colonial Society of Massachusetts, *Publications,* XXXVIII, 134-218; Vaughan, *New England Frontier,* pp. 235-338; Beaver, *Church, State,* pp. 24-40.

31. Kellaway, *New England Company,* p. 63.

32. Harry M. Ward, *The United Colonies of New England — 1643-1690* (New York: The Vantage Press, 1961) is a book with many glaring mistakes. It is a full-length study and lists all of the men who served as Commissioners of the United Colonies, with a brief biographical sketch, pp. 400-411. Another list may be found in Weis, "The New England Company of 1649," p. 207. See also *Acts of the Commissioners of the United Colonies of New England,* Vols. 9, 10 of *Records of the Colony of New Plymouth,* ed. by Nathaniel B. Shurtlett and David Pulsifer (12 vols.; Boston: Press of W. White, 1855-61).

33. Beaver, *Church, State,* p. 53.

34. See Gookin, *Historical Collections,* pp. 141-227.

35. Benjamin Coleman, "Dr. Colman's Return" in Sergeant, *A Letter from the Revd. Mr. Sergeant,* p. 11.

36. The primary account of the beginning and early years of this mission is Hopkins, *Historical Memoirs.*

37. *An Account of the Rise, Constitution and Management of the Society in Scotland for Propagating Christian Knowledge* (Second edition; Edinburgh: Printed for William Brown and Company, 1720), p. 12.

38. *An Account of the Society in Scotland for Propagating Christian Knowledge, From its Commencement, in 1709. In which is included, The present state of the Highlands and Islands of Scotland with Regard to Religion* (Edinburgh: Printed by A. Murray and J. Cochrane, 1774), pp. 7-8.

39. Committee Minutes of SSPCK, quoted in Kellaway, *New England Company,* p. 187.

40. *An Account of the Society,* p. 14.

41. See Beaver, *Pioneers in Mission,* pp. 33-73.

42. *An Account of the Society,* pp. 14-15.

43. John Maclena, *History of the College of New Jersey,* (3 vols.; Philadelphia: J. B. Lippincott & Co., 1877), I, 121.

44. Pilcher, *Davies Journal,* p. 97. Found also in "Journal of Rev. Samuel Davies, From July 2, 1753, to February 13, 1755," in William Henry Foote, *Sketches of Virginia Historical and Biographical,* First series (Richmond, Va.: John Knox Press, 1966), pp. 261-262.

45. *Records of the Presbyterian Church in the United States of America, embracing the Minutes of the General Presbytery and General Synod 1706-1788* (Philadelphia: Presbyterian Board of Publication and Sabbath-School Work, 1904), p. 283.

46. See William DeLoss Love, *Samson Occum and the Christian Indians of New England* (Boston: The Pilgrim Press, 1899), p. 50; Harold Blodgett, *Samson Occum* (Hanover, N.H.: Dartmouth College Publications, 1935), p. 51; and Gideon Hawley, "Biographical and Topographical Anecdotes," in *MHSC,* Series One, III (1794), 192.

47. Kellaway, *New England Company,* p. 189.

48. Love, *Samson Occum and Christian Indians,* pp. 99-100.

49. Beaver, *Church, State,* pp. 7-45, documents the partnership between colonial legislatures and the Indian mission in great detail.

50. See Letter to Wheelock, June 24, 1761, in Love, *Samson Occum and Christian Indians*, p. 90.

51. Blodgett, *Samson Occum*, p. 31.

52. Eleazar Wheelock, *A Plain and faithful Narrative of the Original Design, Rise and Progress and present State of the Indian Charity-School at Lebanon, in Connecticut* (Boston: Printed by Richard and Samuel Draper, 1763), p. 15.

53. *Ibid.*, p. 27.

54. Eleazar Wheelock, *A Brief Narrative of the Indian Charity-School, In Lebanon in Connecticut, New England. Founded and Carried on by That faithful Servant of God, The Rev. Mr. Eleazar Wheelock* (London: Printed by J. and W. Oliver, 1766), p. 5. Wheelock was a close friend and associate of George Whitfield, Whitfield clearly designed his orphanage in Georgia as a New World Halle. Moor's Indian School, as Wheelock's School was called, was on the same kind of plan. See George Whitfield "A Caution against despising the Day of small Things," *Seventy-Five Sermons on Various Important Subjects* (3 vols.; London: Printed for W. Baynes, 1812), III, 366-383, for Whitfield's indebtedness to Francke.

55. See James Dow McCallum, ed., *The Letters of Eleazar Wheelock's Indians* Hanover, N.H.: Dartmouth College Publications, 1932). The story of Wheelock's mission work can be found in David McClure and Elijah Parish, *Memoirs of the Rev. Eleazar Wheelock D.D.* (Newbury port: Printed by Edward Little, 1811); Leon Burr Richardson, *History of Dartmouth College* (Hanover, N.H.: Dartmouth College Publications, 1932), pp. 13-193; and Beaver, *Pioneers in Mission*, pp. 211-234.

56. Besides the two cited in footnotes 36 and 39, they are: Eleazar Wheelock, *A Continuation of the Narrative of the State, &c. of the Indian Charity-School, At Lebanon, in Connecticut; From Nov. 27th, 1762 to Sept. 3d, 1765* (Boston: Printed by Richard and Samuel Draper, 1765); *A Brief Narrative . . . Second Edition with an Appendix* (London: Printed by J. and W. Oliver, 1767); *A Continuation of the Narrative of the Indian Charity-School, in Lebanon, in Connecticut: From the Year 1768 to the Incorporation of it with Dartmouth-College, and Removal and Settlement of it in Hanover, in the Province of New-Hampshire, 1771* (n.p., n. printer, 1771); *A Continuation of the Narrative of the Indian Charity School* (n.p., n. printer, 1773), and *A Continuation of Narrative of the Indian Charity-School Begun in Lebanon* (Hartfor d: Printed by Ebenezer Watson, 1775).

57. See Leon B. Richardson, *An Indian Preacher in England* (Hanover, N.H.: Dartmouth College Publications, 1933); Love, *Samson Occum and Christian Indians*, pp. 130-151; and Blodgett, *Samson Occum*, pp. 84-104.

58. Wheelock, *A Continuation of the Narrative . . . 1771*, p. 17.

59. See Charles Chauncy, *All Nations of the Earth blessed in Christ, the Seed of Abraham* (Boston: Printed and sold by John Draper, 1762). Also in Beaver, *Pioneers in Mission*, pp. 201ff.

60. Letter of Buell to Eleazar Wheelock, January 13, 1761, quoted in Love, *Samson Occum and Christian Indians*, p. 85.

61. The debate was carried on into 1764 in both Boston and Great Britain. See *The Boston Evening Post*, July 30, 1764, or *The Boston Gazette*, July 2 and 9, 1764, for items reprinted from the *St. James Chronicle* and the *London Dailey Advertiser*.

62. Jonathan Mayhew, *Observations on the Charter and Conduct of the Society for the Propagation of the Gospel in Foreign Parts* (Boston: Richard and Samuel Draper, 1763). For a full account of Mayhew's part in this whole debate see Alden Bradford, *Memoir of the Life and Writings of Rev. Jonathan Mayhew, D.D.* (Boston: C. C. Little & Co., 1838), pp. 240-278.

63. See Kellaway, *New England Company*, pp. 194-196, for a detailed account of the beginning of this Society from the point of view of the New England Company. Beaver, *Pioneers in Mission*, pp. 185-188.

64. Letter to Hollis, Bradford, *Life of Jonathan Mayhew,* p. 197.

65. Beaver, *Pioneers in Mission,* pp. 185-209.

66. John Adams mentioned this incident in his "A Dissertation on the Canon and Feudal Law," in Geor ge A. Peek, Jr., *The Political Writings of John Adams: Representative Selections* (New York: The Liberal Arts Press, 1954), p. 21.

67. See for example *New England First Fruits,* p. 23.

68. Perry Miller, *The New England Mind: From Colony to Province* (Boston: Beacon Press, 1961), p. 95. See also Miller, "Jonathan Edwards and the Great Awakening," in *Errand,* p. 163.

69. Thompson, *Thomas Bray,* p. 39.

70. Whitfield, *Seventy-Five Sermons,* II, 277-283.

71. Samuel Davies, *Sermons on Important Subjects* (4 vols., 7th ed.; London: Printed for W. Baynes, 1815), I, 85.

72. Williams, *Wilderness and Paradise,* p. 110.

73. Edwards, *Works,* II, 245, 646-647, 839.

74. *Ibid.,* p. 817.

75. *Ibid.,* p. 250.

76. *Ibid.,* p. 851.

77. *Records of Presbyterian Church,* pp. 10, 49-53.

78. A. D. Gillette, ed., *Minutes of the Philadelphia Baptist Association from A.D. 1707, to A.D. 1807; Being the First One Hundred Years of Its Existence* (Philadelphia: American Baptist Publication Society, 1851), pp. 27, 31, 33, 35.

79. *Records of Presbyterian Church,* pp. 54, 74-76.

80. *Ibid.,* p. 138. The most readable and balanced view of colonial Presbyterianism is Leonard J. Trinterud, *The Forming of an American Tradition* (Philadelphia: The Westminster Press, 1949).

81. Trinterud, *Forming an American Tradition,* p. 137.

82. *Ibid.,* p. 122.

83. See Samuel Miller, *Memoirs of the Rev. John Rodgers, D.D.* (New York: Published by Whiting and Watson, 1813), p. 41, and also in Foote, *Sketches,* Series One, p. 128.

84. See Gewehr, *Great Awakening in Virginia,* for an excellent and exciting account of this expansion.

85. *Records of Presbyterian Church,* pp. 246, 266, 269.

86. *Ibid.,* pp. 278, 294.

87. *Ibid.,* pp. 257-258.

88. See Brainerd's commission in *John Brainerd's Journal (1761-1762) in Transcriptions of Early Church Records of New Jersey* (Newark, N.J.: Historical Records Survey, 1941), pp. 31-32.

89. *Records of Presbyterian Church,* p. 324.

90. See Clifford Merril Drury, *Presbyterian Panorama* (Philadelphia: Board of Education, 1952), p. 8, and Guy Soulliard Klett, "Introduction," in Guy Soulliard Klett, ed., *Journals of Charles Beatty, 1762-1769* (University Par, Pa.: Pennsylvania State University Press, 1962), pp. xxiff.

91. *Records of Presbyterian Church,* p. 326.

92. *Ibid.,* p. 370.

93. *Ibid.,* p. 484. See William Warren Sweet, *Religion on the American Frontier,* Vol. I; *The Baptists* (New York: Harper & Bros., 1936), Vol. III; *The Congregationalists* (Chicago: University of Chicago Press, 1939), Vol. IV; *The Methodists* (Chicago: University of Chicago Press, 1941), III, 8.

94. Gillette, *Minutes,* p. 3.

95. Winthrop S. Hudson, *Religion in America* (New York: Charles Scribner's Sons, 1965), pp. 73-74. See also Lumpkin, *Baptist Foundations,* pp. 154ff.

96. Gillette, *Minutes,* pp. 41, 43, 57.

97. Robert B. Semple, *A History of the Rise and Progress of the Baptists in Virginia* (Richmond: Published by the Author, 1810), p. 289.

98. Gillette, *Minutes,* p. 71.

99. David Benedict, *A General History of the Baptist Denomination in America and Other Parts of the World* (2 vols.; Boston: Printed by Manning & Loring, 1813), II, 309ff. Gano had accompanied Benjamin Miller and David Thomas to Virginia in 1751 to assist in properly organizing the Virginia churches. He had begun to preach while on that journey.

100. Wood Furman, *A History of the Charleston Association of Baptist Churches in the State of South-Carolina; with an Appendix Containing the Principle Circular to the Churches* (Charleston, S.D.: Press of J. Hoff, 1811), p. 10.

101. Semple, *Baptists in Virginia,* p. 291.

102. Gillette, *Minutes,* p. 95.

103. Semple, *Baptists in Virginia,* p. 295.

104. Gillette, *Minutes,* p. 129.

105. David Jones, *A Journal of Two Visits Made to Some Nations of Indians on the West Side of the River Ohio, in the Years 1772 and 1773* (Sabin Reprint No. II; New York: Reprinted for Joseph Sabin, 1865), p. vii.

106. Goen, *Revivalism and Separatism,* pp. 224ff.

107. Gillette, *Minutes,* pp. 95, 97.

108. See R. A. Gould, *Chaplain Smith and the Baptists: or, The Life, Journals, Letters, and Addresses of the Rev. Hezekiah Smith, D.D., of Haverhill, Massachusetts, 1737-1805* (Philadelphia: American Baptist Publication Society, 1885).

109. Isaac Backus, *A History of New England. With Particular Reference to the Denomination of Christians called BAPTISTS* (2 vols.; 2nd ed.; Newton, Mass.: Published by the Backus Historical Society, 1871), II, 154-155, 408-409.

110. Ebenezer Frothingham, *The Articles of Faith and Practice, with the Covenant that is confessed by the Separate Churches,* in Heimert and Miller, *The Great Awakening,* p. 452.

111. Backus, *History of New England,* II, 94.

112. This is the burden of the first volume of his *History of New England* and is a major point in his *A Fish Caught in his own Net* in William G. McLoughlin, ed., *Isaac Backus on Church, State, and Calvinism* (Cambridge: Belknap Press of Harvard University Press, 1968), pp. 166-388.

113. See Benedict, *History of Baptists,* II, 37ff; Semple, *Baptists in Virginia,* pp. 1-288; Lumpkin, *Baptist Foundations;* Jesse Mercer, *A History of the Georgia Baptist Association* (Washington, Geo.: n.p., 1838), pp. 13ff; and James D. Mosteller, *A History of the Kokee Baptist Church in Georgia* (Ann Arbor, Michigan: Edwards Brothers, Inc., 1952), pp. 1-68.

114. Letter of Shubal Stearns, quoted in Isaac Backus, *Church History of New England, From 1620 to 1804* (Philadelphia: American Baptist Publication Society, 1853), p. 228.

115. John Leland, *The Virginia Chronicle,* in *The Writings of the Late Elder John Leland,* ed. by L. F. Green (New York: Printed by G. W. Wood, 1845), p. 105. John Leland (1754-1841), Baptist leader in Virginia and Jeffersonian republican, returned to Connecticut in 1791 where he continued itinerant preaching and the struggle for separation of church and state. Though a tireless evangelist and church planter, he became an antimissionary leader because he opposed societies.

116. Gillette, *Minutes,* p. 120.

117. Lumpkin, *Baptist Foundations,* p. 47.

118. Sweet, *Religion on the American Frontier,* I, 36-53, devotes an entire chapter to "The Frontier Baptist Preacher and the Frontier Baptist Church."

119. Mercer, *Georgia Baptists,* p. 16.

120. Leland, *Writings,* p. 530.

121. The Company did give some limited support to missions among the Indians in New York and for a short time jointly supported one man in the South. See Kellaway, *New England Company,* pp. 260ff.

122. Beaver, *Church, State,* p. 45.

123. Backus, *History of New England,* I, 470ff.

124. *The Records of the General Association of Ye Colony of Connecticut, Begun June 20th, 1738, Ending June 19th, 1799* (Hartford: Press of the Case, Lockwood & Brainard Company, 1888), p. 10.

125. *Ibid.,* p. 76.

126. *Ibid.,* pp. 79-80.

127. *Ibid.,* p. 85.

128. Joseph S. Clark, *A Historical Sketch of the Congregational Churches in Massachusetts from 1620 to 1858* (Boston: Congregational Board of Publication, 1858) has been most helpful to me in tracing church growth in Massachusetts in the Eighteenth Century.

129. George Spalding, *Historical Discourses Delivered on the Hundredth Anniversary of the Piscataqua Association of Ministers* (Dover, N.H.: Morning Star Job Printing Office, 1882), p. 11. See also *The Piscataqua Evangelical Magazine,* II (1806), 85ff for an account of Little's work.

Chapter 4

The Mission Mobilized

While the interest of religion ought to be our first and ruling object, we ought not to forget how necessary it is, for that great purpose, to preserve our character as a body, and our consequence in the republic.

John Rodgers — 1789

Alexis de Tocqueville's observed, in 1833, that the population of the United States doubled every twenty-two years and that the twelve hundred mile frontier advanced at the rate of seventeen miles each year.[1] After the Revolution there was an unprecedented rush over the Appalachian Mountains. Easy land acquisition, feeble administrative machinery and speculation lured thousands into Kentucky and Tennessee. After the decisive Battle of Fallen Timbers in 1794, people flooded into western New York and Ohio. Within twenty-five years a great wedge of population extended to the Mississippi from St. Louis southward.

So the churches gave themselves to frontier work. This awesome task swallowed up their resources. The Indian mission starved. A generation passed after the Peace of Paris before American churches really focused primary attention on the heathen. Though some mission work was done following the Revolution, American churches prepared, unconsciously, for a missionary movement to get really under way. This chapter intends to describe this mobilization for missionary endeavor.

Congregationalists: Continuing the Pre-War Missions

The most pressing missionary problem after the Revolution were the Indian missions begun before American independence. They had been supported primarily by the New England Company and the SSPCK, now sustaining them fell to the churches in New England. Re-establishing communications and securing renewed support from the SSPCK guaranteed that these missions could continue. This also led to the founding of the first continuing organization for a uniquely missionary purpose in America.

The SSPCK Returns

The most successful Indian missionary in the years immediately preceding the Revolution was Samuel Kirkland, sent by Eleazar Wheelock to the Oneidas. In spite of war, political intrigue, animosity of Anglican agents in the area, and abject poverty that was the lot of Wheelock's missionaries, he made significant inroads in that tribe.[2] In 1770, Kirkland broke with Wheelock, and until 1773, he was paid by the Commissioners of the New England Company and the legacy of Daniel Williams controlled by the Harvard Corporation. In 1773, the Boston Board of the SSPCK began to support Kirkland.

Kirkland was a staunch revolutionist. When forced from the country of the Six Nations, he immediately offered himself to the Continental Congress. Through most of the war he was employed by the Congress as an agent-for-Indian-neutrality, chaplain to the troops and missionary.[3]

In 1779, the American Army devastated most of the Indian country in Northern New York. When Kirkland returned to his mission in 1784, food was so scarce that he had to return to New England for another year.

Kirkland wrote to Governor James Bowdoin, president of the Boston Board of Correspondents of the SSPCK when the Revolution began, detailing his time since 1774, when his accounts had last been settled. Former Correspondents of the SSPCK recommended that the Society pay Kirkland "seven hundred and ninety pounds sterling" and re-employ him as a missionary to the Oneidas.[4] The SSPCK agreed to pay fifty pounds annually toward Kirkland's salary, and the Harvard Corporation again joined in his support.

In this correspondence, the SSPCK rekindled its interest in undergirding a mission among the American Indians. Some members of the Boston Board were dead, and others did not wish to continue to serve. So in 1787, the Society appointed several new members to their Board of Correspondents in Boston. Peter Thacher, chosen secretary, became the chief statesman of Indian evangelization in New England during the next ten years.[5]

Other Indian missions were destitute at the end of the Revolution. This Board of Correspondents gradually began to support most of these. Gideon Hawley who had been settled among the Marshpee Indians in Barnstable County in 1756, continued there through the Revolution. On Martha's Vineyard and adjacent islands, the Mayhew family continued to give leadership to Indian churches. At the end of the Revolution, Zechariah Mayhew was still there. Both missions received limited support from the SSPCK.[6]

The Oneida country of northwestern New York was the primary theatre of Indian missions in the two decades before the turn of the century. Not only Samuel Kirkland, but the ministries of two other important missionary-pastors converged in this area. Before the war, Samson Occum and other New England leaders devised a plan for uniting the several scattered groups of New England Indians and moving with them to the Oneida lands. Joseph Johnson, Occum's son-in-law, rallied the Christian Indians in seven different southern New England communities. They secured land from the Oneidas in January, 1774, and the first contingent moved to Brothertown before the Revolution actually began.[7]

When the Revolution came, many Brothertown Indians moved back as far as Stockbridge, where they remained for the duration. When hostilities ceased, the refugees and some Stockbridge Indians returned to Oneida. Samson Occum arrived in 1784 with another large group of New England Indians. The Stockbridge Indians began to make plans to remove to the same vicinity. Two communities, Brothertown and New Stockbridge, were created, and a church was formed in each place.

In 1775 John Sergeant Jr. assumed responsibility for the Indian congregation in Stockbridge. Stephen West had tried to get free of the mission for years.[8] Though Sergeant actually began carrying most of the load as Indian teacher in 1773, a separate Indian church was not formed until the removal to New Stockbridge in 1788.[9] Sergeant was then ordained an evangelist, commissioned by the Board of the SSPCK, and given a salary of $400 annually. He did not move his family to New Stockbridge until 1796, but when he received what he called his "new appointment," he went to the Oneida Country in a position of strength.[10]

Before 1788, Occum spent more time among the Brothertown and New Stockbridge Indians than did Sergeant. In 1787 in addition to a call to settle as the pastor in Brothertown, he was also issued a call by the Indians of New Stockbridge. That year he went as far south as Philadelphia trying to raise support for his mission among the Indians. The two Indian churches provided Occum with a document that described their problem:

> The Fountains abroad, that use to water and refresh our Wilderness are all Dryed up, and the Springs that use to rise near are ceased . . . And our Wheat was blasted and our Corn and Beans were Frost bitten . . . this year. And our moving up here was expensive . . . And these things have brought us to a resolution to try to get a little help from the People of God.[11]

The pleas were of no avail. Occum had limited success in Philadelphia. Support of Indian missions in this period fell primarily to New England churches, and New England leaders were unwilling to consider Occum on a par with English missionaries. Their support went to John Sergeant.

Sergeant's arrival at New Stockbridge proved divisive for the Indian church there.[12] Part of New Stockbridge remained with Occum, reuniting with Sergeant's group after Occum's death in 1791. Sergeant succeeded, with the help of Kirkland's financial and family problems, in undermining that missionary's relationship with the SSPCK. Kirkland was abruptly dropped by the SSPCK in 1795. In 1796 when Sergeant finally moved to New Stockbridge, Occum was dead and Kirkland was supported only by the Harvard Corporation. Sergeant was the only missionary in the Oneida country with adequate support.

The First American Society

When letters arrived in Boston in 1787, appointing new SSPCK correspondents, another idea was generated. The SSPCK was interested only in Indian missions. The attention of men in Boston had been turned dramatically to the frontiers. Something had to be done for the new communities springing up on the edge of the wilderness. This conviction grew out of events begun in 1786.

The Republic loosely formed by the Articles of Confederation struggled with overwhelming problems. By 1787, its "very life was on trial." The "mortal danger" was that the people "had ceased to care whether the Republic lived or died." [13] After two years of depression, in January, 1787, Western Massachusetts erupted. Shay's Rebellion startled New England and the Continental Congress in New York. Contemporary observers and modern historians have emphasized the importance of this relatively small uprising in helping to shape the new nation.[14]

The letters from Scotland added to the shock of the Boston leaders. These men, which included some who had been members of the aborted society of 1762, were "ashamed that more solicitude for this object should be discovered by foreigners than by themselves."[15] Nascent nationalism emerged. Further, the events of the past months spotlighted the frontier. They decided to establish a society like the SSPCK "but on a more extended plan; with powers to send Missionaries to the new plantations on (their) own borders, as well as to the native Indians."[16] The act incorporating the Society for Propagating the Gospel among the Indians and others in North America (SPGNA) was passed November 19, 1787.

The first task of the new society was to raise funds. Specie was so short in New England and the political conflict was so sharp, that this proved all but impossible. In 1790 Peter Thacher, who was also elected secretary of this society, published *A Brief Account of the Present State of the Society for Propagating the Gospel among the Indians and Others in North America.* "The principle efforts of the Society," Thacher wrote, "have been directed to our countrymen and friends in the three eastern counties of this commonwealth." If western Massachusetts could break into rebellion, the easternmost districts of Maine were capable of the same thing.

> Crimes of the most atrocious nature, and such as naturally arise
> from a state of barbarism, have encreased among them, and fur-
> nished large . . . business to the courts of law; And unless some
> effectual means are soon taken . . . it is the opinion of the most
> intelligent persons among them that consequences fatal to the
> peace and possibly to the existence of the government will issue.[17]

However, funds had enabled them only to "distribute books."

The purpose of Thacher's tract was to sell the mission to the General Court of the state. The SPGNA requested funds to undergird its mission to the settlements. The General Court allowed one hundred fifty pounds annually for three years.[18] In 1791 and 1798, Thacher produced reports with similar requests.[19] For more than a decade missionaries of this Society sent to the frontier settlements were supported by monies appropriated by the state legislature. Thacher continued as secretary of both the Boston Board of the SSPCK and the SPGNA until his death in 1802. Jedidiah Morse, Thacher's assistant since 1796, succeeded him as secretary of both boards. This joint secretaryship guaranteed a close working relationship and combined support for several missionary projects by both societies.

In 1789, the SPGNA suddenly received funds to conduct an Indian mission. John Alford left a legacy for charitable purposes in the hands of Richard Cary of Charlestown to be expended in various ways, mostly educational. In 1786, Cary engaged Daniel Little of Wells, Maine, to go on a mission to the Penobscot Indians.[20] In May, 1789, Cary gave these funds to the Society solely for the support of Indian mission work. Thus, before the SPGNA could begin to send missionaries to the frontier, it had an endowment enabling it to undertake Indian education and evangelization. Some monies were also raised by an annual collection.

The mission to frontier settlements began in earnest in 1791. Aging Daniel Little was the first missionary. During the years that followed, Abiel Abbott, James Lyon, Paul Coffin, Little's brother-in-law, were also enlisted.[21] Little had an important missionary career in eastern Maine.[22] Besides his brief mission there before the Revolution, he returned in 1785, assisted by the Piscatequa Ministerial Association. He preached through the settlements again in 1786 on his way to the Penobscots and again in 1787 as he trekked to the Indians as an agent of the Massachusetts General Court. In January, 1788, the General Court published Little's Journal for 1787, and he was honored as the "Apostle to the East."[23]

By 1797, the SPGNA was well organized and well funded. Membership was composed of the elite of Boston and vicinity. This society is among the ten most prestigious organizations in Boston during this period.[24] James Bowdoin, governor in 1787, was elected to membership at the first meeting after he left office. The SPGNA was a product of the liberal, social intercourse that existed among the clergy in the vicinity of Boston before the wedge of theological controversy began to mark distinctions. The society has continued to the Twentieth Century. Control eventually passed to the Liberals and Unitarians in the Nineteenth Century.

Other Missionary Beginnings

When the General Association in Connecticut met in June, 1786, Joseph Bellamy was moderator. Missions monies put in trust eight years before were offered to Isaac Lewis if he should "be inclined" to preach in the "New-formed or forming Settlements for five Sabbaths."[25] In 1787, the New Haven West Association sent one of their members to Vermont for a few weeks of preaching. When the General Association met in 1788, this Association addressed them on the subject of sending missionaries to Vermont.[26] Consequently, the General Association encouraged each local association of ministers to follow the example of New Haven West. Jonathan Edwards Jr., Timothy Dwight, Joseph Huntington and Cotton M. Smith were appointed a committee to discover what suitable measures should be taken to "send suitable missionaries to preach the Gospel, gather churches and administer Gospel ordinances" in ?these new communities in the wilderness.[27]

The General Association was continually involved in appointing missionaries, collecting of funds, and encouraging missionary endeavor after 1788. It was no new thing in 1798, when the General Association met, carried on its regular business, and then adjourned to form itself into the Missionary Society of Connecticut.

In Massachusetts, also, various ministerial associations began to take up missionary projects. The Essex North Association voted in May, 1791, to send one member of their body to "preach the gospel gratis" in New Hampshire. David Tappan was their first missionary.[28] Elijah Parish undertook the same mission in 1792. The Berkshire Association, composed of ministers in Berkshire County, Massachusetts, and Columbia County, New York, undertook limited missionary efforts before a missionary society was formed there in 1798.[29] The Mendon Association, whose members led the way in forming the Massachusetts Missionary Society in 1799, also supported each other in preaching in destitute places.[30] These local associations and many others like them provided the foundations for the increase of missionary organizations that were to come.

Baptist: Itinerant Preachers and Missionary Associations

1787 has been called the most crucial year in American history.[31] That year the weak, struggling, infant nation made a significant change. In the Constitutional Convention, leaders from the several, loosely related, sovereign states turned from the failure of confederation to a federal system. The *United* States of America became a reality.

1787 was a significant year for Baptists in the new nation. When the Philadelphia Association met October 2-5, good reports abounded. William Fristoe told of a great revival in progress in Virginia. A letter from John Leland reported the union of Separate and Regular Baptists in that state and gave further information on the great ingathering there. A letter from the Charleston Association told of Baptist growth in South Carolina. James Manning was present with good news from New England. Messengers from western Pennsylvania, Kentucky and Georgia all had wonderful accounts of the expansion of the Church. The Association rejoiced

> in the prosperity of Zion throughout this continent: and (was) encouraged to believe that the purity of the doctrines and ordinances of the gospel of Christ are prevailing more and more.[32]

Reports of revivals and church extension and the new federal constitution were both viewed as signs that the great missionary hope of the Church was being fulfilled. The Association celebrated both church extension and national stability as joyous events, "portentous . . . of the speedy accomplishment of the promises made by the Father to Christ, the King of Zion.[33]

The Second Great Awakening did not become a general movement among all evangelical groups in all parts of the nation until 1797. Before that Baptists had already experienced significant growth. Itinerant preachers, often traveling at their own expense, and small associations, with great enthusiasm for gathering new congregations, were the chief instruments of this expansion. By 1795, there were forty-eight Baptist associations, forming a network of interrelated and corresponding churches, scattered from one end of the nation to another. All were involved in some measure in sending out itinerant preachers to evangelize destitute places.

In New England, the process of gathering Congregational eggs in Baptist baskets continued. From 1779 to 1785 there were a series of revivals in which Baptists reaped a harvest. The emphasis of the Great Awakening on a regenerate church membership bore late fruit.[34] In 1780 alone, 800 members were added to the churches of the Warren Association.

All the growth was not in the shadow of Standing Order churches. Because of a plea from Caleb Blood in 1779, the Warren Association sent out its first missionaries. Job Seamans and Biel Ledoyt were sent to the Connecticut River Valley in Vermont and New Hampshire. Several churches were organized, and the Shaftesbury Association was formed in 1781. In 1783 Thomas Baldwin began his career as church planter, pastor and missionary statesman in Canaan, New Hampshire, where he was ordained an itinerant evangelist.[35] Job Macomber, preaching in New Gloucester, District of Maine, traveled to Lincoln County and gathered a church in Thomaston on the northeastern frontier. He wrote Isaac Backus of the great opportunity there. Backus shared the letter with Isaac Chase. Chase was ordained for itinerant service in that eastern district in 1783. The following year he wrote Backus:

> I would inform you that the dear Redeemer reigns in these parts
> . . . It hath been a very stupid, barren wilderness in time past; but
> thanks be to the God of love, he hath done great things for us,
> and caused the wilderness to bud and blossom as the rose.[36]

Seven years later, when the SPGNA began actively sending missionaries to the easternmost counties in Maine, they found "a considerable number of townships and Plantations . . . whose religious teachers (were) illiterate men chiefly of the Baptist perswasion." Their efforts, Daniel Little explained to Peter Thacher, had created some "happy effects," but

> in their various   peregrinations, they have propagated narrow
> and party notions; have spread a spirit of bigotry and enthusi-
> asm, and under pretence of superior divine teaching, have les-
> sened the credid (sic) of literature and a learned ministry; of-
> fering their service gratis, by way of contract or contempt of
> ministers supported by an equal tax.[37]

Baptist itinerating evangelists arrived in the most remote settlements of eastern Maine ahead of the missionaries of the SPGNA. When the Baptists arrived in 1783-1784, there were thirty incorporated towns which had no Congregational minister.[38] The Bowdoinham Baptist Association was formed in 1787, four years before the SPGNA sent its first official missionaries there.

By 1795, there were 325 Baptist churches and twelve associations in all parts of New England. These associations functioned as sending societies and instruments of church extension. Backus opined in 1795 that the associations had not only promoted "acquaintance and communication" but also had helped to supply destitute churches and "animated (many) . . . in preaching the gospel through the land, and in our new plantations in the wilderness."[39]

An awakening among Baptists in Virginia began in 1785. The Methodists had experienced a great revival in Virginia in 1776-1776. The War and the growth of anti-Tory feeling caused it to wane. Baptists declined in the same period. The General Assembly exempted all the people in Virginia from supporting the established Church in 1776. John Leland asserted that

> the Presbyterians, the Baptists, the Quakers, the Deists, and the covetious (sic) all prayed for this, and soon obtained it.[40]

Leland later explained that as the Baptists

> gained this piece of freedom, so the cares of war, the spirit of trade, and moving to the western waters, seemed to bring on a general declension. The ways of Zion mourned. They obtained their hearts desire (freedom) but had leanness in their souls.[41]

All that changed in 1785 when the "glorious work of God broke out, on the banks of James River, and from thence . . . spread almost over the state." This revival awakened both Separate and Regular Baptist congregations. The result was a union of the two groups in 1787. This union provided the pattern of cooperation in church extension as Baptists continued to grow on the southern frontier. The activities of the "United Baptist Churches of Christ in Virginia" were confined to a defense of the religious liberty established in Virginia both by state and federal constitutions. The revival in Virginia did not result in missionary organization. In 1811, Virginia Baptists still had no missionary society. The missionary significance of the revival was its pattern of union and the scores of Baptist preachers and laymen who moved across the mountains to participate in the gathering of churches on that new frontier.

In western North Carolina Baptists greatly declined before 1797. Decline began after the War of Regulation in 1771. Dispersion from North Carolina intensified the planting of churches on the frontiers of South Carolina and Georgia. In eastern North Carolina, there was significant growth. The Kehukee Association had ten churches in 1777. Revival came in the late 1780s. By 1794 there were three associations and almost one hundred churches.

The same growth took place among the Baptists in South Carolina and Georgia. Charleston Association continued to send missionaries into Georgia. In 1784, the Georgia Baptist Association was organized. By 1797, two other associations were formed, and Baptists had gained a firm hold in Georgia. The churches in South Carolina and Georgia became large and stable. They developed a number of well-trained and articulate spokesmen. Richard Furman, Abraham Marshall, Silas and Jesse Mercer, and Henry Holcombe provided stalwart and aggressive leadership. Baptist leadership in the South passed from Virginia and North Carolina to Georgia and South Carolina. These men provided missionary enthusiasm and foresight that structured the national missionary organization of Baptists in America.

Baptist expansion in the Middle States was not as pronounced as in New England and the South. The Baptist revival in Virginia moved up into the Red Stone Association of Western Pennsylvania. There was steady church growth on the eastern tributaries of the Ohio River. The Baptist explosion in New England spilled across into the Hudson Valley. New England Separatists moved in vast numbers into Upper New York. Baptists experienced growth on both sides of the Hudson as they reaped a harvest among the uprooted and unchurched New Englanders. The growth in the coastal area around New York, Philadelphia and down to Baltimore was important, not just because of new churches. Strong churches and associations were gathered. These later formed the backbone of missionary support for national missionary organization.

The expansion of Baptists in this period was the work of missionaries or itinerants sent out by associations. This practice occurred with increasing regularity. Self-supporting, itinerant evangelists, almost always in fellowship with some local association, continued their incessant labor in preaching, baptizing and forming churches. Further, Baptist connectionalism laid the groundwork for future organizations for specifically missionary purposes. Almost invariably, newly gathered churches formed themselves into new associations. The new bodies quickly established correspondence and usually exchanged messengers with other associations. By the turn of the century these associations began to form themselves into missionary societies. Through correspondence already established, the means was found to gather Baptists into a national missionary body.

Presbyterians: National Body with Missionary Intent

When peace was made in 1783, the Synod of New York and Philadelphia was in trouble. Plagued by non-attendance before the Revolution, Synod attendance reached an all-time low during the war. When it convened in 1778, only fourteen were present.[42] This problem was one of the contributing factors in the decision to abandon the undelegated synodical organization for a delegated general assembly.[43] Missionary exertions by the Synod came to a virtual standstill. No missionary was sent out after 1777.

Still Presbyterians were involved in church extension, especially in the wilderness during this period. Samuel Stanhope Smith called for intensification of missionary work in Virginia in 1779. He emphasized the need of men to settle on the frontier rather than being itinerant. The Synod recommended that all the presbyteries "turn their attention to this object" and send out missionaries who would "endeavour to form congregations and to effect a settlement among them." Men sent out, the Synod agreed, should have "popular talents and piety," and the capacity to direct the "education of youth."[44]

Missionary initiative passed from the Synod to the local presbyteries. This new, diffused missionary philosophy prevailed for ten years. Synodical action was confined to (1) permitting the ordination of licentiates, *sine titula,* for the express purpose of itinerating on the frontiers, and (2) erecting new presbyteries on "missionary ground" in the wilderness. The second action is the most important missionary activity of the Synod. These new presbyteries were often formed of men who had received ordination without a call to a specific church. They moved to the frontiers to perform their ministry.[45] During the decade before the founding of the General Assembly, in missionary matters, the presbytery held sway.

The first new presbytery was erected in 1781, along Red Stone Creek in Western Pennsylvania. Four ministers, Joseph Smith, John McMillan, James Power and Taddeus Dod, made up the membership. Power, the first Presbyterian minister to settle west of the mountains, arrived in November, 1776. He first visited the Red Stone country in 1774 as a missionary of the New Castle Presbytery.[46] The same year, the Synod granted permission to the First Philadelphia Presbytery to ordain Robert Keith, *sine titula,* "in case of him going out to Canetuck" and to the New Castle Presbytery to so ordain "Mr. Power . . . as he purposes to remove to the western parts of this province."[47] Power was followed by John McMillan and Joseph Smith, both of whom had previously served as missionaries of the New Castle Presbytery. Thaddeus Dod was ordained, *sine titula,* by the Presbytery of New York in 1778. All four men had served as a missionary on the frontier or had been especially set aside for a frontier ministry when he was ordained. By 1789, there were thirty-four congregations in the Red Stone Presbytery.

Other presbyteries followed Red Stone. The Presbytery of South Carolina was set off from the Orange Presbytery in North Carolina in 1784. A year later Hezekiah Balch, Charles Cummings and Samuel Doak were formed into the Abingdon Presbytery, the mother of Presbyterian churches in Tennessee. In 1786, the Transylvania Presbytery in Kentucky and the Lexington Presbytery in western Virginia were erected. At its first meeting the Transylvania Presbytery instructed its ministers to spend at least four weeks in the next year preaching among destitute congregations.[48]

The second part of the synod's instruction in 1779 became a reality. Each new presbytery formed one or more schools. Schools and academies already in existence were strengthened. These frontier schools, especially those taught by John McMillan (Canonsbury Academy) in Red Stone, William Graham (Liberty Hall Academy) in Lexington, John Blair Smith (Hampden Sydney) in Hanover, and Samuel Doak (Martins Academy) in Abingdon, trained men who multiplied Presbyterian churches in all the states contiguous to the Ohio and Mississippi Rivers.

Another factor significantly shaped the missionary character of frontier presbyteries and schools. Revival broke out in the 1780s. Limited revivals began in the Red Stone Presbytery in 1781 and continued intermittently among the churches until 1785.[49] However, in 1787, the great revival in Virginia among the Baptists and Methodists suddenly erupted among the Presbyterians at Hampden Sydney College. One student, Cary Allen, was struck down at a meeting conducted by Hope Hull, a Methodist, while at home on a short vacation.[50] When he returned to college, President John Blair Smith "was exceedingly fearful it was all a delusion, and put him through the most rigid examination."[51]

William Hill, also a student, was converted. He was instrumental in reclaiming James Blythe, a student from North Carolina. These three and Clement Read began meeting weekly together for prayer. The second prayer meeting, held in the College, became so loud that it almost caused a riot. President Smith invited the praying group to his own home and opened the meeting to everyone. The revival began.[52]

This revival among the Presbyterians never became general except in Virginia and North Carolina. However, its effects in raising up young men who served as missionaries and missionary statesmen in the Presbyterian Church throughout the National Period is phenomenal.[53]

Drury Lacy was serving as Smith's assistant at the College. He and Smith were the first leaders in the movement. In 1788, Nash LeGrand was converted at a prayer meeting conducted by Allen and Hill. LeGrand carried the revival into North Carolina and was one of the most successful preachers in the entire movement. William Graham brought a group of his students over the mountain. Archibald Alexander was in the group.[54] They returned to Liberty Hall Academy and scattered revival fires in the Shenandoah Valley. John Lyle was converted and trained under Graham. Robert Marshall was awakened under John McMillan's preaching in Red Stone. James McGready, converted and trained in Red Stone in the earlier revival, visited Hampden Sydney on his way to North Carolina when the revival was at high tide. He joined Nash LeGrand in spreading the revival in North Carolina. By 1789, all of these men had begun their ministry, and all were destined to serve as Presbyterian missionaries along the southern frontier.

When the General Assembly met for the first time in May, 1789, the mission to the frontier was one of its early concerns. The Assembly asked Patrick Alison and Samuel S. Smith to "devise such measures as may be best calculated to carry the mission into execution." That afternoon the Committee returned its report:
1. Each Synod should recommend two men to serve as missionaries of the General Assembly.
2. These men should organize churches, administer ordinances, ordain elders, collect information on the state of religion, and suggest missionary strategy.
3. Each presbytery should promote an offering for the missionary enterprise in each of its churches.[55]

In 1790, only the Synod of New York and New Jersey had fully complied with instructions. The Synod of Philadelphia had named the aging George Duffield as a possible missionary, but he had died before the Assembly met. There was no word from the Synod of the Carolinas. The Synod of Virginia indicated that it had "substantially complied."[56] The General Assembly appointed a Committee on Missions to assign Nathan Ker and Joshua Hart to the frontier settlements of New York and Pennsylvania. The synods were again requested to submit the names of men qualified to serve as missionaries. From the beginning, the delegated national body made it clear that it had primary jurisdiction in the matter of church extension.[57]

Communication with the southern synods was extremely difficult. When the General Assembly convened in 1791, there was an urgent request from the Synod of the Carolinas that special arrangements be made for missionary exertions there. The distance was so great, the field so vast and currency so scarce that the General Assembly agreed to allow the Synod to

manage the matter of sending missionaries to places destitute of the gospel . . . as may appear to that Synod most conducive to the interest of religion in their bounds, provided . . . the Synod send annually to this assembly a particular account of their proceedings . . . with regular statement of the money . . . collected . . . and dispersed.[58]

Virginia had already acted independently in 1790. The action of this Synod may have encouraged the Carolina Synod to pursue the possibility of managing the missions in its own area. When the Virginia Synod met in 1790, it adopted its own plan. The Synod assumed responsibility for the frontier area inside its own boundaries. To execute the mission, a standing Commission of the Synod was appointed, consisting of four ministers and four elders, to serve as a missionary board or society. This Commission was charged by the Synod with the responsibility of appointing missionaries, assigning their fields, and instructing them as to policy and procedure. The presbyteries were asked to recommend suitable men to the Commission and to collect funds. The Commission had the same control over the missionaries that the presbyteries had over their ministers.[59] A missionary serving under the Commission was not listed as a regular member of his presbytery but as one subject to the direction and discipline of the Commission.

John B. Smith, William Graham, James Mitchel and William Wilson were the ministerial members of the first Commission. Nash LeGrand was appointed as the first missionary in April, 1790. In October, Cary Allen, William Hill and Robert Marshall were commissioned. In 1792, Allen and Marshall were sent to Kentucky. Marshall remained to become one of the most influential and controversial leaders in the new state. Other young men, most converted in the revival, crossed the mountains to Kentucky. Allen died there in 1794. James Blythe and John Lyle later became important leaders of Kentucky Presbyterianism.

The Synod of the Carolinas followed the example of Virginia. It appointed a standing Commission of the Synod to handle its missionary affairs. Four missionaries, James Templeton, Robert Hall, Robert Archibald and John Bowman, were appointed in 1792 for service on both sides of the mountains. Year after year, the Synod of the Carolinas had at least four missionaries, preaching four months each, on the Carolina-Georgia frontier and over into eastern Tennessee.[60]

Controversy hindered Presbyterian growth on the southern frontier after 1790. In 1789, Adam Rankin began his acrid attack on the use of Isaac Watts' versified psalms. The trouble began in the Transylvania Presbytery, was aired at the meeting of the General Assembly in the same year, and finally resulted in Adam's expulsion from the Presbyterian ranks.[61] The issue, however, continued to be divisive in the churches in the wilderness, from western Pennsylvania to Georgia. In 1796, Hezekiah Balch's radical Hopkinsianism became a fiery issue.[62] The Synod of the Carolinas attempted to deal with it in 1796 and 1797. In 1798, the General Assembly heard Balch, rebuked him, and ordered a retraction of some of his positions. But back to Tennessee, he continued to expound his New Divinity and to divide the churches. These controversies helped to keep the Revival of 1789 from becoming general, and Presbyterian growth was retarded until after 1800.

For several years the Assembly struggled to maintain control of these synodical missions. Full and complete reports were required each year. However, this level of direction deteriorated. The practical result was that the General Assembly conducted the missionary endeavor in the North and Northwest, while the southern synods managed all missionary affairs in the South. By 1795 dissatisfaction with these arrangements was often expressed. Each year a Committee of Missions was appointed to formulate a report to the General Assembly of all the missionary work conducted throughout the synods.[63] This Committee also appointed, commissioned, and instructed the Assembly's missionaries and made suggestions for making the missions most effective. In 1798, the Assembly appointed a Committee to discover "what alternatives may, with probable advantage, be made in our present plan for managing the missions."[64] There was a new spirit in the land. Societies specifically designed for arousing missionary interest and sending out missionaries had come into being in both Europe and America. Some of the members of the Presbyterian churches in America had been active in the organization of these bodies. In reply to a letter from the General Association in Connecticut, the General Assembly explained the operations and extent of its missionary endeavor. It also expressed a hope to begin a mission to the Indians in the near future.[65] The time was ripe for more concentrated and persistent missionary efforts.

Reformed Dutch: Independence and Missionary Interest

The General Synod of the Reformed Dutch Church also developed missionary awareness and activity in the years immediately following the end of the Revolutionary War. These were the same years that this Church was declaring its independence from the Reformed Church in Holland. In 1771, a Plan of Union was adopted which was designed to heal the crippling divisions among the Dutch churches over their relationship to the Classis of Amsterdam and the Synod of North Holland. The wounds were not immediately healed. Twelve years later, the Synod was still attempting to get some of the consistories to sign the articles of union. That year, 1783, a committee was appointed to look into the matter of the churches still "outstanding."[66]

When this Committee reported to the Synod in 1784, it went far beyond its assignment. It presented a report of the condition of the Reformed Dutch Church in America. The Committee found one hundred regular congregations, but only fifty-three that had a regular "ministry of the holy Gospel." The Committee also called attention to the "new settlements" which were then "occurring in the respective states of the land." These places presented a favorable opportunity "for the extension of our churches and the diffusion of the pure doctrines of grace." "With Divine blessing" and ministers willing to be missionaries, the report concluded, "the number of congregations could be doubled in a short time." The state of the church and the abounding opportunities demanded that "some popular and reasonable measures" be adopted by the Synod to meet these circumstances.[67]

Two years later the Synod took tentative action. Four of its members, Eilartus Westerlo, Dirck Romeyn, Henricus Schoonmaker and Hermanus Meyer, were requested individually to present a written plan in which each would

state the appropriate means by which the . . . extension of the
Church, shall, with the Lord's blessing, be capable of being
attained.[68]

The four plans were to be studied, and the following year the Synod would adopt
one or formulate its own composite plan for the missionary undertaking.

Two years passed. In 1788, a very simple program was adopted: each church
was to take an offering specifically designated for church extension, to be passed
through the Classis to the General Synod. The General Synod would then send out
the missionaries.[69]

In 1789 the monies were brought in. John H. Livingston, Jacob R. Harden-
berg and Solomon Froligh were appointed a Committee to manage the missionary
affairs. The Classis of Albany was asked to choose one of its members as the first
missionary. Two years later, the Synod put the matter of church extension in the
hands of the Deputati Synodi. Still little seemed to get done. A congregation on
the Susquehanna, which requested "ministerial helps," was turned down in 1791
because to send some one was "for the present impractible." However, in October,
1792, Andrew Gray, minister at Poughkeepsie, was sent to the Susquehanna for
six weeks. When Gray reported in 1793, he had "resuscitated" one congregation
and organized a new one.[70]

The Synod was encouraged by the success of Gray. A special committee
was appointed to "obtain missionaries, and make arrangements for supplying their
pulpits." Two missionaries were sent out "for the purpose of extending the interest
of our Dutch Church in the back country."[71] By 1797, when the Synod met to
begin its new pattern of meeting every three years instead of annually, it approved
the appointment of missionaries for each year in the interim.

In general, however, the Dutch Church continued to be very slow in assum-
ing missionary responsibility. It was a small church. The cultural struggle in which
the chur ch found itself hindered aggressive missionary activity. However, there
were articulate leaders in this Church that played a significant part in missionary
organization at the turn of the century. More important, several of these men made
a significant contribution to the developing theology of the missionary enterprise
in America.

Fifteen years after the signing of the Peace of Paris, the attention of the
American churches was focused on the wilderness. All groups had taken some
steps to send the gospel of Christ to the white settlements. Some supported, and
others wished to support, missions to the heathen tribes. Church leaders had a
great dream but did not know how to bring it to pass. Shortly before the turn of
the Nineteenth Century the American churches entered an age of performance.

NOTES FOR CHAPTER 4

1. Alexis de Tocqueville, *Democracy in America,* (2 vols.; New York: Vintage Books, n.d.), I, 413-414.

2. Kirkland's story had been told in Samuel K. Lothrop, *Life of Samuel Kirkland* in Jared Spark, ed., *The Library of American Biography*, (21 vols.; Boston: Charles E. Little and James Brown, 1847), XI, 139-368; Robert John Lennox, "Samuel Kirkland's Mission to the Iroquois," (unpublished Ph.D. dissertation, University of Chicago, 1932); and the years after the Revolution have been documented in Joseph D. Ibbotson, *Documentary History of Hamilton College* (Clinton, N.Y.: Published by the College, 1922), pp. 25-103.

3. Beaver, *Church, State,* pp. 55ff.

4. Lothrop, *Life of Kirkland,* quotes minutes of the Board, pp. 252-254.

5. Peter Thacher's relationship to the SSPCK and SPGNA are described briefly in *MHSC*, Series One, VII (1802), 277-284.

6. See Gideon Hawley, "Letters Concerning Life in Marshpee," *MHSC*, Series One, IV (1795), 50-67 and Hawley, "Biographical and Topographical Anecdotes," pp. 188-193. See also "A discription of Marshpee in the County of Barnstable, September 16, 1802," and "Report of a Committee on the State of the Indians in Marshpee and Parts Adjacent," in *MHSC*, Series Two, III (1815), 1-17.

7. Love, *Samson Occum and the Christian Indians,* pp. 130-230; Blodgett, *Samson Occum,* pp. 139-199.

8. Stiles, *The Literary Diary,* I, 209-212. "Br. West," Stiles concludes, "is tired of Indian Service."

9. *Ibid.,* p. 413. See also Electa F. Jones, *Stockbridge, Past and Present* (Springfield, Mass.: Samuel Bowles & Co., 1854), pp. 86-87.

10. Letter of Sergeant to Peter Thacher, May 19, 1788, quoted in Love, *Samson Occum and the Christian Indians,* p. 280.

11. Quoted in *ibid.,* p. 276, and Blodgett, *Samson Occum,* p. 198.

12. This has been adequately documented without trying to damage Sergeant's reputation and contribution. See Blodgett, *Samson Occum,* pp. 200ff., Love, *Samson Occum and the Christian Indians,* pp. 280-282, and Lennox, "Samuel Kirkland's Mission," p. 207ff.

13. Forrest McDonald, *The Formation of the American Republic: 1776-1790,* A Pelican Book (Baltimore, Maryland: Penguin Books, Inc., 1965), p. 133.

14. McDonald's entire chapter, *ibid.,* "The Critical Period of American History," pp. 133-154, illustrates how Shay's Rebellion stimulated action toward adoption of the Federal Constitution. Andrew C. McLaughlin, *The Confederation and the Constitution: 1783-1789* (New York: Collier Books, 1962), pp. 110-118, does the same. Thomas Jefferson thought the Rebellion was wholesome. He said, "God forbid we should ever be twenty years without such a rebellion," and "No country should be long without one." Letters to William S. Smith, Nov. 13, 1787, and to James Madison, Dec. 20, 1787, in Adrienne Kock and William Peden, eds., *The Life and Selected Writings of Thomas Jefferson* (New York: Modern Library, 1944), pp. 436, 440.

15. [James F. Hunnewell], *The Society for Propagating the Gospel among the Indians and Others in North America: 1787-1887* (Boston: Printed by the Society, 1887), p. 17.

16. *Ibid.,* p. 5.

17. [Peter Thacher], *A Brief Account of the Present State of the Society for Propagating the Gospel among the Indians and Others in North America* (Boston: Published by order of the Society, 1790), p. 1. Thacher (1752-1802) was pastor of the Brattle Street Church in Boston from 1785 until his death.

18. Peter Thacher, *A Brief Account of the Present State, Income, Expense &c. of the Society for Propagating the Gospel among the Indians and Others in North America* (Boston: n.p., 1795), p. 1.

19. *Ibid.,* and Thacher, *Brief Account of the Society for Propagating the Gospel Among the Indians and Others in North America* (Boston: n.p., 1798), p. 2.

20. Richard Carey, *To the Members of the Society for Propagating the Gospel among the Indians and Others in North America* (Boston: Printed by S. Hall, 1789), p. 2.

21. Three of Paul Coffin's "Journals" of his later missions can be found in Maine Historical Society, *Collections,* VII, (1856), 301-405.

22. Accounts of Daniel Little's life and ministry can be found in Edward E. Bourne, *The History of Wells and Kennebunk* (Portland, Me.: B. Thurston & Co., 1875), pp. 708-723; Clifford K. Shipton, ed., *Sibley's Harvard Graduates* (15 vols.; Boston: Massachusetts Historical Society, 1962), XII, 41-48. Portions of his Journal for 1786 and 1787 can be found in Maine Historical Society, *Collections,* VII, (1859), 8-19.

23. Quoted in Shipton, *Harvard Graduates,* XII, 43.

24. Conrad Wright, *The Beginnings of Unitarianism in America* (Boston: Starr King Press, 1955), p. 264.

25. *Records of the General Association,* p. 120.

26. Leonard Bacon, S. W. S. Dutton, and E. W. Robinson, eds., *Contributions to the Ecclesiastical History of Connecticut; Prepared Under the Direction of the General Association* (New Haven: Published by William L. Kingsley, 1861), p. 327.

27. *Records of the General Association,* p. 125.

28. *Contributions to the Ecclesiastical History of Essex County, Mass.* (Boston: Congregational Board of Publication, 1865), p. 30.

29. [David Dudley Field], *A History of the County of Berkshire, Massachusetts* (Pittsfield, Mass.: Printed by Samuel W. Bush, 1829), p. 60.

30. Mortimer Blake, *A Centurial History of the Mendon Association* (Boston: Published for the Association by Sewall Harding, 1853), p. 60.

31. Clinton Rossiter, 1787: *The Grand Convention,* Mentor Book (New York: The New American Library, 1968), pp. iiff.

32. Gillette, *Minutes of the Philadelphia Baptist Association,* p. 228.

33. *Ibid.,* p. 230.

34. Goen, *Revivalism and Separatism,* pp. 208-215, is most conclusive in showing that it was the "logical termination of their quest for the true church" that led the Separatists into Baptist ranks and not economic motives.

35. Henry S. Burrange, *A History of the Baptists in New England* (Philadelphia: American Baptist Publication Society, 1894), p. 90.

36. Backus, *History of New England,* II, p. 485.

37. A letter from Daniel Little to Peter Thacher in Thacher, *A Brief Account . . . 1790,* p. 2.

38. Backus, *History of New England,* II, p. 281.

39. *Ibid.,* p. 413.

40. John Leland, *The Virginia Chronicle* (Norfolk, Va.: n.?., 1789(, p. 5. This is the first edition of

Virginia Chronicle, only seven pages long, written in the style of the King James Bible, and divided into verses like the Bible.

41.   Leland, *The Virginia Chronicle,* in *Writings,* p. 105.

42.   *Records of the Presbyterian Church,* p. 481.

43.   Trinterud, *Forming an American Tradition,* pp. 279-308, goes into great detail at this point.

44.   *Records of the Presbyterian Church,* pp. 484-485.

45.   See, for example, *ibid.,* pp. 495, 507, 516.

46.   Joseph Smith, *Old Redstone; Or, Historical Sketches of Western Presbyterianism: Its Early Ministers, Its Perilous Times and Its First Records* (Philadelphia: Lippincott, Grambo & Co., 1854), p. 228. This is a valuable work that contains the minutes of the first Redstone Presbytery.

47.   *Records of the Presbyterian Church,* pp. 473-474.

48.   Sweet, *Religion on the Frontier,* II, 132.

49.   Smith, *Old Redstone,* p. 144.

50.   Foote, *Sketches of Virginia,* Second series, p. 225.

51.   *Ibid.,* First series, p. 414.

52.   Gewehr, *Great Awakening in Virginia,* pp. 177-185.

53.   Many biographical sketches of these men are available. Foote's two volumes on Virginia have sketches on each man that include original material.

54.   Alexander's personal account of this development of the revival is preserved in James W. Alexander, *The Life of Archibald Alexander, D.D., LL.D.* (Philadelphia: Presbyterian Board of Publication, 1875), pp. 48-81.

55.   *Minutes of the General Assembly of the Presbyterian Church in the United States of America from Its Organization A.D. 1789 to A.D. 1820 Inclusive* (Philadelphia: Presbyterian Board of Publication, 1847), pp. 10, 11.

56.   *Ibid.,* p. 23.

57.   Not until 1831 did the General Assembly adopt the overture "That the Presbyterian Church in the United States is a Missionary Society; the object of which is the conversion of the world." See William Maxwell, *A Memoir of the Rev. John H. Rice, D.D.* (Philadelphia: Published by J. Whetham, 1835), pp. 388ff.

58.   *Minutes of the General Assembly,* p. 38.

59.   *Ibid.,* pp. 43-45.

60.   Minutes of the Synod of the Carolinas in William Henry Foote, *Sketches of North Carolina, Historical and Biographical* (New York: Robert Carter, 1846), pp. 286ff.

61.   Extracts from the Minutes of the Transylvania Presbytery in Sweet, *Religion on the Frontier,* II, 135. See also *Minutes of the General Assembly,* p. 11.

62.   Minutes of the Synod of the Carolinas, Foote, *Sketches of North Carolina,* p. 293.

63.   *Minutes of the General Assembly,* p. 155.

64.   *Ibid.,* p. 146.

65.   *Ibid.*, p. 157.

66.   *The Acts and Proceedings of the General Synod of the Reformed Protestant Dutch Church in North America* (New York: Board of Publication of the Reformed Dutch Church, 1859), p. 104.

67.   *Ibid.*, pp. 114, 115.

68.   *Ibid.*, p. 150.

69.   *Ibid.*, p. 187.

70.   *Ibid.*, pp. 199, 231, 248.

71.   *Ibid.*, p. 290.

Chapter 5

The Missionary Explosion

The rapid multiplication of missionary societies constitutes an epoch in Christendom which will be memorable for ever.

Ebenezer Porter — 1810

About 1795 American churches moved from mobilization to execution. Essential ecclesiastical structures had been created. The task of gathering churches in the wilderness of the new nation was under way. After fifteen years of limited effectiveness and sporadic aggressiveness, muscular Christianity came to the fore. Missionary zeal was one salient characteristic of this new situation. "Let us not overlook," John M. Mason said in 1802,

> as an unimportant matter, the very existence of that missionary spirit that which has already awakened Christians . . . and bids fair to produce in due season, *a general movement of the church* upon earth.[1]

Missionary organizations sprang up everywhere. A monumental enterprise was launched to reap a harvest from the American wilderness.

A New Day

Something happened in 1797. Though not an epochal year which begins a new age, nevertheless, it brought distinct change. The revival that had been sporadic and scattered since the Revolution became a general awakening. The Second Great Awakening did not have the same dramatic beginning as the Revival of 1740. But by the time of the tremendous spiritual eruption on the Kentucky frontier in 1800, the northern seaboard had already felt the throb of new life.[2] The first issue of the *Connecticut Evangelical Magazine* came out in July, 1800. The editors referred to "the late wonderful out-pouring of the Holy Spirit and revival of experimental religion, in large districts of the American Church."

> There have not been so great and extensive a work of divine grace in this land since the years 1742 and 1744, and . . . we still hope these showers may soon increase to a universal rain of divine grace on all churches . . . thro' this land and the world.[3]

As the new magazine reached its readers, the Gasper River revival was under way in south central Kentucky.

A correspondent in a later issue reported that in northern New York

there have been great effusions of the divine spirit in the wilderness within a year and a half past. I hear of wakenings in almost every direction . . . It is a time of harvesting souls; the year of redemption is come . . . and Jerusalem breaks forth in songs, and deserts learn joy.[4]

The Revival spread to Virginia and the Carolinas in two years. By 1803, it reached the recesses of Georgia. The clerk of the Georgia Baptist Association appended a brief report to the published minutes of 1803.

Doubtless there is a glorious revival of the religion of Jesus. The wicked of every description, have been despoiled . . . even deists . . . have had their right arm broken, their hope disappointed, and their prognostications metamorphosed into falsehoods . . . O most mighty Jesus, ride prosperously . . . THY KINGDOM COME! COME! COME![5]

American churchmen, by 1797, generally adopted a new attitude toward "infidelity." Defense turned to offense. Optimism gripped Evangelicals. Infidelity was no longer the fearsome enemy against which bulwarks must be raised but rather a vulnerable enemy against which the churches could be rallied. Timothy Dwight charted the new course. After becoming president of Yale in 1795, he invited the insipient Deism into the open. Then, systematically and convincingly, he demolished it.[6] Dwight's forthright attack gave courage to others.

The Whiskey Rebellion in western Pennsylvania, the new appraisal of the French Revolution that developed about 1795, and the excitement over the Bavarian Illuminati generated by Jedidiah Morse in 1798 combined to encourage almost all Christians, liberal and orthodox, dissenting and Standing Order, to close ranks against this enemy. Circular and synodical letters, magazine pieces and published sermons consolidated efforts and provided ammunition for the battle. William Staughten's Circular Letter for the Philadelphia Baptist Association in 1796 is typical of the spirit with which the conquest of Deism began.

The popularity of infidelity, Staughten judged, could be charged to the "revolution of empire." The "progress of civil liberty" which resulted from the French Revolution was to be applauded. But it was deposable that "papal superstition and protestant insensibility" convinced the leaders of the Revolution that "all religion is vain." This philosophy permeated "infidelity." Every Christian should arm himself with the word of God. The defeat of infidelity was the dispersion of truth.

Like idolatry, persecution and superstition in past ages, Deism was the popular tool of Satan for that particular day. The churches should not be discouraged. "At present, infidelity prevails; but it is an evil, and every evil . . . has the principle of decay within itself." Christians need not fear that "the ark is taken — the kingdom of Jesus overthrown."

> Universal empire and permanent prosperity, are promised to the great Redeemer . . . The present spread of infidelity, far from portending the destruction of Christianity, establishes its truths by fulfilling its predictions.

As persecution in the first century was the means God used of dispersing his Church and sending his Word into all lands, "in the present age, infidelity appears to answer the same grand design, by uniting them."[7] Infidelity was an instrument in the hands of evangelical leaders for mustering Christian forces in the winning of America.[8]

A spirit of optimism moved across America in 1797. The Crises of 1794 passed when John Jay was sent to England, though Jay's Treaty was extremely unpopular. Peace was made in the West in 1795, and the English abandoned their forts on American soil. New lands were opened across the mountains. The fear of Indian reprisals was past. The great debate between Federalists and Republicans was yet to take place. The Alien and Sedition Acts had not been imposed. America had overcome the dismal doldrums of the Confederation. A decade of functioning under the federal constitution had brought stability and optimism to the new nation.

In 1797, there was exciting news from England. In October, 1792, a small group of English Baptists formed the Particular Baptist Society for Propagating the Gospel among the Heathen (BMS).[9] This new society stimulated other Evangelicals in England. In July, 1794, John Ryland received Carey's first letter from India. He showed the letter to David Bogue, Independent pastor at Gosport, and James Steven, pastor of a Scottish church in London. Bogue, Steven and John Hey, a Bristol pastor, began to pray for God to arouse their fellow Independents in England to missionary exertions.[10]

In September, 1794, *Evangelical Magazine* contained an article by David Bogue. Addressed "To the Evangelical Dissenters who practice Infant Baptism," it called for a missionary organization for English Independents because "all other bodies of professing Christians have done . . . something for the conversion of the Heathen."[11] Meetings began in January, 1795, that resulted, nine months later in a great four-day convention in London. On September 21, the London Missionary Society (LMS) was organized.

The BMS did not stimulate American Baptists to form their own missionary organization. They started collecting funds for Carey's support in India, but no one suggested that Americans form their own society.[12] The organization of the LMS had a tremendous effect in America, especially among Pedobaptists. Many missionary societies organized in America in the next decade were stimulated by the enthusiasm and excitement generated by that Society. This was true for several reasons. American evangelicals had a long and warm relationship with English Independents. The LMS was a successful ecumenical effort that combined evangelicals of all stripes. The organizational meeting was a great event in the history of evangelical Christianity. Thousands attended the services conducted in various parts of London. Unprecedented and unexpected interest was expressed in sending the gospel to heathen nations. American Christians were moved to action.

Finally, American churches had been preparing for revival and church extension through several years of concerted prayer. The Northampton Baptist Association in England, home of the BMS, began systematic prayer for a general revival and the spread of the Church in 1784. The Association issued a new edition of Edwards' *Humble Attempt* in 1789.[13] In 1794, a new American edition of *Humble Attempt* inspired concerted prayer among all branches of American Christianity. That year the Hartford North Association of ministers in Connecticut sent an invitation to "every Christian denomination throughout the United States" to attempt to "carry into execution" Edwards' suggestions for concerted prayer. January, 1795, was the suggested date.[14] The response was eager. Baptists, Presbyterians, Dutch and Associate Reformed Churches, Standing Order Churches in New England, and Methodist groups joined in regular meetings for prayer in various parts of America. These monthly or quarterly prayer meetings often were composed of the devout from various denominations. More often, the meetings tended to form along denominational lines. The Concert for Prayer became a wide-spread phenomenon after 1795, and one of the constellation of factors contributing to revivals and missions the next quarter century.

New Patterns

The vigorous missionary organizations in England stimulated new patterns of organization and cooperation in America. The SPGNA was not the pattern for American missionary organizations. Its model was the New England company and SSPCK. It was a closed corporation. Its members were to have "perpetual succession."[15] In the new pattern, missionary societies had a much more open policy of membership and a broader base of support. Back of the society method was objection by congregational type churches to owning property and conducting business beyond the local parish. Societies were preferred to larger ecclesiastical fellowships because they permitted independent action, made an appeal to the benevolent in all walks of life, and opened doors for cooperation across sectarian lines.

These new organizational patterns never became universal. Eventually, missionary organizations were largely returned to denominational control. Ecclesiastical bodies continued to carry on missionary activity. But, in the 1790s, leaders made a determined effort to engender cooperation among all groups in the missionary enterprise.

New patterns also developed in terms of cooperation. The ideal was that all "who are desirous of the Spread of the Gospel of our LORD JESUS CHRIST" join in various societies for the great common purpose.[16] In 1802, the newly formed Standing Committee of Missions of the Presbyterian Church stated, in a letter to several European missionary societies, the common theological foundation of the various missionary organizations in America.

The leading religious opinions embraced by the various denominations who, . . . are engaged in missionary undertakings, are those
which were generally taught and embraced at the reformation from
popery: and in which the trinity and equality of persons in the
undivided Godhead — the deep depravity of man by nature — the
imputed righteousness of Christ, . . . — and the renovation of the
human heart by holiness — form the prominent and commanding
features of the whole system. It should be mentioned, however,
that these doctrines are held with various modifications by the
several christian denominations that have been specified."[17]

In practice, the "various modifications" were difficult to overlook especially
if they related to the proper subjects and mode of baptism. Before 1805, even such
obviously sectarian societies as the Massachusetts Missionary Society and the Massachusetts Baptist Missionary Society were open to anyone who should pay the annual
dues.[18] (The Baptist Society did require that eight of its twelve trustees be Baptists.)
But missionary partnership could not span the chasm between Baptists and Pedobaptists, or between Orthodoxy and Unitarianism. Cooperation between Reformed
groups (Dutch Reformed, Associate Reformed and Presbyterian) and the Congregational general assemblies could and did continue. After the fir st decade of intensive
organization of missionary societies, societies tended to be formed along clearly
drawn lines.[19] Broad cooperation among Baptists and Pedobaptists Orthodox and
Unitarian could only continue in societies that did not send out missionaries or
organize churches. The Bible and Tract societies are obvious examples.

The New York Baptist Missionary Society illustrates this trend. In 1810, its
directors explained why Baptists withdrew from the New York Missionary Society
and formed their own. The issues were baptism and the nature of a visible church.

Neither our Presbyterian brethren nor we could in conscience
sacrifice our views of the commandments of Christ; nor was a
spirit of prophecy necessary to foresee that similar difficulties
must of necessity be continually arising, as the labors of our
missionaries should be owned in the conviction of sinners, and
that consequently the union would tend rather to impede than
to promote the object of the institution.[20]

The New York Missionary Society (NYMS)

The first of the new missionary societies intended to be a perfect pattern of
the LMS in America. In 1796, the news of the organization and early activities of
the LMS reached New York. A number of ministers in that city

being informed of the exertions which were then, and had been
for some time, making in Great Britain, to spread the knowledge
of the Gospel among the heathen, became impressed with the
duty of making a similar attempt in America.[21]

A meeting was held, on September 21, 1796, and the NYMS was constituted, exactly one year after the formation of the LMS. A great public meeting was planned for November 4, when Rev. Alexander McWhorter delivered the first of many profound missionary sermons that were to mark the anniversaries of this society. The NYMS was launched with great public fanfare and broad support among most evangelical groups in the city.

The NYMS had superior leadership. John Rodgers, senior pastor of the Presbyterian Church in New York, was the first president. John H. Livingston, renowned Reformed Dutch pastor was vice president. John M. Mason, influential pastor of the Associate Reformed Church, was secretary and the most important spokesman for the society. Benjamin Foster, pastor of the largest Baptist Church in the city, was one of the directors. The constitution insisted that members might "be admitted from all religious denominations indiscriminately."[22] The strongly Calvinist "religious principles" incorporated in the constitution effectively excluded the Methodists.

The new society directed its attention both to the white settlements and Indians. Indians were its primary target. The Society had difficulty finding a suitable missionary. Some support went to John Sergeant and Paul, an Indian preacher on Long Island. However, late in 1798, Joseph Bullen from Vermont, indicated his interest in becoming a missionary. He was appointed on December 3, 1798. When they met on February 6, 1799, the directors had a letter from Bullen "declaring his acceptance."[23] Bullen was commissioned on March 21, 1799, and he and his son went to the Chickasaw nation in western Georgia for an exploratory mission. The following year, a large mission family of seventeen members, including Deacon David Rice and his family, moved to Chickasaw country. The ultimate results of the mission were disappointing. In five years it was abandoned.[24]

In 1796, the New York Baptist Association encouraged Elkanah Holmes, pastor of the Baptist Church on Staten Island, to execute his plan to preach among the Six Nations.[25] It supported Holmes for a six-month preaching mission each year. In three years, the work among the Tuscaroras was large enough to require greater support. The Association turned to the NYMS.[26] The Association and Society jointly supported Holmes for two years. In 1802, discontent in Holmes' church over his absence for six months each year became vocal. On April 27, 1802, he became a "permanent Missionary" of the NYMS. He eventually left the employ of the Society, but this became the most important mission of the Society. The NYMS continued to support preachers among the heathen until 1817, when its stations were transferred to the United Foreign Missionary Society.

The Northern Missionary Society (NMS)

The second missionary society formed on the new pattern was constituted a few months after the NYMS. A large cluster of Reformed Dutch, Associate Reformed and Presbyterian churches were located in the Albany area. John Blair Smith resigned as president of Hampden-Sydney College in 1789 to give himself to promoting the revival in Virginia. He succeeded George Duffield as pastor of the Pine Street Presbyterian Church in Philadelphia in 1791. In 1795, he was named president of Union College in Schenectady. In this post he became the catalyst for the creation of the Northern Missionary Society.

The society was organized in Lansingburgh, by ministers and laymen from all three Reformed connections in the Albany area, on January 11, 1797.[27] Funds were collected, and the society soon had its agents meet with the chief of the Oneida Indians. The tribe gave the society 400 acres on which to begin their mission. Though the avowed purpose of the NMS was to propagate the gospel among both Indian and white settlers, its energies were almost completely directed toward the Oneidas.

There were early efforts to unite the Northern and New York societies. In its first report the NYMS, the Board revealed that the NMS, "founded on the same doctrines, devoted to the same objects, and desirous of cooperating in the same plan," proposed uniting the two societies. The NYMS agreed on articles of union, but the NMS never approved them.[28] The NMS did not have the resources or leadership that characterized the NYMS. Smith returned to Philadelphia in 1799. Jonathan Edwards Jr. soon filled his office, but the NMS never attained the eminence of the NYMS. Its work was also turned over to the United Foreign Missionary Society after 1817.

The Philadelphia Missionary Society

In January, 1798, Morgan J. Rhees returned to Philadelphia after traveling extensively through the northern United States. He preached three sermons on the missionary obligation of Christians. The first dealt with the character of the primitive missionary, and "additional motives were urged to encourage a mission among the American heathen." The preacher, just returned from Ohio country, was concerned for the evangelization of the Indians. The second sermon asserted that God was no respecter of persons, that he communicated his grace to men by means of preaching, and that "preachers are sent and supported by men as well as by God." The third sermon was directed to "infidels" and "libertines" and showed the sufficiency of revelation. The result was the organization of the Philadelphia Missionary Society.[29]

Its founders hoped that all evangelical Christians would flock to the support of this society. Its missionaries were to go only as Christians and ignore all party names. They were to teach the industrial and agricultural arts as well as the Christian faith.[30] However, the society had too much of a Baptist flavor for the Presbyterians in Philadelphia. In 1800, the First Baptist Church suggested that the Association form its own missionary society. In 1802, the plan was recommended to the churches. A year later plans for such a society were adopted.[31] This missionary society within the associational organization handled the missionary activities of the association. The Philadelphia Missionary Society faded out of existence.

The Missionary Society of Connecticut (MSC)

Missionary concern grew among the Standing Order churches of Connecticut for a decade. Missionary activities increased. The art of cooperation in missionary matters matured.

In 1797, the Fairfield West Association proposed to the General Association that a society be formed in the state "for the purpose of enlarging the Redeemer's kingdom and propagating the gospel among the heathen.[32] The same year, the Hartford North Association "resolved themselves into a missionary society."[33] These two events were separated by significant action at the meeting of the general body on June 20, 1797. With the proposal from Fairfield West before it, the General Association named a committee to "draught an address to the several associations on the subject of a Missionary Society." A committee of correspondence was appointed to receive reactions, and a document was ordered published to give "a general view of the measures adopted in Great Britain and America, for the spread of the gospel in pagan countries."[34] The document received wide distribution. Response was so positive that, in October, the Hartford North Association formed a society which merged with the larger society the following year.

When the General Association met on June 19, 1798, after adjourning, its members formed themselves into the Missionary Society of Connecticut. This new organization was not fashioned after the older societies of England and America, nor was it in the mold of the LMS or NYMS. "The General Association of the State of Connecticut shall be the Missionary Society," the constitution stated. This body then appointed twelve trustees who managed the affairs of the society. Members of the General Association were members of the Society. Affiliation did not depend on monetary commitment. The Board reported each year to the General Association. The object of the MSC was

> to christianize the Heathen in North America, and to support and promote Christian Knowledge in the new settlements within the United States.[35]

The following year, the General Association instructed the Trustees, at the insistence of Jonathan Edwards Jr. that one-half of the monies collected be used for Indian evangelization.[36] The MSC became a tremendous force for church extension among the white settlers. Some time elapsed before it began an Indian mission. Its missions to the Red Indians were never very successful.

The Society continued the practice of the Committee on Missions. A settled pastor was sent for several months of itinerant preaching in the frontier areas. However, in 1799, it adopted a new practice. A man was sent to live on the frontiers. Seth Williston, who had served several years as a sometime missionary, was the first man sent out as a permanent evangelist. In 1800, the Society began sending its missionary to a frontier community, where he would settle, give part time to his own community and then itinerate in the surrounding vicinity. Joseph Badger was the first and best known of these missionaries. He had a tremendous career in church extension on the Western Reserve.[37] That year Salmon Giddings crossed the Mississippi as the first Protestant missionary in St. Louis. A year later, Elias Cornelius was in New Orleans as a representative of the MSC.[38]

In 1800, the Society took its first steps toward a mission to the Indians. The Trustees

> determined, that a discreet man, animated by the love of God
> and souls, of a good common education, who can be obtained
> for a moderate compensation, be sought for to travel among
> the Indian Tribes South and West of Lake Erie.[39]

David Bacon was enlisted and sent to Detroit. Later he moved to Michigan. The mission failed. Bacon and his family, after great privation, finally returned to civilization.

The MSC was not fashioned after the new organizational pattern. It certainly cannot be characterized as an ecumenical organization. However, in 1801, the MSC joined with the General Assembly of the Presbyterian Church in a Plan of Union. This Plan was one of the most significant ecumenical endeavors in the first twenty years of the Nineteenth Century.[40]

This Society led the way in Congregational participation with Presbyterians for planting churches on the northwestern frontier. The wisdom of the Union has been much disputed, both by Presbyterians and Congregationalists.[41] It had tremendous influence in the development of Christianity in western New York, Pennsylvania, Ohio, Indiana and Illinois.

The Massachusetts Missionary Society (MMS)

The first concrete evidence of the separation about to take place in New England was the organization of the Massachusetts Missionary Society on May 28, 1799. Nathaniel Emmons and Samuel Austin were the moving spirits in its organization and gave this society dynamic leadership. Doctrinal controversies had plagued New England before the Revolution. They might have come to overt rupture before 1805 had it not been for the War and the struggle with Deism that followed.[42]

The new society disavowed party spirit or intention to weaken already existing societies.[43] However, in 1804, in a Convention Sermon, Emmons sharply criticized "universal toleration" and "unlimited catholicism."[44] The principle he espoused were already practiced in the MMS. Jedidiah Morse was the only well known man in the society who was not a Hopkinsian.[45] Morse continued as secretary of SPGNA and Emmons also continued as a member of that older society. The two societies jointly supported several missionary ventures.[46] But the MMS provided a vehicle through which Hopkinsians and Old Calvinists could work together. Thus, it presaged the new alignment which was to develop in New England after Harvard was lost by the Orthodox in 1805.

The MMS was open to all who would give two dollars each year and subscribe the Constitution. While membership was primarily Hopkinsian, some Baptists joined in the support of this society.[47] The MMS aided Indians and settlers. With the Northern Missionary Society, it supported Jacob Cram among the Tuscaroras and with the Western Missionary Society in 1809, it supported Joseph Badger among the Ohio Indians.[48] Its frontier missionaries went to Maine and Nova Scotia, to western New England, upper New York, and into Canada.[49] Strong leadership united in the MMS was destined to have an important place in the extension of the American mission to foreign lands.

The Massachusetts Baptist Missionary Society (MBMS)

In 1802, Baptist leaders in Boston decided to organize for missionary purposes. A month before the general election, the two churches issued a call for others to join them in this organization. They were "animated by the laudable exertions" of other Christians both in America and Europe. The new society was organized on March 26, 1802. That day it elected its first trustees and appointed missionaries to Maine, New Hampshire, western New York and Upper Canada.[50]

The MBMS was quite different from any earlier or later Baptist missionary organizations. It did not come into being by action of the Warren Association from which it drew its primary constituency. It set no moral or denominational requirements for membership. The sole stipulation was an annual gift of one dollar or more. Its purpose was not to plant and strengthen Baptist churches, but to

> furnish occasional preaching and to promote the knowledge of
> evangelical truth in the new settlements within the United States;
> or farther, if circumstances should render it possible.

Circumstances immediately made missionary labor possible outside the United States. Joseph Cornell was their first missionary into Canada.[51]

This Society did not intend to engage in a mission to the Indians. However, in December, 1805, Elkanah Holmes addressed a passionate letter to an officer of the MBMS, requesting that Lemuel Covell become a permanent missionary to both the Indians and the white settlers in New York and Canada.[52] The Society demurred. In 1806, Baptists withdrew from the NYMS. Holmes continued in the employ of the NYMS until September 30,1807. On December 9, the MBMS asked the newly organized New York Baptist Missionary Society to cooperate in support of Holmes. In March, 1808, joint support began. The mission to the frontiers continued without abatement. In 1812, the Trustees reported that missionaries had been on the field a total of seventy-four months, over six years of missionary service in one year.[53]

The MBMS became the most extensive and effective missionary society that Baptists formed for churching of the wilderness. Charleston, Philadelphia and Boston were the three centers where Baptist missionary leadership developed. Leadership in the Boston vicinity was as strong as the other two areas combined. Baptists in New England were an important force in stimulating Baptist missionary organizations.

The Presbyterian Standing Committee of Missions

The growing missionary activity of the General Association of Connecticut had a powerful influence on the northern leaders of the Presbyterian General Assembly. These two bodies had a heritage of close cooperation. In 1766, the Synod of New York and Philadelphia and the General Association formed a General Convention which met annually until 1775. The purpose of this alliance was to build Christian fellowship, develop concerted opposition to an Anglican bishop in America, and bless "the benighted heathen on our borders with the glorious light of the gospel."[54]

In 1790, the General Assembly appointed a committee to renew this fraternal correspondence. A three-point plan was adopted two years later. Committees of correspondence were established by each body for exchanging information. Three delegates were appointed to deliberate with the other. Finally, a committee to certify traveling ministers was appointed by each church body.[55]

The Committee of Correspondence of the General Association sent its missionary report to the General Assembly in 1798. In reply, the General Assembly has an account of its own missions, but indicated some changes were anticipated in its missionary structure.[56] A committee was appointed to study the matter. The committee recommended that resident missionaries be employed to live near frontier settlements. Besides regular duties, they would determine places of need, gather helpful information, handle emergencies and generally direct missionaries appointed for brief preaching tours. Jedediah Chapman was named to one of these posts the next year.[57] He had an illustrious career in northwestern New York.

The General Assembly incorporated in 1799. Its body of eighteen trustees became, in effect, a small executive committee that received, dispersed and controlled the properties and funds of the national body. In 1800, the trustees sent a report to the General Assembly that directly effected the missionary outreach of that body. It proposed a far more extensive missionary fund, suggested a significant Bible and literature distribution program, and urged that an order of "catechists" be appointed. These men would not need extensive academic training or have "clerical functions," but could give "private instruction," deliver occasional addresses and lead devotional exercises in the new communities and churches of the wilderness. The program was adopted. The fund-raising enterprise was entered with verve. Its primary purpose was to fund the missionary work.

> The General Assembly . . . have it in contemplation to attempt, more extensively than heretofore has been done, the Christianizing of the Indians, the instruction of the black people, and the propagations of Christian knowledge . . . among those who are uninstructed.[58]

When the General Assembly met in 1801, the missionary spirit was high. Joseph Clark opened the meeting with a sermon on Matthew 28:18-20. The General Association of Connecticut sent word that it wished to meet with Presbyterian representatives "to consider the measures proper . . . for establishing an uniform system of church government" among the new churches of the frontier. A committee was instructed to draw up such a plan. On May 29, the Plan of Union was approved, subject to adoption by the Connecticut body, to go into "immediate operation."[59] The Plan was adopted by the General Association a few weeks later. Identical agreements were reached with all the state-wide Congregational bodies over the next ten of the Great Lakes states throughout the first half of the Nineteenth Century.

Between 1796 and 1801, the number of Presbyterian missionaries greatly increased. By 1801, the Synod of Virginia had two Commissions to care for their missionary needs. The newer one managed missionary affairs west of the Allegheny Mountains. The mission of the Synod of the Carolinas had almost died in the Hopkinsian Controversy. But. in 1800, it sent two missionaries to preach at the Natchez, on the banks of the lower Mississippi.

In 1801, the trustees of the Corporation of the General Assembly again made sweeping suggestions about the missionary enterprise. They raised the question of taking over the Synodical missions. They recommended that John Chavis, "a black man of prudence and piety, . . . be employed as a missionary among people of his own color." Chavis served the General Assembly for years as an evangelist and church planter among black people in the southern and middle states. They also called for an extensive survey of missionary needs and resources in every presbytery of the General Assembly. The trustees were clearly encroaching on the duties traditionally assigned to the "Committee for the missionary business" which was appointed each year. In 1802, matters came to a climax. A standing committee was appointed to handle the funds, and a second motion was adopted by which the Assembly gave

> the general management of the missionary business to a standing committee on missions and that an annual missionary sermon be delivered.[60]

A new day had come for the missionary program of the Presbyterian Church. The Standing Committee included Ashbel Green, Phillip Milledoar, Jacob J. Janaway, Elias Boudinot, who was the president and prime mover of the corporation trustees, and Ebenezer Hazard. All were able, dedicated and active men. They aggressively set themselves to developing an extensive missionary program. On March 13, 1803, the Standing Committee outlined their missionary program in a "Circular Letter to Missionary Societies."

> There are four descriptions of people to whom the Assembly . . . are endeavouring to send missions. 1. To those who are settled on our frontier . . . 2. To certain places in the more settled parts, where the gospel has not been regularly established . . . 3. To the black people, or negroes, of the United States . . . 4. To the Indians, or Aborigines, of our country.[61]

In 1802, the Commission of the Synod of Virginia west of the mountains sent missionaries to the Ohio and Michigan Indians. But the Standing Committee looked in vain for a missionary to the Indians that it might employ. In a letter to the presbyteries, the Committee explained:

> Missionaries for the Indians are a great desideratum with the Assembly. The hope of contributing to send the gospel among the Heathen tribes, prompted the liberality of many who have contributed most largely to the funds which the Assembly have at command; and it was with deep regret that the last Assembly found that they had not a single candidate for an Indian mission.

When the General Assembly met in 1803, Gideon Blackburn was the delegate from the Union Presbytery of eastern Tennessee. The Standing Committee met with him about the possibility of undertaking a mission to the Cherokees. In its report to the General Assembly, the Standing Committee announced the appointment of Blackburn as missionary to the Cherokee tribe. This mission was not intended to major in evangelism, but education.

> The preaching of the word is not the immediate object of the present mission but to prepare the way for its reception at a future and . . . not too distant day.[62]

In Gideon Blackburn the Standing Committee enlisted one of the most colorful and versatile men of his day. Blackburn did not become the apostle to the Cherokees. He overextended his own private capital in the Cherokee school enterprise. The support of Jedidiah Morse and the *Panoplist* and numerous appeals to New England philanthropists did not keep him from going under. In 1810, he abandoned the mission.[63] The Indian mission was just the beginning of his career. He was missionary to middle and west Tennessee, a prominent pastor and college president in Kentucky, and preacher, land speculator and college founder in Illinois. What Peter Cartright was to the Methodists, what John Mason Peck was for the Baptists, Blackburn was to the Presbyterians of the Ohio River Valley.

These seven new missionary organizations broke new ground among the American churches at the turn of the Nineteenth Century. None were exactly the model of the future. Cooperation at its best was limited and often did not prove to be sufficiently pragmatic to be continued. Nevertheless, along with the Revival, a missionary spirit burst upon American Christianity. It became incarnate in these early institutions. These were only the beginning.

Old Structures Continue and Societies Proliferate

During the era that American Christianity was creating new forms of missionary structure, many churches continued to labor at church extension within the larger ecclesiastical bodies. After 1800, there was a rapid change in the missionary pattern of these bodies. The new pattern erected societies for specifically missionary purposes that were controlled by the constituents of the denominational body.

Reformed Dutch Church

When the General Synod of the Reformed Dutch Church met in 1797, it appointed a Committee to confer with representatives of the Associate Reformed and Presbyterian Churches about the possibility of renewing a fraternal correspondence that had been in existence for several years in the previous decade. These representatives met together on June 19-20, 1798. At that meeting, a "Plan of correspondence and intercourse" was adopted, which, though it did not recommend the organic union of the three bodies, called for a much more intimate "brotherly correspondence" than many of the members of the Synod had envisioned. When the General Synod met in 1800, the plan had already been debated throughout the Church. Many consistories had instructed their delegates to vote against the plan.

The mood of the Synod was tense, and the plan was rejected.[64]

Discouragement and dissension marked the Reformed Dutch Church in 1800. Almost all ecclesiastical bodies in America were rejoicing in new life surging through their chur ches. But the General Synod wrote in the "Pastoral Letter:"

> We call upon you deeply to lament . . . the visible declension of the vital piety through our land in general, and, we are sorry to add, throughout our churches. We cannot but regret . . . the small number of conversions (and) . . . the few accessions of professors even to the visible church.

In this Synod, which was permeated with pessimism and division, the Committee on Missions made a pathetic report. The Classis of Albany had sent Robert McDowell to Canada in 1798, where he met with astounding success. He had settled there among three new congregations. The Committee had in hand urgent letters from him, pleading that missionaries be sent to assist in forming new churches. There were also three letters from a congregation in Mercer County, Kentucky, begging for ministerial assistance. The Committee observed:

> A great harvest is . . . springing up in that growing country, and your Committee would be happy if your Rev. Body could send forth labors into it. [65]

The Committee recommended that the Classis of Albany superintend the missionary region "North and West." The Kentucky problem was turned over to the Particular Synod of New York. No real recommendations were made to involve the whole Synod in the mission task. Three years later the General Synod was unable to meet because of the division in the Classis of Albany. When it finally convened in May, 1804, nothing had been done about Canada, and the opportunity in Kentucky had passed.[66]

The General Synod met again in 1806. It had a passionate letter from McDowell, who was present for some of the proceedings. The letter warned that unless immediate action were taken the opportunity for the Dutch Church would be lost. "The Baptists," McDowell explained,

> frequently send missionaries through this country; and missionaries from Connecticut have lately visited those places.

Three missionaries were sent to Upper Canada for an eight-week mission.

Potentially more significant, the General Synod appointed eight members of the Particular Synod of Albany as a "standing committee on missions." It was given complete care of the missionary enterprise and required to report annually to the two particular synods. The Standing Committee seldom functioned. No missionaries were sent out in 1807 or 1808. Only four were appointed between 1809 and 1812. In 1812, the Committee on Missions candidly appraised the missionary record of the Reformed Dutch Church.

It is . . . believed that all has not been done which ought or might have been done, and that it is very problematical whether what has been done has been done to the most advantage to the cause.[67]

Reformed Dutch leaders committed to aggressive missionary action had to find channels other than their own General Synod.

The Congregationalists

There was a great difference between the Massachusetts Missionary Society and Missionary Society of Connecticut. The MSC was a true representation of the Standing Order in Connecticut. The MMS had its roots in the Mendon Association of Congregational Ministers, organized in 1751, and the clannishness of Hopkinsians in Massachusetts at the turn of the century. Nathanael Emmons was the patriarch of the Association and the most respected leader of Samuel Hopkins' disciples in the Bay State. He was the principle leader of the MMS through years of effective service.[68] Other ministerial associations created missionary societies in Massachusetts. Outside this state, missionary organizations usually followed the Connecticut pattern, i.e., one major society for each state.

Actually the first missionary society organized in New England after 1797 was in western Massachusetts. Stephen West, close associate of Samuel Hopkins, and Edwards' successor at Stockbridge, and the honorable Timothy Edwards were the most conspicuous leaders. The Berkshire Ministerial Association was formed in 1793. Several Congregational pastors in Columbia County, New York, participated in the ministerial fellowship of the Berkshire Association. On February 21, 1798, these pastors led in the organization of the Congregational Missionary Society of Berkshire and Columbia "for the purpose of sending the gospel to new and destitute settlements in our land."[69] First missionaries were sent primarily into Vermont and northern New York. By 1805, missionaries were being sent into western Pennsylvania, Ohio and western New York. The society's income began to decline by 1810. Its missionary fields were again confined to New York and Vermont.[70]

In New Hampshire, a General Convention of Ministers was founded in 1747. A petition from this group, in 1758, led to the chartering of Dartmouth College. This ministerial convention "engaged in the work of supplying the back settlements" during the 1700s.[71] The practice culminated in formation of the New Hampshire Missionary Society in September, 1801. In 1809, the General Association of New Hampshire was formed, replacing the old General Convention of Ministers. Meetings of the new General Association and the New Hampshire Missionary Society were held together, one following the other. The northern parts of the state were the primary fields of missionary labor.[72]

In Northampton, Hampshire County, Massachusetts, the Hampshire Missionary Society was organized in January, 1802.[73] The immediate object of the Society was to carry the gospel to the "New Settlements." However, in 1805, the Society began underwriting the education of two Indian youths. The goal of the Society was to help the white settlers to so "imbibe the spirit of Jesus" that "by their example" they would "allure pagans to revere the name and religion of

Jesus."[74] New York and Maine provided mission fields. Ten years after the organization of the Society, it had experienced slow but steady growth. In 1811, the Society had its missionaries in the fields for a total of 129 weeks.[75]

Samuel Hopkins' concern for the Negroes in America characterized the Missionary Society of Rhode Island, constituted May 5, 1803. Its purpose was

> to promote the Gospel in any part of the state where there may be opportunity for it and to assist Africans in coming to a knowledge of the truth in any way which may consist with our means and advantages.

In 1804, Hopkins, the first president, was dead. The funds of the society were $400, half of which had remained from monies collected by Hopkins and Stiles in their earlier efforts at African evangelization. The Society reported that they had "no particular plans."[76] It never began any significant work.

On September 1, 1803, Jedidiah Morse and several others constituted the Massachusetts Society for Promoting Christian Knowledge.[77] Its primary purpose was to "promote *evangelical truth and piety*" by the distribution of tracts and books. The constitution provided also for the support of schools and "pious *Missionaries.*" In 1811, the Society began to appoint missionaries. It carried on extensive missions in the eastern counties of Maine and northern New Hampshire. One of the major thrusts of the Society was to congregationalize Rhode Island. It also supported missionaries in New York state.[78]

Ministers in Lincoln and Kennebec Counties, Maine, organized a tract society in 1802. At the annual meeting of this Society, in Hallowell, on June 18, 1807, it became the Maine Missionary Society.[79] This Society's purpose was to preach the gospel in Maine. It cooperated closely with the MMS, the Hampshire Missionary Society, and, later, the Massachusetts Society for Promoting Christian Knowledge. In 1814, it employed six missionaries for a total of sixty weeks in the state.[80]

Six Vermont pastors met in Eleazar Wheelock's old study on August 27, 1795, and concluded that a "General Convention of Ministers" for Vermont was needed. The Vermont General Convention of Congregational and Presbyterian Ministers and Churches was organized the following year.[81] Missionaries of the MSC in Vermont encouraged the formation of this body. Eleven years later, in 1807, this General Convention organized itself into the Vermont Missionary Society.[82]

In the Summer, 1806, delegates from the Marlborough and (old) Worchester Ministerial Association met to discuss the possibility of forming a missionary society. Another meeting was called early in 1807. Clergy and laymen from Middlesex and Worchester Counties met to form the Evangelical Missionary Society of Massachusetts.[83] The emphasis of this society was on the "waste places" of the frontier. Its goal was to give a missionary a permanent location rather than have him itinerate.[84] From its beginning, this Society's membership was a mixture of liberal and orthodox. But, in 1817, the Unitarian party took over control of the organization.

No attempt will be made to tell of the myriads of missionary societies that were organized by women in New England, and copied in every part of the United States. The story of Cent and Mite Societies would make a large book. Children's societies and societies of young men followed in their train. All of these groups were formed for the gathering of funds and prayer. They did not send out missionaries during these early years. Their number is too vast to count.[85]

The voluntary society was particularly adapted to Congregationalists. These societies became an important tool for winning the American West.

The Baptists

For Baptists, church extension by means of itinerant preachers and missionary associations continued. But 1797 to 1817 was preeminently a time of missionary organization. An account of this organization in every one of the Baptist associations is impossible here. The pattern was almost always the same. An association usually had some preachers who were committed to itinerant preaching. The associations eventually began to provide monetary assistance for those who went on preaching missions. Next, a plan was adopted to raise funds and manage the missionary endeavor. In some cases, a growing concern for Indian evangelization resulted in the association undertaking a mission to some tribe.

This pattern can be illustrated with the developments in a few associations. The Bowdoinham Association was founded in 1787 with three churches. Each annual association was a time of commitment for the "ministerial brethren" to itinerate and evangelize. Revival came to the churches in 1798-99. When the Association met in 1799, a plan called "The Gospel Mission" was devised to raise a missionary fund from among the churches for the support of one or more missionaries throughout the year. Isaac Chase, Baptist pioneer in the District, was ready to give himself wholly to "itinerant labors."

This plan continued until 1804. That year, the Association had forty-eight churches, and division was necessary. The churches in Lincoln County formed their own association. However, before the meeting broke up, a more general plan for missionary cooperation was developed. The Maine Missionary Society was formed.[86] Five years later, when the Standing Order churches formed their "Maine Missionary Society," this older body called itself the Maine Baptist Missionary Society.

The Shaftsbury Association was formed in 1781 among five small churches: two in Vermont, one in Massachusetts, and two in New York. Twenty years later, in 1801, the association had forty-six churches. That year, the Shaftsbury Association became explicitly what it had been emphatically for two decades, a missionary body. Lemual Covell, who already had been active in itinerating and church planting in northern New York and Upper Canada, moved that a fund be raised

for the purpose of sending missionaries to preach the Gospel in

distant parts of our frontier settlements, and, as far as we may
have opportunity, among the *natives* of the wilderness.[87]

In 1802, a "plan" was adopted, remarkedly like the constitution of a missionary society, that committed the Association to missionary exertions, but retained ultimate authority in the Association. The *"design"* of this proposal was

to enable the Association to send able and faithful ministers to
preach the gospel, and endeavor to build up the visible cause of
the Redeemer in such parts of the United States, or the Canadas
as are destitute . . . and as far as they can have access among the
natives of the wilderness.[88]

Every aspect of this plan was carried out. Churches were gathered across New York state, Vermont, western Massachusetts, and Upper Canada. At one time, before the Association began to divide into other associations, five churches from Canada were part of its fellowship. For several years after 1801, one of their missionaries worked with Elkanah Holmes among the Tuscaroras.[89]

When Elkanah Holmes broke with the NYMS, in 1807, members from the New York portion of Shaftsbury Association formed a "New York Baptist Missionary Society" to help keep Holmes among the Indians. In June, 1808, trustees of this society met with the Missions Committee of the Association and worked out a program of cooperation. Actually, the Association then had two missionary bodies functioning within its structure, one working primarily with settlers, the other with Indians. In 1811, the name of the Society was changed to the New York Northern Baptist Missionary Society, to avoid the duplication of names with the older society in the city.[90]

Thirteen churches constituted the Otsego Baptist Association in 1795. It experienced phenomenal growth. By 1805, there were fifty churches. On August 27, 1807, members of this Association organized the Lake Baptist Missionary Society. John Peck became its principle leader and one of the most active missionaries on the frontier.[91] By 1814, church extension had been so succesful that the Society called its members to turn their attention to the "South-west and Western parts of our country."[92]

In 1802, the Charleston Association employed a missionary to travel through destitute western communities. It also sent John Rooker, from the Bethel Association, to begin a mission to the Catawba Indians. A year later he was back with a glowing report. His preaching had been well received. The Indians were eager for a school to be established among them.[93] For several years the Association entered heartily into the Indian mission as well as participating in the task of gathering churches among the Blacks and in the white settlements.[94]

The Georgia Baptist Association, founded in 1785, experienced fifteen years of growth even before the Froudier Revival filtered down from Kentucky. By 1799, it had become three associations. In October, 1800, the Association resolved:

That as a spirit of Itineracy has inflamed the minds of several

ministers, who are desirous to enter into some resolutions, suitable
to carry into effect a design of travelling and preaching the gospel,
a meeting be, and is hereby appointed, at Powel's Creek, on Friday
before the first Sunday in May Next, for that purpose; that the same
day be observed as a day of fasting and solemn prayer to Almighty
God, for prosperity on the design.[95]

Henry Halcomb, pastor in Savannah and editor of the *Georgia Analytical
Repository,* reported on the meeting the following year. The meeting was designed
to promote

itinerant preaching, through, and to the utmost boundaries of the
state, and the formation of a Missionary Society, to support, if not
more, a couple of pious, and suitably-gifted ministers of the gospel,
in confining their labors to our dark, and almost barbarous frontier,
where, from a variety of obvious circumstances, there can be no
standing ministry.[96]

Another meeting was called in Powelton on April 29, 1802. A General
Committee for Georgia Baptists was formed, composed of the representatives from
each association. The General Committee became a strong force in coordinating
and encouraging missionary endeavor. By 1810, a small association had been organized in the Natchez, in Mississippi Territory, and a Baptist preacher had been sent
from Savannah to New Orleans.[97] Baptists in Georgia began early to cooperate in
churching the wilderness.

The Presbyterians

The Presbyterian Standing Committee of Missions set the pace for missionary endeavor in the Presbyterian Church after 1802. But synodical missions continued. By 1800, controversy in the Synod of the Carolinas had subsided. The Synod
recognized anew the "importance and necessity of carrying on the missionary business." James Hall, of North Carolina, was sent to the Natchez in Mississippi Territory. In two years, the Commission of Synod was again set up to handle the missionary affairs. In 1803, William C. Davis was ordered to "act as a stated missionary
to the Catawba Indians" and superintend a mission school in that nation. By 1805,
the Indians "grew weary," and the mission was closed.[98]

James Hall was the primary missionary supported by the Synod through
the next six years. In 1807, he and William H. Barr went to the Natchez. When
the Synod met in 1808, both insisted that it would be more advisable for the Synod to "cherish our own vacancies, than to attempt to establish new societies."
In 1811, the Synod overturned the General Assembly that it might "resign the
missionary . . . business into the hands of the General Assembly." The national
body accepted this resignation.[99]

The Synod of Virginia reported in 1802 that it had, through the Commission of the Synod west of the Allegheny Mountains, appointed nine missionaries
in 1801. Three men were sent to the "Shawnese, and other Indians about Detroit
and Sandusky." One young man was sent to teach agriculture and tool making.

"The prospects" were "flattering, as well among the Indians as the frontier whites."

In 1802, the Synod of Virginia was divided. Two new synods were erected within its western boundaries. Here most of the missionary labor had been directed. The formation of the Synods of Pittsburgh and Kentucky destroyed the aggressive missionary character of the Synod of Virginia. In following years, only two to four missionaries were appointed. In 1807, the Synod asked to be relieved its missionary responsibilities. The request was refused, but for all practical purposes, missionary extension by the Synod ceased.[100]

The Synod of Kentucky was formed when the Revival was at its highest. The influx of members was so vast that in 1803, its members reported to the General Assembly that they found

> themselves unable to answer the demands upon them for missionary labors, and pray the Assembly to attend to their destitute situation, and to send out missionaries to spread the gospel among the multitudes.[101]

Kentucky, along with Indiana and Illinois, became one of the primary fields of the General Assembly's Standing Committee of Missions.

The story was different in the Synod of Pittsburgh. The men who made up this Synod, from the Presbyteries of Redstone, Ohio, and Erie, were the principle active agents in the Virginia Synod's western commission. When they met on September 29, 1803, to constitute the Synod, they formed themselves into the Western Missionary Society (WMS). The Society's object was to

> diffuse the knowledge of the gospel among the inhabitants of the new settlements, the Indian tribes, and, if need be, among some of the interior inhabitants, where they are not able to support the gospel.[102]

Activity for two years was confined to the new settlements. But in 1805, the Wyandot Nation decided it would receive a "Gospel minister among them" on a permanent basis. Joseph Badger, missionary of the MSC, and James Hughes, staunch Presbyterian, attended the powwow. Badger had been unhappy with the MSC because his salary had been cut in 1803. His family had suffered considerable privation.[103] He resigned as missionary of the Connecticut Society and offered himself to the WMS. He was commissioned as their missionary to the Wyandots on February 6, 1806.[104]

The goal of the mission was not just evangelism, but also instruction in farming and the rudiments of English education. A farm was secured at Lower Sandusky. It provided a home for the missionary, income for the mission, and served as a school of agriculture.

The Standing Committee invested $400 annually in this mission. But the Synod of Pittsburgh, acting in its capacity as the Western Missionary Society, conducted the most active synodical mission in the first two decades of the new century.

In 1801, a correspondent of the *Connecticut Evangelical Magazine* observed that there was "a greater obligation of Christians in America, than on any other in the world" to participate in sharing the gospel with those who did not know of its benefits. The reasons for this special obligation were several. The peace that America had enjoyed until that time put the churches under particular accountability. The Indians constituted a great mission field right in the nation's back door.

> But it is not the Heathen only who claim our liberality. Perhaps
> the state of our new settlements is a higher call to Christian exer-
> tion . . . The American church is placed in a new and interesting
> situation; and there is a new and more solemn obligation, than was
> ever found on Christians before, . . . arising from the removal of
> our children into the wilderness, where many of them cannot enjoy
> the hearing of the word and the administration of the ordinances,
> without our assistance in the present moment.[105]

The task of planting churches throughout the American wilderness called for the utmost in missionary endeavor. The ways that the American churches organized to meet the challenge fashioned the missionary character of American Christianity.

John Mason Peck, in 1815, represented Luther Rice at the Madison Baptist Association in upper New York. The response to his report and sermon was overwhelming. Peck noted in his journal:

> It appears that we can hardly be enthusiastic on the subject of
> missions. Here is full scope for the most benevolent and feeling
> heart to exercise itself . . . When I reflect that but a few years
> since all this country was one vast wilderness — properly mis-
> sionary ground — I must exclaim: What hath God wrought.[106]

With these words, Peck brought two important themes together that mark the response of the American churches to the American wilderness in the early National Period. By 1817, the missionary cause had become the great passion of the American churches. Radical commitment to church extension was never de-nominated "enthusiastical." Further, thirty years of missionary endeavor produced results. What had been missionary ground — wilderness, became the base from which missionaries were sent — a garden. There had already been a great harvest. Missionary success was the earnest of ultimate victory.

NOTES FOR CHAPTER 5

1. John M. Mason, *Messiah's Throne. A Sermon, Preached before the London Missionary Society, at their Eighth Annual Meeting, in Tottenham-Court Chapel, on the Evening of Thursday, the 13th of May, 1802,* in *The Complete Works of John M. Mason,* ed. by Ebenezer Mason (4 vols.; New York: Baker & Scribner, 1849), III, 270-271. Mason was pastor of the Associate Reformed Church in New York, preacher extraordinary, theological professor and one of the founders of the New York Missionary Society.

2. Most studies of this Awakening date its beginning in 1797. See Charles Roy Keller, *The Second Great Awakening in Connecticut* (New Haven: Yale University Press, 1942); and Catharine C. Cleveland, *The Great Revival in the West* (Chicago: University of Chicago Press, 1916).

3. *CEM,* I, (July, 1800), 6.

4. *Ibid.,* p. 77.

5. Jesse Mercer, *History of Georgia Baptist Association,* pp. 42-43.

6. See Charles E. Cuningham, *Timothy Dwight 1752-1817* (New York: The MacMillan Company, 1942), pp. 193-234. Dwight's most important works on this subject are: *The Nature and Danger of Infidel Philosophy, Exhibited in Two Discourses* (New Haven: Printed by George Bunce, 1798); and *A Discourse of Some Events of the Last Century* (New Haven: Printed by Ezra Read, 1801).

7. Gillette, *Minutes,* pp. 319-321.

8. I am indebted to Marty, *The Infidel,* for the clue that "infidelity" was useful to American churchmen.

9. One of the earliest published accounts of the foundation of the BMS is in John Rippon, *The Baptist Annual Register* (4 vols.; London: n.p., 1793-1802), I, 37ff. Hereafter *Baptist Register.*

10. Richard Lovett, *The History of the London Missionary Society 1795-1895,* (London: Henry Frowde, 1899), p. 5.

11. *The Evangelical Magazine,* September, 1794, p. 379.

12. The Philadelphia Association, for example, encouraged the churches to support Carey and actually collected money in 1794. Gillette, *Minutes,* p. 298.

13. See Beaver, "Concert for Prayer," pp. 420-427.

14. William Linn, *Discourses on the Signs of the Times* (New York: Printed by Thomas Greenleaf, 1794), pp. 174-175, contains a long quotation from this communication.

15. [Hunnewell], *Society for Propagating the Gospel,* p. 5.

16. Nathaniel Emmons, *To ALL, who are desirous of the Spread of the Gospel of our LORD JESUS CHRIST* (no bibliographical infor mation, dated May 28, 1799), p. 1.

17. Standing Committee of Missions, MSS Minutes, Archives, Board of National Missions of the United Presbyterian Church, New York, in 3 vols., "Committee of Missions 1802-1807," "Committee of Missions 1807-1815," and "Committee of Missions 1812-1830," I, 16.

18. See the constitutions of these two societies. Emmons, *To ALL,* p. 3, and *MBMM,* I (September, 1803), p. 6.

19. I speak of the period before 1825. Beginning in 1826, various denominational bodies did cooperate in the work of the ABCFM: Dutch Reformed until 1845, German Reformed until 1863, and New School Presbyterians until 1870. However, before that date the ABCFM was essentially a Congregational society that did not have the support of all the various elements of the Standing Order churches

in New England. William Bently habitually referred to it as a "Hopkinsian society" and the Philadelphia newspaper, on departure of the first missionaries, referred to the ABCFM as a "Congregational" society. See *Philadelphia Gazette,* February 22, 1812.

20. Quoted in Albert L. Vail, *The Morning Hour of American Baptist Missions* (Philadelphia: American Baptist Publication Society, 1907), p. 181. This is the only attempt I am aware of to present a comprehensive account of the missionary activity of Baptists along church, association, and society lines in this early period. The book has few citations but is still very useful.

21. *The New York Missionary Magazine and Repository of Religious Intelligence,* I (January, 1800), 9. Hereafter *NYMM.*

22. See "The Address and Constitution of the New-York Missionary Society," in *The Evangelical Magazine,* June, 1797, pp. 245-255.

23. New York Missionary Society, MSS Minutes, Archives, Houghton Library, Harvard University, February 6, 1799.

24. Beaver, *Pioneers in Mission,* pp. 235-248, gives an account of this mission and the instructions given to Joseph Bullen.

25. *Minutes of the New York Baptist Association,* 1796, p. 3.

26. NYMS "Minutes," April 7, 1802.

27. John Blair Smith, *The Enlargement of Christ's Kingdom, the object of a Christian's Prayers and Exertions* (Schenectady: Printed by C. P. Wyckoff, 1797).

28. "Report of the Directors of the Missionary Society," Appended to John M. Mason, *Hope for the Heathen* (New York: T. & J. Swords, 1797), pp. 47-49.

29. See Rippon, *Baptist Register,* III, 535ff, and William Staughton, *Missionary-Encouragements: A Discourse, delivered on Wednesday Evening, the 16th of May, 1798* (Philadelphia: Printed by Stephen C. Ustick, 1798), p. 42.

30. Vail, *Morning Hour,* pp. 92-93.

31. Gillette, *Minutes,* pp. 350, 370, 381.

32. Bacon, *et al., Contributions,* p. 38.

33. *Ibid.,* p. 242.

34. *Records of the General Association,* p. 173.

35. *Ibid.,* p. 120.

36. *Ibid.,* p. 182.

37. *Memoir of Rev. Joseph Badger* (Hudson, Ohio: Sawyer, Ingersoll and Co., 1851) is the only lengthy account of his life. Some of Badger's correspondence can be found in Sweet, *Religion on the Frontier,* III, 77ff.

38. Keller, *Second Great Awakening,* pp. 73-77.

39. *CEM,* I (1800), 14.

40. This document has been reprinted many times. It can be found in Williston Walker, *The Creeds and Platforms of Congregationalism* (New York: Charles Scribner's Sons, 1893), pp. 530-531; or in Sweet, *Religion on the Frontier,* II, 15.

41. The great debate took place in the late 1820s and early 1830s leading up to the schism of 1837. See

Samuel J. Baird, *A History of the New School, and of the Questions Involved in the Disruption of the Presbyterian Church in 1838* (Philadelphia: Claxton, Remsen & Haffelfinger, 1868); Lewis Cheeseman, *Differences between Old and New School Presbyterians* (Rochester: Published by Erastus Darrow, 1848); and Zebulan Crocker, *The Catastrophe of the Presbyterian Church in 1837* (New Haven: B. & W. Noyes, 1838) tell the different viewpoints of the Presbyterians. The critique of the Congregationalists came some time later when a denominational consciousness was developing among them. See W. S. Kennedy, *The Plan of Union: Or a History of the Presbyterian and Congregational Churches of the Western Reserve* (Hudson, Ohio: Printed by the author, 1856).

42. Wright, *Beginning of Unitarianism,* p. 251.

43. Emmons, *To ALL,* p. 5.

44. Emmons, *Works,* I, 309.

45. Morse was more a New Divinity man than an Old Calvinist, except that he did not hold the Edwards-ean view concerning the proper candidates for communion.

46. *The Panoplist,* X (July, 1810), 281.

47. See R. Pierce Beaver, *All Loves Excelling* (Grand Rapids: William B. Eerdmans Publishing Co., 1968), p. 19.

48. *Panoplist,* IV (June, 1808), 41; VI (August, 1810), 92.

49. This information can be found in almost every annual report of the trustees. The long report of 1814 is illustrative because that year they had supported Mills and Schermerhorn, and had begun partial support of settled pastors, plus the funding of itinerates. See *ibid.,* X, 281-285, 328-330.

50. *MBMM,* I, 5, 7-8, 159.

51. *MBMM,* I, 6, 11-12.

52. *MBMM,* I, 191.

53. *MBMM.* II, 93, 220.

54. *Minutes of the General Convention of Delegates Appointed by the Synod of New York and Philadelphia and the General Association of Connecticut 1766-1775* (Philadelphia: Presbyterian Board of Publication and Sabbath-School Work, 1904), bound with *Records of Presbyterian Church,* p. 10.

55. *Minutes of the General Assembly,* pp. 29, 33, 52.

56. *Ibid.,* pp. 141-142, 147.

57. *Ibid.,* pp. 184, 209.

58. *Ibid.,* pp. 193, 197, 206.

59. *Ibid.,* pp. 212, 225.

60. *Ibid.,* pp. 224, 229, 250.

61. Standing Committee, MSS Minutes, I, 20.

62. *Ibid.,* pp. 11, 63, 70.

63. *Ibid.,* II, 109.

64. *Acts of Reformed Dutch Church,* pp. 288-289.

65. *Ibid.,* pp. 305, 308.

66. *Ibid.,* p. 331.

67. *Ibid.,* pp. 353, 425.

68. Blake, *Mendon Association,* p. 59.

69. Field, *County of Berkshire,* p. 148.

70. *Panoplist,* VI (March, 1811), 316.

71. George Punchard, *History of Congregationalism from About A.D. 250 to the Present Time* (5 vols.; Boston: Congregational Publishing Society, 1880), IV, 668.

72. *Panoplist,* IX (Sept., 1813), 284.

73. *CEM,* III (Dec., 1802), 237-38.

74. *Panoplist,* I (Nov., 1805), 272, 275.

75. *Ibid.,* VII (Oct., 1811), 157.

76. *CEM,* V (April, 1805), 129.

77. William B. Sprague, *The Life of Jedidiah Morse* (New York: Anson D. F. Randolph & Company, 1874), pp. 128ff.

78. *Panoplist,* I (Sept., 1805), 428-431.

79. See Mary Ellen Chase, *Jonathan Fisher: Maine Parson 1798-1847* (New York: The Macmillan Company, 1948), pp. 175ff, for an account of the work of this society from the viewpoint of one of its trustees and most active missionaries.

80. Brown, *Sermon before Maine Missionary Society,* p. 26.

81. Punchard, *History of Congregationalism,* IV, 676.

82. Walker, *History of Congregational Churches,* p. 313.

83. Joseph Allen, *History of Worchester Association of Ministers* (Boston: Nichols and Noyes, 1868), p. 33.

84. *Report of Rev. Mr. Puffer, to the Corresponding Secretary of the Evangelical Missionary Society. Also, the Report of the Trustees of Said Society At their Annual Meeting, October 5, 1808* (Worchester, Mass.: Isaiah Thomas, June, 1808), p. 11.

85. See Beaver, *All Loves Excelling,* pp. 13-57 for an account of the involvement of women in the early National Period.

86. Joshua Millet, *A History of the Baptists in Maine* (Portland: Printed by Charles Day & Co., 1845), pp. 192-200.

87. Quoted in Stephen Wright, *History of the Shaftsbury Baptist Association* (no biographical information in my copy), p. 81.

88. *Ibid.,* pp. 87ff.

89. Henry Crocker, *History of the Baptists in Vermont* (Bellows Falls, Vt.: Ph. H. Gobie Press, 1913) gives a rather full account of this participation. The second chapter contains the Journal of missionary Caleb Blood which details his work with Holmes while on his mission. See pp. 35-54.

90. Stephen Wright, *Shaftsbury Baptist Association,* p. 129.

91. See Letter of John Peck to John Mason Peck in Babcock, *John Mason Peck,* p. 54.

92. *The Vehicle or New-York Northwestern Christian Magazine,* I (Nov., 1814), 100.

93. *MBMM,* I, 21, 42.

94. Furman, *Charleston Association,* p. 34.

95. Mercer, *Georgia Baptist Association,* p. 39.

96. *GAR,* I (July and August, 1802), 55.

97. *MBMM,* I, 308.

98. Foote, *Sketches of North Carolina,* pp. 304, 451, 455. Hall was also under appointment of the General Assembly. *Minutes of the General Assembly,* p. 224. James Bowan and William Montgomery accompanied him.

99. *Ibid.,* pp. 461, 472, 473.

100. *Minutes of the General Assembly,* pp. 238, 377, 380.

101. *Ibid.,* p. 280.

102. Sweet, *Religion on Frontiers,* II, 605.

103. *Memoir of Badger,* pp. 109ff.

104. Sweet, *Religion on Frontiers,* II, 607.

105. *CEM,* I (March, 1801), 324.

106. Babcock, *John Mason Peck,* p. 46.

Chapter 6

The Mission Becomes Global

The apostolic age is returning.

Edward Griffin — 1816

The American Board of Commissioners for Foreign Missions (ABCFM) issued a small book in 1818 that caught the imagination of evangelicals in both America and Britain.

Written by Gordon Hall and Samuel Newell, the ABCFM's premier missionaries in Bombay, it was entitled *The Conversion of the World: or The Claims of Six Hundred Millions of Heathen, and the Ability and Duty of the Churches Respecting Them.* The book introduced a plan that, if carried out faithfully by all churches, would so multiply the number of missionaries and native preachers around the world that the command of Christ to teach all nations could be literally obeyed. Within twenty years the churches could convert the world.[1]

The plan, so stimulating and visionary at the time, had no lasting significance. Chur ches did not respond to the astounding challenge of the two brash, Yankee missionaries. The plan was naive and impractical. Nor were American Christians ready to make the commitment of money and personnel that the proposal demanded. However, that such a book could be addressed to the American churches, that Christian leaders would urge its consideration on American Christians, and that it would be quickly reprinted in England is important. These facts suggest something about the character of American Christianity in 1818.

The book was not addressed to Congregationalists, or even to all evangelical pedobaptists. "They address themselves immediately to the American *Churches* and *Christians,* without distinction of denomination."[2] The little book presumed the missionary shape of American Christianity. It presumed that American Christians were concerned about converting the entire world to Christ and willing to commit men and money to the task. This chapter will describe the process by which the American churches assumed a global task.

Heritage of the Indian Mission

The overseas mission of the American churches was not suddenly created

180

in the years following 1810. The formation of overseas societies represents a re-
surgence of the great impulse to win ungospelized nations to Christ, a return to
the task of converting the heathen peoples of the world. This impulse permeated
the Puritan mission of the Seventeenth Century. It occupied a significant place in
the missionary thought of the Eighteenth Century. It is this concern that provides
continuity between the Protestant World Mission, as it developed in the Nineteenth
Century, and the Colonial Indian Mission. The great influx of people into the American colonies and nation after 1750, the development of larger ecclesiastical bodies,
the spiritual destitution of the new frontier settlements, and the particular emphasis of revivalistic theology on personal conversion combined with the problems in-
herent in a struggling new nation to thwart this desire and to give it second place
to the task of churching the wilderness. Preoccupation with forming churches
among people nominally Christian is the major innovation of American missionary
activity in the Eighteenth Century. The earliest overseas societies herald the return
of the mission to the heathen to a place of prominence in the American churches.

The passion to convert the heathen was not lost in the flurry of missionary
organization of the early National Period. This cause was a constituent purpose in
almost every society organized after 1787. In some it was the sole reason for being.
The missionary associations and synods did not completely overlook the heathen.
There was no distinction between "home" and "foreign" missions in this period.
The societies that were constituted before 1810 understood their work to be one
with the work of the Baptist Missionary Society, the London Missionary Society,
and other organizations in western Europe that labored to win the people of non-
Christian lands to Christ.

The attention of the American societies quite naturally turned to the Red
Indians. These pagan tribes were immediately accessible to the American churches.
Many viewed the contiguous relationship as providential. Conversion of the American Indians was the peculiar responsibility of the American churches. But, there
was a partnership between the different missionary societies in one great task. William Carey wrote to the New York Missionary Society in this vein in 1800.

> The various tribes of American Indians appear to have a claim
> upon the American churches; or rather, perhaps we may say,
> that one great end of the existing of the churches in America
> is, to spread the glorious gospel among the heathens in their
> vicinity . . . churches may be looked upon as little encampments
> from which we are to sally out, in attack upon the great enemy.[3]

Thomas Haweis, one of the early leaders of the LMS, wrote to a friend in
Connecticut, June 26, 1799:

> It revives our inmost souls to see the spreading of the sacred flame
> in America, and the blessed hope, that tossed from the torpor of
> apathy, we are all beginning to feel the value of those souls that
> the son of God came down to save by his own most precious blood
> . . . Between the Allehany mountains and the Columbia river, which
> we hope ere long to visit, there will be a glorious space to traverse,

till we meet, in what point who can tell! But I trust the sound
will spread like the undulations of the pool till it shall reach
from the west to the east and from the east to the west.[4]

When the Andover students queried the General Association of Massachusetts, in 1810, the crucial question was not whether American churches
should evangelize the heathen, but "whether they ought to direct their attention
to the eastern or western world."[5] The new missionary endeavor was new only
because it was to take place in a new sphere. The ABCFM's second report explained:

On our own continent . . . there are many millions of men "sitting
in darkness and the region and shadow of death," and our brethren
in England may wonder that . . . we should turn our views to any
other part of the world. But attempts which have been made to
evangelize the aboriginal tribes of the North American wilderness,
have been attended with so many discouragements, and South
America is yet so unpromising a state, that . . . for the Pagans on
this continent but little can immediately be done. Hence, though
the hope is entertained, that the time is coming when the benevolent exertions . . . for spreading the knowledge of his name, may
be successfully employed nearer home; yet at present the Eastern
world is thought to offer a more promising field.[6]

One attempt had been made earlier to involve American Christians in sup-
porting an overseas mission addressed to pagan peoples. Samuel Hopkins and Ezra
Stiles instigated the formation of the African Education Society in 1773, for the
education and maintainance of Blacks preparing for missionary service in Western
Africa.[7] In 1788, John Erskine suggested that Stiles, Hopkins, Jonathan Edwards
Jr., and Samuel Wales jointly request that the Society in Scotland for Propagating
Christian Knowledge (SSPCK) fund this missionary effort. The group refused. In
1791, the secretary of the SSPCK wrote Hopkins requesting specific recommenda-
tions for suitable missionaries. Hopkins probably never replied. He insisted that he
did not know suitable men to recommend as a board of commissioners in New
England.[8]

The most important factor in establishing continuity with the early Indian
mission and in creating a purposeful unity between all the missionary societies of
the early National Period was theological. Missionary men conceived that the mission of the church in the world, the divine assignment to bring the peoples of the
earth to Christ, was identical with God's great work of redemption. Missionary
sermons, circular letters, magazine articles of the period, and, in fact, constitutions
of the various societies, abundantly attest this assertion. Samuel Spring said in 1802,
"The peculiar fruits of the cross will be displayed by the reformation of the world."[9]
Jonathan Allen told the young women who first went out to India:

My dear children — you are now engaged in the best of all causes.
It is that cause for which Jesus the Son of God came into the world
and suffered and died.[10]

Leonard Woods encouraged their husbands:

> The cause which you have enlisted, is the cause of divine love.
> You have chosen the noblest and most honorable work on
> earth.[11]

The way of speaking about the mission shifted somewhat in the overseas societies. The American experience — actual flesh and blood conflict with a literal, endless wilderness — compelled the missionary spokesmen to reserve the wilderness/paradise motif almost exclusively to the frontier mission after 1800. For the mission to the heathen, in all parts of the world, a familiar and related concept became prominent. "Darkness" described the pagan world. "Light" was the inevitable consequence when the gospel was faithfully proclaimed. The darkness/light theme assumed various expressions. "Blindness," "superstition," and "ignorance" were the conditions of heathen nations. Christ brought them "vision," "enlightenment," and "knowledge." The ABCFM's instruction to its first missionaries is typical.

> The great object of your Mission is to import to those who sit in
> darkness, and in the region and shadow of death, the saving knowl-
> edge of Christ.[12]

Occasionally the wilderness/paradise theme did become manifest in discussions of the overseas mission. Pliny Fisk said of his impending mission to Palestine:

> While you continue here to cultivate the vineyard of the Lord, we
> will go to plant . . . a branch of his vine in the land where it first
> grew.[13]

Warren Fay, discussing the success of the overseas missionaries, asked:

> Is it expected, that the Missionaries in the vast wilderness of Pagan-
> ism will see a verdant landscape blooming at their feet, . . . as soon
> as the first blow is struck, and the noise of the axe is heard? . . .
> shall not the Missionary . . . be allowed time to clear away the
> growth of a century, and break the ground, and scatter the seed,
> and nurture the rising plants, before you pronounce his labor
> unsuccessful and useless?[14]

Heman Humphrey developed the most extensive statement of the overseas mission in the context of the desert/garden concepts. In sermon at the ordination of the Sandwich Island missionaries, Humphrey exploited this theme to its fullest. As surely as God gave Canaan to Israel, he had also given the world to the Church. The Church had a "great work to accomplish in subduing the world 'to the obedience of Christ.' " In the covenant of redemption, Christ secured all the kingdoms of the earth. Thus, Christ gave the world to the Church in every promise "in which the universal spread of the gospel is mentioned."[15]

The missionary men of the American churches considered the heathen mission as one, whether conducted by American societies, European societies, or their Puritan precursors. Moreover, the mission was God's appointed means of setting up Christ's kingdom in the world. That great goal was "the end of God's creating the world."[16] The converting of the nations was the mission of God. In 1806, Eliphalet Nott expressed this concept of the mission well.

> I have read you from the records of eternity, the CHARTER of the Kingdom of Jesus Christ. A charter that covers all nations, extends over every clime, and comprehends the islands of every sea. That wilderness, inhabited by savages, belongs to Jesus; it is his husbandry, and in spite of *HELL*, he will one day gather its precious fruits.[17]

Toward Overseas Societies

The year 1810 is not the date American churches first began participating in the rising Protestant World Mission. It does mark the beginning of the first great missionary thrust of the American churches toward peoples outside the North American continent. Much has been written attempting to ascertain the social, economic and religious factors that led to this development. Four factors are axiomatic. The renewed vigor of the churches as a result of the Second Great Awakening and the influence of European missionary activity have been discussed at length. The growth of American foreign trade and the development of American nationalism merit attention. Also, the new alignment of religious parties in New England and the youth movement that developed in the college revivals after 1805 are also significant in the rise of the overseas mission.

The Growth of Foreign Trade

Historians have alleged that the development of international commerce had a direct influence on American missionary activity.

> An influence making for aroused interest in carrying the gospel to the "heathen" outside America was the widening of geographical knowledge . . . American shipping and commerce, cut off in the years immediately following independence by lack of trade agreements with other nations, sought profitable trade in China, India, and the Malay peninsula; and the knowledge of these distant lands and people thus brought to America served to add to the feeling of concern and responsibility for the carrying of the Gospel to needy people everywhere. It was therefore no accident that the first foreign missionaries to go out from America were ordained in the Congregational Church at Salem at whose docks lay many China clipper ships, whose captains and crews and cargoes had done so much to arouse New England interest in distant lands.[18]

Winthrop Hudson observed that

> the religious enthusiasm of the Second Awakening could not be contained within the national boundaries. News of the Orient

had been seeping back into New England during the early years of the Awakening. This was the era of the clipper ships and the Pacific trade, and every ship that returned to Salem or Boston brought tales of distant lands and strange people . . . In 1810 the "banding" of a number of students . . . led to the founding of the American Board of Commissioners for Foreign Missions.[19]

Overlooking the error concerning clipper ships, the first of which was not launched until 1843, the question is, did the growth of American international commerce stimulate markedly the commitment of the American churches to an overseas mission?

No direct relationship can be found between the development of foreign commerce and American missionary interest or activity. The period between the signing of the preliminary peace treaty between England and America in November, 1782, and the proclamation of peace in April, 1783, gave American merchants an opportunity to make arrangements for the resumption of legal trade. The Articles of Confederation did not provide for the regulation of commerce; commerce was left in the hands of the merchants. A great influx of imported goods and outflow of specie resulted in financial depression. The development of foreign trade was the reaction that came from the depression. New ways had to be discovered to conduct trade in the new political situation after Independence.[20] Trade began immediately after the end of the war and was a part of the economic recovery that began well before the federal constitution was adopted.[21] Overseas missionary activity developed much later. It did not follow the pattern of the development of foreign trade which one might expect if there were a direct relationship between the two.

The trade that developed in the Orient and the south sea islands had most significance to American missionary activity. American trade in these areas of the world was a consequence of efforts to trade with China. The first American ship arrived in Canton in 1784. In 1789, the *Columbia* landed on the American continent's Northwest Coast to acquire furs for China. American ships began landing in Hawaii in 1790. These three points were important to American trade. Decisions to send missionaries to these places did not grow out of this prolific commercial contact. In each case, a direct, dramatic event, not related to trade, stimulated the assumption of missionary activity.[22]

Several factors explain this lack of direct relationship. A large portion of those men involved in foreign commerce during this period were Quakers. In the early National Period, Quaker merchants were not interested in missionary schemes.[23] The development of liberal Christianity in New England followed class lines. Unitarianism developed among the elite, decision-making classes.[24] Merchants generally were members of this group and of churches that, at least, leaned toward Unitarian Christianity. Unitarianism was never aggressively involved in overseas missions. Finally, the seamen and traders who carried American commerce to these places were not usually noted for their religious commitment nor sympathetic with the work of missionaries.

The great growth of international commerce after 1785 did have its effect
on the rising Protestant World Mission in America. The influence, however, was not
direct and general but indirect and specific. First, foreign commerce made a structural and functional contribution to the sending of overseas missionaries. Missionary work invariably began where American traders had already gone. The trader was
a kind of pathfinder for the missionary. The fir st American ship reached the Pegu
harbor near Rangoon in 1793, ten years before the Judsons arrived. Gordon Hall
and Samuel Nott settled in Bombay in 1813 to begin their mission. As early as 1786,
another New Englander from Salem had already made his residence in Bombay for
purposes of trade.[25]

Missionary leaders realized early that discovery and trade greatly assisted the
expansion of Christianity. Many missionary sermons echo the words of John Emerson:

In no period to which history has presented the record, has the world
witnessed such a *rage,* for traveling and making discovery, which
prove successful, although undertaken and prosecuted without any
religious motives, or any regard to the spread of the gospel, yet by
removing obstacles, prepare the way for the conveyance of religious
knowledge into places which not long since were wholly unknown
to the rest of the world, and which, had it not been for the modern
improvements in navigation and the rage for exploring unknown
regions, would have been as yet undiscovered. Thus our enterprising
navigators have been unintentionally paving the way for the progress
of the Lord's work, whenever the set time to favor Zion comes.[26]

A second contribution of foreign trade to the development of American
missions is related to missionary support. A general relationship exists, though
certainly not a definite ratio, between the ability of churches to undertake a strong
mission program and the availability of funds. International commerce not only
contributed to the growing prosperity of the country, it also made men rich who
had a strong commitment to the extension of the Christian faith. John Norris of
Salem is a classic example. Norris was a major supporter of Andover Theological
Seminary. When the ABCFM was searching for monies in 1812 to outfit their
newly appointed missionaries, his widow made a contribution of $30,000.[27] This
is only one example of substantial support for the overseas missionary undertaking
that came because of the growth of foreign commerce. Many individual merchants
personally encouraged the missionary enterprise.

The frontier mission did not generate the dynamic and stewardship needed
to carry the financial load for evangelizing the heathen at home, for producing Bibles
and literature needed for the work, or in providing educational preparation for those
chosen to labor in the mission. "Actually, it was to require the launching of an overseas mission to open the wellsprings of giving and to develop resources adequate even
for domestic needs."[28] The overseas societies caught the imagination of the churches.
Rich and poor contributed to the missionary effort. The most significant contribution
that the growth of American trade made to the rise of the overseas societies was to
provide a significant source of wealth for the support of the growing enterprise.

The Beginning of American Nationalism

American nationalism began to flourish after the War of 1812. But budding nationalism was a factor in the close association between missionaries and the Continental Congress during the Revolution and played a formative part in the creation of the earliest American missionary societies.[29] By 1806, due primarily to maritime struggles with both Britain and France, a large portion of the population began to demand action to defend the nation's honor.[30] This nascent nationalism was emphatically expressed by missionary statesmen and volunteers. Samuel J. Mills Jr., was the personification of missionary intensity. When he heard, in 1809, that Adoniram Judson Jr. was considering the possibility of becoming a missionary of the LMS, Mills' reaction was sharp.

> What! Is England to support her own Missionaries and our likewise?
> O shame! If brother Judson is prepared, I would feign press him for-
> ward with the arm of an Hercules, if I had the strength; but I do not
> like this dependance on another nation.[31]

Jacob Norton, in a flurry of nationalistic pride, predicted in May, 1810, before the ABCFM was formed in September, that Americans would soon "go forth into every region of the inhabitable globe, with the everlasting gospel."[32] Gordon Hall, in a sermon delivered two days before he sailed for India, insisted that the blessing of God on the United States had put the young nation under a singular obligation to send the gospel to all nations.[33] Looking back on the first decade of American involvement in overseas missions, Sereno E. Dwight averred that the peculiar duty of the American churches was to furnish missionaries for the worldwide task.

> Here lies the duty of the Church of America. She alone is able to
> furnish in the requisite numbers the Missionaries of the Cross. The
> call of God on this subject is distinct and loud.[34]

The ABCFM expressed this spirit in 1811. The Board called for "American funds for the support of American missionaries."[35]

When the United Foreign Missionary Society (UFMS) was formed in 1817, American nationalism was becoming vocal. Its Board of Managers commended the ABCFM because it had "done much to redeem the American character" with its missionary exertions. The goals and responsibilities of the UFMS were described in highly nationalistic terms.

> As soon as the southern forests yield to the hand of cultivation,
> our limits will extend to Mexico; and the whole region of death
> from the river Del Norte to Cape Horn, . . . will reach from our
> own door. Who on earth, rather than ourselves, are the people to
> pour the river of life through that desolate region?[36]

Developing American nationalism was a factor in the formation of the overseas societies.

New Alignments in New England

The Unitarian Controversy is alleged to have altered the ecclesiastical scene in New England as profoundly as did the Great Awakening. It made a distinct contribution to the formation of the earliest overseas missionary society. In 1790, the clergy of the Standing Order churches in Massachusetts were divided theologically into Arminians, Anti-trinitarians, moderate Calvinists and Hopkinsians. Only the Hopkinsians were clearly identified as a group. The Arminians and Anti-trinitarians joined forces in the election of Henry Ware in 1805 as theological professor at Harvard. The election became an act of party warfare.[37] The consequence was the union and cooperation of Hopkinsians and moderate Calvinists in the Bay state, much as the old Calvinists, Edwardseans and Hopkinsians had formed an evangelical party in Connecticut.

All theological types cooperated in the Society for Propagating the Gospel among the Indians and Others in North America (SPGNA). It was a product of the pervasive social intercourse that existed among the clergy of the Boston vicinity before controversy forced distinctions. The secretaryship of Jedidiah Morse and the close association of the SPGNA with the SSPCK helped keep the American society basically orthodox until after 1817. Only in the SPGNA did the Liberal Party, both Trinitarian and Unitarian, continue in the mainstream of American missionary activity. This involvement and cooperation waned decidedly after 1805.

The reason for this diminishing involvement by the Liberal Party can be found in the change in structure of cooperation in Massachusetts after 1805. The conflict over the election of Henry Ware caused the parties to draw lines. The Orthodox did not withdraw from membership in the SPGNA. They did shift their primary allegiance and best efforts to the Massachusetts Missionary Society, in 1799, to the Massachusetts Society for Promoting Christian Knowledge, in 1803, and, finally, to the ABCFM, in 1810.

The chief statesman in bringing about this new coalition was Jedidiah Morse.

> Dr. Morse early formed the purpose of doing his utmost to effect an important change in the ecclesiastical condition of Massachusetts — first, by separating the Unitarians from the Orthodox, and then, by drawing the Orthodox of different shades into more intimate relations.[38]

Morse established direct contact with Hopkinsians through the MMS. He was a director. He maintained close contact with Old Calvinists and New Divinity leaders in Connecticut. He formed close friendships with Presbyterian leaders and Evangelical spokesmen in Scotland and England. And he aggressively enlisted the moderate Calvinists in Massachusetts on the side of Orthodoxy.

Morse began to edit and publish the *Panoplist* in 1805. One of his private goals for the magazine was "an amicable coalescence, at a future time, with the great Body of Hopkinsians."[39] Morse won the friendship of Leonard Woods, the most able young Hopkinsian in New England, and enlisted his aid in the *Panoplist,* though Woods was a chief contributor to the *Massachusetts Missionary Magazine.* Woods was a key figure in the enlistment of Hopkinsians in the General Association of Massachusetts. This organization was the fir st attempt to bring the two groups together in an institutional framework.[40] Through the instrumentality of Morse and Woods, the moderate Calvinists and Hopkinsians discovered that each group was planning to establish a theological school. A cooperative endeavor was proposed. Woods' attachment to the scheme was the primary factor that persuaded the Hopkinsians to join in the creation of Andover Seminary.[41] The new alignment in New England prepared the way for the first overseas society. It was natural, when the time came to form a society for conducting a mission to the heathen, both East and West, that students from Andover Seminary would apply to members of the General Association of Massachusetts, who, in turn, would form a board of commissioners in which Hopkinsians and other Calvinists could cooperate.

The Student Movement

A student movement was the catalyst which actually initiated the organization of the overseas societies. It began in New England, spread to the Middle States, and eventually provided the personnel that enabled the American churches to man their farflung missionary endeavor before the Civil War. The student movement directly influenced the creation of the first three overseas societies.

The ground-swell of student missionary commitment provided the spark that the American churches needed to turn their energy to the heathen peoples of the world. Neither the example of European societies nor the birth of a more fervent nationalism was sufficient. This eruption of youthful enthusiasm and life commitment by college and seminary students occasioned the new surge of American missionary efforts.

Letters and journals of the early volunteers and youthful advocates of the overseas mission suggest two main ideas captured their imagination. First, they were determined that American churches conduct a mission to convert the heathen. The students correctly perceived that the mission to the frontier settlements had starved the mission to pagan peoples. They called for a return of the spirit of Eliot and Brainerd. This interest turned the attention of the students to peoples outside of North America. In 1809, Samuel J. Mills Jr., met Henry Obookiah in New Haven. Obookiah was a Hawaiian lad who had come to New England on a merchant ship. Edward Dwight, then tutor at Yale College, had begun privately to teach him the rudiments of an English education and of the Christian faith. Mills and Obookiah became friends. Mills wrote to Gordon Hall, soon after he met Henry Obookiah, explaining that Obookiah had expressed a desire to return to teach his own people.

> What does this mean? Brother Hall, do you understand it? Shall he be sent back unsupported, to attempt to reclaim his countrymen? Shall we not rather consider these southern islands a proper place for the establishment of a mission? Not that I would give up the heathen tribes of the West. I trust we shall be able to establish more than one mission in a short time . . . We ought not to look

merely to the heathen on our own continent, but to direct our
attention where we may, to human appearance, do the most
good, and where the difficulties are the least . . . O that we
might glow with desire to preach the Gospel to the heathen
that is altogether irristible.[42]

The second concept to which the students were committed related to the
missionary calling. They were convinced that the missionary vocation should be
for life. The frontier mission was conducted by itinerants who labored on "missionary ground" for only a few months each year. The mission in which these students wished to engage was a life-long affair. Harriet Atwood wrote to a friend in
Boston:

What will you say to me when I tell you, that I *do* think, seriously
think of quitting my native land forever, and going to a far distant
country . . . Should I refuse to make this sacrifice, refuse to lend
my little aid in the promulgation of the Gospel amongst the heathen,
how could I ever expect to enjoy . . . peace of conscience, though
surrounded by every temporal mercy? . . . I must relinquish their
society (friends and family), and follow God to a land of strangers,
where millions of my fellow sinners are perishing for lack of vision.[43]

Adoniram Judson recalled this passion twenty-five years later when he
recounted how the original group came together at Andover.

Some . . . had thought chiefly of domestic missions, and efforts
among the neighboring tribes of Indians, without contemplating
abandonment of country, and devotement for life. The reading
and reflection of others had led them in a different way; and
standing on the ground of *foreign* missions and *missions for life,*
the subject assumed in our minds such an overwhelming importance and awful solemnity, as bound us to one another, and to
our purpose more firmly than ever.[44]

The student movement was born in the revival, that swept college and seminary campuses after the turn of the century. In 1802, a significant student awakening occurred at Yale.[45] One-half of the seniors were converted, and one-third of the
class entered the ministry. Several, including Jeremiah Evarts, became prominent
leaders in the missionary movement. In 1806, a revival gripped the campus of little
Williams College in Massachusetts. Samuel J. Mills Jr. according to one of his class-
mates, was the chief instrument of the awakening.[46] Mills had been converted in
1798, in a revival in his father's parish in Torringford, Connecticut. He went to
Williams College convinced of a divine call to preach the gospel to the heathen. For
many of the students who were converted in the revival, the period was also an
awakening to missionary responsibility. A number of students left Williams College
for further theological study already devoted personally to "a mission or missions
to the heathen."[47]

In 1808, another revival broke out at Yale. Samuel J. Mills was there for

some months in 1809, primarily interested in the enlistment of students in the
missionary cause. More revivals followed at Yale. The actual sailing of the missionaries for India stimulated additional interest. Revivals followed on most college
campuses north and east of Philadelphia shortly after their departure. In a report
in 1815 concerning the revivals of that year in Dartmouth, Princeton and Yale,
the editors of the *CBM* explained:

> most of our important Seminaries of education have been blessed
> with the rich effusions of his grace. As the evidence of this, many
> of the younger pastors of our chur ches, who afford a fair prospect
> of being eminent blessings to the cause of the Redeemer, as well as
> many in civil life . . . fix the commencement of their Christian life
> at those interesting periods.[48]

The report might also have said that most of the missionaries involved in the overseas mission began their lives as Christians and their devotion to the missionary
vocation in the college awakenings.

The energies of the youth movement were turned toward the heathen mission through two principle agencies. Samuel J. Mills Jr. had led in the organization
of the *Sol Oriens* Society on September 8, 1808, at Williams College. This society
grew out of a group that met weekly to pray for a revival on the campus. This society, which soon changed its name to the Society of Brethren, functioned to effect
a mission to the heathen in the persons of its members. After the Brethren moved
to Andover and had stimulated the formation of the ABCFM, these same young
men gave leadership to the organization of the "Society of Inquirey on the subject
of Missions." This society was the first agent behind the "tremendous missionary
and intercollegiate activity emanating from Andover" during the next fifty years.
Interested students, challenged by the example of Andover, organized "Societies
for Inquirey" on almost every evangelical educational institution in America. The
societies usually met monthly, discussed some missionary problem or debated a
missionary question, and regularly corresponded with other Societies of Inquiry
in other schools.[49] What was born in spiritual awakening was channeled into the
missionary enterprise.

The second agent used to inform and enlist the students was the literature
that the movement produced. Missionary sermons had been published and distributed energetically for fifteen years before the overseas societies were formed. These
sermons, printed in tract form, compose the largest part of the early missionary
literature in America.[50] Evangelical and missionary magazines had been regularly
published in the same period. These continued for many years to be powerful tools
for raising both money and men. When William Staughton and Luther Rice launched
The Latter Day Luminary, in 1818, they called magazines the "signal fires of the
present time," which "convey . . . the joyous news that the feast of the Lord is
come."[51]

The overseas missionaries and their friends very early produced their own
literature. Their letters, published and republished in the missionary magazines
and annual reports, were avidly read. Written both by the missionaries and their

wives, these letters added excitement and romance to the overseas mission. Soon the overseas mission developed a hagiology. In 1815, two books had been issued which detailed the brief life of Harriett Newell.[52] The year that *The Conversion of the World* came from the press, E. W. Dwight issued a memoir of Henry Obookiah who died before he could return to the Sandwich Islands.[53] That same year, 1818, Samuel J. Mills Jr. died at sea on a return trip from West Africa. Gardiner Spring's account of his life, in 1820, made him the third member of this body of saints.

Through revivals, missionary organizations and propaganda, the student movement was the catalyst for the formation of the overseas societies and provided the personnel for the growing missionary endeavor.

The First Three Overseas Societies

By 1817, the die was cast that molded American Christianity with a pronounced missionary character. When that year ended, this country had three organizations designed to conduct "foreign" missions. These were only the beginning. Methodists followed with an overseas society in 1819. Episcopalians organized their Domestic and Foreign Missionary Society in 1821. American involvement in the rising Protestant World Mission continued to mount for a hundred and fifty years. A functioning board of foreign missions became a distinctive responsibility for mainstream denominations in America. So, 1817 was a plateau from which "foreign" missions became the *cause celebre* of the American churches.

The first three societies set the pattern in terms of structure and objectives. The formation of these societies was a climax to all that had happened in the past quarter century. The "missionary spirit" that was abroad in the land reached its ultimate incarnation in the overseas societies. The apostolic age was returning.[54]

The American Board of Commissioners for Foreign Missions

The ABCFM was formed by the action of the General Association of Massachusetts at its annual meeting in Bradford, June 29, 1810. The action was in response to the "*statement* and inquiries" presented under the name of four students from Andover Seminary the day before. Careful preparation preceded the petition. The number signing the document was limited to four to avoid undue alarm. Professor Moses Stuart arranged an earlier interview between the students and three of the most influential leaders of Congregationalism in Massachusetts. Samuel Worcester, Samuel Spring and Jeremiah Evarts were won to the cause before the General Association met. Worcester and Spring were named to the committee to study the students' request.

The petition did not suggest that an overseas society be formed. But, when the Association reconvened, it voted to form a "Board of Commissioners for foreign Missions." The century-old concept of a Board of Commissioners was combined with the idea of an overseas mission. The new Board was to elect nine members annually, five by the General Association of Massachusetts and four by the General Association of Connecticut. Its purpose was to devise ways and means "for promoting the spread of the Gospel in heathen lands."[55]

The ABCFM was not, in its first years of activity, the ecumenical organization that it became after 1820, nor was it originally designed on that scale. It did not even have the support of all the Standing Order Churches in Massachusetts. The General Association of Massachusetts was a small, struggling organization in 1810. Ignored and avoided by many moderate Calvinists, despised as sectarian by Liberals, and highly suspect to many Hopkinsians, this body had to go into print in 1809 to justify its existence.[56] Only ten of twenty-four ministerial associations sent delegates in 1810. The General Association was presumptuous to place itself beside the General Association of Connecticut, which was by law a representative body of Standing Order Churches in that state and had just begun the second century of its existence.

The ABCFM considered itself a New England society through much of its first ten years. During the era of the War of 1812 and the agitation for New England secession from the Union, there was reluctance to be anything but a New England society. Parts of the "Address to the Christian Public" in 1811 suggest a New England nationalism.

> It appears that *a great and effectual* door for the promulgation of the Gospel among the heathen is now opened to all Christian nations: but to no nation is it more inviting, than to the people of New England . . . No nation ever experienced the blessings of the Christian religion more evidently, and uniformly, than the inhabitants of New England.[57]

In 1812, the ABCFM became an incorporated, self-perpetuating body politic. Immediately, Board members were elected from Philadelphia and New York. However, during its first ten years the Board never met outside New England, only four non-Congregational Board members ever attended its annual meetings, and its officers continued to be men of the New England Standing Order.

During the first decade, the affairs of the Board and its missions were handled well. New England Christians responded liberally. The missionaries performed with energy and creativity. Indeed, the influence of the ABCFM broke the boundaries of New England parochialism.

By 1817, the ABCFM had a much broader view of itself. Not limited to certain geographical boundaries or to a single denomination of Christians, it still welcomed the United Foreign Missionary Society to share the "great work of beneficence."[58] Looking back over the first ten years, Samuel Worcester, pastor in Salem and first secretary of the ABCFM, exclaimed,

> For this great object, this Board . . . possess advantages, which cannot be too highly prized. Its constitution is eminently adapted to vigorous action . . . It is limited to no section of the country, — to no denomination (sic) of Christians. Its members, chartered and corresponding, and its patrons, auxiliaries and agents are in all the States of the Union, and of nearly all the considerable religious communions. In its form and spirit —

its arrangements and provisions — its whole design and system of action — it is a NATIONAL INSTITUTION.[59]

Until 1870, the ABCFM was a great ecumenical society in which various denominational bodies cooperated.

At the Board's first meeting, a constitution was adopted. The "object of this Board was to devise, adopt, and prosecute, ways and means for propagating the gospel among those who are destitute of the knowledge of Christianity." The ABCFM was never strictly an overseas society. A mission to the heathen was its goal. At the first meeting the prudential committee was instructed to research "the state of the unevangelized nations on the western and eastern continents." "In our own country," the Board explained,

> the missionary spirit is excited, and much has already been done
> for imparting the gospel to . . . our new and frontier settlements.
> But for the millions on our own continent and in other parts of
> the world, we have yet those exertions to make, which comport
> with the Savior's emphatical directions.

The justification of a new society was those young people who had presented themselves "devoted for life to the service of God, . . . and ready to go into any part of the unevangelized world, where providence shall open the door for their missionary labors."[60]

The first eight missionaries sailed for India in February, 1812. Problems discouraged the mission for four years. War with England was declared a few weeks before the missionaries arrived in Calcutta. The war was an economic disaster for New England. The East India Company was totally hostile to the mission. The missionaries were dispersed to various ports. Not until 1813 did those remaining with the mission receive permission to remain in Bombay. The missionary band was quickly depleted. The Judsons and Luther Rice became Baptists. Harriet Newell died on Ceylon. Shortly after Samuel Newell arrived in Bombay, the Samuel Notts returned home.

By 1817, the status of the mission greatly improved. A second group of missionaries arrived in Ceylon in 1815. They were well received, and their mission was under way. In November, 1816, Horatio Bardwell and family arrived in Bombay. The translating and printing aspect of the mission got under way. More important, the mission received full approval for British authorities.

The Board's western mission began more slowly. The prudential committee recommended in 1811 that the Board settle on a specific missionary station in the East "and upon some place within the territories of the Indians of this continent for a missionary station in the West." The next year, the Board joined with the Hampshire Missionary Society in the educational expenses of Eleazer Williams in anticipation of a mission among the Cahnawaga people in Canada. The war and Williams' personal problems made this impossible. The Board planned for Edward Warren and Benjamin C. Meigs to undertake an Indian mission. Warren's health failed him. By 1815 the prudential committee had suspended but not "ultimately relinquished" plans for a western mission.[61]

The following year, 1816, the committee reported a new and exciting "Plan for evangelizing American pagans." While evangelizing the scattered tribes of the American West was not of the same magnitude as the eastern world, it had peculiar claims on the American churches. Few instances since the apostolic age could be compared to the labors of "Eliot, the Mayhews and Brainerd, among the Indians."

> It is no wonder that since their day little has been achieved; for little, very little, has been attempted. The spirit of Eliot, of the Mayhews, and of Brainerd, has for a long time slept. Never indeed has the work of civilizing and christianizing our Indian tribes been taken up on a well concerted and extended plan, and conducted with vigor and perseverance; never has such an experiment been made as is now contemplated. To establish schools in the different parts of the tribe . . . for the instruction of the rising generation in common school learning, in the useful arts of life, and in Christianity, so as . . . to make the whole tribe English in their language, civilized in their habits, and Christian in their religion; this is the present plan.[62]

Cyrus Kingsbury was on his way to Tennessee to survey the Cherokee Nation when the ABCFM met.

In Kingsbury the ABCFM had a devout Christian and indefatigable worker. In 1817 the Cherokee mission was launched. It became one of the most significant missions of the ABCFM in the Nineteenth Century.

One other project received the support of the ABCFM before 1818. In 1809, Samuel J. Mills Jr. met Henry Obookiah at Yale. Obookiah attended Bradford Academy briefly and spent some time at Andover. During this time he was converted. He and Mills dreamed of heading a mission to the Sandwich Islands. While interest was being aroused about Obookiah, three other Hawaiians were discovered. In 1816, a group of interested people led by Joseph Harvey and Charles Prentice proposed that a school be established to train these young men and others like them for missionary service among their own people. The Board elected seven men to form a plan for "establishing and conducting a school for the education of heathen youths in this country."[63] The Foreign Mission School was opened in Cornwall, Connecticut, in October, 1817. For a decade this institution continued to have the support of the ABCFM.

By the end of 1817 the ABCFM was well established. It supported missionaries in Bombay, on the Island of Ceylon and among the Cherokees. It had launched an educational institution in New England and had collected over $30,000 in that year for the mission cause. Some of the young men who were involved in the creation of the ABCFM had become the instruments for the formation of two other overseas societies in the United States.

The Baptist Board of Foreign Missions

The General Missionary Convention of the Baptist Denomination in the United States of America for Foreign Missions was formed in Philadelphia on May 20, 1814, at a "meeting of the Delegates from associated bodies of the baptist denomination . . . for the purpose of diffusing evangelic light, through the benighted regions of the earth."[64] The Convention was designed to meet once in three years. A twenty-one member "Board of Commissioners," denominated "Baptist Board of Foreign Missions," was given responsibility to conduct missionary affairs.

Baptists in America had been talking about getting together for forty years. After the Continental Congress refused to disallow religious taxation, in 1775, the Warren Association sent a letter to all the Baptists on the continent proposing a general meeting of delegates from all the associations to discuss means of securing full religious freedom.[65] Members of the Philadelphia Association called for a "general conference" in 1799, and requested that the different associations react to the suggestion. The following year, the call was renewed, and the Association, in response to a query of William Staughton's church in Philadelphia, also voted

> to invite the general committee of Virginia and different Associa-
> tions on the continent, to unite with us in laying a plan for form-
> ing a missionary society, and establishing a fund for its support,
> and for employing missionaries among the natives of our continent.[66]

Nothing came of these movements toward a national union. However, what Baptists would not do for separation of church and state or for frontier and Indian evangelization, they were persuaded to do for Luther Rice, Adoniram and Ann Judson and the Eastern mission.

Baptists had been involved, in a limited way, in the support of the mission of English Baptists for over twenty years. Since the earliest news arrived in America about William Carey and his associates, Baptist associations had collected monies for the mission. Direct and sometimes lengthy contact with English Baptist missionaries on their way to India by way of the United States also provided other opportunities to give monetary support to the mission in India.[67] However, little consideration was given to forming an American society. Carey himself discouraged such plans. He wrote to William Staughton, July 30, 1807,

> It has always been by opinion, that all in America, whose hearts
> the Lord stirs up to this work, should either go to the Indians . . .
> of their own country, or to the neighboring islands, Cuba, St.
> Domingo, &c.[68]

Staughton, who had been present in 1792 when the Baptist Missionary Society was organized in England, published, in 1811, *The Baptist Mission in India,* a book detailing the rise and progress of the English mission and "intended to animate to Missionary Co-operation."[69] He was after American support for the English mission.

The earliest efforts of American Baptists for foreign missions was in coopera-
tion with the BMS. Beofre Adoniram Judson sailed for India, he suggested to Lucius
Bolles, young pastor of the Baptist Church in Salem, Massachusetts, that American
Baptists form a society "in imitation of the exertions of their English brethren."[70]
Bolles and his church organized the Salem Bible and Translation Society in April,
1812, before the ABCFM missionaries arrived in Calcutta. The object of the
Society was to

> raise money to aid the translation of the scriptures into the Eastern
> languages . . . Or, if deemed advisable . . . to assist in sending . . .
> Missionaries from this country to India.[71]

The same day that Judson wrote Samuel Worcester that he and his wife had become
Baptists, he also wrote Thomas Baldwin and Lucius Bolles expressing a hope that a
Baptist society might be formed to support them.[72] In six weeks Luther Rice had
joined Baptist ranks. Judson wrote again that if Baptists in America adopted a plan
to support them it would be better to have a separate American Baptist society.
Nevertheless, an organization auxiliary to the BMS would be acceptable.[73] Carey
wrote suggesting the same procedure. He put into words what many Baptists in
America already believed.

> The change of sentiment in brethren Judson and Rice, is a strong
> inducement for you . . . and lays the churches in America under
> obligations different from any under which they lay before.[74]

By the time Rice returned to America on September 7, 1813, the possibility
of organizational cooperation had vanished. War made it a moot question. Thomas
Baldwin and Daniel Sharp had already led in the formation of the Baptist Society
for Propagating the Gospel in India and other Foreign Parts, in January, 1813. The
Constitution of this Society looked toward a more extensive organization.

> Should Societies be formed in other places . . . the Board will
> appoint one or more persons to unite with delegates from other
> Societies in forming a *General Committee* . . . more effectually
> to accomplish the important objects contemplated by this
> institution.[75]

Baldwin was especially firm in his insistence that Boston and New England
not make plans to undertake the overseas mission alone.

Luther Rice spent only three weeks in New England. On September 29, he
left Boston to visit the Middle States. His reception among Baptists there was so
great that he was encouraged to go on toward the South to form "foreign" societies
and enlist Baptists there in a plan for a general committee. In Charleston he met
W. B. Johnson who suggested that the general meeting be held in Philadelphia. But
Johnson, and others in the South, wanted a different approach. They did not want
a general committee of delegates from the newly formed societies. They wanted an
organization, as Johnson said in an "Address" to the people of South Carolina,
through

which the energies of the whole Baptist denomination throughout
America, may be elicited, combined and directed in one sacred
effort for sending the word of life to idolatrous lands.[76]

Consequently a "convention" was formed in Philadelphia, not a society or
committee. The goal was to enlist the resources of the entire denomination. This
structure became a source of conflict and one of the factors that contributed to
the division of the Convention.[77]

During the first three years the Board of Missions was occupied primarily
in developing financial support for the mission and sending new missionaries to
Burma. The travel and activities of Luther Rice in this period is fantastic. He itinerated over the entire nation leaving new societies in his wake. William Staughton
reported to the Convention in 1817 that "the whole Baptist denomination throughout our country appear to have caught the holy flame."[78]

In December, 1815, George H. Hough, his wife, and Mrs. Charlotte H.
White, the first single woman missionary, sailed for Burma. The appointment of
Mrs. White met opposition both at home and in Burma.[79] She never arrived in
Rangoon. In Calcutta she met and married an English Baptist missionary.

During the first three years, the Board of Missions designed a much more
extensive operational program to recommend to the Convention. From the beginning, it was understood that the activities of the Convention might not be confined
only to an overseas mission. The first "Address" that the Board directed to the
American public stated plainly that in the future the Indians would receive the
attention of the Convention. Hope was also expressed that something might be
done toward improving ministerial education.[80] At the Convention in 1817, the
recommendations of the Board

> that the powers of this Convention be extended so as to embrace
> home missions and plans for the encouragement of education

were adopted.[81]

Actually, the Board had already taken major steps in anticipation of the
approval of the Convention. Luther Rice had enlisted John Mason Peck and John
E. Welch for a Western Mission in 1815.[82] They had been studying in Philadelphia
under Staughton for a year when the delegates convened. James A. Ranaldson had
made application to the Board for appointment as a missionary in the vicinity of
New Orleans. Humphrey Posey had expressed a desire to work among the Cherokees. Isaac McCoy had requested an appointment to a mission in the vicinity of
Vincennes. When the Convention adjourned on May 14th, the Board went immediately to work to launch its Western Mission.

On May 16, James A. Ranaldson was employed as a missionary in the New
Orleans vicinity and instructed to "visit such Indians as are most contiguous" to
discover if missionary schools might be started among them. The evangelization of
Red Indians was especially emphasized. The Board adopted a resolution of Daniel

Sharp to accept the first suitable person to "offer for Indian service." On May 17, Welch and Peck were appointed to St. Louis and also instructed

> to enquire into the state of the Indian nations in that section of
> the country with a view to the establishment of a Mission among
> them.[83]

The two young men were ordained and had departed in one week.

The manning of the Western Mission continued for the rest of the year. Isaac McCoy was appointed for a frontier mission on September 5, 1817. Before his commission arrived he had determined to attempt a mission to the Indians. McCoy had a long and controversial career as an Indian missionary.[84] On October 13th, Humphrey Posey was employed to begin a mission among the Cherokees.[85]

Immediate steps were taken by the Board to begin a theological institution. Cooperation with the Baptist Education Society of Philadelphia, of which Staughton was president, was inevitable. By the time of the Annual Report of 1818, the Institution for Improving the Education of Pious Young Men had been formed with Staughton as principal and Ira Chase as professor.[86]

In April, 1816, a group of Black Baptists in Richmond formed the African Baptist Missionary Society. Before the Convention met in 1817, its trustees addressed the Board, wanting to cooperate in establishing an African mission manned by American Blacks. The Convention instructed the Board, if it were possible, to "institute an African Mission."[87] In 1819, Lott Carey and Collin Teague, members of the African Society, were nominated to the Board as missionaries. In 1821 they sailed for a mission in Monrovia.

The general character of the Convention was restricted again in 1820. In 1826 it was limited strictly to heathen missions. However, by 1817, the Board of Foreign Missions was established as the principal missionary agency of American Baptists and had undertaken a diversified missionary program.

The United Foreign Missionary Society

The United Foreign Missionary Society was formed July 28, 1817, in New York City. Prepared by a joint committee from the Presbyterian, Reformed Dutch, and Associate Reformed Churches, its constitution had been approved by the highest judicatories of those Churches. The object of the new society was to "spread the Gospel among the Indians of North America, the Inhabitants of Mexico and South America, and in other portions of the heathen and anti-christian world." The Board of Managers, set up to conduct all the missionary business of the Society, explained:

> The period of harmony, and of evangelical exertion has at length
> arrived. It will give pleasure to the friends of Zion to hear, that the
> three great Denominations in America who are allied to each other
> by the form of their ecclesiastical government, as well as by a com-

mon faith, have entered unitedly and in earnest, on the business
of Foreign Missions.[88]

Complex factor s combined to bring this third overseas society into existence. After the ABCFM was formed, there was a groundswell of interest among
Presbyterians in an overseas mission. Samuel Worcester wrote Eliphalet Nott,
moderator of the General Assembly, early in 1812. He urged the General Assembly to form an institution like the ABCFM that Congregationalists and Presbyterians might cooperate to "promote the great object of missions amongst unevangelized nations." The General Assembly did not undertake that task. "The numerous and extensive engagements . . . in regard to domestic missions" made it impossible.[89] When Archibald Alexander delivered the missionary sermon for the General
Assembly in 1814, he acknowledged the responsibility of American Christians for
the American Indians and Blacks, but the vast numbers of pagans in the East and
their responsiveness to the Gospel prompted him to hope for something new.

> Undoubtedly a new era has commenced, in regard to the propagation
> of the gospel. And shall our church, as numerous as any . . . remain
> idle spectators of the exertions of others? . . . Can we be contented
> to prosecute the great business of missions, in the same cold and cir-
> cumscribed manner? . . . I sincerely hope, that the General Assembly
> . . . will, at their present sessions, take the subject of foreign mission
> into serious consideration.[90]

Nothing was done, but individual leaders in the Presbyterian Church continued
to cooperate with and promote the ABCFM's work.

The interest in overseas missions was tempered by an intensified reaction
to New England theology, particularly Hopkinsianism. Gardiner Spring was in-
stalled as pastor of the Brick Church in New York, in August, 1810. The young
pastor, son of Samuel Spring and graduate of Andover, was immediately suspect.
In 1811, Ezra Stiles Ely, Alms House and Hospital preacher in the city, published
a book contrasting statements of Calvin and Hopkins.[91] It was aimed, said Gardiner Spring, "to prejudice and ignorance, and . . . the youthful pastor of the Brick
Church."[92] This marked the beginning of five years of agitation against Hopkinsians in New York.

In 1814, the theological students of John M. Mason, Associate Reformed
leader in the city, attacked Hopkinsianism as an error on a par with Socinianism.
These views, they asserted, would bring Christ to the death of the cross, "all upon
an uncertain speculation, to save all men, or no man, just as the caprice of mortals
shall determine."[93] Early in 1816, Hopkinsian Samuel Whelpley issued a series of
pamphlets which were an open attack upon traditional Calvinism at the point of
original sin, inability, and atonement. According to Calvinists, he insisted,

> man is . . . condemned, incapacitated, and eternally reprobated
> for the sin of Adam; . . . is condemned over again, for not doing
> that which he is totally . . . unable to do; and . . . is . . . trebly
> condemned, for not believing in a Saviour, who never died for

him, and with whom he has no more to do than a fallen angel.

He insisted that Hopkinsianism was true Calvinism and that those who taught otherwise were persecuting bigots.[94]

The controversy surfaced in missionary circles that year. The Young Men's Missionary Society, auxiliary to the NYMS, attempted to appoint Samuel Cox, one of Gardiner Spring's students as a missionary. Though Spring was chairman of the Committee of Missions, Cox was summarily rejected by the Society. The minority organized the New York Evangelical Missionary Society for Young Men.[95]

Gardiner Spring weathered the storm. He became a staunch defender of the mission boards of the General Assembly against voluntary societies. In 1817, however, his leadership among Presbyterians was not established.

Ezra Stiles Ely, now a pastor in Philadelphia, carried the fight to the Synod of Philadelphia in 1816. In the Synod's Pastoral Letter, he said,

> all the Presbyteries are more than commonly alive to the importance
> of contending earnestly for the faith . . . and of resisting the introduc-
> tion of Arian, Socinian, Arminian and Hopkinsian heresies, . . . by
> which the enemy of souls would . . . deceive the very elect.[96]

The General Assembly of 1817 rebuked Ely and the Synod for their untempered zeal. However, it was this same General Assembly which took action to work officially in a more closely controlled and more theologically orthodox foreign missionary society.

The American Bible Society (ABS), organized in 1816, set the stage for the formation of the UFMS. This organization should be considered on a par with the overseas societies as a manifestation of the missionary spirit. Missionary leaders considered the ABS of equal importance to the missionary society in the conversion of the world. The General Assembly spelled out the relationship in 1818.

> Bible societies in our day are related to missionary societies, as
> the gift of tongues was related in the commission of the apostles
> in the primitive church.[97]

Bible societies provided a new form of inter-denominational cooperation at a time when non-sectarian societies were breaking up and new societies controlled by a particular denominational viewpoint were springing up everywhere.

The Bible Society, like so many other developments that strengthened the mission of the American churches, arose through the inspiration of the overseas mission. In 1805, Benjamin Wickes, ship's captain and friend of missionaries, arrived in Philadelphia with ten thousand guineas to be sent to India for use in Serampore in the translation of the Bible into the languages of the Hindus. Invitations were published for Americans to enlarge the fund. The purpose was to promulgate the "pure word of eternal life contained in the Scriptures, without any gloss or comment."[98] This led to the formation of the Philadelphia Bible Society in December, 1807.

This society did not intend to be of national scope because the founders feared it would be "unwieldy and languish in all places, except the centre of its operations."[99] They urged the formation of other societies in the principle towns of the nation. The response was astonishing. Societies were organized in all parts of the countries, even on the most remote frontiers.

Samuel J. Mills Jr. and John D. Shermerhorn were sent on an intelligence mission through the West in 1812. They were supported by a number of Congregational societies. Soon after their return, Mills returned to the Mississippi Valley with David Smith, a Presbyterian, taking with him thousands of Bible portions. The report of the journey and personal promotion by Mills led to the formation of the American Bible Society in May, 1816, just before the convening of the Presbyterian General Assembly.[100]

The ABS was a true nonsectarian body. Its membership encompassed all denominational types, including Quakers and Methodists. Its principal officers, however, were Elias Boudinot, Presbyterian; John M. Mason, Associate Reformed, and John B. Romeyn, Dutch Reformed. The organizational meeting was a spectacular event and suggested to the more progressive leaders of classical Calvinist churches that a much more significant level of cooperation might be achieved. When the UFMS was formed, its Board of Managers said it was the most important event in the history of the city of New York, "except that which gave birth to the American Bible Society."[101]

Finally, the influence of Samuel J. Mills Jr. was a significant factor in the formation of the UFMS. Mills lived in the Middle States during 1816-1817. He possessed a unique ability to enlist important men in missionary projects and to work behind the scenes in missionary enterprises. His letters and journals reflect intense missionary zeal. Historians invariably name him as one of the most influential promoters of missionary endeavor in the early National Period. Little has been said of Mills' nationalism, which was certainly one of the factors behind his lifelong commitment to missionary   endeavor. He viewed the scarcity of Bibles across the mountains as "a foul on our national character" that "Christian America must rise and wipe . . . away."[102]

While living in the Middle States he associated with Edward Dorr Griffen and James Richards. While living at the home of Richards, in Newark, the plan of the UFMS was fashioned.[103] Mills' influence turned the attention of the UFMS to Mexico and South America. An effort to evangelize the southern parts of the Western Hemisphere was one of Mills' dreams that he never saw fulfilled.[104]

Mills was present at the General Assembly in 1816. A committee was appointed to discover if missionary affairs might be conducted with more efficiency. The formation of Bible societies, some said, reduced the need for missionary exertions. The committee responded. Instead of relaxing missionary efforts, Bible Societies should "infuse new life and vigour into the missionary cause." Two recommendations were made. First, the Standing Committee of Missions should be made a Board of Missions "with full powers to transact all the business of the missionary cause" among the frontier settlements. Second, a committee should be appointed to confer with the Reformed Dutch and Associate Reformed Churches about the possibility of the three churches uniting in the formation of a society for foreign missions.[105]

The Committee found the General Synods of the Dutch and Scotts Reformed Churches receptive. A constitution was drawn up by representatives of each group. When the three churches had their next general meetings, the constitution was approved. Delegates met in New York in July, 1817, and the UFMS became a reality.

The UFMS was not an established society by the end of 1817. Its Board immediately adopted the missions of the New York and Northern Missionary Societies. But the UFMS never attained the stature of the other two overseas societies. In 1826 the ABCFM assumed its missionary stations. However, when the UFMS was formed, all of the great evangelical Calvinistic church bodies in America had united in concerted action to send the gospel of Christ to the nations of the world. Other American denominational bodies emulated this commitment to an overseas mission.

In the Wake of the Overseas Mission

Several important developments followed in the wake of the overseas societies. The resources for funding the "foreign" mission and the various missionary activities on the American continent were provided after the beginning of the overseas missions. That this would happen was the constant claim of those men who called the churches to undertake the global task. These men stressed again and again this principle: *"That the readiest and most efficacious method of promoting religion at home, is for Christians to exert themselves to send it abroad."*[106] What often happened is illustrated in the experience of James Ranaldson, missionary of the Triennial Convention in the vicinity of New Orleans. He was instructed to contact the Greeks, but he found that this was impossible for him. He helped to form the Mississippi Society for Baptist Missions, Foreign and Domestic, which sent a missionary to the Creeks. He gathered a church among them in a few months. In his report, Ranaldson said:

> The society having attributed a great share of their success to the agency of your missionary, agreed to remit the sum which was appropriated for his use by the Baptist Board of Foreign Missions . . . I hope the employment of domestic missionaries will never diminish your treasury, but rather replenish it.[107]

Second, a proliferation of voluntary societies eventually produced an age of benevolence in American Christianity. All kinds of societies for multivarious purposes arose from one end of the young nation to another. The missionary men considered all these concerted efforts as part of the divine plan to renovate the world. In 1825 Warren Fay explained the relationship between the different societies.

The various benevolent institutions, which adorn this age, are

component and intimately connected parts of one great system
. . . Bible Societies, Education Societies, Tract Societies, Domestic
Missionary Societies, and all the benevolent institutions . . . are
necessary, and even indispensible, to form that vast moral machinery, which is designed, in its combined operation, to enlighten, and
bless, and save the world.[108]

Third, the growing tendency toward national organizations was amplified
by the formation of the overseas societies. The success of the overseas efforts,
which ultimately increased funds for all missionary causes, suggested that national
societies were needed for the work of church extension and other benevolent undertakings throughout the nation. Other factors also contributed to this development. The rising tide of cultural nationalism progressively increased after the
Revolution. It ripened into full-grown militant nationalism after the War of 1812.
Nationalism played a significant part in the development of national organizations.[109]

The organization of the ABS was interpreted as an event in which the
"American nation (arose) in the majesty of its collected might" to take its place
among the other Christian nations of the world "for extending the empire of religion and civilization."[110] Colin B. Goddykoontz, in a dissertation prepared under
the direction of Frederick Jackson Turner, insisted that the entire "home missionary movement was an expression of nationalism."[111]

Finally the formation of the overseas societies contributed to the division
of the missionary movement into missions to the heathen, at first including the
American Indians, and home or domestic missions. Later the Indian mission was
also handed over to the domestic mission. In 1826, the older Pedobaptist societies
affiliated with the American Home Mission Society. That year the work of the
Baptist Board of Foreign Missions was restricted solely to heathen missions. In
1832, the American Baptist Home Missionary Society was formed. Severed from
integration with missions to the heathen, home missions often deteriorated into
competitive extension of denominational empire. After a fashion, the wilderness
vanished.

NOTES FOR CHAPTER 6

1. American Board of Commissioners for Foreign Mission, "Advertisement" in Gordon Hall and Samuel Newell, *The Conversion of the World: or the Claims of Six Hundred Millions of Heathen, and the Ability and Duty of the Churches Respecting Them* (2nd ed.; Andover, Massachusetts: Flagg and Gould, 1818), pp. 21-22. The book was reprinted in London the following year.

2. *Ibid.,* p. 6.

3. William Carey, Letter to the NYMS, Oct. 15, 1800, in John Abeel, *A Discourse, Delivered April 6th, 1801, in the Middle Dutch Church, before the New York Missionary Society, at their Annual Meeting* (New York: Isaac Collins and Sons, 1801), p. 63.

4. *CEM,* I (July, 1800), 31.

5. *First Ten Annual Reports of the American Board of Commissioners for with Other Documents of the Board* (Boston: Printed by Crocker and Brewster, 1834), p. 10. Hereafter *ABCFM Annual Reports* and year of report.

6. *Ibid.,* 1811, p. 18.

7. Hopkins, *Works,* I, 138. The story of this missionary effort has already been told in Chapter II.

8. *Ibid.,* pp. 136, 143, 144.

9. Samuel Spring, *A Sermon, Delivered before the Massachusetts Missionary Society, at Their Annual Meetings May 25, 1802* (Newburyport: E. M. Blunt, 1802), p. 6.

10. Jonathan Allen, *A Sermon, Delivered at Haverhill, February 5, 1812, on the Occasion of Two Young Ladies Being About to Embark to India* (Haverhill, Mass.: W. B. & H. G. Allen, 1812), in Beaver, *Pioneers in Mission,* p. 276. Allen was pastor of the church at Bradford, Mass., the home of Ann Hasseltine. He was of the Hopkinsian persuasion.

11. Leonard Woods, *A Sermon, Delivered At the Tabernacle in Salem, Feb. 6, 1812* (Boston: Samuel T. Strong, 1812), in Beaver, *Pioneers in Mission,* p. 266.

12. *ABCFM Annual Reports,* 1812, p. 41.

13. Pliny Fisk, *The Holy Land, an Interesting Field of Missionary Enterprise. A Sermon, Preached in the Old South Church Boston, Sabbath Evening, Oct. 31, 1819, Just Before the Departure of the Palestine Mission* (Boston: Samuel T. Armstrong, 1819), p. 36. Fisk was one of the first two missionaries sent by the ABCFM to the Middle East.

14. Warren Fay, *The Obligations of Christians to the Heathen World. A Sermon Delivered at the Old South Church in Boston, Before the Auxiliary Foreign Mission Society of Boston and Vicinity, at Their Annual Meeting, January 3, 1825* (Boston: Printed by Crocker and Brewster, 1825), p. 15.

15. Heman Humphrey, *The Promised Land. A Sermon Delivered at Goshen (Conn.) at the Ordination of the Rev. Messrs. Hiram Bingham & Asa Thurston, as Missionaries to the Sandwich Island, Sept. 29, 1819* (Boston: Samuel T. Armstrong, 1819), pp. 5, 7. Humphrey, successful pastor at Pittsfield, was to become second president of Amherst College in 1823.

16. Edwards, *History of the Work of Redemption,* in *Works,* I, 584.

17. Eliphalet Nott, *A Sermon Preached before the General Assembly of the Church in the United States of America by Appointment of their Standing committee of Missions, May 19, 1806* (Newburyport, Mass.: Reprinted for Samuel Dole, 1801), p. 21. Nott, after serving as missionary of the MSC and pastor of the Presbyterian Church in Albany, had been elected president of Union College in 1804.

18. William Warren Sweet, *Makers of Christianity: From John Cotton to Lyman Abbott* (New York: Harper Brothers, Publishers, 1942), pp. 212-213.

19. Hudson, *Religion in America,* p. 156.

20. Samuel Eliot Morison, *The Maritime History of Massachusetts* (Boston: Houghton Mifflin Company, 1941), pp. 27-40. See also Curtis P. Nettels, *The Emergence of a National Economy, 1775-1815,* Vol. II of *The Economic History of the United States* (New York: Holt, Rinehart and Winston, 1962), pp. 45-64.

21. Merrill Jensen, *The New Nation* (New York: Vintage Books, 1965), pp. 194-195.

22. The work of Samuel J. Mills Jr. and the conversion of Obookiah led to the founding of the Sandwich Island Mission in 1820; a plea from Robert Morrison and a financial offer by resident merchant D. W. C. Olyphant, not interest aroused by years of China trade, led to the founding of the Canton mission; and the romanticized account of a visit of Nez Perces to St. Louis finally led Methodists and Congregationalists to launch missions to the Northwestern Coast in 1834 and 1836.

23. See Letter of Moses Brown to Samuel Hopkins in Mack Thompson, *Moses Brown, Reluctant Reformer* (Chapel Hill, N.C.: University of North Carolina Press, 1962), p. 186.

24. Wright, *Beginnings of Unitarianism,* pp. 6-8.

25. Morison, *Maritime History,* pp. 82, 95.

26. John Emerson, *The Duty of Christians to Seek the Salvation of Zion Explained and Urged, Sermon, Preached at Northampton, Before the Hampshire Missionary Society, at their Annual Meeting, August 31, 1809* (Northampton: William Butler, 1809), pp. 14-15.

27. William E. Strong, *The Story of the American Board* (Boston: The Pilgrim Press, 1910), p. 13. See also Woods, *History of the Andover Seminary,* p. 76.

28. Beaver, *Pioneers in Mission,* p. 250.

29. Beaver, "Missionary Motivation through Three Centuries," p. 133.

30. Francis S. Philbrick, *The Rise of the West: 1754-1830,* Harper Torchbooks (New York: Harper & Row, Publishers, 1965), p. 273.

31. Gardiner Spring, *Memoirs of the Rev. Samuel J. Mills* (London: Printed for Francis Westley, 1820), p. 29.

32. Jacob Norton, *Faith on the Son of God Necessary to Everlasting Life. A Sermon Delivered Before the Massachusetts Missionary Society, at Their Eleventh Annual Meeting, in Boston, May 29, 1810* (Boston: Lincoln & Edmands, 1810), p. 25.

33. Gordon Hall, *The Duty of the American Churches in Respect to Foreign Missions. A Sermon Preached in the Tabernacle, Philadelphia, on Sabbath Morning, Feb. 16, 1812; and in the Presbyterian Church, on the Afternoon of the Same Day* (2nd ed.; Andover: Flagg and Gould, 1815), p. 9.

34. Sereno E. Dwight, *Thy Kingdom Come: A Sermon Delivered in the Old South Church, Boston, Before the Foreign Mission Society of Boston and Vicinity, January 3, 1820* (Boston: Crocker and Brewster, 1820), p. 28. Dwight, son of Timothy Dwight, was pastor of Old South Church in Boston, missionary statesman and biographer of Jonathan Edwards. He was later to become president of Hamilton College.

35. *ABCFM Annual Reports,* 1811, p. 23.

36. United Foreign Missionary Society, MSS Records of the Board of Managers of the United Foreign Missionary Society (1817-1822), Houghton Library Archives, Harvard University, Cambridge, Massachusetts.

37. Wright, *Beginnings of Unitarianism,* pp. 252, 280.

38. Sprague, *Life of Jedidiah Morse,* p. 57.

39. Letter of Jedidiah Morse to George Burder, June 1, 1805, in *ibid.,* p. 65.

40. Leonard Woods wrote a series of articles, beginning in April, 1807, for the *Panoplist* which presented the arguments for and advantages of a General Association.

41. Woods, *History of the Andover Seminary* tells the story of the developing cooperation in great detail. The "Appendix," pp. 448-636, is composed of letters that verify Woods' theme.

42. Spring, *Memoirs of Mills,* pp. 37-38.

43. Leonard Woods, *A Sermon, Preached at Haverhill (Mass.) in Remembrance of Mrs. Harriet Newell, Wife of the Rev. Samuel Newell, Missionary to India To Which are Added Memoirs of Her Life* (4th ed., enl.; Boston: Printed for Samuel T. Armstrong, 1814), p. 102. Harriet Newell was the first American to die in overseas missionary service.

44. Francis Wayland, *A Memoir of the Life and Labors of the Rev. Adoniram Judson, D.D.* (2 vols.; Boston: Phillips, Sampson and Company, 1853), I, 53.

45. *CEM,* II (July, 1802), 30-33.

46. Spring, *Memoirs of Mills,* p. 11.

47. Strong, *Story of American Board,* p. 7.

48. *CEM,* Second Series, VIII (June, 1815), 232-233.

49. I have read most of the extant minutes and correspondence of the Societies of Inquirey in Andover and Princeton, upon which I base these observations. See Clarence P. Shedd, *Two Centuries of Student Christian Movements* (New York: Association Press, 1934), pp. 32-90, which tells the entire story with some detail.

50. For a discussion of the "Role of Missionary Sermons," see Beaver, *Pioneers in Mission,* pp. iff.

51. *The Latter Day Luminary,* I (Feb., 1818), vii.

52. Besides Woods, *Sermon Preached at Haverhill,* see Timothy Dwight, *Memoirs of the Life of Mrs. Harriet Newell, Wife of the Rev. Samuel Newell, to Which is Annexed a Sermon* (Lexington, Ky.: T. T. Skilman, 1815).

53. [E. W. Dwight], *Memoirs of Henry Obookiah, a Native of Owhyhee and a Member of the Foreign Mission School, Who Died at Cornwall, Conn., Feb. 17, 1818, aged 26 Years* (New Haven: n.p., 1818).

54. Edward Griffin, "Speech," in American Bible Society, *Proceedings of a Meeting of the Citizens of New-York and Others, convened in the City-Hall on the 13th of May, 1816; at the Request of the Board of Managers of the American Bible Society* (New-York: Published by order of the Board of Managers, 1816), p. 7.

55. *ABCFM Annual Reports,* 1810, p. 10.

56. *CEM,* Second Series, III (May, 1810), 184-189.

57. *ABCFM Annual Reports,* 1811, p. 28.

58. *Ibid.,* 1817, p. 163.

59. *Ibid.,* 1820, pp. 316-317.

60. *Ibid.,* 1810, pp. 11, 12, 13.

61. *Ibid.,* 1811, p. 24; 1815, p. 123.

62. *Ibid.,* 1816, p. 135.

63. *Ibid.,* 1816, p. 128.

64. Baptist Board of Foreign Missions, *Proceedings of the Baptist Convention for Missionary Purposes; Held in Philadelphia, in May, 1814* (Philadelphia: Printed for the Convention by Ann Coles, 1814), p. 6.

65. Backus, *History of New England,* II, 204, and Alvah Hovey, *A Memoir of the Life and Times of the Rev. Isaac Backus, A.M.* (Boston: Gould and Lincoln, 1859), pp. 226-228.

66. Gillette, *Minutes,* p. 350.

67. For a very full discussion of the level of this involvement see Vail, *Morning Hour Baptist Missions,* pp. 238ff.

68. Letter of William Carey, July 30, 1807, in *MBMM,* I (March, 1808), p. 1.

69. William Staughton, *The Baptist Mission in India Containing a Narative of its Rise, Progress, and Present Condition. A Statement of the Physical and Moral Character of the Hindoos, their Cruelties, Tortures and Burnings, with a very Interesting Description of Bengal, Intended to animate to Missionary Co-operation* (Philadelphia: Published by Hellings and Aitken, 1811).

70. Letter of Judson to Lucius Bolles, Sept. 1, 1812, in *MBMM,* III (March, 1813), 268.

71. *MBMM,* III (Sept., 1812, 215.

72. See various letters, *MBMM,* III (March, 1813), 266-267.

73. Letter of Judson to Thomas Baldwin, Oct. 22, 1812, in *MBMM,* III (June, 1813), 292.

74. Letter of William Carey to Thomas Baldwin, Oct. 20, 1812, *MBMM,* III (June, 1813), 290. See also his letter to William Staughton, Oct. 20, 1812, *MBMM,* III (Sept., 1813), 322.

75. *MBMM,* III (March, 1813), 286.

76. Quoted in Hortense Woodson, *Giant in the Land* (Nashville: Broadman Press, 1950), p. 35.

77. See W. W. Barnes, *The Southern Baptist Convention, 1845-1953* (Nashville: Broadman Press, 1954), pp. 12ff., and Robert G. Torbet, *Venture of Faith* (Philadelphia: Judson Press, 1955), pp. 105ff., for a discussion of problems leading to the ultimate division.

78. Baptist Board of Foreign Missions, *Proceedings of the General Convention of the Baptist Denomination in the United States, at their First Triennial Meeting, Held in Philadelphia, from the 7th to the 14th of May, 1817: Together with the Third Annual Report of the Baptist Board of Foreign Missions for the United States* (Philadelphia: Printed by Order of the Convention, 1817), p. 131. See the detailed accounts of the travels and activities of Rice in the first three annual reports of the Board of Missions.

79. See Staughton's defense of the appointment in a Letter to Judge Tallmadge, August 14, 1815, and Judson's dissatisfaction with the appointment in Letter to Lucius Bolles, Nov. 9, 1816, American Baptist Foreign Mission Society, Archives, Valley Forge, Pa.

80. Baptist Board of Foreign Missions, *Proceedings,* 1814, p. 42.

81. *Ibid.,* 1817, p. 124.

82. Letter from Luther Rice to John Mason Peck, Nov. 30, 1815, in Babcock, *Memoir of Peck,* p. 49.

83. Baptist Board of Foreign Missions, MSS Minutes, American Baptist Foreign Missionary Society, Archives, Valley Forge, Pa., pp. 81, 83.

84. Isaac McCoy, *History of Baptist Indian Missions: Embracing Remarks on the Former and Present Condition of the Aboriginal Tribes; their Settlement within the Indian Territory, and their Future*

Prospects (Washington: William M. Morrison, 1840), pp. 43-44.

85. Baptist Board of Foreign Missions, MSS Minutes, pp. 86, 88.

86. Baptist Board of Foreign Missions, *Annual Report,* 1818, pp. 193ff.

87. Baptist Board of Foreign Missions, *Proceedings,* 1817, pp. 134, 180.

88. United Foreign Missionary Society, MSS Records, p. 6.

89. [William M. Engles, ed.], *Minutes of the General Assembly 1789-1820* (Philadelphia: Presbyterian Board of Publication, 1847), pp. 491, 515.

90. Alexander, *A Missionary Sermon,* p. 21. Alexander was first professor at Princeton Theological Seminary.

91. Ezra Stiles Ely, *A Contrast between Calvinism and Hopkinsianism* (New York: Published by S. Whiting and Co., 1811).

92. Gardiner Spring, *Personal Reminiscences of the Life and Times of Gardiner Spring* (2 vols.; New York: Charles Scribner & Co., 1866), I, 129.

93. Letter from John Knox, Thomas Gifford, jun., and Paschal N. Strong, March 8, 1814, to Society for Inquiry in Missions, Princeton Theological Seminary, Princeton, N.J., in Society for Inquiry in Missions Correspondence, Archives, Princeton Theological Seminary, Princeton, N.J.

94. [Samuel Whelpley], *The Triangle: A Series of Numbers upon Three Theological Points, Enforced from Various Pulpits in the City of New York* (New York: John Wiley, 1832), pp. 5, 16.

95. Gardiner Spring published a pamphlet entitled *An Explanation of the Origin and Design of the New York Evangelical Missionary Society for Young Men,* which is in Spring, *Personal Reminiscences,* I, 249-262. It presents his side of the controversy. For the other side see *History of the Young Men's Missionary Society of New York and the Hopkinsian Question* (New York: n.p., 1817).

96. *Minutes of General Assembly,* 1816, p. 655.

97. *Ibid.,* 1817, p. 679.

98. *MBMM,* I (Sept. 1812), 221.

99. *Panoplist,* IV (Jan., 1808), p. 377.

100. See American Bible Society, *Proceedings,* p. 8.

101. United Foreign Missionary Society, MSS Records, p. 6.

102. John F. Schermerhorn and Samuel J. Mills, *A Correct View of that Part of the United States which Lies West of the Allegany Mountains with Regard to Religion and Morals* (Hartford, Conn.: n.p., 1814), and Spring, *Life of Mills,* p. 77.

103. Spring, *Life of Mills,* p. 82.

104. See Letter of Mills to Elias Cornelius, October 3, 1816, in *ibid.,* pp. 85-86.

105. *Minutes of General Assembly,* 1816, pp. 632-634.

106. *ABCFM Annual Reports,* 1814, p. 76.

107. Baptist Board of Foreign Missions, *Annual Report,* 1818, p. 224.

108. Fay, *Obligations of Christians, p. 6.*

109. I have been instructed concerning American nationalism by George Dangerfield, *The Awakening*

of American Nationalism, Harper Torchbooks (New York: Harper & Row, 1965); Frederick Merk, Manifest Destiny and Mission (New York: Vintage Books, 1966); and Carlton J. H. Hayes, Nationalism: A Religion (New York: Harper & Row, 1960).

110. American Bible Society, Proceedings, p. 8.

111. Colin Brummit Goodykoontz, Home Missions on the American Frontier (Caldwell, Idaho: The Caxton Printers, Ltd., 1939), p. 422. Goodykoontz is very valuable but not always exact. He has Adoniram Judson Jr. going on a mission to northern Vermont in 1800, p. 136.

Part III

Missionary Thought

The apostolate or mission of the Church has its roots in the creative, the revelatory-illuminating, and the redemptive-revelatory work of God. It is one form of God's love reaching out to all men. The creation will not be complete until the advent of the new heavens and new earth in the kingdom which the Church proclaims. Moreover, through all the painful consequences of man's rebellion against God, the Holy Spirit ever brings new light about the purposes of God, the nature of man, and the ultimate liberation that will come with the kingdom. Despite all its miserable failure and imperfections, there can be seen in the household of faith the fruits of the divine reconciliation and a foretaste of the redeemed humanity. As God sent His Son, so the Son has sent his body, the Church, empowered by the Holy Spirit, to preach the Gospel of reconciliation to the whole world. The Church exists primarily to witness to this good news, and every other function of the Church is subsidiary and contributory to this purpose.

R. Pierce Beaver — 1961

Introduction

The leading religious opinions embraced by the various denominations who are engated in missionary undertakings are those which were generally taught and embraced at the time of the reformation from popery.

The Presbyterian Standing Committee of Missions — 1802

When the Hopkinsians formed the Massachusetts Missionary Society in 1799, they did not restrict participation to their own sect. Neither did they emphasize tenets that distinguished Hopkinsianism from the older, more moderate Calvinism. Nathanael Emmons explained that all who held to the authority of the Holy Bible and were candid about the doctrines it contained were forced to agree on some fundamental axioms: that mankind is in a state of apostacy from God; that the Gospel of Christ is the only remedy for that rebellion and its terrible consequences; that the Gospel must be known, received and obeyed to be effective; that man's virtue and happiness are in direct proportion to the influence of the Gospel in his life; that belief in the Gospel brings new life to the individual; and that the efficacious influence of the Gospel all over the world will produce the glory that the Scriptures promise to God. These were the essential precepts of an evangelical faith. "On these grounds," Emmons continued,

> the grand commission, which Christ gave to his primitive disciples, . . . was delivered. On these grounds the apostles of the Lord exhibited all that fidelity and zeal, in obedience to this charge, which are related in the New-Testament; and on these grounds, zeal in every believer for the spread of Christianity has an adequate sanction.[1]

Three years later, in 1802, the new Standing Committee of Missions of the Presbyterian Church sent a letter to the various European missionary societies. After introducing the various societies and ecclesiastical bodies in America engaged in missionary labor, the letter reported:

> The leading religious opinions embraced by the various denominations who . . . are engaged in missionary undertakings, are those which were generally taught and embraced at the reformation from popery: and in which the trinity and equality of persons in the undivided Godhead — the deep depravity of man by nature — the

213

imputed righteousness of Christ, as the only meritorious cause of a sinner's justification in the sight of God — and the renovation of the human heart by the influence of the Holy Spirit of grace, as essentially necessary to genuine holiness — form the prominent and commanding features of the whole system.[2]

In 1806, William Rogers wrote the Circular Letter of the Philadelphia Baptist Association on the subject of Christian missions. The letter discusses the doctrinal precepts upon which mission work is to be undertaken. Rogers' missionary axioms were: (1) a deep conviction of the fallen state of the human race; (2) the total inability of men to deliver themselves; (3) the full ability of Christ to save all sinners; (4) the ultimate triumph of the salvation of Christ in all the earth; and (5) the preaching of the Word of God as the means of achieving this great work.[3]   These five principles constitute a minuscule theology of missions acceptable to the strictest Hopkinsianism and the most orthodox Presbyterian.

The missionary spokesmen of the early National Period were careful to set the mission in theological perspective. Sermons at anniversary meetings of the societies and at ordination of missionaries, addresses to the public and annual reports of societies and boards, circular and pastoral letters from associations and synods stressed the theology of missions. They answered opposers, enlisted the lethargic, and encouraged the faithful from a Biblical viewpoint. Examination of such documents reveals a more Calvinistic framework than these three summaries would indicate. It was, however, Calvinism modified by a strong evangelical impulse. In spite of various modifications, men who led the early missionary enterprise were aware they had much in common. These fundamental theological precepts are what John M. Mason called *"the doctrines of the Gospel of peace."*[4]

NOTES FOR INTRODUCTION

1. Nathanael Emmons, *TO ALL, Who are desirous of the Spread of the Gospel of our LORD JESUS CHRIST* (Boston: n.?., 1799), pp. 6-7.

2. Standing Committee of Missions, MSS Minutes, I, 26.

3. Gillette, *Minutes,* pp. 426-429. William Rogers was a Baptist pastor in Philadelphia and professor of Oratory and English at the University of Pennsylvania.

4. Mason, *Hope for the Heathen,* p. 136.

Chapter 7

Mission and the Work of Redemption

This is the cause which Jehovah has supported from eternity. It is the cause for which Jesus died. It is the cause which the Holy Ghost has been carrying on in all ages.

Asa Lyons — 1815

The missionary cause is the work in which the Holy Trinity is engaged.

Joseph Harvey — 1815

Jonathan Edwards defined the "work of redemption" as the saving work of God carried on from the fall of man to the end of the world. As the progression of events by which God effected the redemotion of his particular people, it was "the greatest of all God's works . . . and . . . the end of all his other works." This great work of God, according to Edwards, has two facets. One consists in the converting, sanctifying and glorifying of individuals, a work on different subjects but common to all ages of man. This aspect began at the fall and continues to the end of the world. The second, however, pertains to God's grand design in creation, history and providence. It is carried on, during the same period of time, but

> by many successive works and dispensations of God, all tending to one great end and effect, all united as the several parts of a scheme, and all together making up one great work.

This latter aspect of the work of redemption was the primary concern of Edwards in his famous sermon series on 1739. He was interested in the "one great scheme" by which God was accomplishing his "greatest of all works." For it was in the accomplishment of this work that God received his greatest glory. This great design not only relates to the atoning work of Christ, but also to

> what the Father, or the Holy Ghost, has done, as united or confederated in this design of redeeming sinful men . . . for it is all but one work, one design.[1]

Further, Edwards contended, it was possible for the Church to join with God in the accomplishment of this great master plan.

217

The publication of the *History of the Work of Redemption* in America in 1782, and regular new issues throughout the early National Period, provided a theological source book for rising missionary statesmen. The mission of the Church was grounded in the nature of the Triune God. Missionary labors were God's chosen means of performing his most glorious work. The mission was an essential part of the mission of God. It was integral to his great work of redemption.

The Sovereign Purpose of Jehovah

The precise plan for the reclamation of the world was determined by the sovereign decrees of God from eternity. Ultimate achievement was guaranteed by God's sovereign power. This plan would come to its final consummation through the instrumentality and expansion of his Chur ch, the means established by God's sovereign pleasure and wisdom. The rise of missionary organizations was no accident of history or the product of human ingenuity. That the gospel of mercy will be taken to all nations and every nation will eventually bow to Christ was settled before the foundations of the world.

The success of the mission was certain in spite of political and social situations. Nor was the weakness and poverty of the Church a deterrent. John M. Mason told Christians in 1797 to look for an interposition of the arm of God to effect "this prodigious revolution" no matter how "mean the instruments." Jehovah directs the complicated movements of the universe. The unpromising situation of the heathen is no obstacle to the sovereign God. He orders the dispensations of providence to achieve the glory of the Messiah.

> The vicissitudes of kings and kingdoms, and all the stupendous events which shine in ancient annals, were important chiefly as they served to prepare the way, and to spread the triumphs of Him who was a light to lighten the Gentiles.[2]

Samuel Miller insisted that the "whole system of Creation, of Providence and of Redemption, was fixed in the counsels of God." The time and place of each event is known and fixed. The God who made the universe, who constantly governs it and guides all its intricate variations, has foreseen every event and adjusted every instrument. Interwoven in his plan, from its beginning to consummation, was all the means necessary to meet every exigency.[3]

This representation of God's immutable plans and operations, Miller admitted, gave offense to some. It appeared inconsistent with the freedom of human volitions and actions. The Bible recognized no such inconsistency. It asserted the doctrine of God's sovereign will and purpose while at the same time it spoke of man as a "free accountable agent." There was no objection to either God's sovereignty or man's accountability that could not be fully answered by both Scripture and reason.[4]

The early exponents of the missionary movement held consistently to the sovereign election of God in salvation. Among these men was an occasional advocate of a general atonement, but most insisted that the purpose of God in redemption had not been left to the caprice of sinful man but determined by the unmerited choice of God.

Alexander Proudfit, before the Northern Missionary Society, related the doctrine of election to the missionary responsibility of the Church.

> The scriptures represent all the adorable persons of the Godhead as equally concerned, and sustaining their respective capacities, in the economy of our redemption. Moved by pure unmerited mercy, the Father from eternity, made a sovereign and absolute choice of a portion of our family whom he predestinated to glory; these he gave as an inheritance to his eternal Son.

This doctrine did not militate against human agency, hamper the gospel call, nor render the hope for a saving response presumptious. "Salvation is not offered to any as *predestinated,* nor refused to any as *passed by.*" The gospel invitation is as unhindered as if the decree of election did not exist. Since the gospel is freely offered to all, the refusal of it cannot arise from one's non-election. That is not known. It springs from the enmity of his heart against God. Absolute election does not encourage continuation in sin or the neglect of the gospel ordinances. The Bible repeatedly commands men to make their calling and election sure and to avail themselves to the means of grace. "Duty and privilege, the means and the end, are connected inseparably in the counsel of God."[5]

Rather than discourage the missionary enterprise, the sovereign purpose of God was the ground of hope for the missionary undertaking. God surely had a people among the heathen. He had decreed that he would call them to his Son through the exertions of his Church. Jonathan Allen spoke in 1812 from John 11:52, "that also he should gather together in one, the children of God, that are scattered abroad." The sermon outline is remarkably similar to the outline of the *History of the Work of Redemption.* Its central assertion was that

> God has, according to his eternal counsels, among the sons of men, a chosen people . . . All these . . . sooner or later must be collected together . . . This grand event will, finally, be accomplished. The arrangements for it, in the divine government, are already made, the wheels to bring it about are all in motion; and not one of them will ever stop, till the important object is obtained.[6]

The missionary movement was an essential part of the divine arrangements.

In 1813, William Bullen Johnson wrote a circular letter of the Savannah-River Baptist Association, entitled "The Importance and Advantages of Itinerant and Missionary Efforts." It is one of the most profound documents produced in the early National Period setting the mission in theological perspective. Noting contemporary political and religious developments, Johnson remarked:

> In these commotions . . . we, as Christians engaged in the cause of

our God and Saviour, have a deep interest. For we know that it is
God who rules in the heavens and governs in the earth; that in both,
he arranges . . . his designs according to his preconceived and unfrus-
trable purposes. These commotions, therefore, are under his immediate direction, and made to subserve his will . . . They must of course,
then, deeply interest every heart concerned for his glory and the
honour of his service. And the more so, as, in effecting his designs
and in bringing to its full completion his infinitely wise plan, Jehovah is graciously pleased to employ his servants as instruments.[7]

The sovereign purpose of God can not be thwarted. Like a great master
builder he has established his ultimate objective. He has determined the schedule
of completion. All events of history and prehistory are parts of the one great
blueprint. He has decided what materials shall constitute his Kingdom. The nations of the world are his building stones. He has settled on the instrument of its
erection. "The Gospel," published throughout the world by God's own people,
"is the grand instrument, ordained by infinite wisdom, to turn people from darkness to light, and from Satan to God."[8] The mission was a cardinal part of the
work of redemption.

The Mediatorship of Jesus Christ

The crucial period in the total scheme of redemption came between the
incarnation and ascension of Jesus. In that period Christ made the purchase of
redemption. Missionary activity was related to God's design for world redemption
at this point. The mission, in a fashion, continued the mediation of Jesus Christ.
The conversion of the world was a consequence of the death of Christ.

The peculiar fruits of the cross will be displayed by the reformation
of the world. Though great things were effected for Zion's prosperity directly upon Christ's ascension, and during the successful times
of the Apostles, and the subsequent days of reformation; though
millions have been savingly enlightened since the christian era . . .
he is not yet satisfied, and contemplates the latter day glory as the
answerable reward of his death . . . The Lord has promised that his
church shall embrace the nations.[9]

The "plentious provision" Christ made for the salvation of the world shall
not be wasted. This atonement is as sufficient for Asiatics and Africans as for
Americans. It is a warrent from God to strive for the salvation of the whole world.
Wherever the preaching of the cross shall stir up people to seek salvation, their
salvation shall be found.[10] The missionary cause was the cause for which the son
of God came into the world and suffered and died.[11]

The work of Jesus Christ in the saga of redemption was achieved in his
office as mediator between God and man. Edward Dorr Griffen, in one of the superior sermons of the Nineteenth Century, affirmed that the only explanation for
the exercise of God's power in the creation of the universe was the "eternal pro-
pensity" in God to "overflow and fill with happiness numberless vessels fitted to

receive it." This divine predeliction to manifest the richness and perfections of his nature to his creatures was

> not for ostentious display, but to enrich the universe with the knowledge of his glory, and to lay a foundation for general confidence and delight in him.

This was the glorious and eternally proposed by the goodness of God.[12]

> The principle means that God ordained to accomplish his purpose was
the

> appointment of his Son to act as his viceregent in the creation and government of the world, to assume a created nature in personal union with himself, and thus to fill up the infinite chasm between God and his creation, and be the grand connecting length between finite and infinite nature.[13]

All things were made by and for the Son. All the work of creation and all measures of the divine government of the world are a part of one plan. The execution of the plan was committed to Christ. Therefore, whatever valuable use the earth may have, whether to bring glory to God or good to the creature, can only be realized *"through the mediation of Christ."* The material creation may be a path to happiness and heaven for man; it may illustrate to principalities and powers the wisdom and goodness of God. But it will only do that in consequence of the mediatorship of the Son.

> The whole plan of this world, including creation and providence, including every event from its beginning to the final judgment, was involved in the plan of redemption.

All are designed to be serviceable to Christ and the kingdom he purposed to set up to accomplish his plan.

> Only by setting up his kingdom can Christ bring to consummation the glorious purpose of his mediatorship. Therefore, "he has marched down the tracts of ages . . . with his eye unmovedly fixed upon this single cause." Revolutions and rebellions, the councils of kings and the debates of senates, harvests and famines, volcanoes and earthquakes, are all made to advance his interests.

> His Kingdom . . . is the only cause on earth that is worth an anxious thought, . . . the only interest which God pursues or values, and the only object worthy of the attention of men.

The cause of Christ is the only cause which will prevail "amidst the wrecks of time."[14]

> This mediatorial kingdom, planned before the creation of the universe, but purchased by the death of the Son of God, has a glorious destiny. It is destined to banish the effects of the fall, to restore mankind to God, and to cover

all lands. In the establishment of this kingdom, the Church has been called to share. This was the significance of the missionary exertions of the Church.

Richard Furman preached from the Great Commission at the opening of the organizational meeting of the Baptists' Triennial Convention. The promised presence of Christ with his people, Furman alleged, revealed his

> determined purpose of accomplishing the great Design of his Mediatorial Kingdom; by bringing to their completion, the schemes of Providence and Grace, in the advancement of the Divine Glory. On this grand object the Redeemer's heart had been set from eternity . . . All the terrors attendant on his state of Humiliation, even the bitter Death of the Cross, could not deter him from prosecuting the great Design; and he will not leave his work incomplete.

From that observation, Furman drove his point home. "Electrified" as they were, by the combined voice of Scripture and Providence, he urged those assembled to act for God in the "best of all Causes." The Redeemer's work must not continue incomplete.[15]

In the same vein, Heman Humphrey assured his hearers in 1819:

> Immense regions . . . are still unsubdued . . . In the highest and most perfect sense the world belongs to Christ. All things were made by him and for him . . . The covenant of redemption . . . secures to him, as Mediator, the ultimate possession of all the kingdoms of men. (The Church) can possess nothing but what she holds under him and for his glory. Wherever she raises her standard, it is in his name . . . In this subordinate sense the world belongs to the Church. It is . . . given to her as a possession in every promise . . . in which the universal spread of the Gospel is mentioned! It is hers to share in the conquests, as well as to fight under the banners of her King.[16]

The Influences of the Spirit

The Holy Spirit's ministry in the mission of the Church is not as fully developed and defended in the missionary documents as the relationship between the mission and the sovereign purpose of Jehovah and the mediatorship of Christ. One obvious reason is because the Spirit's ministry in the work of redemption was often an excuse for refraining from missionary activity. Opposers objected to sending missionaries to the heathen because the conversion of the nations was solely God's work, specifically the task of the Holy Spirit. The exponents of the mission counteracted with voluminous emphasis on the necessity and effectiveness of human resolution and effort in the cause of God. However, the essential character of the Spirit's ministry was presupposed. What the Father had planned in eternity and what the Son had purchased by his death had to be secured by the power of the Holy Ghost. John Blair Smith urged

Christians to

> ardently solicit the Almighty Spirit, who is the great agent in
> the establishment of the empire of Jesus Christ in the hearts of
> men, to accomplish his work in the most extensive manner.[17]

Alexander Proudfit discussed the "peculiar principles of the Gospel" most necessary in missionary proclamation.

> For the Holy Ghost, the third person in the godhead, is reserved
> the application of the purchased redemption. His office in the
> economy of grace is not less important than, nor less clearly pointed
> out, than those of the Father and the Son.[18]

The ministry of the Spirit in the work of redemption had direct connection with the Church's mission at three points.

The Holy Spirit is the sole agent of conversion. The conversion of the world is his own peculiar work. Though the proclamation of the gospel is performed by human agency, only the Holy Spirit actually produces regeneration. "With the rod of revelation the minister of the gospel may smite the rock of the human heart, but the power of God only can make the waters of repentence flow. The renovation of the human heart by the influences of the Holy Spirit" is essential to true holiness and one of the great evangelical precepts common to the missionary churches. The New York Missionary Society instructed its first missionary to the Indians to teach, among other cardinal doctrines,

> the application of the redemption of Christ by the Holy Spirit, and
> the absolute necessity of his agency to change the hearts of men.[19]

In 1820, Sereno Edwards Dwight perceived a new alignment in Christendom in which the "true nature of Christian Catholicism" was beginning to be understood. "The line of demarcation," he said, "which the Church is now drawing, is between those who admit the doctrines of human depravity, vicarious atonement, regeneration and the influences of the Holy Spirit, and those who reject them."[20] The goal of the work of redemption could only be achieved by the application of that salvation to the hearts of individuals. Only the Spirit could perform this work. Aging John Leland emphasized this in his sermon before the Baptist Convention in Philadelphia, in 1814. Christ, Leland said, "sends his Holy Spirit with his work to convince of sin, to discover the glories and fulness of Christ, to apply the blood of sprinkling to the wounded conscience, (and) to lead the soul to Christ."[21]

The Holy Spirit relates also to the Church's mission as the dispenser of revivals and the prime mover behind the missionary and benevolent activity of his people. Like the proponents of the Great Awakening, missionary leaders of the Second Great Awakening interpreted revivals as a foretaste of a much greater day. The revivals, along with missionary societies and all other benevolent societies, promised that after the "winter years, the Springtime of the world shall come."[22] They were signs, as Nathanael Emmons said, that God was "now visibly arising to plead his own cause."[23] Samuel Miller asked in 1802,

> Is he not giving us a pledge that his spirit hath not forsaken his Church, by reviving his work in different parts of our land; by exciting his people . . . to form missionary plans, and engage in missionary enterprises . . . and by lifting up a standard against infidelity and vice?[24]

The work of the Spirit most directly related to the mission of the Church is in the partnership between the Church and the Spirit in the great age of the Church's enlargement. The era when the kingdoms of the world actually become the kingdom of Christ will become a reality, according to Joseph Harvey, by the use of "appointed means, and the instrumentality of human exertions." But such an achievement also requires the special effusions of the Holy Spirit.

> We have seen that the kingdom of Christ in this world will be established on the basis of a new creation. The event described . . . implies a radical and universal change in the human character. For this work, means and human exertions alone are insufficient. This is the peculiar work of the Holy Ghost . . . We are informed that the period immediately preceding the Millennium will be greatly distinguished by these operations. . . . Many days of Pentecost will yet be seen on earth, in which multitudes will be born again. . . . Thus by the powerful operations of the spirit in blessing human exertions, will the kingdom of Christ suddenly break forth on every side. Revival will meet revival. . . . This is the preparatory work; and what follows, is the Millennium itself.

The latter day glory of the Church will be accomplished as a result of a regular system. The means is the word of God; the friends of Christ are the instruments; and the "efficient Agent is the Holy Spirit."[25]

In two missionary sermons Jedidiah Morse expounded the concept of a great "Gospel Harvest" that would introduce the Millennium. The Scriptures speak, he said, of a two-fold harvest of the whole world. The first, during the time of the apostles, was partial. The second, yet to come, will be far more complete and glorious than anything that has happened previously in the history of the Church. The result will be that the "whole world . . . shall become one universal, purified church, of one heart and one soul, and constitute . . . the 'inheritance' and the 'possession' of Christ."[26]

Morse found four features that marked the first harvest. The First Century world was dominated by only two languages; it was subject to one great empire; it contained a wide Jewish dispersion; and the Hebrew scriptures had been translated into Greek. The growth of French as the diplomatic language of the world and the rise of English as an international language of commerce, the hegemony of Protestant nations through a worldwide colonialism, the presence of clusters of Jews in most nations, and the explosion of Bible translating activities around the world convinced Morse that a new apostolic age had dawned. Missionary success actually proved that the time of the "grand gospel harvest" had begun. Some debated whether the miraculous effusions of the Holy Spirit would again take place as in the first century. Morse and most other missionary spokesmen did not expect it.[27] Nevertheless, the gathering of the great harvest of the world was the work of the Holy Spirit. Only his sovereign choice made the Church his threshing tool.

The Glory of God

The work of redemption is God's greatest work, the one work for which all other works consist. Its triumphant completion is the end for which God created the world. Developments of divine providence always tend to the consummation of God's redemptive plan. This is the work of God that brings him most glory. Nothing else that God has done or can ever do will so demonstrate the glory of God's wisdom and strength. Church participation in the work of redemption is the most glorious of all the works of the Church. For in that participation, the work of redemption is completed, and that work perfected which brings most glory to God.

The glory of God is the first and greatest missionary motive in the early National Period. Perception of the Church's opportunity to share in the work of redemption was the first grand, exciting concept that captur ed the imagination of those who early identified with the missionary enterprise. The missionary movement was regarded as God's own action. It was innately related to the glorious design of God for the redemption of the universe. In 1805, the preacher before the Piscataqua Missionary Society showed to his hearers that "the glory of God, a regard to his honor and praise in the spread of the gospel, ought to be the governing motive, in all missionary exertions."[28] Concern for the glory of God obligated the Church to disinterested zeal in the missionary cause.

> His operations, both in creation and Providence, illustriously
> display his infinite perfections . . . Yet it is reserved for the
> Gospel to exhibit the most illustrious, the most astonishing
> display . . . In the Gospel exclusively, is brought to human
> view, that mystery of condescension and grace, God manifested
> in the flesh . . . This may justly be pronounced the glory that
> excelleth.[29]

There is, however, a discernable waning of the glory of God as the most important missionary motive throughout and beyond the period of this study. What is of interest here relates to a shift of emphasis in the concept of the work of redemption. Edwards and the earliest missionary preachers stressed the grand design of God in creation, providence and history as the most glorious aspect of the work of redemption. Most statements after 1810 gave major exposure to conversion, sanctification and glorification of individual men. This was a legitimate and significant part of God's great redemptive design. The work of divine grace on the heart of man changed him from an obstreperous rebel to an obedient child. It fitted him for eternal bliss with God.

That which prepared a man for heaven, also enabled him to live the most useful and felicitous life on earth. The improvement of the condition of man, first spiritually and then socially and materially, displaces the magnificent, progressive consummation of the work of redemption as that which gives most glory to God.[30] This was predictable. Missionary advocates insisted that the Gospel, God's divine instrument for accomplishing redemption, directly affected both the individual man and his society. Eliphalet Nott helped to set the pattern, in 1806, when he explained that the success of the missionary undertaking would be glorious primarily because of its effect on the heathen world.

> Every enterprise tending to meliorate the condition of man, reflects glory to its author . . . Christian, can you conceive of any thing more glorious, than extending the blessing of Christianity to those tribes of wretched pagans who dwell upon your borders?[31]

This shift of emphasis from one aspect of the work of redemption to another tended to bolster the Christian's compassion for his fellow man, second only to the glory of God as the primary missionary motive.

NOTES FOR CHAPTER 7

1. Edwards, *Work of Redemption, Works*, II, 534, 615-616.

2. Mason, *Hope for the Heathen,* pp. 133-134.

3. Miller, *A Sermon before NYMS,* pp. 10, 12. Miller was long-time pastor of the Presbyterian Church in New York City and second professor appointed to Princeton Theological Seminary.

4. *Ibid.,* p. 17.

5. Alexander Proudfit, *A Sermon, Preached Before the Northern Missionary Society in the State of New-York, at their First Annual Meeting. In Troy, February 8; and by Particular Request, in Albany, March 6, 1798, at a Special Meeting of the Society* (Albany: Printed by Loring Andrews and Co., 1798), pp. 9-12. Proudfit was pastor of the Associate Reformed Church in Salem, N.Y.

6. Allen, *A Sermon, in Haverhill,* p. 269.

7. *MBMM,* IV (Sept., 1814), 35. Johnson was a Baptist pastor in South Carolina, and one of the founders of the Southern Baptist Convention.

8. Allen, *Sermon in Haverhill,* p. 273.

9. Spring, *A Sermon before the MMS,* p. 6. Samuel Spring was the Hopkinsian pastor of Newburyport, Mass., one of the founders of Andover Seminary and the ABCFM.

10. Woods, *Sermon Delivered at the Tabernacle,* p. 260.

11. Allen, *Sermon in Haverhill,* p. 276.

12. Edward D. Griffen, *The Kingdom of Christ: A Missionary Sermon Preached before the General Assembly of the Presbyterian Church, in Philadelphia, May 23rd, 1805* (Philadelphia: Jane Aitkens, 1805), pp. 6-7. Griffen was a noted evangelist, pastor and teacher. He served as pastor in Newark, N.J., through two very successful periods, interrupted by his professorship at Andover and pastorate at Park Street in Boston.

13. *Ibid.,* p. 8.

14. *Ibid.,* pp. 13-17.

15. Richard Furman, "Sermon," in Baptist Board of Foreign Missions, *Proceedings of the Baptist Convention,* pp. 20ff. Furman was the pastor of First Baptist Church, Charleston, S.C., and first president of Baptist Triennial Convention.

16. Humphrey, *Promised Land,* pp. 6-7.

17. John Blair Smith, *The Enlargement of Christ's Kingdom, The Object of a Christian's Prayers and Exertions. A Discourse, Delivered in the Dutch Church, in Albany, Before the Northern Missionary Society in the State of New-York, at Their Organization, Feb. 14, 1797* (Schenectady, N.Y.: Printed by C. P. Wyckoff, 1797), p. 14.

18. Proudfit, *Sermon before NMS,* p. 17.

19. New York Missionary Society, "Instructions to their Missionaries among the Indians," in Beaver, *Pioneers in Mission,* p. 243.

20. Dwight, *Thy Kingdom Come,* p. 22.

21. Leland, *Writings,* p. 379.

22. Griffen, *The Kingdom of Christ,* p. 19.

23. Nathanael Emmons, *A Sermon, Delivered before the Massachusetts Missionary Society, at their Annual Meeting in Boston, May 27, 1800* (Charlestown, Mass.: Samuel Etheridge, 1800), p. 29.

24. Miller, *Sermon before NYMS,* p. 46.

25. Joseph Harvey, *A Sermon, Preached at Litchfield, Before the Foreign Mission Society of Litchfield County, at their Annual Meeting, February 15, 1815* (New Haven, Conn.: Hudson & Woodward, Printers, 1815), pp. 6-7. Harvey was pastor at Goshen, Conn., and founder of the For eign Mission School.

26. Jedidiah Morse, *A Sermon, Delivered Before the American Board of Commissioners for Foreign Mission, at their Annual Meeting in Springfield, Massachusetts, September 19, 1821* (Boston: Board of Commissioners by George Clark, 1821), p. 6.

27. Jedidiah Morse, *The Gospel Harvest, Illustrated in a Sermon, Delivered at the Old South Church in Boston, before the Society for Foreign Missions of Boston and the Vicinity, at their Annual Meeting, January 2, 1815* (Boston: Printed by Nathaniel Willis, 1815), p. 18.

28. *The Piscataqua Evangelical Magazine,* II (1805), 206.

29. Proudfit, *Sermon before NMS,* pp. 21-22.

30. See "The Waning Glory of God," Chapter IV of Haroutunian, *Piety Versus Moralism,* pp. 72-96.

31. Nott, *Sermon before the General Assembly,* pp. 22-23.

Chapter 8

Mission and Man

The Religion of Christ is the only effectual remedy for human depravity, and this depravity is the source of all disorders and misery.

Samuel Miller — 1802

The cause of missions has for its object the extension of the Saviour's reign, and raising millions of our fellow men from deplorable darkness and desolation, to temporal and eternal blessedness. Yes, it is the Great Cause, in comparison with which All Others Sink Into Nothing.

Samuel Miller — 1823

The missionary spokesmen of the early Nineteenth Century had a global awareness. Their world swarmed with tribes and peoples who had never heard the gospel of Jesus Christ. American churchmen turned their attention to the East partly because the American West was sparsely populated with generally nomadic nations. On the other hand, the Orient contained cities and nations of enormous size. "Nations, countless as the stars of Heaven," one of the preachers told his congregation,

> inhabit this Globe, who have neither heard his fame or seen his glory. They are without God, and without Christ, in the world. They are become vain in their imaginations. They have changed the glory of the incorruptible God into an image made like to corruptible man. With rude admiration, they gaze on the natural sun, breaking from the east, and kindling day around them; but never have their eyes beheld the sun of righteousness, whose benign glories dissipate the more malignant gloom of spiritual darkness.[1]

It was to these millions that the churches addressed their mission. When Hall and Newell prepared *The Conversion of the World,* they estimated that six hundred million men were not even nominal Christians. Missionary preachers had speculated about these numbers for some time and attempted to compute the corresponding responsibility that this multitude placed on the Church. After 1818, six hundred million is almost a certified number. It appears over and over again in the sermons as a measure of the colossal need of the world and the Gargantuan task of the Church.

The mission began in hope. The sovereign decrees of God guaranteed success. In the struggle with Universalist ideas in the last half of the Eighteenth Century, Evangelicals asserted that the Lord would save a greater part of mankind,
even though, up to that time, a relatively few of the total number of men who
had lived were counted among the elect. Joseph Bellamy supported these speculations with a mighty pen. He concluded that in the great days of the Church's expansion over all the world and in the thirty-five generations of the millennium,
millions would be saved.[2] The leaders of the missionary movement took up this
welcome news. They expected the pagan millions to believe in Christ.

Salvation in the aggregate, nevertheless, would be accomplished by individual conversion. The condition of unregenerate man was deplorable.

> Ever since man revolted from God, and joined apostate angels, in
> rebellion against his Maker, and involved himself and his posterity
> in guilt and ruin, darkness has covered his understanding.[3]

Those who attempted to set the mission in theological perspective had to concern
themselves with the nature of man without Christ.

Human Depravity

Preachers of the missionary sermons, with few exceptions, were profoundly convinced of the depravity of human nature. There were shades of disagreement as to its character and extent and, occasionally, a lack of clarity about
how it is communicated to individuals. This divergence from precise, doctrinal
harmony may mark the decline of Calvinism in American theology. However,
these distinctions were not noticeably drawn among those who vitally participated
in promotion of missionary endeavors. The emphasis among the missionary men
overlooked sectarian distinctives in commitment to the great cause of world redemption. Whether New Divinity, classical Reformed Calvinism, or modified Calvinism of the Baptist variety flavored the theological posture of a given board or
society, it insisted that its missionaries stress "the depravity and moral impotence
of sinners."[4] The glory of God was the ultimate object to be achieved by missionary efforts. The condition of man, because of his sin, was the immediate occasion
for such activity.

> Blind to his true interests ever since the fall, man hath erected the
> standard of opposition against the divine government . . . Not a
> rebel of the fallen race lays down his arms without opposition.[5]

The fall of Adam, and the condemnation of mankind in him, was the beginning of
that stupendous and glorious drama which preceded the redemption of the world
by the Son of God and all the marvelous workings of the Spirit of God since then.[6]

Occasionally a missionary sermon before the SPGNA gave primary emphasis to the education and civilization of the pagans and had little to say about their

conversion. John Lathrop was pessimistic about achieving much among American aborigines until they were civilized. While a missionary of Eleazar Wheelock, in his youth, he had seen too many native youths, trained for mission service, abandon their work and "become *Indians again.*"[7] William E. Channing preached the annual sermon before this society in 1809. It was not published. An early collection of some of his miscellaneous works contains an abbreviated paper, which contains the essence of that sermon. In the paper, he raises serious questions about the value of the missionary undertaking and suggests that the pagans do not need to be converted, at least to that brand of Christianity most engaged in the missionary enterprise.[8] In 1811, James Kendall presented a long apology for the salvation of the devout and sincere heathen who had never heard of Christ. However, he ended the defense by saying:

> When we consider the darkness, the ignorance, the error, and
> sin in which the heathen world are generally involved, and the
> superior advantages, which they enjoy who live under the light
> of the gospel . . . the few examples of virtue and piety, that
> may be found amidst the darkness of paganism, will not be
> urged as a reason, why we should feel no concern, and take no
> pains, to furnish them with the means of better light, a purer
> faith, and a sublimer worship.[9]

The major thrust of these sermons is atypical, even among sermons delivered before the SPGNA.

The typical missionary preacher, theologizing about the plight of man, drew pictures of total depravity. Mankind's moral perversion was comprehensive both in its nature and extent.

> Blindness covers the understanding, perverseness occupies the
> will, and the affections are corrupted. From this evil heart pro-
> ceed all the streams of abominable conversation found amongst
> mankind: all nations of the earth are infected with this malady.[10]

The several consequences of the fall, John M. Mason said, left man in hopeless ignorance of the true God. "Los of ability to discover the chief good, was at once the just reward, and the native consequence of revolt." The heavens declare the glory of God, but benighted pagans are not able to "decipher their language." Fallen man cannot discover completely correct ideas about the external characteristics of God from natural revelation. Insight into God's moral character and his love and forgiveness is totally impossible. The inseparable companion of this perverted understanding is "an erring conscience."

> The general sentiment of right and wrong, though sufficient, if
> violated, to leave men without excuse, will by no means con-
> duct to the proper discharge of duty.

Finally, mankind without the benefit of special revelation does not know how God should be worshipped. Pagan rites follow the absurd, blasphemous or obscene. The result on social character is atrocious.

Unrestrained by any just apprehensions of God, of his law, or
his government, the most baleful passions domineer in the heart,
and the most horrible excesses pollute the life. Moral distinctions
confounded, the sense of relative obligation extinguished, crimes
the most atrocious perpetuated . . . upon principle, are . . . the
result of being without God.[11]

In 1814, Elijah Parish presented human depravity in a different manner.
Because of man's native depravity a special divine revelation is necessary. Natural
man can never have "just ideas of the Divine Being." No pagan nation has ever
held consistent ideas of the holiness, justice, or providence of God. An occasional
individual may attain a sublime concept of deity, but it is as "rare and useless,
compared with the permanent light of the Christian world, as the lucid flashes of
the electric cloud compared with the splendors of the shining sun." Reason is impotent. It cannot provide mankind with correct views of immortality, of their
need of the office of a Mediator. Neither civilization nor the arts improve man's
religious knowledge. Man is not able to change the moral character of his own
heart or reform the actions of his life.[12]

In 1815, before the Vermont Missionary Society, Asa Lyon devoted his
entire sermon to the "Depravity and Misery of Man." Lyon inferred that modern
communication, travel and education had enabled observers to become acquainted
with man "in his various dispersions through nearly the whole world."

As a physical, a religious, a moral, a social and a civilized being,
he has passed under our accurate observation. In every situation,
we can trace some faint remains of the image and superscription
of the Creator; but can discover more abundant testimony that
his glory has departed.

Man's natural powers are strong, and he is capable of "refined and exalted happiness," but he pursues paths which lead to distress and misery. The increasing
knowledge of man is but a notice of his depravity and imperfections.[13]

Viewing man from his intellectual and physical character, Lyon found
evidence that all men had descended from the same parents. However, his mental
and physical attainments all over the globe were vastly diversified. Whatever man's
situation — luxury or poverty, education or ignorance — it tended to have some
perverted dimension. Men go mad with learning and lazy with plenty. "Man is
everywhere stripped of his primeval glory, the gold is become dim and the most
fine gold changed." Man is involved in worship wherever he is found, but it is
tainted by his depravity. He tends to worship for purely selfish reasons and often
fashions his gods after his own image. Morally he shows the same ambivolence.
"Qualified, by nature, to be subject to moral law," man nevertheless perverts
moral principles. Man tends to justify as virtuous the evil and selfish in himself.
The good things he does arise from wrong motives.

The moral glory of man is departed. Man's condition is pitiful and melancholy. Blind to his true condition and the true God, he cannot perceive the good.

Captive to his own selfishness he cannot will the good. Enmeshed in perverted affections, he cannot love the good.

Where is hope and help? The preachers asseverated that it could only be found in Jesus Christ. His good news was the "sovereign remedy for all these evils."[14]

Immortal Souls

The depravity of man is only one aspect of his condition. His treasonous relationship with his creator does not affect the eternality of his soul. Men are created to live forever. Two very significant articles appeared in the *Connecticut Evangelical Magazine* in 1801. The first was primarily concerned with the missionary responsibilities of the American churches. The second discussed additional motives for support of the missions. The "worth of the souls of men" received first consideration. The souls of the heathen and the people of the new settlements were as valuable as the souls of people in established communities.

> Heaven will be as precious, and the loss of its glory as great and
> irreparable an evil to them, as to yourselves. Who can conceive
> of the quantity of happiness or misery, that must be experienced
> by an immor tal soul through eternity! . . . This will be obtained
> or lost by each one of those immortal souls, for whom your charity
> is solicited, and the greater part of them know it not.[15]

Ebenezer Porter brought human depravity and the immortality of the soul together in his sermon before the Missionary Society of Connecticut in 1810. What could be said, he asked, of the immense multitudes of Asia, Africa and North and South America who are immersed in the gloom of absolute heathenism?

> I will say they are *men*, sprung from the same stock, polluted
> with the same depravity, and destined to the same eternity with
> us. Their souls are immortal, like ours; and like ours, must be
> ransomed by an interest in the one all-sufficient atonement, or
> perish without hope. The trump of God will wake them from
> the dust of the earth, to share in all the realities of an intermina-
> ble hereafter; to mingle in the groans of the damned, or the shouts
> of victory that shall encircle the throne of the Lamb.[16]

Eternity is the destiny of every man, either an eternal misery or blessedness.

Leonard Woods was a most eloquent artist of the immortal soul. Man, he insisted, was as frail as the "tender grass" but fashioned for immortality.

> The lamp which the Lord hath lighted up in his breast, will burn
> forever. The mind will be ever vigorous and active. No labor can
> exhaust it. No length of ages can waste its vigor. No pressure of
> guilt or suffering can destroy its activity.

This kind of mind lives in every human being. The sophisticated citizen and the brutal savage, the heathen and the Christian, are all immortal. All are "on a level in point of accountableness to God and immortality of the soul."[17]

The soul's immortality had tremendous implications for the missionary movement just as did man's depravity. Immortality gave the soul infinite value. It helped give meaning to the death of Christ. An infinite sacrifice was made for something of infinite value. Human depravity left man hopeless and helpless, justly deserving the "damnation of Hell" but unable to alter his character or change his destination.[18] Immortality made man God's highest creation and of supreme significance. The salvation of a world of immortal souls was an object infinitely surpassing in magnitude the highest comprehension. An obligation equally great bound every Christian to exert himself to the uttermost to accomplish it.[19]

The possibility of mercy and the promise of heaven or inevitable judgment and eternal perdition were man's only options. The immortality of the soul combined with the man's utter sinfulness to form a powerful motive to missionary action. Gordon and Newell closed their little booklet in 1818 on this note.

> O, Christians, fly to the work! . . . the Heathen are before you; —
> their present miseries, and their future impending ruin, call you to
> hasten to them the word of life; — your Redeemer bids you go and
> pluck them as brands from the burning. . . . While you delay, the
> Heathen perish, and you rob the Saviour of the joy and praise of
> receiving the Heathen for his inheritance . . . You and they are sum-
> moned to judgment. How can you meet them there? — They knew
> nothing of that tremendous day — but you did; and you knew that
> if they died unwashed in the blood of Christ, that day must seal their
> eternal perdition. . . . Now they know that while you and they were
> upon the earth . . . you had it in strict charge from the Judge him-
> self to make it known to them, that they, as well as you, might be
> prepared to meet it in peace. But you neglected the charge; and
> now nothing remains for them, but the dreadful doom.[20]

Benevolent Compassion for Mankind

The threat of judgment and hell is not the primary motive that rises out of the concept of man held by the spokesmen of the missionary movement. In the sermons and other promotional literature of the mission before 1820, one must search carefully to find such references. The emphasis of the literature of the first generation of missionary advocates is on mercy and compassion. The mission is the product of disinterested love. It stems from and fosters a benevolent compassion for mankind. Compassion for one's fellowman, the desire for his salvation, a passion that his lot in life be improved, is the second great motive of the missionary movement of the early Nineteenth Century. Samuel Hopkins' concept of disinterested benevolence is the most potent theological construct in this missionary attitude.

Hopkins identified seeking the glory of God, devotion to the establishment of the kingdom of Christ, and pursuit of the greatest good for mankind. All three were essential expressions of disinterested benevolence. In the propaganda materials of the mission, prepared for popular consumption, it was difficult to maintain this ontological identification. In meeting objections to the missionary movement, it was much easier to present the enterprise to lukewarm church members and outspoken critics as an effort to meet the spiritual needs of pagan man, of caring for his immortal soul, than to become involved in the metaphysical ramifications of the glory of God.

Personal salvation, the preachers were sure, soon produced a desirable effect in the social and moral behavior of depraved man. But priorities must be maintained.

> Happiness is the object of general pursuit, and whatsoever is essential to it is, by a very familiar figure, called the desire of all. This is the hinge upon which missionary efforts ought to turn. It is the only consideration sufficient to . . . support those efforts against the opposition which always awaits them. The civilizing of a nation is an important object; the salvation of an individual is of more importance: for deliverence of millions from a savage state is a blessing not to be compared with the rescue of a single soul from eternal misery.[21]

Attention gradually shifted, in the period of this study, from the glory of God to the salvation of man as the most important motive of the missionary enterprise. Several factors contributed to this shift. The visibility of communities, proliferating and mushrooming, on the advancing frontier created a state of emergency. The potential of the new settlements as wombs of a new paganism begat genuine concern. But theologically, the ground for such a shift was disinterested benevolence or holy love.

Leonard Woods is probably the most able exponent of disinterested benevolence as the foundation of the missionary enterprise. For him, like Hopkins, disinterested benevolence described the nature of God and the essence of true religion. Every true worshipper of God, he told one congregation, resembles him in love and can only be satisfied with that which infinite love designs. The Christian *is* concerned with the temporal needs of his fellowman.

> But, when their spiritual interest is before him; when he contemplates the value of their souls, and the prospect which the gospel opens of immortal happiness in the world to come; his bowels of compassion are moved; his tenderest affections kindled; pure and heavenly love pervades and warms his soul. He longs for the eternal felicity . . . of the world.

With this disinterested love the Christian presents himself to God as a living sacrifice, willing to suffer anything for the advancement of his cause. *"His heart beats high for the conversion of the world."* This love is the "true spirit" of the Christian faith. It is the "affection which glows in every new born soul," the principle which "governs and animates the church of Christ."[22]

Woods' sermon in memory of Harriet Newell is a sonnet-in-prose to disinterested benevolence. Holy affection, he said, is the work of divine grace in the heart of man. It is the essence of being in Christ and finds expression everywhere true Christians live and serve. But, it is most evident in the lives of those who suffer persecution and/or serve as missionaries. To them belong the greatest pleasures of benevolence.

Let them see the glory of God displayed in the salvation of sinners;
let them see the Church look forth as the morning; let them enjoy
communion with Christ; and they have enough.

Harriet Newell manifested disinterested benevolence as she, through the grace of God, entirely consecrated herself to *"the establishment of the kingdom of Christ in pagan lands."* Divine love was so exquisitely displayed in her that the hardships of the missionary life were associated in her mind with the glory of God and the conversion of the heathen. They gave her enjoyment and delight rather than aversion and dread. She was a woman eminent in benevolence and piety and entirely devoted to the best of all causes.[23]

Many other missionary preachers agreed with Woods. Benevolence was the true spirit of the gospel of Christ. "God is a being of infinite benevolence," Horatio Bardwell said.[24] The Gospel of Christ is the only remedy, the divine sovereign remedy, for man's depravity. John Williams insisted that "the true knowledge of God, in Christ, by his Spirit and gospel, is the source of all virtue and happiness in individuals, families, cities and nations."[25] John M. Mason explained:

Exposed to this melancholy fate, the heathen claim our sympathy.
. . . Are they shut out forever from the divine compassions? No!
To the praise of his grace, Jehovah hath thoughts of mercy, rich
mercy towards them. He will destroy . . . the covering cast over
all people, and the veil that is spread over all nations.[26]

According to William W. Miller, a layman, speaking before the Auxiliary Missionary Society of Morristown, New Jersey, the gospel of Christ teaches the immortality of man and discloses the only plan for reconciling the sinful creature to the creator. Yet some Christians felt "no anxious desire to convey" these truths to others.

Where is your benevolence? And if you have no benevolence,
where is your christianity? It is but a name; benevolence, is the
animating principle of our holy religion; it gives it all its life and
energy and beauty.[27]

"The interposition of the Son of God in behalf of sinners," Eliphalet Nott averred, "is the highest act of benevolence that the universe ever saw." Great glory and benevolence belong to those who tell of that divine intervention.[28] Jeremiah Day asked, "What other pursuit is to be compared with this great enterprise of

Christian benevolence?" Not military victories or commercial successes or scientific discoveries. Nothing compares to that "compassionate love" that takes the message of divine mercy to the corners of the world.[29] The object of the gospel is so great that no means should be spared to insure its success. Nothing is too important to be consecrated to this sacred and benevolent cause.[30]

Two great motives head the list of those things that stimulated the American churches in missionary cause at the beginning of the Nineteenth Century. The missionary leaders recognized their preeminence. "The glory of God, and the welfare of mankind are the leading principles which govern the Christian's heart."[31]

Alexander Proudfit suggested that the concern for the salvation of men was related to the concept of biblical anthropology.

> With a concern for the glory of God, we may connect, as a second
> obligation for preaching the gospel, compassion for our fellow mor-
> tals. Sympathy for the object in distress, and a painful solicitude
> for its relief, are equally dignified and universal characteristics of
> human nature. . . . But . . . it is the soul, the precious, never, never
> dying soul, which claims our compassion and our aid. Do not your
> hearts melt within you while your eye rolls over that western wil-
> derness? There you behold millions of your fellow mortals, perish-
> ing without vision; stung deep they often are with remorse for guilt;
> but strangers to that Jesus whose blood speaks reconciliation and
> peace.[32]

Compassion, actuated by benevolent love, the essence of the Christian faith, dictated selfless involvement in preaching the gospel to the nations.

In one of the most creative defenses of the missionary movement produced in the first quarter of the Nineteenth Century, Alexander McClelland asked the critics of the enterprise to consider the redeeming quality of the principles and motives from which the endeavor originated. The objective and motives of the movement were beyond criticism and above all praise. The objective was to "raise to the Deity a tribute of glory" from his creation by extending the knowledge of his Son. Further, the mission aims to emancipate the family of man from the thraldom of ignorance and sin. Christians have been impelled to become involved in this arduous task by

> motives as pure as the object is glorious; by the disinterested desire,
> that "the will of God be done on earth, as it is in Heaven," by con-
> sidering the deplorable condition of those who have no God, and
> by the conviction, that as God has made of "one blood all nations
> of the earth," so all are capable of being restored to the felicity
> and prerogatives of their exalted nature.[33]

NOTES FOR CHAPTER 8

1. Proudfit, Sermon before NMS, p. 22.

2. Bellamy, The Millennium, Works, I, 510. See also C. C. Goen, "Jonathan Edwards: A New Departure in Eschatology," in Church History, XXVIII (March, 1959), 38.

3. John Williams, A Discourse, Delivered April 5, 1803, in the Baptist Church, in Gold-Street, Before the New-York Missionary Society, at Their Annual Meeting (New-York: Isaac Collins and Son, 1803), p. 5. Williams was pastor of the Gold Street Baptist Church in New York and longtime correspondent of William Carey.

4. Abiel Flint, "The Charge," in Samuel Miller, A Sermon, Delivered in the Middle Church, New Haven, Conn., Sept. 12, 1822, at the Ordination of the Rev. Messrs. William Goodell, William Richards and Artemas Bishop, as Evangelists and Missionaries to the Heathen (Boston: Crocker and Brewster, 1822), p. 41.

5. Abeel, Discourse before NYMS, p. 24. Abeel was an associate pastor of the Reformed Dutch Church in New York.

6. Haroutunian, Piety Versus Moralism, p. 34.

7. John Lathrop, A Discourse Before the Society for Propagating the Gospel among the Indians, and Others, in North-America. Delivered on the 19th of January, 1804 (Boston: Manning and Loring, n.d.), p. 19.

8. William Ellery Channing, "Means of Promoting Christianity," Discourses, Reviews, and Miscellanies (Boston: Carter and Hendee, 1830), pp. 527-529.

9. James Kendall, A Sermon Delivered Before the Society for Propagating the Gospel among the Indians and Others in North America at Their Anniversary, November 7, 1811 (Boston: John Eliot, Jr., 1811), p. 15. Kendall was at the Church in historic Plymouth.

10. Williams, Discourse before NYMS, p. 11.

11. Mason, Hope for the Heathen, pp. 126-130.

12. Elijah Parish, Sermon Preached at Boston, November 3, 1814, Before the Society for Propagating the Gospel among the Indians and Others in North America (Boston: Printed by Nathaniel Willis, 1814), pp. 3ff. Parish was pastor of the Congregational Church in Byfield, Mass.

13. Asa Lyon, The Depravity and Misery of Man. A Sermon Delivered Before the Vermont Missionary Society at Their Annual Meeting at Woodstock, September 15, 1814 (Middleburg, Vt.: Printed by Timothy C. Strong, 1815), p. 5. Lyon was pastor in South Hero, Vermont, and at the time he delivered this sermon, served as judge of the Vermont Circuit Court.

14. Ibid., pp. 10-12.

15. CEM, I (April, 1801), 361.

16. Ebenezer Porter, "A Sermon delivered at the New Brick Meeting House, in Hartford, on the evening of May 15, 1810; at the request of the Trustees of the Missionary Society of Connecticut," in CEM, III (July, 1810), p. 244. Porter was pastor at Washington, Conn., and in 1812 became Professor of Sacred Rhetoric at Andover.

17. Woods, Sermon Delivered in Salem, pp. 258-259.

18. [And.], "On Human Depravity," CEM, III (April, 1810), p. 127.

19. Hall and Newell, Conversion of the World, p. 86.

20. Ibid., pp. 88-89.

21. Abeel, *Discourse before NYMS,* p. 12.

22. Woods, *Sermon Delivered in Salem,* pp. 257-258.

23. Woods, *Sermon Preached at Haverhill,* pp. 4, 6, 7, 11, 15, 22.

24. Horatio Bardwell, *The Duty and Reward of Evangelizing the Heathen: A Sermon Delivered in Newburyport, Lord's Day Evening, October 22, 1815* (Newburyport, Mass.: Printed by William B. Allen & Co., 1815), p. 6.

25. Williams, *Discourse before NYMS,* pp. 6-7.

26. William W. Miller, *An Address, Delivered Before the Auxiliary Missionary Society of Morris at Their Meeting Held at Morris-town, Oct. 24, 1820* (Morristown, N.J.: Printed by Jacob Mann, 1820), p. 17. Miller was a Presbyterian layman in Morristown, N.J.

27. Mason, *Hope for the Heathen,* p. 131.

28. Nott, *Sermon before the General Assembly,* p. 26.

29. Jeremiah Day, *A Sermon, Delivered in Boston, Sept. 17, 1823, Before the American Board of Commissioners for Foreign Missions, at Their Fourteenth Annual Meeting* (Boston: Printed by Crocker and Brewster, 1823), p. 9. Day was Dwight's successor as president of Yale.

30. Parish, *Sermon Preached in Boston,* p. 23.

31. William Linn, *A Discourse, Delivered April 1st, 1800, in the Brick Presbyterian Church, Before the New-York Missionary Society, at Their Annual Meeting* (New-York: Printed by Isaac Collins, 1800), p. 8. Linn was one of the pastors of the Reformed Dutch Church, in New-York City.

32. Proudfit, *Sermon before NMS,* p. 24.

33. Alexander McClelland, *A Sermon in Vindication of the Religious Spirit of the Age: Preached April 9, 1820, in the Middle Dutch Church, New-York, on the Anniversary of the New-York Missionary Society* (New-York: Printed by D. Fanshaw, 1820), pp. 9-10.

Chapter 9

Mission and the Renovation of the World

Those who are engaged in the cause of missions have undertaken to produce the greatest change which has ever been wrought in the character and destinies of the human race.

Elias Cornelius — 1823

The goal of the mission of the American churches in the early National Period was truly magnificent. It comprehended the whole human race. The object was reclaiming all the nations of the world for Christ. Only the renovation of the whole world answered the designs of divine redemption.

The Gospel

In the minds of the champions of missions, the gospel of Jesus Christ became the ultimate weapon. It was irresistably efficacious and perfectly adapted to all the needs of all men in all parts of the world. The immediate goal of the mission was to preach this totally adequate gospel to all mankind.

Elijah Parish defined the gospel as a "scheme of mercy" designed by the infinite God and revealed in his word. "The gospel alleviates," Parish continued, "the heaviest woes of man, and is a source of consolation in his most deplorable necessities."[1] But it consisted of more than the simple account of the life of Jesus. Compared to the promulgations of philosophy and the intellectual disquisitions of sophisticated Armenians and Unitarians, however, the missionary preachers considered the preaching of the gospel a short and simple process. Speaking of the apostles, which modern missionaries were to immulate, John M. Mason said:

> Their guilt and their depravity — their certain destruction without pardon and renovation — the grace of God in sending Christ Jesus to die for sinners — his ability to save unto the uttermost; and the freedom of his salvation to the most worthless and vile, are the truths which won the Gentiles to the obedience of Christ. It is this same gospel which, at this hour, turns men from *darkness to light,* and which is destined to carry the banners of the cross victorious round the globe.

Such a gospel unveiled man's real misery but also introduced the only remedy. It both revealed man's greatest needs and disclosed the means for supplying those needs. "Seconded by the energy of the quickening Spirit," Mason added,

> this precious gospel fastens on the conscience, melts the heart, thrills the very bones and marrow, and transforms the most obdurate rebel into a willing subject of Jesus Christ.[2]

The gospel was the divine medicament, the sovereign, omnipotent antidote, for man's moral and spiritual sickness.[3] The proclamation of this gospel in the power of the Holy Spirit and in the language of the hearers was the appointed means of its propagation throughout the world. The missionary advocates invariably stressed the importance of preaching. Its pre-eminence was emphasized as opposed to the distribution of the Bible and the establishment of schools. Both these were extremely important, but it was the preaching of the gospel, not the knowledge of the gospel, that was necessary for the salvation of men. The public preaching of the gospel was the "great engine of divine grace."[4] The ABCFM reported to the "Public" in 1813,

> Important . . . as the distribution of the Scriptures among the heathen, in their own languages, is held to be . . . it should never be forgotten, that the *preaching of the gospel* in every part of the earth, is indispensable to the general conversion of mankind. Though the Scriptures alone have, in many individual cases, been made the instrument of regeneration, yet we have no account of any very extensive diffusion of Christianity, unless where the truths of the Scriptures have been preached, . . . *the preaching of the gospel* is, after all, the grand means appointed by Infinite Wisdom for the conversion and salvation of men.[5]

The effect of the gospel went far beyond the conversion of individuals. The gospel was also the divine instrument for producing a vital transformation in the total human situation. The gospel of Christ, not human reason or modern science, nor any of the other accruements of civilization, was the only medium potent enough to effect such a comprehensive reformation.

> Every hope of the future melioration of mankind, and of the establishment of general happiness, which does not rest on the future prevalence and influence of the gospel, is delusive. The Religion of Christ is the only effectual remedy for human depravity . . . To think, then, of reforming, purifying and tranquilizing society by literature — by science — by the prevalence of political orthodoxy — by any thing but Christianity, is an expectation which all experience has shown to be a vain dream.[6]

Archibald Alexander refuted the idea that the American Indians had to be civilized before they could be evangelized. The gospel, accompanied by the power of God, had triumphed over such obstacles many times before. Rather than wait for civilization to reach the western wilderness, the gospel should be immediately proclaimed among those tribes. It was the most effective instrument of civilization. "The renovation of the heart, which it produces, will do more to mitigate savage ferocity, than all the arts of the world."[7] Joseph Harvey accentuated this particular influence of the gospel:

> The appointed means of civilizing and christianizing the heathen, and of salvation to every sinner, is the WORD OF GOD. . . . But in order that the word of God should take its full effect, it must be translated into the various languages of the earth; its great truths must be explained. . . . the Heralds of the Gospel must go forth to preach the unsearchable riches of Christ in heathen lands.[8]

The hope of changing savages into civilized men by the force of law or military discipline, or by the influence of agriculture or an acquaintance with the arts was useless phantasy. Only the gospel of Jesus Christ could accomplish this magnificent feat.[9]

Francis Wayland averred that the missionary movement was the most sublime enterprise of human history. One aspect of this sublimity was the gospel's effectiveness in producing moral revolution in the world. "The gospel of Jesus Christ is the remedy devised by Omniscience" specifically for healing the disease of man's moral nature. Only the gospel can persuade men to obey God. "Reason cannot do it; philosophy cannot do it; civilization cannot do it." The preaching of the cross of Christ is the cure for all the remedies of the fall and alone can transform human society.[10]

While the immediate goal of the mission was to preach the gospel of Christ to all the world, the divine effects of the gospel were destined to reach such proportions that an acutal renovation of the world would take place. This ultimate hope was usually described as the conversion of nations, the expansion of the church throughout the world, and the transformation of human society.

The Conversion of the Nations

The goal of the mission was the actual conversion of every nation and tribe to Christ. The globe is to be Christianized. Christianity is eventually to replace all the other religions of the world. The mission aimed at the deliverance of the whole heathen world from the darkness and sin of paganism. Its goal was the diffusion of gospel light into every corner of the world. Samuel Spring explained that the day was approaching when "the temple of Christ will be commensurate with the habitable globe."[11] Ebenezer Porter asserted that the prayer, "Thy Kingdom come," implied that there would be a universal spread of true religion among mankind.[12] For Sereno Dwight that prayer was a petition that the spiritual dominion of Christ over the minds of men might become universal. In other words, it was a prayer "that all mankind may become christian."[13] This was the first great hope of the mission.

The conversion of the nations was related to the eternal covenant between the Father and the Son. The Father had given the nations of the world to Christ as his inheritance. Jehovah was a covenant God. The nations of the world belonged to Christ. The submission of all nations to Jesus was more certain than the law of the harvest. The reward of the farmer may fail. The reward of the labor of Christ shall not! "There must be a harvest of souls," Eliphalet Nott thundered,

> a harvest immense and universal. The veracity of God is pledged to this effect. This pledge secures unalterably the event. The seasons may be interrupted . . . but the promise of God cannot fail.

Jesus Christ must ultimately receive homage from all nations.[14]

The preachers stressed the covenant between the Father and the Son before the foundation of the world. In that agreement, the Father decreed that a particular number of men from all the tribes and cultures of the world would be given to the Son. Some also stressed the covenant relationship between God and his people. Peter Sanborn insisted that the Abrahamic covenant furnished abundant cause for missionary efforts. That pledge of God to Abraham and his descendants assured that the "Gospel net" would ultimately enclose "all the nations and families of the earth." Because of this covenant, those who engage in the missionary enterprise can be sure of success. Essentially it is the promise of Jehovah that he shall "ultimately draw all nations to the cross and gather them into one vast assembly."[15]

Total conversion was anticipated. The ratio of the saved to the lost was to increase greatly as the church moved ever closer to the Millennium. God would remove the veil of darkness and ignorance that covered men outside of Christ. Families in Christian lands who were apostate or blinded by anti-Christian doctrine would see the light. Israel would turn from obstinate unbelief. The lure of Islam would be exploded. Pagan ignorance would be demolished.[16] That the heathen would be converted and Christianity become, "at some future day, the religion of all mankind" was not just ecclesiastical rhetoric.[17] The conversion of the nations would eventually be a material reality.

In 1815, Jedidiah Morse explained that by the conversion and accession to the Christian church, or both Gentiles and Jews, the whole world will be Christendom, and all the kingdom of the earth will become "the kingdoms of our Lord and of his Christ."[18] Six years later, speaking from *Psalm 2,* Morse declared that the Bible promised "that the whole world, at some future period, shall become one universal, purified church, of one heart and one soul, and constitute . . . the 'inheritance,' the 'possession' of Christ."[19] The first missionaries to depart for Palestine were instructed to consider their mission as part of an extended and continually expanding system of benevolent action "for the recovery of the world to God."[20] The friends of missions were engaged in a cause which they assuredly believed would come to actual manifestation.

> They hope they are performing some humble part, in the great scheme of measures for repairing the desolations, not of a temple or a city, but of a world. They are not attempting to lay again,

the foundations of the earthly Jerusalem; but from the wilds of heathenism, to gather materials for the spiritual Sion.[21]

The conversion of the nations described the vastness of the missionary task. Its magnitude was sufficient to call the church to extraordinary exertions. Christians, Leonard Woods felt, had been looking for "some grand object to seize their hearts and engage all their powers." The conversion of the world constituted *"the very object wanted."*[22] The object of the mission was so vast that it defied description. It was an attempt to evangelize whole nations and, ultimately, to renovate a world. In an attempt so noble and sublime all Christian men would want to participate. The "great object of evangelizing *all* nations" was more glorious, more worthy of patronage "than the tongue can express."[23]

"Christians," Alexander McClelland said, "are seriously entering into the grand project of christianizing and civilizing the globe, and are looking forward to a period, when there shall not be a tribe in Tartary's wilds which shall not offer to the Lord offerings of righteousness and praise." They were so confident, he continued, that the conversion of the nations would be brought about by the instrumentality of God's people that they were "standing up to the work like men," with a fixed purpose and a calmness and resolution most astonishing.[24]

The missionary enterprise embraced "every child of Adam." It was as vast as the race. Its goal was to rescue each man from tribulation and wrath and give him a title to glory and immortality. Francis Wayland asked,

What object ever undertaken by man can compare with this same design of evangelizing the world? Patriotism itself fades away before it.

An entire moral revolution in the whole human race will be effected.

Not a nation, but a world is to be regenerated. ... We go forth not to persuade men to turn from one idol to another, but to turn universally from idols to serve the living God. ... And this mighty moral revolution is to be effected, not in a family, a tribe, or a nation, but in a world which lieth in wickedness.[25]

The concept of the conversion of the nations was the context in which individual conversions took place. It actually resulted from the continual conversions of individuals from many nations and became a strong connective to the extreme emphasis on individual conversion which later prevailed. As the great object of the mission and by concept expanded imaginations and loosed tongues of eloquence. "The darkness of a hundred ages," Heman Humphrey pronounced, "is to be pierced and shattered, by the all pervading light of the Sun of Righteousness." Satan, the malignant usurper of the earth shall be ejected from his domain. Millions of captives will be set free. The Holy City is to be rescued from the hands of Islam.

The river of the water of life is to flow in a thousand new channels, bearing upon its unruffled current, the blessings and the triumphs of the Cross. Those who are scorched in equatorial deserts will "sit down under the shadow of Christ with great delight," while all, who shiver amid the ice of the poles, will be warmed into spiritual life. The effeminate Hindoo and the degraded African will be raised to the dignity of men and of Christians. The habitations of cruelty, in far distant continents and islands, will be enlightened by the Gospel and possessed by the church. The wild men of the American forests will be tamed, and all the wilderness will become the heritage of Zion.[26]

In 1826, Edward D. Griffen spoke before the ABCFM. In only thirty years, he observed, tremendous changes had been wrought on and by the Church.

Already the influence of heaven has dropt upon the wilderness and the yell of the war whoop is changed to notes of praise. We must not stop till every Indian tongue has joined the general song. We must not stop till our influence has cheered the whole extent of South America. And then we must go forth to the islands, and hold on our way till we meet our brethren in other fields and unite with them in completing the harvest of the world.[27]

Kingdom and Church

In one word, the goal of the mission was the extension of the meditorial kingdom of Christ throughout the world. However, the inevitable sign of the Saviour's reign in the life of any people was the gathering of churches. The planting of the Church of Christ in all lands of the world was an achievement essential to the total renovation of the world. The increase of Christ's Kingdom was essentially the same as the enlargement of the Church Militant on earth. Richard Fuller, for example, identified the Church as the Kingdom of Christ upon the earth.[28]

John Blair Smith's sermon before the Northern Missionary Society at its organizational meeting was based on Matthew 6:10, "Thy kingdom come," one of the favorite missionary texts. He distinguished, as did most of the missionary preachers, between the "kingdom of glory" and the "kingdom of grace."

The kingdom of glory was the universal dominion of God which embraced all ranks of being, pervaded all space, and had been established from the beginning with incontrollable superiority and glorious sovereignty. The kingdom of grace comprehends the whole plan and administration of Christ's mediatorial office. It is the empire of Jesus Christ over the hearts of converted sinners. The prayer, "Thy kingdom come," concerned this kingdom of grace. It alluded to the concern that Christians "ought to feel for the enlargement of his Church, until the kingdoms of the world become the kingdom of God, and of his Christ."[29]

The gathering of visible churches was the natural outcome of the extension of Christ's dominion of grace over the hearts of men. Smith explained that he did not discuss the "increase and enlargement of what is commonly called the visible Church," as a distinct object of the petition for the coming of the kingdom. "As far as this is valuable," Smith said, it will always correspond, in extent, with the spiritual kingdom of Christ.

> The visible Church of Christ, ought to be, from the very terms, a plain and obvious representation of his kingdom in the soul and conducted according to the simple pattern contained in his word.

Just the formation of external appendages to Christianity was not a worthy goal. A proper visible church was not constituted by merely conducting a form of worship where the doctrines of the gospel are generally espoused and the ordinances loosely administered. Nor did the union of professing Christians for maintaining the external institutions of Christianity necessarily comprise a real church of Christ. Only the just representation to all the world of what Jesus Christ has ordained and of that supreme dominion which was established in the hearts of people fashioned a proper church. Nothing but the exact correspondence of real Christianity in the soul with a visible profession can sufficiently obviate the charge of hypocrisy or reflect the true character of Jesus. Only such a visible manifestation of the Church will convince an unbelieving world of the excellency of the gospel and draw it to Christ. The creation of churches externally regulated and administered in conformity to the prevalence of the dominion of Christ in the souls of men was an essential part of the enlargement of Christ's kingdom. An expansion of such churches was precisely that coming or advancement of his kingdom to which Jesus alluded in the petition from the Model Prayer.

> This is that efficacious leaven which will eventually penetrate the whole mass of men on earth, in the latter days. . . . For the coming of this kingdom we are taught to pray; and for its successful progress and triumphant manifestation every pious heart will ejaculate a hearty Amen.[30]

The planting of churches was a spontaneous consequence of the conversion of the nations. William Lyman, reflecting on the basis of the eternal covenant between the Father and the Son, alleged that the covenant included all the promises of good that God had made to his people. It subsumed both the sending of the gospel to the remotest ends of the earth, thus effecting the conversion and salvation of souls, and the enlargement and purification of the Church.[31] Accession to the church follows immediately on conversion to Christ. The apostles engaged in this activity. They had preached the gospel and gathered churches. This should be characteristic of the church's mission in all ages.[32]

The planting of the churches through all the world, like the conversion of the nations, was one of the certain issues of missionary endeavor. The Lord had promised a latter day period of glory for the Church. After the apostolic age the Church had drifted into error and apostacy. The true Church had become a persecuted minority. To this "little flock," the eternal God had promised an era of prosperity. It would be awakened from its slumber, delivered from its impotency, and divested of the rags of insignificance. God intended to display his glory through the "existence and prosperity of the church."[33] This was in the mind of God infinite ages before time began. Christ's ministry in the world was for the redemption of the Church. "The church is the grand theme of revelation."[34] Missionary preachers believed that they could perceive, in the events of current history, the approach of this great day. "We behold," said Francis Brown, "harbingers of the approach of the King of Zion to build up and beautify his church."[35] Robert H. Bishop, preaching at the annual meeting of the Bible Society of Kentucky, in 1815, declared that "the church of the living God was to be re-established, and re-established with a degree of splendor and permanency never before equalled." The "empire of the church is to be greatly extended," and "the glory of her master" is to be seen and felt through every corner of the world. The Bible predicted that, amid great scenes of war and carnage, there would be extraordinary efforts to extend the knowledge of God among the nations of the earth.

> The church shall awake from the slumber of many generations;
> she shall shake herself from the dust, and raise her triumphant
> head amidst the wreck of empires.[36]

Heman Humphrey found an analogy between the occupation of Canaan by the Israelites and the ultimate expansion of the church over the world. As the nation of Israel was militant, so is the Church now. "As the land of Canaan belonged to Israel, in virtue of a divine grant, so does the world belong to the church."[37] This great hope could not be thwarted forever by Satanic opposition. The enlargement of the Church must become a reality. Christian congregations must eventually be gathered in all communities, in every land. Nothing less was promised in the word of God.

Elijah Waterman, preaching before the MSC in 1803, visualized this missionary goal achieved. With the eye of faith he saw the fruits of successful labor. Missionaries were multiplied. Schools were taught. Churches were formed. The peaceful ordinances of Christ superceded the orgies of demons. Tongues that muttered songs of war sung the songs of Zion.[38] Two decades later, Samuel Miller proclaimed that the period is approaching when there will be a general prevalence of the profession and power of the Christian faith over the whole earth. Not every Christian will be perfect nor every professor truly pious. But the "visible church shall fill the world." All infidelity, heresy, superstition, profaneness and vice shall be banished from the earth. Christianity shall be universally honored. The Church shall be everywhere prosperous.[39]

The Transformation of Society

Along with world-wide national conversions and the gathering of churches in every community of the world, the missionary leaders aimed for a total reformation of human society. This goal, like the gathering of churches, was not to be sought for itself or to be considered separate and apart from real conversion to Jesus Christ. However, it was not in any respect a secondary goal. It was, in fact, the inevitable consequence of the gospel's effect on men in the great day of the Church's prosperity and extension through the world. Reshaping human society is a subordinate goal of the mission only in the sense that it follows after the other two.

John N. Abeel laid great stress on the proper order. "The common progress of society," he admitted, might eventually bring civilization to a nation. But the gospel can achieve this much sooner. The effect of the gospel on a nation is to "soften their manners, purify their social intercourse, and rapidly lead them into the habits of civilized life." But the gospel has this effect only when it is gladly received and permitted to have its perfect work. Therefore, the grand object is not to bring pagan men to ordered society but to bring them to Christ and salvation.

The salvation of an individual has two wonderful effects. It delivers a soul from eternal misery and is, thus, essential to his future happiness. It also improves his moral and social demeanor and is most desirable in the human situation. The first is important because it is both prior and eternal. The gospel cannot have the latter effect until it has had the former.[40]

In the same vein, the ABCFM attempted to enlist all philanthropists and patriots into the missionary cause. Making disciples to Christ is the most effective means for truly helping man and the surest way to develop a nation of honor and strength.

It is now generally seen and felt . . . that Christianity is the only remedy for the disorders and miseries of this world, as well as the only foundation of hope for the world to come. No other agent will ever control the violent passions of men; and without the true religion, all attempts to meliorate the condition of mankind will prove as illusory as a feverish dream. The genuine patriot, therefore, and the genuine philanthropist, must labor, so far as they value the prosperity of their country and the happiness of the human race, to diffuse the knowledge and the influence of Christianity, at home and abroad.[41]

It is apodictic that the mission shall benefit human social and moral conditions. The immediate effect of conversion to Christ is the reshaping of human attitudes and behavior. William Staughton listed all the traits of Indian character that Christians found offensive. The gospel of Christ had answers for all levels of debauchery.

The gospel is suited to the removal of the vices which disgrace the Indian tribes; and where it is received in power, instead of the brier, will come up the fir-tree, and instead of the thorn, the myrtle tree. Instead of uncleanness, there will be purity; instead of drunkenness, sobriety; instead of treachery, integrity; instead of cruelty, mercy; instead of indolence, industry; instead of theft, honesty; and instead of contempt for females, the mother, the wife, the daughter, and the sister will be loved and respected as tender, faithful friends.[42]

The Christian faith, William Linn said, following the same line, contributes to the temporal happiness of men "by enlightening their minds, subduing their passions, and directing them in the discharge of their duties" to God and one another.[43] The religion of Christ is "a system of religion, admirably calculated to improve the minds, the morals, and the manners of men, and, by consequence, to promote their present interest and happiness."[44]

To prove the point, the preachers called attention to the effects of the gospel on the heathen in the recent history of the mission. Jeremiah Day, in 1823, insisted that the good that the mission had brought to the heathen in temporal affairs made it more than worth the sacrifice. In India, "the devoted widow is rescued from the funeral pile," and mothers are restrained from abandoning infants to the tide of the Ganges. Red Indians have left the path of war, and "cruel Africans" have laid down their murderous knives. In the islands of the Pacific houses of Christian worship are being built, and the people observe a "more unviolated Sabbath, than the descendants of the pilgrims of New England."[45] Edward D. Griffen insisted that even were the gospel unrelated to man's eternal salvation, it would still be of tremendous service to man in his day-to-day life. The Christian faith is a foundation of hope, a purifier of manners, a tamer of the passions, a means of civilization, and a handmaid to science.[46] To lift up ones temporal life was of the nature of the gospel of Jesus Christ.

The ultimate goal, however, was the final demise of the great crimes of society that had so long plagued man. When the knowledge of Christ has been universally received, when the nations have been converted and churches have been erected among all peoples, the final victory over social and moral evils will take place. This is the final renovation of the world for which the mission was aimed. Its achievement was nothing less than the introduction of the Millennium.

John Williams, Baptist pastor in New-York, assured his hearers, in 1803:

When this glorious period shall arrive, the darkness . . . among the nations shall be expelled by the . . . gospel. For the inhabitants of the world shall know the Lord from pole to pole! Idolatry shall be no more . . . Envy shall cease . . . All the instruments of war shall be converted into implements of industry and husbandry. Our Indians shall bury their tomahawks in the dust forever, and love as brethren. The vices which now afflict the nations shall be removed . . . Happy Period![47]

Joshua Bates explained to the SPGNA, in 1813, that he could not say what the precise state of the world would be during the time of the universal prevalence of Christianity. "That there will be a great change in the social condition, if not in the civil institutions and political relations of the inhabitants of the earth, is . . . probable. . . . Consider for a moment," he added,

what must be the happy effects of a universal prevalence of these principles. . . . How great must be the sum of human happiness, when all, in the exercise of Christian benevolence, seek the happiness of all! How great too must be the increase of personal felicity to each individual Christian, when all are Christians . . . If in the present mixed state of society, where the iniquity of the unprincipled aboundeth, and the love of many real Christians waxeth

cold, the happy effects of Christian faith . . . are enjoyed in a
measure by all . . . what unspeakable happiness will be enjoyed,
when this faith . . . shall be perfect and universal.[48]

"Blessed renovation! Happy World!" was the exultation of Samuel Miller
when he envisioned the goal of the mission "gloriously realized." All the malignant and violent passions which now degrade man shall be taken away. Intemper-
ance, impurity and injustice shall be destroyed. Bigotry, party-spirit, and strife
(civil and ecclesiastical) shall be abolished. War, famine, pestilence, oppression
and slavery shall be no more. In their place will be righteousness, order and peace.[49]

Such descriptions, of course, approach the end-time of earth, the last and
most glorious period of history, the thousand year reign of Christ in the hearts of
all men. This was, in fact, the goal of the mission, to labor with God to bring on
that glorious period. The mission, indeed, brought men to Christ and prepared
them for heaven. But, in the process, and only through that process, the Millennial
reign becomes a reality.

This brings this study to two other questions which must be discussed.
What specifically is the role of the Church in this grand enterprise? How is the
mission of the Church related to the Millennial Age?

NOTES FOR CHAPTER 9

1. Parish, *Sermon Preached in Boston,* p. 3.

2. Mason, *Hope for the Heathen,* pp. 139-140.

3. Lyon, *The Depravity and Misery of Man,* pp. 16, 18.

4. Abel M'Ewen, "A Sermon, delivered at the North Presbyterian Church in Hartford, on the evening of May 16th, 1815; by appointment of the Trustees of the Missionary Society of Connecticut," *CEM,* Second Series, VIII (June, 1815), pp. 205, 208. M'Ewen was pastor of the Congregational Church of New London, Conn.

5. *ABCFM Annual Reports,* 1813, p. 69.

6. Miller, *Sermon before NYMS,* pp. 51-52.

7. Alexander, *A Missionary Sermon,* p. 18.

8. Harvey, *Sermon in Litchfield,* p. 5.

9. Dwight, *Thy Kingdom Come,* p. 13.

10. Francis Wayland, *The Moral Dignity of the Missionary Enterprise. A Sermon Delivered Before the Boston Baptist Foreign Mission Society on the Evening of October 26, and Before the Salem Bible Translation Society on the Evening of November 4, 1823* (3rd ed.; Boston: James Loring, 1824), p. 19. At the time of this sermon, Wayland was pastor of the First Baptist Church of Boston. He became President of Brown University in 1827.

11. Spring, *Sermon before the MMS,* p. 6.

12. Porter, "Sermon at Request of MSC," p. 244.

13. Dwight, *Thy Kingdom Come,* p. 4.

14. Nott, *Sermon before the General Assembly,* p. 9.

15. Peter Sanborn, *The Extent and Perpetuity of the Abrahamic Covenant a Motive to Missionary Exertion. A Sermon Preached Before the Massachusetts Missionary Society, at Their Annual Meeting, May 30, 1815* (Boston: Printed by Samuel T. Armstrong, 1815), pp. 6, 11. Sanborn spent all his life as pastor of the Congregational Church in Reading, Mass.

16. Mason, *Hope for the Heathen,* pp. 136ff. R. Pierce Beaver, "Preaching the Mission to Americans in the National Period," unpublished paper provided by the author, has been most helpful to me in this entire section. See p. 6.

17. *ABCFM Annual Reports,* 1813, pp. 66-67.

18. Morse, *The Gospel Harvest,* p. 14.

19. Morse, *Sermon before the ABCFM,* p. 6.

20. "Instruction of the Prudential Committee of the American Board of Commissioners for Foreign Missions, to the Rev. Levi Parson and the Rev. Pliny Fisk, Missionaries designated for Palestine. Delivered in the Old South Church, Boston, Sabbath Evening, Oct. 31, 1819," in Levi Parsons, *The Dereliction and Restoration of the Jews. A Sermon, Preached in Park-Street Church, Boston, Oct. 31, 1819, Just Before the Departure of the Palestine Mission* (Boston: Samuel Y. Armstrong, 1819), p. 41.

21. Day, *Sermon before the ABCFM,* p. 4.

22. Woods, *Sermon Delivered in Salem,* p. 265.

23. *ABCFM Annual Reports,* 1812, p. 48, 1813, p. 74.

24. McClelland, *A Sermon in Vindication of the Religious Spirit of the Age,* p. 6.

25. Wayland, *Moral Dignity of the Missionary Enterprise,* p. 14.

26. Humphrey, *Promised Land,* p. 11.

27. Edward D. Griffen, *A Sermon Preached Sept. 14, 1826, Before the American Board of Commissioners for Foreign Missions, at Middletown, Connecticut* (Middletown, Conn.: Printed by E. & H. Clark, 1826), p. 25.

28. Fuller, "Sermon," p. 19.

29. Smith, *The Enlargement of Christ's Kingdom,* pp. 3, 11.

30. *Ibid.,* pp. 19-21.

31. William Lyman, "A Missionary Sermon, delivered at Hartford, on May 14, 1811," *CEM,* Second Series, IV (June, 1811), 203.

32. M'Ewen, "A Sermon Delivered in Hartford," pp. 208, 209. See also Morse, *The Gospel Harvest,* p. 14.

33. Bardwell, *The Duty and Reward of Evangelizing the Heathen,* p. 3.

34. Emerson, *Duty of Christians,* p. 11.

35. Brown, *Sermon before the Maine Missionary Society,* p. 18.

36. Robert H. Bishop, *The Glory of the Latter Days, A Sermon, Delivered at the Annual Meeting of the Bible Society of Kentucky, Sept. 1815. With an Appendix, Containing 1. Some Original Thoughts on the Slaying of the Witnesses; and 2. A Concise Account of the Kentucky Bible Society* (Lexington, Ky.: Printed by Thomas T. Skillman, 1815), pp. 4, 10. Bishop was controversial Associate Reformed and Presbyterian pastor, professor at Transylvania College in Kentucky, and president of Miami University.

37. Humphrey, *Promised Land,* p. 5.

38. Elijah Waterman, "Extract from a Sermon delivered at Hartford, on the Evening of May 12th, 1803," *CEM,* IV (July, 1803), 31. He was a pastor at Windham, Conn.

39. Miller, *Sermon Delivered in New Haven,* p. 18.

40. Abeel, *Discourse before NYMS,* pp. 13, 40.

41. *ABCFM Annual Reports,* 1813, p. 50. The conviction that the gospel will transform society, along with developing millennial expectation, came under the influence of Social Darwinianism and fused with the Nineteenth Century infatuation with "progress." Eventually James Dennis could produce three big volumes on missions and social progress.

42. Staughton, *Missionary-Encouragement* (Philadelphia: Stephen C. Ustick, 1798), p. 41.

43. Linn, *Discourse before the NYMS,* p. 9.

44. Abiel Holmes, *A Discourse Delivered Before the Society for Propagating the Gospel among the Indians and Others in North America, at Their Anniversary Meeting in Boston, November 3, 1808* (Boston: Farrand, Mallory and Co., 1808), p. 17.

45. Day, *Sermon before the ABCFM,* p. 17.

46. Griffen, *Sermon before the ABCFM,* p. 6.

47. Williams, *Discourse before NYMS,* p. 14.

48. Joshua Bates, *A Sermon Delivered Before the Society for Propagating the Gospel Among the Indi-
     ans and Others in North America, at Their Anniversary, Nov. 4, 1813* (Boston: Published by Cum-
     mings and Hilliard, 1813), pp. 6-7. Bates was pastor at Dedham, Mass., until 1818 when he became
     president of Middlebury College.

49. Miller, *Sermon Delivered in New Haven,* pp. 21-22.

Chapter 10

Mission and the Role of the Church

The present age is emphatically the age of action.

Samuel Worcester — 1813

The duty of the Church is written in sun-beams.

Heman Humphrey — 1819

The devotees of the missionary enterprise were often highly critical of the apparent lethargy of Christians of earlier ages in propagating the gospel fully to all nations. This view developed from a gap in their knowledge of what had been done. It evinced a lack of appreciation for Roman Catholic missions through the Middle Ages and since the Reformation. In fact, the obvious disparity between the quantity and success of missionary labors performed by Roman Catholics and those performed by Protestants since the Sixteenth Century may have caused the greatest chagrin.

Explanations of the absence of large intensive efforts by Protestants to convert the heathen usually followed one of two lines. Some, like Nathanael Emmons, ascribed it purely to negligence:

> Had christians in every age possessed the spirit of the apostles and the primitive believers what great things would they have done to promote the cause of Christ? Or had they been as wise as the men of the world . . . to promote their temporal interests, the gospel would have long since been carried to the ends of the earth . . . Nothing has been wanting, since the revival of learning, the invention of printing, and the discovery of the magnet, to prevent the universal spread of the gospel, but merely christian resolution and zeal. This long and great negligence calls for the humiliation of Christians.[1]

The second theory did not discountenance the first. Negligence may have been the immediate occasion of the sparsity of missionary endeavor. But a more exact approximation of the situation considered the timetable of God. Francis Brown, exhibiting remarkable misinformation for one who was the following year

255

to become president of Dartmouth College, insisted that "nothing of any considerable magnitude had been done by those, who ought to have stood foremost" in such an undertaking. Who would have believed that even "our own Mr. Edwards" would have had no thought of translating the Bible into the language of the heathen or of establishing missions among them he querried. Such lack of action would be surprising "if events had not taught us that the Lord's time had not yet come."[2]

Whatever caused the failure of Protestant forerunners, missionary spokesmen all agreed that a new day had dawned. The time for waiting had passed. The time of action had come.

The Age of Exertion

When Samuel Miller preached his first missionary sermon in 1802, he was not ready to say that the period of the great expansion of the Church, preparatory to the Millennium, had actually dawned. He warned against rushing too quickly to identify current historical events with events foretold in prophecy. Many had fallen into that trap in 1798, when the Pope had been forced to give up his throne by Napoleon's armies. The papal defeat had been interpreted as the fall of Antichrist. More recent developments had dashed such hopes.

Miller was sure that such an age would come and that its time was fixed. Its certainty involved the church in two specific duties. The duty of waiting, with "a firm and unwavering expectation," for the fulfillment of the prophecy was self-evident. Waiting cultivated "a spirit of patience and entire submission to eternal Sovereignty." The second duty was diligent exertion. Efforts to promote the Church's expansion through the world and to hasten the events of prophecy were by no means inconsistent with waiting.

> It is required of every Christian that he be active, that he aspire to
> the honour of being a *worker together with God,* and that he employ
> every power conferred upon him in hastening the desired period.
> While he is bound on one hand to wait with patience . . . he is equally
> bound . . . to labour with as much zeal and diligence as if everything
> depended on human exertions. Neither the existence of divine pur-
> poses, nor the necessities of divine operations, exclude human agency.[3]

Twenty-one years later, Miller preached at the ordination of three missionaries to the South Seas and the Levant. Stupendous events had transpired in those two decades. One development was that missionary endeavor had become the most celebrated cause of the American churches. Some of the early leaders were dead. Could Timothy Dwight or Samuel Worcester return with a word from the other side, Miller was sure, they would verify that the cause of missions had an importance and glory "unspeakably greater" than had been perceived in the preceding years. Only about one hundred eighty years remained before the dawn of the Millennium. Even greater things must take place in that relatively brief period of time. The age of efforts had come. The Church had already begun to flex its muscles. "Let us," he said, "hold on our way, with all the alacrity and confidence of those who anticipate a speedy and glorious conquest."[4]

Other missionary leaders were more emphatic than Miller. By the time the overseas mission was under way, many American churchmen were convinced that the time of waiting had passed. "Other times," the ABCFM's "Address to the Public" claimed in 1813, "have been times of preparation; the present age is emphatically the age of action. Shall we remain idle in this harvest time of the world?"[5] Answering the objection that the conversion of the nations is God's work and that the churches must wait for God to do it, Joseph Harvey countered,

> True, my brethren, this is *God's* work. — That is our encouragement. But it is *Man's* work also . . . And by attention to the subject we may, perhaps, discover that the time for *waiting* is past, and the time for acting has arrived.[6]

In 1820, Sereno E. Dwight concluded that to live in such a day "involved no trifling responsibility." The kingdom of Satan was overturning. The kingdom of Jesus was rising in its ruins. It was not a time to be idle. The age of exertion had come.[7]

This new age was often contrasted or compared with the age of the apostles. Many believed that in the time of the apostles the gospel had actually been preached to the whole world.[8] But the full consequences of the promises of God for Christ and his Church had not been realized. The apostolic age was instructive for the Church in the period of its greater and more glorious expansion.

The promoters of the mission insisted that the Nineteenth Century churches were not to expect the gospel to be propagated by means of the miraculous. Abiel Holmes gave a major portion of his missionary sermon of 1808 to this aspect of missionary endeavor. Before Christ, the dispensation of true religion was restricted to the Hebrew nation. With the commission of Christ to the apostles, a new dispensation was established in which no nation was debarred from the privilege of faith. At Pentecost, the apostles were endued with "miraculous gifts" to enable them successfully to execute their commission. So empowered, the name of Christ was proclaimed with "a celerity utterly astonishing." No adequate causes could be found to explain it without reference to divine agency.

> But it was not the divine purpose to continue the propagation of the gospel by supernatural means. The age of miracles was to terminate, when, by the establishment of Christianity, the design of them should be effected.

Other gifts — pastors and teachers to instruct in the great truths and duties of Christianity — were imparted to the Church for the propagation of Christ through all the successive generations of the human race. Therefore, "industry and zeal" must take the place of miracles in this present age. "The Bible," Holmes reported, "is translating into barbarous languages; and the various nations of the earth will soon, as formerly at the memorable Pentecost, hear in their own tongues the wonderful works of God."[9]

John Emerson, the following year, further developed this concept. The servants of Christ must use fully all instituted means and adopt every reasonable and scriptural measure calculated to achieve the desired end.

It is plainly the will of providence, that the gospel should be propagated in the world, not indeed as in the apostles (sic) days, by extraordinary means; the age of miracles having terminated with their special design, but by those more common and ordinary ones.

The same God who granted supernatural gifts also gave other gifts which were permanent and designed to continue to the end of the world. The apostles were, therefore, the first instruments for laying the foundations, but "his ordinary stated ministers are appointed to raise the superstructure of this spiritual building."[10]

Prayer was of crucial importance, but prayer had to be accompanied with correspondent labor or else be abortive. It was unreasonable to think that men who prayed for daily bread would not expect to labor at an honest calling. It was just as unthinkable for Christians, who prayed for the kingdom of God to come, to be unwilling to labor in the kingdom's behalf.

The principles of reason . . . and the dictates of common sense, . . . the directions of scripture, and the obvious designs of providence, at once show the importance of christians' laboring in all suitable means for the bread and water of life, in order that we and others may not famish and die eternally.

In contrast to the primitive age of Christianity, miracles are not to be expected. God will effect his purpose by ordinary means. Erudition acquired by study will supersede the gift of tongues. The written words of the Bible dispersed by Christian preachers and accompanied by the influences of the Holy Spirit will be as effective as the words delivered from the inspired prophets of old. "Human exertions will supply the place of supernatural interpositions."[11]

Others were not so impressed with the effectiveness of the miraculous gifts. Supernatural abilities notwithstanding, the proclamation of the gospel in the apostolic age was accomplished by human instruments. In 1798, Alexander Proudfit castigated those who would "deliberately mock the Most High, or wantonly insult" the misery of fellow mortals by advising that the whole matter be left to "Holy Providence."

Jehovah it is true worketh, but it is equally true he worketh by means. The Gospel has never yet been propagated by miracle. As far as its joyful sound has extended through the earth, it has unvaryingly been effected through the intervention of means.

The time had come for the Church to "awake from security," to "shake off the lethargy of former years," and begin to labor in proportion to the magnitude of the enterprise and to the assurance of success.[12]

A quarter century later Proudfit reasserted his position. All the achievements essential to the conversion of the world must be "obtained through the co-operating agency of the Lord the Spirit, by means." The word of God, either read or preached, would be the instrument. "The kingdom of Messiah was never extended, nor its trophies multiplied, by miracles. The administration of his covenant is wholly an administration of means."[13]

Eliphalet Nott, preaching before the Presbyterian General Assembly, in 1806, described the Messiah's reign as one to be introduced "BY HUMAN EXERTIONS." After reviewing the successes of the apostolic age, he observed that wherever Christianity had been extended — in Europe, Asia, or Africa — during the first centuries of the Church it was extended "through the intervention of human agency." Even among the American tribes during the Colonial Period the method was the same. He concluded that no new method of salvation is to be expected. Converts to Christianity have always been made by the "exertions of the saints." Such will be God's method in time to come.[14]

All agreed that in missionary endeavor "the excellency of power" must be of God. They also agreed that this work is to be accomplished by human instrumentality. Heman Humphrey admitted that the whole enterprise might be accomplished by a miracle in a single day. But just as God had chosen to employ his people to drive out the nations in the conquest of Canaan, so God had decreed that the Church must inherit the Gentiles. The Church should not expect miracles or angels to perform this enormous task. The Church must go and take possession.

> How was the Gospel first propagated, even in the age of miracles?
> By toil, by perseverance, by encountering a thousand dangers: by
> assailing the strong holds of Jewish infidelity and Pagan Idolatry.
> Had the Apostles shut themselves up in Jerusalem what would
> have been the consequence? In vain would they have *waited* for
> the conversion of the heathen.

Later history certified the truth. The Reformation was accomplished by the power of God through the agency of valiant champions of the truth. In the same manner, by the use of means and instruments, the whole world must be subdued and rendered fruitful.

> The Bible must be translated into all languages, and the means
> of sending it to every human habitation must be provided. The
> Gospel must be carried to the heathen, before we can expect
> them to embrace it . . . Missionaries must be *sent*. The conver-
> sion of the world is to be effected, by the blessing of God upon
> the prayers and labors of the Church.[15]

The Command of Christ

The command of Christ is the authority for the Church's exertions. After 1810, obedience to the Great Commission of Jesus is a major motive for engaging in missions. Hardly a sermon can be found that does not stress this command.

Obedience to the command of Christ is also a significant factor in the earlier sermons. In 1797, John M. Mason summed up and underscored all other missionary motives with the command of the Lord Jesus Christ. It left no room for evasion. Disobedience to it could only be called sin. Excepting only the Moravians,

> all denominations of Christians among us have violated their faith
> to their Lord; and are now chargable with habitual disrespect to
> his authority. Instead of going, with generous emulation, to the aid
> of the heathen, we have gone, one to his farm, and another to his
> merchandize; we have clamoured for the shibboleths of party, and
> have been unanimous . . . in declining, on carnal and frivolous ex-
> cuses, that work of faith, that labor of love.[16]

The divine commission, according to Levi Frisbie in 1804, retains its gracious and sacred authority. On these grounds, the Church must proclaim the gospel to all classes and nations of people.[17]

The Great Commission, given by Christ, made it impossible for the Church to excuse itself. The Biblical material made evident that the responsibility for evangelizing the world was applicable to all generations of Christians. "The explicit command of the great God our Saviour" makes the obligation "inviolably binding on us," Alexander Proudfit asserted.[18] Richard Fuller's sermon in 1814 had a portion of the Great Commission as its text. In the Commission, he said, the Lord has "empowered his faithful Ministers to preach the gospel, and administer New-Testament Ordinances in every age and nation, till Time shall be no more."[19]

A few days later, Archibald Alexander, preaching on the same theme in the same city, affirmed that this command marked a "new and important era in the history of the church and of the world." It constituted the "public and formal abrogation of the Mosaic economy." It is evident that the commission did not apply to the apostles only. It obligated their successors also because the work it prescribed was too great to be completed by so few. Further, every minister of the gospel derives his authority to preach and baptize from this commission of Christ to the apostles. This command made the office a divine, not merely a human, appointment.

> Now, that instrument which gives authority, must be allowed to
> regulate its exercise. If we receive the office, we . . . take upon us
> the obligation to fulfil (sic) its duties . . . The conclusion . . . is in-
> evitable, that every minister is bound, by the very nature of his
> office, to use his best efforts to propagate the gospel through the
> whole world.[20]

The command of Christ defined the extent and duration of the efforts of the Church. Leonard Woods insisted that the command of Christ absolutely obliged Christians to *"seek the conversion of the world."* When the command was given, Christ had "all nations and ages before him." With all "the love and authority of the King of Zion," he gave the command to *"evangelize all nations."*[21]

> *The friends of missions, if they regard the command of their*
> *Savior, will not rest, till they have gone into all the world, and*
> *preached the Gospel to every creature. They will not cease their*
> *labors, till the tribes of the wilderness rejoice in his salvation;*
> *till every island of the sea has received his law; "till Ethiopia*
> *shall stretch out her hands unto God"; till the myriads of Asia*
> *shall unite in ascriptions of praise to the Redeemer.*[22]

Just to acknowledge the obligation did not fulfill the command of Christ. Nor did a few acts of obedience satisfy all of the claims of Christ's authority. The command of Christ was not fully obeyed until every idol was destroyed, every family illumined with Bible truth, and until every heart had experienced renovating grace. When the unbeliev of Judaism, the delusions of Islam and the ignorance of Paganism was decimated, and when the knowledge of God had covered the earth, then the obligations of Christ's command would be no more.[23]

The command of Christ involved the entire church in the missionary cause. Obedience to the divine command, Leonard Woods asserted, is a business in which every Christian ought to take part. It is folly to think the command is binding only on Christ's special ambassadors and not on "private Christians." The ambassadors must be sent and supported. "The christian community at large has a deep concern in the command of Christ."[24]

For Richard Furman, only deliberate disciples were members of the visible church. All were, by definition, members of that "holy society standing in special relation to the Son of God, as his Kingdom on earth." They were fitted to his service and used by him as "honoured instruments for maintaining his Cause, and for displaying his Glory among mankind." In this station, the saint has an arduous service to perform in the "Cause of God." The command of Christ is binding on him, as a member of Christ's Church, to labor for the increase of his Lord's kingdom at large. The weakest Christian may contribute to the interests of this kingdom.[25] Archibald Alexander also asserted that the command of Christ was obligatory on the "private members of the Church." They are not required to preach, but their duty is apparent.

> If a king should send forth heralds, through the whole extent of
> his dominions, to announce some important intelligence . . . it
> would be the duty of all, not only to avoid throwing any obstacle
> in the way of the royal messengers, but to facilitate their progress
> by every means in their power, and to give them every encourage-
> ment . . . whilst engaged in the king's business. Well, Zion's king,
> . . . hath sent forth his heralds, and commissioned them to go to the
> ends of the earth, announcing every where the glad news of salvation:
> are not all the subjects of this King . . . under obligations to promote
> this object?[26]

The command of Christ clearly defined the role of the Church in the mission to the world. It constituted a divine imperative for missionary endeavor. When the first foreign missionaries were ordained in 1812, Samuel Worcester saluted the young men as the first-fruits of the obedience of the American churches.[27]

Co-workers with God

As significant as was obedience to the Great Commission of Christ, it does not completely delineate the concept of the role of the Church in the mission. For the champions of the mission, the glory of the Church's role was to be fellow laborer with God in the work of redemption. They were amazed that the omnipotent God ordained that impotent men shall be co-workers with him in bringing the world to salvation. William Staughton, before the Philadelphia Missionary Society in 1798, asserted that the "honor of being fellow-workers with God" was one of the high motives to missionary endeavor.[28] In 1801, Samuel Niles told the Massachusetts Missionary Society that, though God is not dependent on his creatures to achieve his designs of mercy and though human efforts have no innate efficacy in themselves, men are still co-workers with God in the salvation of sinners.

> Divine wisdom sees a propriety in employing men and means, to spread the knowledge of the truth, convince sinners of wickedness, and convert them from it. Human exertions always have been, and always will be . . . improved in this great work, till the elect are gathered in, and the heavens be no more.[29]

Eliphalet Porter, preaching before the SPGNA in 1807, averred: "We ought to esteem it, not merely our duty, but our privilege and glory to be labourers together with God, in diffusing the light and blessings of Christianity."[30]

Samuel Spring envisioned the American churches as designed, in the providence of God, for a very special kind of partnership with him in world redemption. Who knows, he asked, whether we "on this narrow strip of the continent are brought upon the stage at this revolutionary period to cooperate with Christ in a peculiar manner to enlighten Gentiles and restore the Jews?" God was calling for laborers. No Christian had a warrent to prefer the honor that "opulence and pleasure" might give to that honor that God would give to those who labored with Him.[31] Christians, another preacher proclaimed, might consider themselves "the agents of heaven" as they exercised their privilege of propagating the gospel.[32]

In 1814, Samuel Worcester found it a pleasing thought that the "Redeemer will graciously bestow upon Christians in America the honor of becoming joyful instruments in promoting his cause." How noble the distinction if America should be known in the far corners of the world as a nation that refused to covet territory or to harbor ambitions of political dominion or commercial status and, instead, became engrossed in dispensing Christ's "unsearchable riches."[33] Such were the glorious possibilities of laboring with God in the work of redemption.

Leonard Woods said that God offered "the privilege of aiding in the great work of *converting the nations*; — a work, which he has reserved to these *last, best days*; — a work, which the holy apostles would almost wish to live again to promote; and in which the hosts of heaven exceedingly rejoice." It is "honor and happiness" to take part in this work.[34] Ebenezer Porter, in 1810, observed that though the head of the Church is not dependent on human instruments, "he is pleased to use them as the stated medium of his operations." Porter hailed the new day of cooperation in the work of God that had dawned for the American churches.

> We have seen the missionary flame . . . kindle across continents
> and oceans, till the same holy fervor . . . warms the hearts of God's
> people on every side of the globe. We have seen the Christian world
> awake from a slumber of two thousand years, to a system of efforts,
> for the revival and spread of religion. The rapid multiplication of
> missionary societies, praying societies, bible societies . . . constitute
> an epoch in Christendom which will be memorable for ever.

This was all a part of great opportunity offered the church in joining with God in his redemptive labor.[35]

No one was more eloquent in describing the glory of being a fellow worker of God than the youthful Horatio Bardwell. In the accomplishment of the system of redemption, Bardwell explained,

> the great Head of the church most reasonably requires the concur-
> rence and co-operation of his creatures. The divine constitution,
> respecting the church, is such, that human instrumentality is neces-
> sary. Men must be co-workers with Christ. Not because God is not
> able to carry on his own work . . . but because thus it hath seemed
> good in his sight. . . . How great is the honour, to be employed in
> the same work with the Lord Jesus Christ! — In the same work,
> which engages the attention of saints and angels in heaven! . . . in
> this glorious cause . . . we are permitted, yea, commanded to en-
> gage: — and through Christ strengthening us, we can do much.[36]

Such was the grandeur of the undertaking, such the exalted privilege of partnership with God that those involved in the missionary enterprise felt, "not merely that it is our duty, but our glory, to be agents in advancing the stupendous work."[37]

The Duty of the Churches

"The duty of the Church," Heman Humphrey avowed in 1819, "is written in sun-beams."[38] His metaphor encompassed both the magnificence of the missionary effort and the clarity of specific responsibility incumbent on the churches. All the boosters of the missionary cause agreed with him. There is almost unanimous accord in the literature of the mission concerning the explicit employments in which the churches were called to engage.

In general, of course, there was only one great obligation. It was the duty of the churches to send missionaries and Bibles. For this reason missionary societies and boards and Bible societies came into existence. They enabled the churches to fulfill their world-wide responsibility. What could not be done by individual churches could be done together.

> While acting alone, man is imbecile and defenseless; his sphere is
> limited; his efforts are inefficient . . . but united with others . . .
> they produce a field of light and glory. In all their important con-
> cerns, . . . they have spontaneously united together to accomplish
> their great enterprises.[39]

The ABCFM expressed this single goal in their "Address to the Christian
Public," 1813:

> The object of the Board is *one* — the promulgation of Christianity
> among the heathen. The means, by which this object is designed to
> be effected, are of two kings; — the publication and distribution of
> the Scriptures in the different languages of the nations; and the sup-
> port of faithful missionaries to explain, exemplify, and impress on
> the mind, the great truths which the Scripture contain.[40]

Gordon Hall and Samuel Newell were most emphatic in their definition of the duty
of the churches.

> Let the churches, then, consider the part that belongs to them in
> the business of evangelizing the world. It is their business to send
> forth preachers.

In 1818, these young men in Bombay noted that progress in Bible distribution far exceeded that being made by missionary societies. The fault was not that
too much zeal for giving the Bible to every creature was evident, but that there
was too little zeal for sending missionaries to preach and teach the Bible. "Sending
teachers without the Bible was the error of the church of Rome: let it not be the
error of Protestants to send the Bible without preachers."[41]

The work of the Holy Spirit is to raise up the missionaries. The work of
the churches is to send them out. In the performance of this duty, the churches
had three principle functions. Henry Kollock spelled them out in 1803: *"we
should pray earnestly, labor diligently, and give liberally for the attainment of
this glorious object."*[42]

Church members should pray. The call to prayer was no sanctimonious
cliche invented to soften the hearts of the hearers for a more concrete and cost-
ly request. It is hard to overestimate the part played by the Concerts for Prayer
in the establishment of the missionary character of the American churches.[43]
"God has promised that the gentiles shall be brought in," the preachers declared, "and yet for this he will *be enquired of by the house of Israel."*[44] The
first duty of the church was to pray.

Church members should become involved in the machinery of the missionary enterprise. Christians were called upon to promote the entire benevolent
movement by their own participation and through the enlistment of others. Not
only missionary societies, but Bible, education, tract and charity organizations
were all part of the same divine enterprise. Christians were called upon to conduct their lives in a manner consistent with their profession of Christ. "In some

instances," Asa Lyon said,

> while missionaries were recommending the gospel, others, profes-
> sing the same religion, . . . were exciting, by their crimes, the
> strongest prejudices against it. . . . In vain may we hope for success
> to the christian preacher, while the christian dealer is defrauding,
> intriguing and practicing every species of deceit and wickedness.[45]

Church members should give monetary support to the missionary endeavor.
The sermons, having as one of their specific designs, the opening of the wellsprings
of liberality, almost invariably end on this note. To motive the preacher adds eloquence, to eloquence, passion, and to passion, harangue, as the benevolent plea is
brought to a climax. Prayers are of no avail if the churches will not give of their
plenty. Property must be committed to the missionary cause. "Since miracles have
ceased," one preacher said, "the treasure, which Jesus would use in his cause, is to
be drawn, not from the mouths of fishes, but from the hands of men." Christians
are but stewards of earthly substance until the Lord needs it.[46] In 1817, the Board
of Missions of the Presbyterian Chur ch called for a serious study of tithing as a
means to underwrite the mission.[47] *The Conversion of the World* called for the
same level of financial support.[48] Warren Fay insisted that the whole matter of
funding was not a question of expediency or of policy. Christian missions are as
binding upon the churches as the support of the ministry at home.[49] Giving was
an essential participation in the mission. Through it the Christians were obedient
to their Lord and shared in the divine system of redemption.

The role that the Church was to play in the missionary enterprise had tremendous rewards. Horatio Bardwell described them well.

> Will it not be a source of unspeakable consolation to us, in our
> dying hour, to reflect, that we have done something in this
> glorious work of enlightening the heathen? In heaven . . . how
> glorious the thought, of meeting the souls of pagans, ransomed
> by the blood of Christ and saved by our instrumentality! . . . if
> *we* refuse to engage in this great harvest, the work will go on.
> . . . The work is the Lord's.[50]

NOTES FOR CHAPTER 10

1. Emmons, *Sermon before MMS,* p. 24.

2. Brown, *Sermon before the Maine Missionary Society,* p. 13.

3. Miller, *Sermon before NYMS,* p. 40.

4. Miller, *Sermon Delivered in New Haven,* p. 34.

5. *ABCFM Annual Reports,* 1813, p. 74.

6. Harvey, *Sermon in Litchfield,* p. 4.

7. Dwight, *Thy Kingdom Come,* p. 35.

8. Morse, *The Gospel Harvest,* p. 8.

9. Holmes, *A Discourse before the SPGNA,* pp. 10-13, 35-36.

10. Emerson, *Duty of Christians,* p. 7.

11. *Ibid.,* pp. 8, 9, 13.

12. Proudfit, *Sermon before NMS,* pp. 24-25.

13. Alexander Proudfit, *The Universal Extension of Messiah's Kingdom; A Sermon, Delivered in the North Church, New-Haven, Conn., Sept. 12, 1822, Before the American Board of Commissioners for Foreign Missions, at Their Thirteenth Annual Meeting* (Boston: Crocker and Brewster, 1822), p. 13.

14. Nott, *Sermon before the General Assembly,* pp. 20-21.

15. Humphrey, *Promised Land,* pp. 12-14.

16. Mason, *Hope for the Heathen, p. 151.*

17. Levi Frisbie, *A Discourse Before the Society for Propagating the Gospel among the Indians and Others in North America, Delivered on the 1st of November, 1804* (Charlestown, Mass.: Samuel Etheridge, 1804), p. 30. Frisbie was pastor at Ipswich, Mass.

18. Proudfit, *Sermon before NMS,* p. 21.

19. Fuller, *"Sermon,"* p. 15.

20. Alexander, *A Missionary Sermon,* pp. 6, 11, 12.

21. Woods, *Sermon Delivered in Salem,* p. 261.

22. Day, *Sermon before ABCFM,* p. 8.

23. Elias Cornelius, *A Sermon, Delivered in the Tabernacle Church, Salem, Mass., Sept. 29, 1823, at the Ordination of the Rev. Edmund Frost, as a Missionary to the Heathen: and the Rev. Messrs. Aaron W. Warner, Ansel D. Eddy, Nathan W. Fiske, Isaac Oakes, and George Sheldon, as Evangelists* (Boston: Printed by Crocker and Brewster, 1823), p. 6. At the time of this sermon, Cornelius was pastor at Salem, Mass.

24. Woods, *Sermon Delivered in Salem,* pp. 260-261.

25. Furman, *"Sermon,"* p. 19.

26. Alexander, *A Missionary Sermon,* pp. 14-15.

27. Samuel Worcester, "The Right Hand of Fellowship," in Woods, *A Sermon Delivered in Salem,* p. 41.

28. Staughton, *Missionary-Encouragement,* p. 43.

29. Samuel Niles, *A Sermon Delivered Before the Massachusetts Missionary Society at Their Annual Meeting in Boston, May 26, 1801* (Cambridge, Mass.: William Hilliard, 1801), p. 36.

30. Eliphalet Porter, *A Discourse Before the Society for Propagating the Gospel among the Indians and Others in North America, Delivered Nov. 5, 1807* (Boston: Munroe, Francis & Parker, 1808), p. 4. Porter was pastor of the old Eliot Church in Roxbury.

31. Spring, *Sermon before MMS,* pp. 23, 25.

32. Kendall, *Sermon before SPGNA,* p. 25.

33. *ABCFM Annual Reports,* 1814, p. 90.

34. Woods, *Sermon Delivered in Salem,* p. 268.

35. Porter, "Sermon at Request of MSC," pp. 245, 249.

36. Bardwell, *Duty and Reward of Evangelizing the Heathen,* pp. 5-6.

37. Miller, *An Address at Morris-town,* p. 11.

38. Humphrey, *Promised Land,* p. 19.

39. Parish, *Sermon Preached in Boston,* p. 23.

40. *ABCFM Annual Reports,* 1813, p. 67.

41. Hall and Newell, *Conversion of the World,* pp. 12, 18, 84.

42. Henry Kollock, *Christ Must Increase. A Sermon Preached Before the General Assembly of the Presbyterian Church in the United States of America; by Appointment of Their Standing Committee of Missions, May 23, 1803* (Philadelphia: Jane Aitken, 1803), p. 15. Kollock was, at the time he preached this sermon, pastor of the Presbyterian Church in Elizabethtown, New Jersey.

43. I refer again to Beaver, "Concert of Prayer," pp. 420-427, for an assessment of this endeavor.

44. Nott, *Sermon before the General Assembly,* p. 27.

45. Lyon, *Depravity and Misery of Man,* p. 19.

46. *Ibid.,* p. 21.

47. *Minutes of the General Assembly,* 1817, p. 659.

48. Hall and Newell, *Conversion of the World,* p. 29.

49. Warren Fay, *The Importance of the Last Promise of Jesus Christ to Christian Missionaries. A Sermon, Delivered at Springfield, May 10, 1826, at the Ordination of the Rev. Rufus Anderson, as an Evangelist: and of the Rev. Messrs. Josiah Brewer, Eli Smith, Cyrus Stone, and Jeremiah Stow, to the High and Sacred Office of Christian Missionaries* (Boston: Printed by Crocker and Brewster, 1826), p. 25.

50. Bardwell, *Duty and Reward of Evangelizing the Heathen,* p. 19.

Chapter 11

Mission and the End of History

History is but a development of prophecy.

Samuel Miller — 1802

Those committed to early missionary organization and activity in America gave much thought to eschatology. John Leland's sarcastic retranslation of Matthew 10:7 in behalf of the missionary movement is a pungent witness to this preoccupation.

> And as ye go, preach to the people, your money is essential to the salvation of sinners, and therefore, form into societies, and use all devisable means to collect money for the Lord's treasury; for the millennium is at hand.[1]

This engrossment with last things, however, should not imply an inattentiveness to things essential. Eschatology structured and gave meaning to the mission. The Millennium was less than two centuries away according to the best calculations. Churches had to be planted among every people before that great day dawned. The miraculous could not be expected. They were confident that God would accomplish his purpose of bringing in the Gentiles and converting the Jews by human means. God had set about his work. The Church was called to join with him. The march of God in history, his determined ordering of providence, would make the kingdoms of this world become the Kingdom of his Son. When the Salem Bible Translation and Foreign Mission Society met on January 4, 1817, James Coleman, theological student and budding missionary to Burma, spoke. "The preacher brought to view," a hearer reported, "the glorious millennial day, when the knowledge of the Lord shall fill the whole earth, and perfect peace and happiness prevail: That this great event was to be brought about by the spread of the Gospel of Christ, and that christians were under infinite obligation to their Lord and Saviour, to be workers together with him."[2] This grand motive helped inspire effort, give courage in times of difficulty, define missionary goals, and undergird every other missionary impulse.

Not a single sermon or missionary report can be discovered that does not stress eschatological considerations. John H. Livingston's sermon before the NYMS

in 1804 on this subject is the Goliath among many lesser giants. He recognized
that there were other missionary motives.

> The glory of God, the love of Christ, and the salvation of sinners,
> suggest constraining motives for propagating the Gospel. The com-
> mand to *teach all nations*, and the promise that the word shall *not
> return void*, present a warrant and encouragement to vigorous exer-
> tions for converting the heathen.

But when he turned his attention to *Revelation* 14:6-7, he found a prophecy from
which he could "deduce a NEW MOTIVE for strenuous and persevering exertions"
in missionary engagements.[3]

Livingston was wrong, of course. The eschatological hope was not a *new
motive*. There was an eschatological note in the early English apologies for explo-
ration and colonization. The Great Migration of 1630 had profound eschatological
overtones. John Eliot related his mission to the Indians directly to the outpouring
of God's Spirit in the Latter Days. Eschatological hope waned somewhat after the
Restoration of 1660, but Cotton Mather worked sedulously to promote the mission
and vividly related it to the coming of the Lord.

The prophetical expositions of Jonathan Edwards, and his disciples Joseph
Bellemy and Samuel Hopkins, became structurally determinative for the missionary
endeavor of the early National Period. In *An Humble Attempt* and *History of the
Work of Redemption,* Edwards explicitly established the relationship between eschatology and missions. The works of Bellemy and Hopkins, and many other lesser
known men, built upon Edwards' eschatological superstructure.

Edwards' millenial thought does represent a new departure in eschatology
for Eighteenth Century Americans. From the time of the Restoration, Americans
seldom postulated a Millennial Age of the Church that was not brought on with
the dramatic interruption of history by the return of Christ. "Edwards foresaw a
golden age for the church on earth, within history, and achieved through the ordinary processes of propagating the gospel in the power of the Holy Spirit."[4] In his
broad outline of history and the consummation of all things, Edwards basically
follows Calvin. In the period of the Reformation, however, the Church was under
the cross. In the time of the Great Awakening, in Edwards' considered opinion,
the Church was in the period preparatory to the dawn of a thousand year reign of
peace and prosperity for the Church. The passing of two centuries in the timetable
of God made all the difference in the world.[5]

Edwards asserted that history, subject as it is, to divine providence, will
eventuate in the triumph of Christian principles and that a holy utopia will come
into being. This concept was immensely effective as an instrument of propaganda.
As presented in the works of Edwards and many other preachers and theologians
in the Revolutionary Era and as constantly promulgated by innumerable preachers interested in the missionary cause in the early National Period, this theory sustained the morale of the evangelical churches and gave them a philosophy of history that made them partners with God in the redemption of the world.[6]

A renaissance of Edwardsean theology followed the end of the American Revolution. This coincided with earthshaking political developments in Europe. World events, that began in 1789, provided new flesh for the old bones of Edwards' eschatological skeleton. Samuel Hopkins' *Treatise on the Millennium* was completed in 1792 and published the next year with his *System of Divinity.* It was blatantly out of date even before it was sold. The French Revolution made Hopkins' book obsolete. The *Treatise on the Millennium* has a pre-French Revolution mentality. Edwardsean eschatology, re-interpreted in the light of the earth-shattering developments of the French Revolution, became Livingston's great *new motive* to send the gospel to the whole world.

Certain eschatological problems plagued the Protestant missionary enterprise from its earliest beginnings. Could the nations be converted, the fullness of the Gentiles brought in, before the conversion of the Jews and/or the destruction of the Antichrist? How would the monumental task be successfully completed? Was a new Pentecost necessary for the success of the mission to the Gentiles? Where did the terrible wars prophesied in the Bible fit into the picture?

All these ravelled ends began to fit together during the French Revolution and the era of Napoleon. The world was racked with war. The Papacy sank to its lowest ebb. Surely a blow had been delivered from which it would never recover. The granting of citizenship to Jews in France in 1790 and 1791, and the gradual opening of the ghettoes across western Europe that followed until 1815, brought many conversions to Christianity. The missionary periodicals reported with joy every such conversion that could be discovered.

These events coupled with the struggle with infidelity, the spectacular revivals that broke out over America, the sudden rise of a missionary spirit and missionary success around the world, and the rise of benevolent societies to attempt to assuage every manner of social ill augured but one conclusion. *God was about to bring his work of redemption to its glorious consummation.* The long awaited day was about to dawn. The kingdoms of this world were about to become the kingdoms of God and his Christ. *Revelation* 14 was being fulfilled before the eyes of the Church. The angel had begun to fly, having the everlasting gospel to preach to all who were on the earth. The Church must arise from its torpidity and join God in his glorious work.

The presentation of the eschatological implications of the mission usually followed a simple pattern. First, the reality and certainty of the coming Millennial Age was presented. The second step attempted to discover the approximate time when that age would arrive. Concern with the signs of the time was an exercise in decoding providence and history. Finally, the Church was called to arise and enter into God's work. The basis of this plea was that, in the years immediately preceding the actuality of millennial bliss, there would be a time when the Church would be highly motivated and unbelievably successful in labors to bring the world to Christ. These three areas deserve amplification.

Millennial Triumph

The advocates of the mission spared no ink or paper in their assertions concerning both the reality and the certainty of the Millennial Kingdom of Christ on the earth. This Kingdom was to be brought about, not, in the opinion of most spokesmen, by a literal return of Christ, but by the successful labors of the Church in missionary endeavor. The ambiguity of the wilderness/paradise theme reasserts itself in reference to the mission of the Church at this point. For ages the Church had hidden in the wilderness. Now God began to call his Church out of the wilderness to bring it quickly to its millennial triumph. The missionary movement was "one great means" for introducing the glories of the millennial period.[7]

The missionary spirit which pervaded the churches, John H. Livingston remarked, was an undeniable earnest for the enlargement of the Redeemer's kingdom. The missionary awakening was the most significant development since the Reformation. Related to the ultimate consequences of history it was superior to the Reformation.

> A new era is formed in the Church, and with it a new argument to prove that she is rising to higher prosperity. This is another step in the gradual plan to bring her out of the wilderness.

When the Millennial Age dawns, the poverty and impotency of the Church will vanish. For a thousand years the Christian faith will have prevalence in the world. This divine kingdom was not construed as a fifth monarchy, a temporal, earthly dominion like the four great world empires described in *Daniel* and *Revelation.* Nor was it a chiliastic kingdom brought on by the appearance of Christ returning from the heavens. Rather, this new age shall be "the abundant grace and spirit of Jesus with his Church." The Redeemer will reign in the hearts of men. In this period the knowledge and influence of the everlasting gospel will be extensively experienced. The whole earth will profess the Christian religion and all nations submit to the righteousness and authority of Jesus. The world will become the garden of the Lord. "The Redeemer's kingdom on earth will perfectly correspond to the sublimest descriptions of its extent and glory."[8]

This was no new doctrine. William Linn said every single person present at the NYMS meeting in 1800 believed "a time will come when the Christian religion will prevail over the whole earth."[9] John M. Mason explained that the millennial victory of the Church would be a complete victory over the enemies of Christ, "a universal prevalence of righteousness and peace, and, a signal manifestation of the glory of God."[10]

Leonard Woods agreed that Christians held this conviction in theory, but he doubted that it was a *"practical sentiment."* Nevertheless, he was confident:

> The Lord of the universe, in these last days, is about to do a marvelous work, a work of astonishing power and grace. The time of his glory is come. He will soon destroy all idol worship. The thrones of wickedness he will level with the dust. He will dissipate the gross darkness, which covers the nations. He will send out his light and truth, shed down his quickening Spirit, and renovate the world.[11]

A year later he assured those mourning over the death of Harriet Newell that she did not die in vain. The time is at hand when the tribes of India, and all the nations of the earth "shall fall down before the King of Zion, and submit cheerfully to his reign."[12] "Peace and righteousness and felicity will be universal and abundant."[13]

For Richard Furman the advance of the Church through the centuries was both proof and preview of what was to come.

> It is natural to look forward with pleasing anticipation to those blessed days . . . when the triumphs of the Cross shall extend to the remotest parts of the habitable globe, the knowledge of God cover the earth . . . and the Kingdoms of the World become the Kingdoms of our Lord . . . when War shall cease, the Revolutions of Empires terminate, Fraud and Oppression be banished from the earth, and Benevolence, Harmony and Love prevail.[14]

Sereno E. Dwight affirmed that, through the preaching of the gospel, the mosque, the synagogue, and the heathen temple will become centers of Christian worship. There will be "neither Mahammedan nor Heathen, neither Jew nor Gentile, but all . . . one in Christ Jesus."[15]

> On the one hand is the plundering Arab: on the other the pitiless savage. Here are the frozen children of the pole; there, the savage sable tribes of Africa; . . . the long disinherited Jew steals silently to his Messiah . . . Hark! the din of armies . . . cease; discord and war retreat back to hell . . . Brethren, 'tis no illusion; 'tis "the sober certainty" of truth divine. The zeal of the Lord of hosts will perform this — HALLELUJAH![16]

Samuel Miller put it explicitly: "the certain accomplishment of the divine predictions may be inferred *from the character of their Author.*" The divine character is the ground of confidence and the firm and eternal pillar on which the Church may build its hopes "without fear of disappointment or shame." The fulfillment of every promise is related to the glory of God. To doubt whether the "King of Zion" will keep them is to doubt whether he will remember his own glory or give attention to its advancement. The promises which God made to his Church,

> are upon solemn record . . . I cannot tell you precisely when the happy period shall arrive; but I can tell you upon authority not to be questioned, that *in due time the kingdoms of this world shall become the kingdoms of our Lord and of his Christ.*[17]

The first point of Eliphalet Nott's sermon before the General Assembly in 1806 was the "Certainty" of the "establishment of the Universal *Reign of the Messiah on the Earth.*"[18] William Rogers explained to the churches of the Philadelphia Baptist Association that same year that the progress of Christ's kingdom is gradual, but at last it will be victorious. "The stone which has already smitten the image is becoming a great mountain and must fill the earth."[19] "Other causes may miscarry," Leonard Woods said, "but this will certainly triumph. The Lord God of Israel has pledged his perfections for its success."[20]

The Signs of the Time

The second step in the pattern of relating eschatology to mission attempts to discover approximately when that age will arrive and at what hour, in the calendar of God, the Church presently functions. This is achieved by deciphering history, decoding the significance of past and current events, and by determining the meaning of Biblical prophecy. By the latter one can, it is asserted, determine what will surely come to pass. By comparing the two, the interpreter can discover the prospect and duty of the Church in its present hour.

Such observations and comparative studies were the solemn duty of the Church. Christians, Samuel Miller said, should observe with "habitual attention," the course of providence and diligently compare it with the designs announced in prophecy. The Bible contains important disclosures of the divine intention for the world. To study these in conjunction with the unfolding of human affairs was therefore a profitable exercise. It enabled one to deduce the condition and prospects of the Church and had a tendency to confirm faith, enliven hope, bind affections more closely to the Redeemer, and promote comfort.[21]

The study of prophecy was approached through many different Biblical passages. The Apocalypse was a primary source for prophetic material. John H. Livingston's sermon was a study of *Revelation* 14. This chapter contains a series of visions, "which follow each other in uninterrupted succession, referring to events which, in that very order, will be accomplished." Livingston's emphasis was on the second vision (14:6-7), but its interpretation depended on the identification of what came before and what follows after. The first vision (14:1-5) had already occurred during the Reformation. It could, therefore, be dated precisely.

The third vision (14:8) predicts the "fall of *great babylon.*" Using the 1,260 prophetic years of Daniel, Livingston insisted that the latest possible date for that event was 1999. By simple arithmetic, then, it could be determined that the second vision had to happen within a period of 500 years. Three hundred years had passed since the Reformation and nothing had happened that would correspond "in respect to the universality, the power, the success, which characterize the preaching of the Gospel described in the prediction." He was compelled to look for these events within the next 200 years.[22] Within 200 years there must be a period when a zealous ministry would arise in the midst of the churches with a new and extraordinary spirit, remarkable for its plans and success. This ministry would arrest public attention and be a prelude to momentous changes in the Church and in the world.

Great events must come to pass before the third vision can be fulfilled: (1) the nations *"who aided antichrist in murdering the servants of God"* must be punished; (2) "the Jews are to be converted"; (3) *"The fulness of the Gentiles* is to be brought into the Church"; and (4) the final destruction of antichrist.

What changes in the moral world, what revolutions in the civil,
are impending! Attend to each of the enumerated articles; estimate their magnitude; . . . then determine whether two hundred
years are not a short space for the consummation of such events?
and, if the extensive propagation of the Gospel is to precede the
conversion of the Jews, the bringing in of the fulness of the Gentiles, and the destruction of antichrist, say, whether or not we may
indulge the expectation, that it will soon commence, if it be not
already begun? We conclude, . . . that the Churches are authorized
to hope that *the vision shall* quickly *speak.*[23]

Livingston was not willing to rest here nor were the other preachers who
developed expositions of this subject. More could be known. Revelation 14:7 asserted that at the time the angel began to fly, the judgment of God would be
poured out on the nations which had been within the pale of antichrist. The simul-
taneous rise of missionary activity with the beginning of devastating wars in Europe
could not be ignored. "Why," Livingston asked,

are convulsed nations rising in a new and terrific form to extermi-
nate each other? . . . is God now coming out of his place to judge
the *earth,* to judge that portion of the world which assisted the
beast in slaying the witnesses? Must this generation — we forebear.
Judge ye. But, be assur ed, that if this work be begun . . . at that
very hour, the angel will begin to fly. When Zion sings of judgment, she always sings of mercy.

Let this suffice. You have attended to the prophecy, and estimated
the period of its accomplishment. You compared existing facts
with the prediction, and drawn a conclusion. Do you now call,
Watchman, what of the night? . . . clouds and darkness still remain,
and the gloom may even thicken at its close; but the rising dawn
will soon dispel the shades, and shine *more and more unto the perfect day.* THE MORNING COMETH![24]

Historical developments were easily correlated with the inferences of prophetic scriptures. The art of printing and the perfection of navigation were, of
course, essential to the universal spread of the gospel. The growing ecumenical
cooperation among evangelical Christians, the rise of missionary and benevolent
societies, the remarkable revivals of the age, the popularity of concerts for prayer,
and an unusual number of conversions among Jews, Moslems and heathen were
interpreted as signs that the day of aggressive action had come.[25]

Political developments of global scope directly related to the four great
events that must precede the arrival of the Millennium. The French Revolution
and the Napoleonic Wars were interpreted as the "shaking of nations" which
must precede the final triumph of righteousness in the world. Leonard Woods
explained that "the civil revolutions and convulsions, and the desolating wars of
the present day, need not dishearten" the Church. They were not only suited to
withdraw Christian affection from the perishable things of the world but also

presaged the Church's prosperity.

> The Lord shook all nations just before the Desire of all nations
> came. He has arisen now to shake terribly the earth; and we ex-
> pect the spiritual coming of Christ, and the millennial glory of
> the church, will soon follow.[26]

A whole series of events encouraged the missionary statesmen to believe
that the Jewish nation was about to be converted and return to Palestine. The
openness of the French Revolution and Napoleon to the Jewish people stimulated numerous developments that encouraged hope. The convocation of the "Grand
Sanhedrin" in Paris, July 15, 1806, was considered by Jedidiah Morse, as a distant indication that the period of Jewish dispersion was drawing to a close.[27]
The conflict of the Ottoman Empire with Russia, in the area of the Black Sea,
and with Persia, on the eastern edge of the Empire, convinced many that Islam
was about to be destroyed. The Wahhabi movement in the Arabian desert intensified these hopes.[28] "Destroy . . . the Ottoman Empire, and nothing but a
miracle," Levi Parsons said in 1819, "would prevent their (the Jews) immediate
return from the four winds of heaven."[29]

The rise of the Protestant World Mission to public attention and aggressive enterprises and the success of the missionaries around the world marked the
new ingathering of the Gentiles to the Church. The act of Parliament that opened
India to missionary endeavor despite the opposition of the East India Company
was hailed as the harbinger of that day when all the governments of the world
would become "nursing mothers" to the Church.

Napoleon's concordat with the Pope in 1801 dashed the hopes of many
that the ultimate fall of the antichrist had come. However, the fact that the Papacy was humiliated by the French Army and was reduced almost to vassalage in
the Napoleonic era convinced the missionary leaders that the Roman Church
would never recover to a position of strength. The decline of papal power
would ultimately result in a total collapse.

All these events augured that God was about to do some great thing in
the world for and with his Church. "When we observe," Samuel Worcester wrote
in 1813,

> that this tone of public feeling has been excited not by a sudden
> impulse of enthusiasm, but by a patient comparison of the word
> of God with his providence, of prophecy with history, by an at-
> tentive consideration of the peculiar *signs of the times,* and by
> the gradual operation of causes above the powers of man to con-
> trive or combine; we are forced to believe, that God has great
> things to be accomplished by the men of this generation, and
> that, after punishing the nations for their sins, he is about to de-
> liver them from the wretched bondage in which they have been
> held.[30]

Set Time to Favor Zion

The last step in the simple pattern of casting the mission in an eschatological mold has been illustrated many times in this study. It was the call for the Church to rise up and enter into God's glorious work of redemption. God was bringing history to a magnificent consummation. The Church was invited, and commanded, to join in the universal task.

However, the most dynamic aspect of the eschatological pattern in producing missionary labor was not the certainty of the millennial triumph of Christ. Rather, it related to the period before the actual dawning of the Millennium, which was the period when God would greatly bless the labors of the Church. This age actually introduced the millennial period. The Millennium was not imminent. It was at least 200 years away, according to the most respectable calculations. The time God had set to favor the Church was at hand. This awareness motivated the Church to extraordinary missionary endeavor.

Livingston's investigation of *Revelation* 14:6-7 convinced him that earlier commentators had failed to grasp the significance of the vision. It was restricted to what happened in the Reformation or identified with the mass of events that will take place after the Millennium actually begins. In reality it comprehended achievements vastly greater than were produced in the Reformation.

> And, so far from actually belong ing to the millennial period, it
> is only the appointed *means* for introducing that state; whatever
> may be its progress or consummation, it must, in the nature of
> things, begin its operations some considerable time before the
> Millennium can commence.[31]

Ten years later, Francis Brown delivered an exposition of Psalm 72:16. He remarked that most authorities asserted that this verse included the entire gospel dispensation and told of the gradual increase of the Christian Church until it filled the whole earth. To him, however, it related to the period included between the dawn of the Millennium and the full splendor of that glorious day. From the time the movement began, the Christian faith, which till then had been in a low state, began to advance and would be propagated with unexampled rapidity through the world.[32]

The signs of the time pointed to an age of success for the Church. Elijah Waterman listed, in 1803, the tokens of success that the mission experienced in those times. He concluded that "the set time to favor Zion had come."[33] Jedidiah Morse anticipated even greater victories. "When the set time to favor Zion shall have arrived," he said, "Christ will open to his missionary laborers, *a door of utterance*" and will give them the same zeal and fervency of love that was conspicuous in the primitive ages of the Church.[34] Joseph Harvey, in his exposition of *Revelation* 11:15, distinguished between the Millennium itself and that period immediately preceding it.

The Millennium properly means the thousand years during which

the saints will reign with Christ on earth. At the commencement of the Millennium then, the affairs of the church will
be settled, all nations united under Jesus Christ . . . But
there must be a period previous to this, scarcely less interesting than the Millennium itself, when the course of events
will assume a decided character, and the light of the Millennium will be clearly seen; when the tribes of Israel will be
restored, and the fulness of the Gentiles gathered in . . .
This latter period may be considered as the dawn of the
Millennium, and will doubtless embrace several years before
the Millennium actually commences.[35]

Harvey went on to show that the Church had at that time entered into
that period which is immediately preparatory to the Millennium, which is the
dawn of the latter day glory. This realization gripped the churches of the early
National Period. The age of the Church's prosperity had actually begun. The
Lord was ready to favor Zion in all her works. The time of harvest had arrived.
There was little reason to expect the Millennium to begin before two centuries
had elapsed. However, the time preparatory to that utopian age was already under way. The "set time to favor Zion" had actually arrived.

The veil begins to be rent from the heart of the Jew: the covering case over all nations is removing. The *glorious period* promised to church is at hand. The *morning* Star has arisen. The *day*
begins to dawn. The shadows are fleeing away; and, at the set
time, the *millennial Sun,* in all His glory, will beam upon the
world.[36]

NOTES FOR CHAPTER 11

1. Leland, Writings, p. 685.

2. *The American Baptist Magazine and Missionary Intelligencer,* I (March, 1817), 71.

3. John H. Livingston, *A Sermon, Delivered before the New-York Missionary Society, at Their Annual Meeting, April 3, 1804. To Which Are Added, An Appendix, the Annual Report of the Directors, and Other Papers Relating to American Missions* (New-York: T. & J. Swords, 1804), pp. 5, 7.

4. Goen, "Jonathan Edwards," p. 26.

5. I disagree with Goen at this point. He finds a serious disagreement between Calvin and Edwards in their concept of the Millennium. See *ibid.,* pp. 34-35. I believe the difference is not one of content but of emphasis. Calvin lived in the period of history, according to both Calvin and Edwards, in which the church was undergoing its most trying time. Calvin's theology was written to people who were under the cross. Edwards lived 200 years later, in one of the centers of the Evangelical Awakening. He wrote his theology for a Church on the brink of the Millennium. Both postulated a triepochal division of history. Calvin's concept of the Millennium, according to Goen, is "Simply a period of church history (the present and last) during which Christ reigns in the hearts of individual believers and over the church, his body." This is hardly different than Edwards' concept.

6. Tuveson, *Redeemer Nation,* pp. 18, 29, 34.

7. Brown, *Sermon before the Maine Missionary Society,* p. 22.

8. Livingston, *Sermon Delivered before NYMS,* pp. 26, 62-63, 77.

9. Linn, *Discourse before NYMS,* p. 8.

10. Mason, *Messiah's Throne,* pp. 265-267.

11. Woods, *Sermon in Salem,* p. 268.

12. Woods, *Sermon in Haverhill,* p. 25.

13. Bates, *Sermon before the SPGNA,* p. 6.

14. Furman, "Sermon," p. 23.

15. Dwight, *Thy Kingdom Come,* p. 28.

16. Mason, *Hope for the Heathen,* p. 141.

17. Miller, *Sermon before NYMS,* pp. 28, 29, 30, 37.

18. Nott, *Sermon before the General Assembly,* p. 7.

19. Gillette, *Minutes,* p. 428.

20. Woods, *Sermon in Haverhill,* p. 25.

21. Miller, *Sermon before NYMS,* pp. 47-48.

22. Livingston, *Sermon before NYMS,* pp. 15, 17, 54-57.

23. *Ibid.,* pp. 19-22.

24. *Ibid.,* pp. 24, 66-67.

25. Benjamin M. Palmer, *The Signs of the Times Discerned and Improved, in Two Sermons, Delivered in the Independent or Congregational Church, Charleston, S.C.* (Charleston, S.C.: Printed by J. Hoff, 1816),

pp. 4-11. He was co-pastor of The Congregational Church in Charleston.

26. Woods, *Sermon in Salem,* p. 265.

27. Jedidiah Morse, *Signs of the Times, A Sermon, Preached before the Society for the Propagation of the Gospel among the Indians and Others in North America, at Their Anniversary, Nov. 1, 1810* (Boston: Samuel T. Armstrong, 1810), pp. 39-40.

28. Dwight, *Thy Kingdom Come,* p. 16.

29. Parsons, *The Dereliction and Restoration of the Jews,* p. 12.

30. *ABCFM Annual Reports,* 1813, p. 74.

31. Livingston, *Sermon before the NYMS,* p. 15.

32. Brown, *Sermon before Maine Missionary Society,* p. 4.

33. Waterman, "Extract from a Sermon," p. 30.

34. Morse, *The Gospel Harvest,* p. 19.

35. Harvey, *Sermon in Litchfield,* p. 8.

36. Sanborn, *The Extent and Perpetuity of the Abrahamic Covenant,* pp. 9, 18.

Chapter 12

Theology Undergirding Mission

In 1855, when Robert Baird, the first great historian of American Christianity, was persuaded to revise his 1844 American edition of *Religion in the United States of America,* he was more enthusiastic about the future of the evangelical churches of the young nation than he had been during his years in Europe. Immense changes had taken place in the past dozen years, in all aspects of the nation's history. Vast land areas had been annexed in the west and southwest. Five new states, including Texas and California, had been added. The question of the northwest boundary had been settled. Eight new territories had been marked off, including one for the American Indians. Expansion of commerce, wealth and population had been phenomenal.

"What progress have our churches and religious societies made within the brief period of twelve years!" he exclaimed. Both church and state had undergone the testing of war with Mexico and the influx of three million "foreigners," mostly "ignorant of the true Gospel, and many of them uneducated, poor and vicious."[1] This crisis, Baird wrongly concluded, was over. He failed to weigh the significance of the rise of the cities and the impact of industrialization. He did not take seriously the varient Christian groups who "protested" the socially established Evangelical United Front. The three largest, mainline denominations had already split over slavery in 1855. Baird did attempt to speak to that issue. But could not see the nation brought to Civil War. All that had happened before, he alleged, was but "the promise of much greater things for the future."[2] In reality the Churches had come to the end of an era.

No section of Baird's work demanded greater revision than Book VIII: "Efforts of the American Churches for the Conversion of the World." Missionary enlargement and extension had continued both in the winning of the American continent and in the enterprise to convert the world. Baird was correct when he reported that "almost every evangelical church" was "doing something for the propagation of the Gospel . . . in heathen lands."[3] Almost one million dollars was being given annually toward the conversion of the heathen. The missionary shape of the American churches was sculptured in granite. It would not suddenly dissolve or easily erode. He did not perceive, however, that the tremendous thrust from the missionary explosion at the turn of the century had just about lost its dynamic.

281

This decline is most evident in Baird's brief note on missionary motivation. Baird mentions only two factors which prompt American commitment to the missionary enterprise. The consequential blessing of God upon a nation which attempts to spread the gospel is his primary motive. Gratitude arising from the indebtedness of the American churches from their beginnings to the "spirit of missions" is a second impulse.[4] This is far short of *gloria dei* and compassion for the souls of men as the grounds of missionary action.

Were Baird merely a historian such shallow concepts of missionary motivation might be excused. But for years he was, himself, the agent of no insignificant missionary society. Social unrest and war disrupted missionary activity after 1845. American Christians became preoccupied with other issues. The movement was temporarily running out of gas. Decline more or less continued for a quarter century. Then, beginning about 1770, and rising to high tide after 1885, missionary enthusiasm came rushing back, inundating the churches.

The purpose of this study has been to uncover the theological foundations of the early missionary societies in America and to describe the birth of the missionary character of the American churches. The effort has led to an investigation of the Puritan superstructure of early American missionary theology. It has necessitated an examination of the theology of the Evangelical Revival in America. The zeal and evangelistic fervor of the youthful missionary movement can only be explained in terms of the Great Awakening and the revivals that broke out all over America during the thirty year period with which this study has concerned itself. The study has necessarily been set in historical context. What actually did the American churches do? How did they organize themselves for missions?

The comprehensive nature of missionary activity is really overwhelming. The study has been confined to Congregationalists, Baptists, Presbyterians and the two smaller Reformed Dutch and Associate Reformed Churches. Nothing has been told of Methodist missionary labor, but by 1820 the Methodists numbered as many adherents as did the Baptists and in the third decade of the century moved ahead as the largest group in America. Little has been said about the evangelization of the Blacks in the South. That in itself is a fantastic story. The study has shown conclusively, however, that missionary activity was common to all groups and, for the Baptists, Congregationalists and Presbyterians, defines the major interest and largest commitment of men and money of each group.

In light of the temporary waning of the mission at mid-century, the question might be asked, How did theological concepts undergird this sixty year missionary thrust. A brief effort to answer this question will serve as a conclusion to this study.

One of the last sermons that Timothy Dwight delivered, the last published in his lifetime, was before the ABCFM in September, 1813. The text was on John 10:16:

And other sheep I have, which are not of this fold.
    Them also I must bring;

And they shall hear my voice;
And there shall be one fold, and one shepherd.

The sermon is a profound affirmation of the missionary theology of the era and suggests four ways that theology undergirded the American missionary movement of the first half of the Nineteenth Century.

First, the theology of the evangelicals of the period magnified the significance of the world-wide mission of the Church. To gather his people from every nation under heaven and in every age of man is one of the reasons that Christ came to earth. "To collect them," Dwight has Jesus say,

is one of the great duties of my office; a part of the glorious
work, which my Father gave me to do: and I shall not leave
it unaccomplished.

Dwight defined this task as one great division of Jesus' meditorial office. The first was to "teach the will of God for our salvation." The second was to "expiate" our sins. The third was "to gather us into his heavenly kingdom."[5]

The mission is, therefore, no periphery activity in the divine sweep of things. It is central to all that God has done, is doing, and is going to be in the world.

The work, to which you are summoned, is the Work of God.
My brethren, it is the chief work of God, which has been
announced to mankind. It is the end of this earthly creation. It is
the end of this earthly Providence. It is the glorious end of Redemption.[6]

With such a view of the mission of the Church, there was no hesitancy in calling the best young men and women to devote their lives to the mission.

Secondly, the theology of the missionary leaders delineated a truly glorious goal for the mission, to be brought to reality as the climax to a certain timetable. The Millennium was not the wild dream of a few questionable visionaries. It was an actual historical period certain to be inaugurated in about two hundred years. Such was the considered view of the most respectable preachers, teachers and laymen who provided leadership for the missionary enterprise. It was God's historical solution to all the great problems that have plagued the Church. The divisions of the Church of Jesus Christ will be no more. The Church will be established in every land and will be truly one.

Still the period is advancing; it is hastening; in which Christians
will be most honourably united in the present world. The morning . . . will actually arise on this dark world, when all distinctions
of party and sect, of name and nation, of civilization and savage-
ness, of climate and colour, will finally vanish.[7]

Nor was the Millennium defined only in religious terms. It was the divine denouement for all the great problems that have festered human society. It was a period in which the disposition of mankind would undergo a transformation. Concepts of racial and social superiority, driving ambition, avarice and "brutal" sensuality must "lose their seat in the heart, and cease to control the life." Insensitivity to the needs of others, injustice and ingratitude must also fade away.[8] The conduct of men will "experience a mighty and wonderful revolution." Profaneness will vanish. Truth will reign over tongue, pen and press. Honesty will characterize human commerce. Oppression will be excluded from government. Wisdom and worth will characterize rulers. Crime will cease. Wars will be no more.[9]

This was no insignificant and irrelevant dream. The task in which they engaged was not a religious game, unrelated to the real world and played by men out of touch with human society. What they were involved in was an essential maneuver in the divine drama of history. And they knew how the battle would turn out and approximately when the victory would be won.

Third, the theology of the early American missionary movement ascribed importance to the place of the Church in the accomplishment of the divine goal. "By whom are these things to be done?" Dwight asked his hearers.

They are to be done by Protestant nations; and, extensively, by us. In other words, they are to be done by those, to whom God has given the means, and the disposition.[10]

The opportunity of becoming co-workers with God in achieving the ultimate triumph of Christ throughout the world was the peculiar privilege of the American churches. Christians from other Protestant lands, particularly England, would also participate, but American Christians were to play a significant part. For this purpose, Dwight called for all Christians to work together.

It is a shame for those, who wear the name of Christians, not to unite with other Christians, in such a purpose, as this. It is not the purpose of a sect, a party, or a name. It is not a purpose of superstition, bigotry or enthusiasm. It is a purpose of God; an object of the highest complacency to Infinite wisdom.[11]

Such theological undergirding gave meaning to the Churches. It explained their reason for being in the world. It provided them an exciting option for vital participation in the redemptive purposes of God.

We profess to love God. Shall we not unite with all the heart, to further the divine purpose, for which he made the earth and the heavens? We profess, that we have believed in Christ. Shall we not advance with our utmost powers the exalted end of his labours, and sufferings? . . . this is the great harvest of the world . . . Who will not unite himself with such labourers in such an employment?[12]

Finally, this theological understanding of God, themselves, and history, enabled the missionary organizations to design a strategy. Since they knew the goal, were aware of the present situation, and had cognizance of the divine timetable, the missionary leaders knew what tremendous things had to be accomplished in the next two centuries. Churches had to be planted and enlarged in every land and among all peoples. The Bible had to be translated and distributed throughout the world. Schools had to be erected to train Christian leaders. These things provided something concrete to which the churches could give their personnel, money and prayers. *"The present is the proper time for this glorious undertaking,"* Dwight thundered.

> Should we fasten upon the year 2000, as the period in which there shall be a complete accomplishment of the predictions concerning this wonderful event, how evidently it is necessary, that all the measures, by which it is to be accomplished, should be now formed, and immediately begin to operate.[13]

There was an urgency that pervaded the entire movement. It was intensified and instructed by the prevalent eschatology. But it was much deeper than the peculiar view of history proclaimed in missionary sermons. It had its roots in the nature and purpose of God. A quotation from the aging Samuel Austin, Hopkinsian pastor and early leader of the ABCFM, will serve as a final word in the attempt to fathom the early American missionary enterprise.

> Let us, in this great and godlike enterprize, come forward with a stronger zeal to the help of the Lord against the mighty . . . The cause . . . is the same precisely in ours, that it was in his (Paul's) hands. It is, as it was then, and ever will be, the cause of humanity, of truth, of virtue, of salvation, of God. It embraces all that is valuable to man for time and eternity. Whoever embarks in this cause, then, must do it with all his heart. He must let his lukewarmness open itself on some temporal concern. Let him be a coward every where else; but let him fight manfully here. Let him be parsimonious in regard to all other demands; but let him be very bountiful here.[14]

NOTES FOR CHAPTER 12

1.   Baird, *Religion in America,* p. 588. A new edition, *Religion in America,* A Critical Abridgement
     with Introduction by Henry Warner Bowder, Harper Torchbook (New York: Harper and Row,
     Publisher, 1970), has been recently issued.

2.   *Ibid.,* p. 631.

3.   *Ibid.,* p. 636.

4.   *Ibid.,* p. 589.

5.   Timothy Dwight, *A Sermon, Delivered in Boston, September 16, 1813. Before the American
     Board of Commissioners, for Foreign Missions, at their Fourth Annual Meeting,* annexed to
     Memoirs of the Life of Mrs. Harriet Newell, pp. 261, 268.

6.   *Ibid.,* p. 290.

7.   *Ibid.,* p. 267.

8.   *Ibid.,* p. 278.

9.   *Ibid.,* pp. 280-282.

10. *Ibid.,* p. 288.

11. *Ibid.,* pp. 289-490.

12. *Ibid.,* pp. 291-292.

13. *Ibid.,* p. 292.

14. Samuel Austin, *Paul, an Example and Proof of the Peculiar Excellence and Usefulness of the
     Missionary Character. A Discourse, Delivered in Hartford, Conn., Sept. 15, 1824. At the Fifteenth
     Annual Meeting of the American Board of Commissioners for Foreign Missions* (Boston: Printed
     by Crocker and Brewster, 1824), p. 28.

Appendix

This paper was presented to the Consultation on The Mission in America in World Context, convened at the Overseas Ministries Study Center in Ventnor, New Jersey, on May 12, 1975.

Appendix

Garden or Wilderness: The Mission to America in Historical and Personal Perspective

This paper addresses two questions: Is the mission to America a part of the world mission of the Church or, if that is conceded, how is it and how has it been conceived a part of the world mission task? My response will be from the historical perspective and be restricted to Protestant Christianity.

The second question is: What is the mission of the Church today to the United States of America? In responding to this question I will share with you my heart. Essentially the mission of the Church is and always has been to announce the good news of Jesus Christ to all peoples and to gather those who hear into churches. I believe this is both primary and perpetual.

American Mission/World Mission in Historical Perspective

Historically, American home or domestic missions was identical with and in no way separate from the rising Protestant World Mission. Unfortunately, this view has not always prevailed. I will attempt to describe the shifts that have occurred and to characterize the emphasis in three different periods.

Subdue The Wilderness 1606-1820

The first two centuries of Protestantism in America, 1606-1820, can be characterized as an effort to subdue the wilderness. The wild woods must become a garden. The desert must become a paradise. The goal of the American churches, for 200 years, was to plant the wilderness with properly ordered churches and, in New England at least, to set them in a correctly ordered society.

English Protestants — especially those with Puritan interests — came to the New World with a rich heritage in the wilderness/paradise motif. Influenced by the Continental Reformation, they viewed the church as always under the cross and always sent through the world. This warfaring-wayfaring character of the church was an essential part of the gospel epic. The world that the church must go through as well as the arena of conflict was "wilderness."

The garden/wilderness theme is not as descriptive of the mission to America in the last 50 years as it was in the first three centuries. Nevertheless, there is no motif more persistent nor useful to those who have written about the Christianization of the nation than that of wilderness and paradise. From 1613 to 1975, the theme has regularly reappeared.

"Wilderness" was an excellent word to describe the physical circum-
stance that the churchman found in America. Confrontation with literal wilderness deepened and developed the metaphor. They hoped that the Biblical promises would come true. The wilderness would blossom, and rivers would run in
the desert.

The ambivalence of the wilderness/paradise motif is striking. By 1720,
"wilderness" began to be interiorized. Emphasis shifted from literal woods to
the heart of man. Let me mark the distinctive thrust of each century and illustrate how men from these periods understood the missionary task of the American churches — especially as it related to their own continent.

Colonization

Every significant colonization effort by the English was cast in religious
motif. Practice did not always follow profession, but among the complex motives
that undergirded the migration to the New World these men believed that in the
providence of God, along with their attempts at planting colonies, producing
profits and extending the possessions of the English crown, there was an overarching divine plan of which they were a part. This was true in Virginia, New
England and even Pennsylvania and Georgia.

Do not ignore the Christian faith of the early Virginians. The documents
of the period testify to the effect of piety in their lives. Alexander Whitaker called
on Christians in England to show the fruits of their faith in "these barren parts of
the world." Whitaker insisted that "the Plantation is Gods" and that it was God's
"Kingdome" that was being erected in the New World. God, Whitaker believed,
was working in the Virginia enterprise "to some higher end then ordinary."

This "higher" goal, that the English colonists perceived, expressed itself in
two forms. The most obvious was the evangelization of the Indians. Prophecy confirmed that it was the intention of God that the whole world submit to Christ.
The Kingdom of God would include all nations. In the mission to the Indians
"the Kingdome of Christ is enlarged. His design is upon all the Kingdomes of the
Earth, that he may take possession of them for himselfe."

It was a source of encouragement to John Eliot that the Bible assured
*"that all languages shall see his glory, and that all Nations and Kingdoms shall
become the Kingdoms of the Lord Jesus."*

The planting of churches among all peoples and the final and complete
triumph of Christ over all the nations are accomplished by the power and grace
of God. These are the particular works of God and bring him greatest glory.
Richard Mather explained that the "Amplitude and large extent of the Kingdom
of Jesus Christ upon Earth . . . is a thing plainly . . . foretold. It must needs be
the Honor of Christ Jesus the King of *Sion*, when multitudes of people do submit unto Him as their King."

Mission was defined as wilderness being transformed into garden. Through the proclamation of the gospel among the heathen, the church becomes God's instrument for making the wilderness a paradise. In the gathering of Indian churches the barren desert becomes a fruitful garden. Henry Whitfield celebrated the transformation of the New England Indians. "In the wilderness are waters broken out . . . the parched ground is become a Poole . . . the Lord hath done a new thing . . . He hath made a way in the Wildernesse, and Rivers in the Desert." Discipling Indians in the American wilderness was a significant event in the economy of God's divine plan.

The second expression of this "higher end then ordinary" was the colonization enterprise itself. The entire colonization effort was habitually drawn within an eschatological frame and was thereby directly and dramatically related to God's ultimate purpose in the world.

The English Protestants of the 17th Century held that the God who made the world sustained the world and would bring his creation to his own predetermined consummation. History was only God's wisdom expressed in time. All the debate about socio-economic and political motives is beside the point. Whether overpopulation, religious persecution, indebtedness or economic ambition, God was at work. Virginia was no simple commercial undertaking. It was a move on the chess board of-time, executed by the hand of God himself, and purposed to achieve his own goals and glory.

This understanding was especially obvious in the Great Migration of 1630. Not just the evangelization of the Indian, but the Great Removal itself was a strategic maneuver in the divine game plan.

The Puritan of the Great Migration divided the time between Pentecost and the Parousia into three great Epochs: the age of the apostles; the period of the manifestation of Anti-Christ; and the era of the great expansion of the church. They were living at the end of the second epoch. The world was about to witness the destruction of Anti-Christ. Great upheavals were evident at the end of this second eschatological age. God would use them, the Puritan believer, to provide a place of refuge for the people of God. He would make their churches a pattern for the churches that would exist around the world in the third epoch. John Winthrop asked: "Who knowes, but that God hath provided this place to be a refuge for many whome he means to save out of the generall callamity, and seeinge the Church hath noe place lefte to flie into but the wildernesse, what better worke can there be, then to . . . provide . . . for her against she comes thether."

The most blatant reflection of this view is Edward Johnson's *Wonderworking Providence of Zion's Savior in New England.* Johnson was sure that the fall of Antichrist was at hand. The Puritan was "prest for the service of the Lord Christ, to rebuilt the most glorious Edifice of Mt. Sion in a Wilderness."

The third epoch, the era of the expansion of the church, was about to dawn. The fulness of the Gentiles was at hand. "All people, Nations and Languages" were "soonly to submit to Christ's Kingdome." The blessing of God on the churches in New England was the forerunner of what he would do over the world. He called on men in every nation to believe in Christ and "gather into churches." The planting and growth of the churches in New England were "but a Porch of his glorious building in hand."

The leaders of the Great Migration felt that they occupied an auspicious place in history. Their mission to America had central significance in God's ultimate plan for the redemption of the world.

The Evangelical Revival

By 1720, a shift was already beginning. New England piety was in decline. Cotton Mather had anticipated the dawn of a new Pentecost and Reformation for two decades. Solomon Stoddard's Church had experienced four of the five "harvests" of his lifetime. The influence of German Pietism was felt in both England and America. Reforming societies had proliferated in England and had sent their emissaries to the New World. The foundations for the larger ecclesiastical bodies in America had been laid. Perhaps 1727 was the pivotal year. John Wesley was in Epworth, but the Holy Club had formed at Oxford. Jonathan Edwards was assisting his grandfather in Northampton. And Nicolas von Zinzendorf was presiding at the rebirth of the Moravian Church. A new day was about to begin.

A series of European wars violently spilled onto the American Frontier and hindered efforts to continue the Indian mission for 75 years. Sporadic efforts to evangelize the Indians increased after 1740 in all parts of the Colonies. But Americans developed a new concept of mission in the Eighteenth Century. It led to a second way of doing mission work, a way other than special societies and boards of commissioners organized for missionary purposes.

This second missionary method, church planting by larger ecclesiastical bodies, is a new thing in American Christianity and marks the beginning of home missions for the American churches.

New ideas are never completely new. The first generation of the New England Puritans conceived both the planting of English churches and the gathering of churches among the Indians as a part of its errand into the wilderness. "To reduce the Quakers to the Christian faith" was an early goal Thomas Bray designed for the Society for Promoting Christian Knowledge. By "Christian faith" Bray always meant Anglicanism. The Society for Propagating the Gospel (SPG), by its efforts to found churches from Maryland north, identified "mission" with the planting of congregations of a particular persuasion. Puritans gathered churches from adherents of the Church of England in the Seventeenth Century. It is ironical that the New England establishment took offense at the work of SPG missionaries in New England after 1760. These examples are not exact parallels. There was a new factor besides the tendency to propagate the organized structure of one's own viewpoint. This new idea, new at least in power and prominence if not in essence, had its rise in the Evangelical Revival.

The emphasis on the *new birth,* which is central to this major Christian movement, essentially constitutes a new definition of the word "Christian." George Whitfield clearly distinguished between the two ways that one may be "in Christ." One was by outward profession — i.e., to be "baptized into Christ's church," or be "called a christian." The second way, and "undoubtedly the proper meaning," is to be in Christ "not only by an outward profession, but by an inward change and purity of heart, and cohabitation of his Holy Spirit." If "we are not inwardly wrought upon, and changed by the powerful operations of the holy Spirit . . . however we may call ourselves Christians, we shall be found naked at the great day." Samuel Davis called the new birth the "grand constituent of a Christian, and prerequisite to our admission into the kingdom of heaven." This essential change in the definition of "Christian" represents a radical interiorization and individualization of the wilderness concept.

The Great Awakening underlined man's depravity and the absolute necessity of an experience of new birth. "Natural man," no matter what his nationality, the availability of means of grace, or relationship to the visible church, is cut off from God. Edwards insisted that "the savages who live in the remote parts of this continent . . . as well as the inhabitants of Africa, are naturally in exactly similar circumstances towards God with us in this land. They are no more alienated or estranged from God in their nature than we."

The only advantage Englishmen had was the means of grace. Thus when settlers moved to the frontiers where there was no stated preaching of the gospel, even that distinction disappeared. Frontier settlements along with Indian villages thus became the proper sphere of missions. Indeed, those who could not testify of the "birth from above," especially for the Separate Congregationalists, the New Light Presbyterians, the Methodists, and the Baptists, became proper subjects of the evangelical invitation. Place of residence and accessibility to a parish church were not matters of consideration.

This new concept of "missions," or of what constitutes "heathen" and "Christian," enabled the ecclesiastical bodies of the Colonies to view church planting among Europeans as an integral part of mission. The young, expanding ecclesiastical bodies, shaped by the Great Awakening and the revivals that followed, placed Indian evangelization and church planting among white settlers into the same missionary basket, often to the neglect of the Indian mission.

Edwards is the theologian of the Great Awakening and of the missionary explosion that took place in America after 1790. For Edwards, the mission of the Church was to be a co-laborer with God in the consummation of the work of redemption. The work of redemption had two facets. The first consisted in converting, sanctifying and bringing to glorification individual men. The second aspect regarded God's grand design in creation, history and providence. In its totality, the work of redemption is God's greatest work — that one of which all others consist. Its completion is the end for which God created the world. The Church's participation in it is the most glorious work of the Church.

After 1786, the Evangelical Revival began a second surge in America. The Methodists and Baptists in the South and in New England, and the Presbyterians on the Southern frontier experienced awakenings in the 1780s. In the 1790s the revival became general. Stimulated by events in England, this surge of new life aroused a fervent missionary spirit and crystallized into numerous organizations for missionary endeavor.

Leaders of the new societies counted their efforts a vital part of the rising Protestant World Mission. During the first two decades, missionary action was confined to the Indians and to the new settlements on the North American continent. But they considered their activity to be one with the divine work of redemption and on a par with that missionary work conducted by European societies.

William Carey said in 1800, that the "various tribes of American Indians appear to have a claim upon the American churches; or rather . . . that the one great end of the existing churches in America is to spread the glorious gospel among the heathen in their vicinity." Carey expressed the conviction of American missionary statesmen.

The distinction between "domestic" and "foreign" missions was unknown before 1815. In 1802, when the Presbyterian Standing Committee of Missions wrote to all the Protestant societies in the world, a "foreign" missionary society was one located in Western Europe. The query of the Andover students in 1810, about the possibility of an overseas mission, was not whether the American churches would evangelize the heathen, but "whether they ought to direct their attention to the eastern or western world."

The new American Board of Commissioners for Foreign Missions justified its existence by explaining it hoped "that the time is coming when . . . exertions . . . for spreading the knowledge of his name, may be successfully employed nearer home; yet at present the Eastern world is thought to offer a more promising field."

In reality, the excitement created by the overseas societies, along with rising nationalism, intensified efforts on the home front. All the major denominational bodies were involved in both an Eastern and Western mission by 1825, and more funds and personnel were available for both.

Let me share two observations. First, no distinction was made between the Eastern and Western Mission. Both were essential parts of the work of redemption. Missionary organizations, and all the other benevolent societies, were intimate parts of one great system designed to enlighten, bless and save the world.

Second, until the second decade of the 19th Century, there was no real distinction between the mission to pagan peoples on the American continent and the mission to the frontier settlements. The condition of both peoples was described as "wilderness" which Christ had promised to subdue. Ira Chase wrote Isaac Backus from Maine, in the 1780s, that the Redeemer reigned in those parts; "it hath been . . . barren wilderness, . . . but thanks be to the God of love, he hath . . . caused the wilderness to bud and blossom as the rose."

By the end of the next quarter century the emphasis began to change.

Perfect Paradise 1820-1920

The third century of the Protestant mission to America could be described as a massive effort to cultivate the divine garden, or to bring paradise to perfection.

The success of the frontier mission in the first two generations after the Great Awakening contributed to the change in emphasis. John Mason Peck noted in his journal in 1815, that one could not become too "enthusiastic on the subject of missions." He reflected that only a few years before all New York State "was one vast wilderness — properly missionary ground." But missionary ground had become a sending camp. Wilderness had vanished. American churchmen, progressively through the 19th Century, thought of the nation in this way. America was a Christian (Protestant) nation.

Nationalism was a major factor. After the War of 1812, it became vocal. "Manifest Destiny" became its rally cry. American nationalism was not as aggressive as that of some nations of Western Europe in empire building overseas. It was aggressive on the North American continent. American missionaries may not have been agents for American emperialistic advance in Africa, Asia, or even in Central America and the Pacific, but that was not true with reference to the Indian nations on this continent.

The mission to America turned from offense to defense. Its major purpose was to maintain, perfect and extend the nascent Protestant empire that was already evident by 1820. Even revivalism, the main evangelistic method of the 19th Century, is an instrument for renewing the establishment. It presupposes something given, something that can be revitalized.

In this process, home mission no longer was a part of the world mission. It did not lose its importance to the American churches. It simply became the technique for maintaining Christian America, which in the providence of God would save the world.

American Christians, since 1820, or certainly since 1886, have suffered from what I call the Babylonian Captivity of the Great Commission. When they hear Matthew 28:19-20, a light begins to flash in the back of their brains that says "foreign missions." The mission to America lost its identification with the world mission of the Church and was only indirectly related to the mission of God.

Keeping Down the Weeds

I could illustrate the defensive posture endlessly. First, major energy was expended on keeping down the weeds. Home missions became the great divine hoe, for keeping the garden clean.

Examine Lyman Beecher's *Building The Waste Places* (1816) and *Plea For The West* (1836), Horace Bushnell's *Barbarism: The First Danger* (1847), and Josiah Strong's *Our Country* (1886), the four books most cited by historians as pivotal in home missions. You will find that their all-consuming passion is to make sure that no alien plants grow in paradise. These four books are especially re-vealing for another reason. All four call for the extension of 19th Century New England culture to the entire nation. The mission to America in these documents is to New Englandize the continent. (Unfortunately, American historiography and American church historiography have been captive to the New England interpre-tation of American history for 175 years. Most books on the mission to America, when they have told the story of the American Home Missionary Society and the Home Mission Councils of the 20th Century think they have told the whole story.)

The Evangelical United Front characterized the first part of this third century of the mission to America. Its myriad societies aimed at reforming Ameri-ca in the major and the minor. No stone was to be left unturned that would keep America from being the perfect example of a Christian nation. The struggle with immigration, the crusade against Romanism, the war with Mormonism, and, of course, the abolition of slavery were, as far as most Protestants were concerned, all from the same piece. Josiah Strong's incredibly influential book, *Our Country,* discusses the challenge of the home mission in terms of the perils to Protestant America. These wild herbs and foreign shrubs had either to be domesticated or uprooted and cast out.

Parceling Out the Field

Along with this effort to keep down the weeds, the home mission forces were busy in parceling out the garden. The field was divided up. The Evangelical United Front collapsed in the 1830s. It was the time of the rise of the Landmark doctrine among the Baptists, the organization of the Missouri Synod among the Lutherans, the ascendancy of High Church claims among the Episcopalians and Old School Orthodoxy among the Presbyterians. Even the Methodists regarded Methodism as the "purest existing type of Christianity, and as a priceless heritage of doctrine and discipline."

A song from an early Methodist song book expresses the attitude of most groups:

> I am a soldier of the cross
> I count all earthly things but dross;
> My soul is bound for endless rest
> I'll never leave the Methodist.
>
> For better church cannot be found
> This doctrine is so pure and sound;
> One reason that I'll give for this,
> The Devil hates the Methodist.
>
> The Devil, Calvin and Voltaire
> May hate the Methodist in vain;
> Their doctrine shall be downward hurl'd
> The Methodist will take the world.

This was in a hymnal entitled, *The Spiritual Song Book Designed For the Pious of All Denominations.*

Denominational exclusivism helped shape the mission to America into competitive church extension along denominational lines.

The garden was parceled up in other ways. Through the debate over slavery and the War most Protestant bodies divided. During reconstruction the South effectively insulated itself from the North and West and was left to the southern churches. Blacks were rejected by churches in the North and South, and the Black population was left to the fledgling Black churches. Racism became a cardinal doctrine of American Protestantism. The great continental paradise was divided up into little plots — each vying for prominence.

Overseas missions gained the ascendancy and came to be *the* mission of the Church. America became the great sending nation that was destined to renovate the world with the gospel and democracy. Home missions must make certain that America remained strong and pure.

The fences around the garden were continually pushed out until the frontier was no more. The churches were urged to resist the other threats to the Protestant Hegemony, to Christian America. Americanization was the emphasis for both the immigrant and the Indian. They must learn the English language and adopt the culture of the eastern seaboard. In this way, America could fulfill her place in the divine plan of God.

Thus, in 1847, Horace Bushnell said that the "bowie-knife type of society" which prevailed in the South and new West must be overcome. The struggle might take a century. But the nation would enter a condition of "Christian culture and virtue and become the most august, and happiest nation in the earth and the leading power of the world's history." This goal made home missions the "first and sublimest Christian duty which the age lays upon us. . . . There can be no other duty at all comparable to saving our country." America is the "brightest hope of the ages." America must become the "new Christian Empire whose name the believing and the good of all people shall hail as name of hope and blessing."

Forty years later, buoyed up on the swells of scientific and cultural racism and militant nationalism, Josiah Strong produced a best seller. The Anglo-Saxon, he said, the true American, has two traits of genius: "self-government" and "pure *spiritual* Christianity." These two traits constitute the great needs of mankind. God was preparing in Anglo-Saxon civilization the die with which to stamp the earth. "The Anglo-Saxon holds in his hands the destinies of mankind for ages to come."

But "the Anglo-Saxon race would speedily decay but for the salt of Christianity." This is just the role of home missions. The churches must Christianize the immigrants so they can be Anglo-Saxonized. The Christians of the United States have it in their hands to hasten or retard "the coming of Christ's Kingdom to the world" by hundreds or thousands of years. "We of this generation and nation," he said, occupy the Gibraltar of the ages which commands the world's future.

The mission to America was no longer integral to the world mission of the Church. The mission to America was subservient to the *mission of the nation.* The national mission had become identical with the mission of God. Such seems almost inevitable when the Church identifies the nation as the garden of God.

You may wish to disagree with my analysis of the 19th Century. Some may say I have been too kind. Others may feel I have ignored the magnificent achievements of the churches during this century. The achievements were magnificent. Looking at the era from another perspective, my assessment might vary considerably. However, in the terms of this discussion, in the 19th Century there was a radical transformation among American churchmen in their understanding of the mission to America. By the end of the century there was a dangerous tendency to identify national destiny with the eternal plan of God. America, not the Church, had become the new Israel of God.

This concept has lingered. After 1890, there was a serious new evaluation of the home mission task in America; this dream of national destiny predominated through World War I. The churches joined enthusiastically in that great American crusade to make the world free for democracy.

Seeking a City

How shall I characterize the last fifty years? How have Protestants viewed the mission to America in its world context during these years of crises and change? During this century, the mission to America has been a search for the city of God. But there has been great variation in defining the city of God.

First, let me note that most attempts at analysis deal only with a portion of American Protestantism. It is amazing to some of us who are not a part of Councilier Protestantism how often spokesmen of their churches speak for *the* Church. Those who write about the American Christian experience seldom get beyond this particular expression of American Protestantism.

There are at least four other segments of American Christianity that must be considered in this analysis. Though this century has seen the rise of Ecumenical Christianity, the vision of the Church's mission to America has become both fractural and myopic. Our views of the mission to America have been defined, most often in reaction — positive or negative — to the imposing view of 19th Century America as the New Israel.

Fragmentation came to American Christianity in the North after 1910. In the Fundamentalist-Modernist Controversy of the 1920s, that fragmentation became violently visible. But the disruption of 1920 hardly disturbed churches in the South or among Blacks.

Northern Evangelicals came out of the Fundamentalist-Modernist Controversy with a major emphasis on overseas missions. They have viewed America as essentially a Christian nation and lamented the lack of fervent evangelism, true doctrine, and separated living. They were and continue to be a vital part of the third great wave of overseas missionary endeavor from America after World War II.

In America their emphasis continues to be personal and proclamation evangelism. Northern Evangelicals have hardly developed a *mission* to America. Few groups within this family have had a concerted strategy for church planting in the United States. Influenced by the moderate wing of the 19th Century Holiness movement, especially Keswick Theology, they have hoped to see the kingdom of God actualized in the lives of individual Christians. They have despaired of social action as the solution to the problem of mankind or as an essential expression of obedience to Christ's missionary command. Holding firmly to a Premillennial view of Christ's coming, there has been a subtle pessimism about the ultimate victory of Christ and his Church among many people. They have perceived that "here we have no lasting city" and have looked "for the city which is to come" (Heb. 13:14).

The Councilier Protestant faction of American Christianity, though it has members North and South, Black and White, European and English-language background, continues to reflect the mentality of the Northeastern Protestant establishment. This century, its concept of mission to America has been characterized more by cooperation and social action than by evangelism and church planting. Though the naivete' of the social gospel was abandoned in the late 1920s and the 1930s, the concern to actualize the Kingdom of God in America has persisted.

The idea of Christianizing the social order arose while the vision of America as the great Christian empire of destiny was most visible and while progressive post-millenialism was most immoderate. This definition of the mission to America still tends to reflect the presuppositions and goals of that era.

J. Paul Douglas said in 1914 that home missions had "overspread the continent with the hearthstone and the spire. . . . They have visioned in beauty and order a Paradise Redeemed . . . the most perfect reflection of the World that Shall Be."

"Now," he continued, "home missions must undertake the final phase of their task, namely, the combination of these fragments of success into a more perfect realization of Christianity in America worthy to be presented to God for ultimate completion."

Throughout the 20th Century, with only brief relapse into realism in the Niebuhrian period and into evangelism and church planting in the revival of the 1950s, Councilier Protestants have pursued the "final phase" of the mission to America, to actualize the Kingdom of God in the social fabric of the nation.

There has been real achievement. Not only have dramatic steps been made in social and racial justice in America in this century, but the social consciousness of other Christians has been aroused. Councilier Protestants have played a vital part in this.

The identification of the mission to America with the social involvement of the churches has stressed ministry and presence as essential missionary actions. Involvement in political issues is preferred to personal evangelism. Systemic evangelism, not individual conversion, will change the world. There is little place for a sovereign God who made the world or a Christ crucified for our sins and raised for our justification. These seek a city of man, made with human hands, where men can be human and God is unnecessary. But in doing this, it is affirmed, the church has found what God is doing in the world and has joined him in his work. The mission to America is seen as a part of the mission of God. But it has largely lost its world context.

A third segment of American Protestantism that needs some analysis is the Black churches. These churches have in the main, of course, become part of Councilier Protestantism in this century. But Black churches have not shaped Councilier Protestantism and have exercised little influence until the last decade.

The fantastic record of Black churches in evangelism and church planting in this century, especially in the inner cities of this nation, has been ignored in most discussions of the mission of the American churches on the continent. Invariably, stories of the home mission enterprise have told about educational and social ministries of White churches to Black people. But no word is said of the multiplication of Christians and churches by Black Christians in the Black community. The numbers and broad base of the Black churches made Black leadership in the Civil Rights Movement a possibility.

The primary mission of the Black churches to America has been confined to the Black community. Only in the Civil Rights Movement and, perhaps, the Black Power Movement in the recent past, has their mission assumed a national dimension. For most Black churches — though identified with the social and political goals of the Black Community, and even with articulations of Black theology — the major emphasis continues to be on warm and personal church-centered evangelism.

A fourth significant segment of American Protestantism which demands attention is a group that might be classified as Southern Biblicists. The Southern Baptist Convention and the Churches of Christ are the best example of this classification. Both have been, through this century, oriented toward southern culture, and during the past quarter century have moved out of the South and Southwest into all parts of America.

I cannot speak about the Churches of Christ, but I can speak with some authority about Southern Baptists. We struggle to actualize a national strategy. We struggle constantly with the conflict between evangelism and culture. In the South and Southwest, where we often constitute a cultural establishment, it is difficult to be prophetic, and we have become middle class. But multiple churches in most communities means that we have effectively addressed ourselves to all segments of society except the Black community. We are making efforts to cross all barriers. There are now ten thousands of Black and Ethnic people who are Southern Baptists.

Northern Evangelicals tend toward premillenialism. Southern Biblicists have tended to be amillenialists. The emphasis has been on personal salvation with no real expectation that the world and human society will be actually renovated, either by the evolution of human society or by the direct intervention of God. They seek a heavenly city, but not one coming down out of heaven.

Bible centered, personal evangelism and a strong emphasis on local churches have made these groups avid and successful church planters. They do give offense to many; but, seeing all men in need of Christ, they view America as a mission field on a par with other nations of the world. The mission to America is a part of the world mission of the Church. Some would object to the way these groups define both "world mission" and "church."

Finally, a fifth segment of American Protestantism that shares the fractured, myopic vision of the mission to America is the Pentecostal churches. At the time the Protestant establishment in the North was moving away from individual salvation and church planting to a social mission toward the alienated of America, and while the Protestant establishment in the South was developing its rationale for evangelizing Whites only, there was an explosion of spiritual faith — largely among the poorer people of this country — that has majored on the conversion of individuals and (in its early stages, at least) crossed racial barriers in North and South.

All the growth of Pentecostal churches has taken place since 1901. The most significant thing that has happened in this century in reference to the World Mission of the Church has not been the Ecumenical Movement, but the birth of Pentecostalism and the multiplication of Pentecostal churches across the world. I graduated from a very respectable Christian college, had two degrees from the second largest theological seminary in the world, and had just about finished a graduate program in the field of Church History at a major university before I ever heard about the great Azuzu Street Revival of 1906, and the effect of that revival in raising up men who would win others to Christ and erect churches all over the world. The equal place of women in the Church that Old Line Protestants passionately debate today was settled at the beginning of the century for Pentecostals. No group has more effectively mobilized the laity in this century nor penetrated the lower classes of American society than the Pentecostals.

They, too, give offense to many. They claim to have a corner on the Holy Spirit, have not bowed the knee to academia, and divide the body of Christ into those who have the gift and those who have it not. Nevertheless, even though Pentecostalism is splintered into many groups, their churches provide an exciting option for many Americans; they are found in all parts of the nation, and they now penetrate — to a degree — all the social levels of American society.

With all the diffusion, how can the mission to America be a part of the World Mission of the Church? American home missions emerged out of the World Mission, just as did the American overseas mission. In fact, the commitment to the overseas mission blessed the home mission by helping to raise the level of stewardship in a way that made home missions much more effective.

In the 19th Century the two were divided. The home mission became the instrument for perfecting the American Protestant Paradise. In a large measure it lost its relationship to the world mission, except as providing a source of money and personnel for the Church's mission around the world.

I share Pierce Beaver's conviction that we can disciple this nation well, thoroughly and continuously only as a part of the discipling of all nations. I believe that we must rethink the definition of "mission." The mission of the Church must be more strictly defined. The mission of the Church is essentially making disciples. We cannot remain silent before social and racial injustice. We are sent to minister, as well as witness. But we cannot overlook the intention of God to take out of the nations a people for his name (Acts 15:14) and our commission to take the good news that Jesus who was crucified, God has raised from the dead and made both Lord and Christ (Acts 2:31).

This brings me to my second question.

Mission To America Today

What is the mission of the Church to America today?

I deny absolutely any distinction between the task of the Church in America and the task of the Church in the world. The mission to America and the mission of the Church are one.

There are several reasons why I say this.

1. I am a true son of the Evangelical Revival. I cannot admit in reading the New Testament or in estimating my own experience that a man is "in Christ" because his parents were Christians, or because he has been baptized, confirmed, absolved, and habitually frequents a place of Christian worship and participates in a sacramental event. A man is not a Christian because he owns right doctrine, lives an exemplary life, or is born in a country whose culture has been molded by Christianity. He is a Christian who has met Christ as Liberator and made him Lord.

Men are not essentially good. There is a fault in the nature of man that runs through his mind, will and emotions. Only the effectual call of God will cause a man to change his mind (i.e., repent) and turn to God (i.e., be converted). Mere reformation is not enough. A new birth is necessary. It is directly produced by the Holy Spirit as men turn in faith to God through Christ.

I am not here contending for one-by-one salvation only. I have seen, in this country, entire households come to faith in Christ together. But I am contending for personal faith and the real indwelling of the Holy Spirit in the life of the believer. Thereby a man becomes the temple of the Holy Spirit, a child of God, and brother to the Carpenter.

The mission of the Church to make disciples of all peoples includes a young man in Central Texas who joined a Southern Baptist church out of fear of Hell, without a lively faith in Christ, as well as a man in another culture who never heard the gospel.

2. I do not believe that America is now or ever has been a Christian Empire, or that God ever shifted his missionary calling to the nation instead of the Church. Making America the "Redeemer Nation" contaminated, compromised and castrated the Church. By identifying America as the New Israel through which God intended

to renovate the world, the Church became impure, immoral and impotent. We have not recovered from that yet. The Church in America is a mixed multitude in a mess, not a company of obedient disciples on a mission. This nation is deluded by allegiance to a civil religion and ensnared by militant hedonism, secular humanism and a new and exotic paganism. Yet most leaders of American churches assume that America is already discipled.

For this reason I do not speak of this age as the post-Christian era in America. America never reflected the mind of Christ. The reign of Christ has never dawned here. I do not expect it by human effort.

Secularism and pluralism are not new things in America — they are just more acceptable options today. Since the Declaration of Independence this nation has been moving, as Franklin Littell has said, from state church to pluralism. There was a period when a certain brand of Evangelical Protestantism had tremendous influence on those who molded American culture. But that was almost as oppressive to other Evangelical Protestants as it was to Roman Catholics and Latter Day Saints.

The churches in America are young churches. America is a mission field, where there are multitudes to be discipled, baptized and taught to be responsible members of responsible churches. We must begin to see the American Church as one among many young churches in the world.

3. Finally, I am convinced that the chief mission task of the Church in America today is related to evangelism and church planting. There are about 210,000,000 people in the United States of America. Something over 60 per cent of that number are related to some sort of religious organization. This would include Buddhist, as well as Baptists and Muslims, as well as Methodists. But 40 per cent, or about 80,000,000 people, claim no allegiance to Jesus Christ or any other Lord. There are only seven other nations in the world with a total population of more than 80,000,000. In terms of warm bodies, the American Church is in the midst of one of the largest mission fields in the world today. And the population is basically responsive.

Look at it another way. The membership rolls of American churches are glutted with people whose only religion is religion-in-general or no-religion-at-all. Southern Baptists have 12,000,000 members. We do not know where 3,000,000 of those are. If they have a vital relationship to Christ, they haven't expressed it recently. One out of four has disappeared. Of the other three who are left, one of them is such a scandal to his community that we wish we didn't know where he was! I doubt if other churches in the United States have a record much better in terms of radical obedience in life and service to Jesus Christ. Fifty per cent of the people who call themselves Christian in America have no vital Christian witness. It is no wonder some Christians feel compelled to turn to politics and violence to effect change.

America must be viewed — to use the term McGavran has made famous — as a vast mosaic. Just because there are five churches in a city of 10,000 does not mean that city is adequately churched. We are in the process of doing a profile of every city in Illinois with a population of 500 or more. We find there may be numerous churches, but the majority only address the gospel to the middle classes. Where Roman Catholics predominate, especially in small cities, they too are mainly affluent and turned toward the community leaders. Among Protestants, only Pentecostal, Black churches and some Baptists address themselves to the "poor folks."

There is competition between churches, but they are all competing for the people in one class. The rest are forgotten or ignored.

We have an objective in Illinois to have some organized ministry or witness in every place in the state. But we are going much further than that. We are determined that the gospel of Christ will be offered in every segment of the society, so that men will not have to cross barriers to come to Christ. They can come to Christ among their peers and family. We refuse the strategy of just one church in a city of 5,000 or more. We are committed to multiple churches in the various segments of society.

The making of disciples and multiplying of churches among all segments of human society is the essential mission of the Church in the world. The mission to America is no different.

Selected Bibliography

Selected Bibliography

Primary Sources

Missionary Sermons

Abeel, John. A Discourse, Delivered April 6, 1801, in the Middle Dutch Church, Before the New York Missionary Society, at Their Annual Meeting. New York: Isaac Collins and Sons, 1801.

Alexander, Archibald. A Missionary Sermon, Preached in the First Presbyterian Church in Philadelphia, on the Twenty-third of May, 1814. Philadelphia: Printed by William Fry, 1814.

Allen, Jonathan. A Sermon, Delivered at Haverhill, February 5, 1812, on the Occasion of Two Young Ladies Being About to Embark to India. Haverhill, Mass.: W. B. & H. B. Allen, 1812.

Austin, Samuel. Christians Bound to Spread the Gospel Among All Descriptions of Their Fellow Men: A Sermon, Preached Before the Massachusetts Missionary Society, at Their Annual Meeting in Boston, May 24, 1803. Salem: Joshua Cushing, 1803.

_____. Paul, an Example and Proof of the Peculiar Excellence and Usefulness of the Missionary Character. A Discourse, Delivered in Hartford, Conn., September 15, 1824, at the Fifteenth Annual Meeting of the American Board of Commissioners for Foreign Missions. Boston: Printed by Crocker and Brewster, 1824.

_____. A Sermon Preached Before the Massachusetts Missionary Society at Their Annual Meeting in Boston, May 24, 1803. Salem: Joshua Cushing, 1803.

Baldwin, Thomas. The Eternal Purpose of God, the Foundation of Effectual Calling. A Sermon, Delivered Before the First Baptist Society in Boston, Lord's Day Morning, February 19, 1804. Second Edition. Boston: Printed by Manning & Loring, 1804.

_____. The Knowledge of the Lord Filling the Earth. A Sermon, Delivered in Boston, June 4, 1812, Before the Massachusetts Bible Society, Being Their Third Anniversary. Boston: Printed by Lincoln & Edmands, 1812.

_____. A Sermon, Delivered in Boston, May 30, 1804, Before the Massachusetts Baptist Missionary Society. Being Their Second Anniversary. Boston: Printed by E. Lincoln, 1804.

Bardwell, Horatio. The Duty and Reward of Evangelizing the Heathen: A Sermon Delivered in Newburyport, Lord's Day Evening, October 22, 1815. Newburyport, Mass.: Printed by William B. Allen & Co., 1815.

Barnard, Thomas. A Discourse Before the Society for Propagating the Gospel Among the Indians and Others in North America, Delivered November 6, 1806. Charlestown, Mass. Samuel Etheridge, 1806.

Bates, Joshua. A Sermon, Preached at Boston, January 4, 1816, Before the Society for Foreign Missions of Boston and the Vicinity. Dedham (Mass.): Printed by the Gazette Office, 1816.

Beecher, Lyman. Resources of the Adversary and Means of Their Destruction. A Sermon Preached October 12, 1827, Before the American Board of Missions, at New York. Boston: Crocker and Brewster, 1827.

Bishop, Robert H. The Glory of the Latter Days, A Sermon Delivered at the Annual Meeting of the Bible Society of Kentucky, September, 1815. With Appendix, Containing 1. Some Original Thoughts on the Slaying of the Witnesses: and 2. A Concise Account of the Kentucky Bible Society. Lexington, Ky.: Printed by Thomas T. Skillman, 1815.

Blood, Mighill. A Sermon Delivered at Thomastown, June 26, 1820, Before the Maine Missionary Society, at Their Thirteenth Anniversary. Bangor (Me.): J. Burton Jr., 1820.

Brown, Francis. A Sermon Delivered Before the Maine Missionary Society, at Their Annual Meeting, in Gorham, June 22, 1814. Hollowell: Printed by N. Cheever, 1814.

Buchanan, Claudius. The Star in the East. A Sermon, Preached in the Parish Church of St. James, Bristol, on Sunday, February 26, 1809. For the Benefit of the Society for Missions to Africa and the East. Hartford: Hudson and Goodwin, 1809.

Buell, Samuel. The Excellence and the Importance of the Saving Knowledge of the Lord Jesus Christ in the Gospel Preacher and Christ Preached to the Gentiles in Obedience to the Call of God. A Sermon Preached in Easthampton, August 29, 1759, at the Ordination of Mr. Samson Occum; New York: James Parker, 1761.

Campbell, John P. A Portrait of the Times, or the Church's Duty. In a Discourse Delivered at the opening of the Synod of Kentucky in the 1st Presbyterian Church in Lexington, October 14, 1812. Lexington, Ky.: Printed by Thomas T. Skillman, n.d.

Cannon, Josiah W. A Sermon Delivered at Northampton, Before the Hampshire Missionary Society, at Their Annual Meeting, August 23, 1821. Northampton: Thomas W. Shepard and Co., 1821.

Chaplin, Daniel. A Sermon, Delivered in Boston Before the Massachusetts Society for Promoting Christian Knowledge; on the Evening of June 1, 1815. Boston: Nathaniel Willis, 1815.

Chauncy, Charles. All Nations of the Earth Blessed in Christ, the Seed of Abraham. A Sermon Preached at Boston, at the Ordination of the Rev. Mr. Joseph Bowman, to the Work of the Gospel Ministry, More Especially Among the Mohawk-Indians, on the Western Borders of New England. August 3, 1762. Boston: Printed and Sold by John Draper, 1762.

Chester, John. A Sermon, Delivered Before the Bershire and Columbia Missionary Society, at Their Annual Meeting in Canaan, September 21, 1813. Hudson (N.Y.): A. Stoddard, 1813.

Codman, John. A Discourse, Delivered Before the Roxbury Charitable Society, at Their Anniversary, September 24, 1817. Boston: Munroe & Francis, 1817.

_____. Idolatry Destroyed, and the Worship of the True God Established. A Sermon Delivered in the Old South Church, Boston, Before the Foreign Missionary Society of Boston and the Vicinity, January 1, 1818. Boston: Lincoln & Edmands. 1818.

Cooper, William. A Sermon, Preached to God's Ancient Israel, the Jews, at Sion-Chapel, White Chapel-Chapel, London, on Sunday Afternoon, August 28, 1796. Concord, N.H.: George Hough, 1797.

Cornelius, Elias. A Sermon, Delivered in the Tabernacle Church, Salem, Massachusetts, September 25, 1823, at the Ordination of the Rev. Edmund Frost, as a Missionary to the Heathen: and the Rev. Messrs. Aaron W. Warner, Ansel D. Eddy, Nathan W. Fiske, Isaac Oakes, and George Sheldon, as Evangelists. Boston: Crocker and Brewster, 1823.

Dana, Daniel. A Sermon Preached in Boston, Before the Massachusetts Society for Promoting Christian Knowledge. May 28, 1817. Andover: Flagg and Gould, 1817.

Dana, Joseph. A Sermon Delivered Before the Meerimack Humane Society, at Their Anniversary Meeting, Newburyport, September 4, 1804. Newburyport: Edmund M. Blunt, Printer, 1804.

Day, Jeremiah. A Sermon, Delivered in Boston, September 17, 1823, Before the American Board of Commissioners for Foreign Missions, at Their Fourteenth Annual Meeting. Boston: Crocker and Brewster, 1823.

Dwight, Sereno Edwards. Thy Kingdom Come: A Sermon Delivered in the Old South Church, Boston, Before the Foreign Mission Society of Boston and the Vicinity, January 3, 1830. Boston: Crocker and Brewster, 1820.

Dwight, Timothy. A Sermon, Delivered in Boston, September 16, 1813, Before the American Board of Commissioners for Foreign Missions at Their Fourth Annual Meeting. Boston: Samuel T. Armstrong, 1813.

Eckley, Joseph. A Discourse Before the Society for Propagating the Gospel Among the Indians and Others in North America, Delivered November 7, 1805. Boston: Printed by E. Lincoln, 1806.

Ely, Alfred. A Sermon, Preached at Northampton, Before the Hampshire Missionary Society, at Their Annual Meeting, August 19, 1819. Northampton: Thomas W. Shepard & Co., 1819.

Emerson, John. The Duty of Christians to Seek the Salvation of Zion, Explained and Urged. A Sermon Preached at Northampton, Before the Hampshire Missionary Society, at Their Annual Meeting, August 31, 1809. Northampton: Printed by William Butler, 1809.

Emmons, Nathanael. A Sermon, Delivered Before the Massachusetts Missionary Society, at Their Annual Meeting in Boston, May 27, 1800. Charlestown, Mass.: Samuel Etheridge, 1800.

Fay, Warren. The Importance of the Last Promise of Jesus Christ to Christian Missionaries. A Sermon Delivered at Springfield, May 10, 1826, at the Ordination of the Rev. Rufus Anderson, as an Evangelist; and of the Rev. Messrs. Josiah Brewer, Eli Smith, Cyrus Stone, and Jeremiah Stowe, to the High and Sacred Office of Christian Missionaries. Boston: Crocker and Brewster, 1826.

_____. The Obligations of Christians in the Heathen World. A Sermon Delivered at the Old South Church in Boston, Before the Auxiliary Foreign Mission Society of Boston and Vicinity, at Their Annual Meeting, January 3, 1825. Boston: Crocker and Brewster, 1825.

Field, Joseph. Prosperity Promised to the Lovers of Jerusalem. A Sermon, Delivered in Northampton, August 22, 1816, Before the Hampshire Missionary Society, at Their Annual Meeting. Northampton: William W. Clapp, 1816.

Fisk, Elisha. A Sermon, Preached in Braintree, Before the Norfolk Auxiliary Society for the Education of Pious Youth for the Gospel Ministry, at Their Third Annual Meeting, June 9, 1819. Dedham: Printed by H. & W. Mann, n.d.

_____. A Sermon, Preached in the Meeting House in Park Street, Boston, May 29, 1822, Before the Massachusetts Society for Promoting Christian Knowledge. Boston: Crocker and Brewster, 1823.

Fisk, Pliny. The Holy Land an Interesting Field of Missionary Enterprise. A Sermon, Preached in the Old South Church Boston, Sabbath Evening, October 31, 1819, Just Before the Departure of the Palestine Mission. Boston: Samuel T. Armstrong, 1819.

Fitch, John. The Kingdom of Christ. A Sermon Delivered Before the Vermont Missionary Society, at Their Annual Meeting, at Pawlet, September 16, 1813. Middlebury: T. C. Strong, 1813.

Frisbie, Levi. A Discourse Before the Society for Propagating the Gospel Among the Indians and Others in North America. Delivered on the 1st of November, 1804. Charlestown, Mass.: Samuel Etheridge, 1804.

Furman, Richard. "Sermon." Baptist Board of Foreign Missions. Proceedings of the Baptist Convention for Missionary Purposes; Held in Philadelphia, in May, 1814. Philadelphia: Printed for the Convention, 1814.

Gile, Samuel. A Sermon, Delivered in the Old South Church, Boston, Before the Foreign Mission Society of Boston and the Vicinity, January 1, 1819. Boston: Lincoln & Edmands, n.d.

Gillet, Eliphalet. A Sermon Delivered Before the Maine Missionary Society at Their Annual Meeting in Bath, January 27, 1810. Hallowell, Me.: N. Cheever, 1810.

Griffen, Edward D. The Claims of Seamen. A Sermon, Preached November 7, 1819, in the Brick Church, New York, for the Benefit of the Marine Missionary Society of That City. New York: J. Seymour, 1819.

_____. Foreign Missions. A Sermon, Preached May 9, 1819, at the Anniversary of the United Foreign Missionary Society, in the Garden Street Church, New York. New York: J. Seymour, 1819.

_____. The Kingdom of Christ: A Missionary Sermon Preached Before the General Assembly of the Presbyterian Church, in Philadelphia, May 23, 1805. Philadelphia: Jane Aitkens, 1805.

_____. A Sermon Preached September 14, 1826, Before the American Board of Missions, at Middleton, Connecticut. Middletown: E. & H. Clark, 1826.

Grout, Jonathan. Missionary Societies Called to Go Forward. A Sermon, Preached at Northampton, Before the Hampshire Missionary Society, at Their Annual Meeting, August 30, 1810. Northampton, Mass.: William Butler, 1810.

Hall, Gordon. The Duty of the American Churches in Respect to Foreign Missions, A Sermon Preached in the Tabernacle, Philadelphia, on Sabbath Morning, February 16, 1812; and in the First Presbyterian Church on the Afternoon of the Same Day. Andover: Flagg & Gould, 1815.

Harris, Walter. A Discourse, Delivered to the Members of the Female Cent Society, in Bedford, New Hampshire, July 18, 1814. Concord (N.H.): George Hough, 1814.

Harvey, Joseph. A Sermon, Preached at Litchfield, Before the Foreign Mission Society of Litchfield County, at Their Annual Meeting, February 15, 1815. New Haven: Hudson & Woodward, Printers, 1815.

Haskel, Daniel. A Sermon, Delivered in Randolph at the Annual Meeting of the Vermont Juvenile Missionary Society, October 13, 1819. Middlebury, Vt.: Francis Burnap, 1819.

Holmes, Abiel. A Discourse, Delivered at the Old South Church in Boston Before the Society for Foreign Missions of Boston and Vicinity, January 1, 1812. Cambridge: Printed by Hilliard and Metcalf, 1813.

_____. A Discourse Delivered Before The Society for Propagating the Gospel Among the Indians and Others in North America, at Their Anniversary, November 4, 1813. Boston: Published by Cummings and Hilliard, 1813.

Howard, John C. A Discourse Delivered Before the Humane Society of the Commonwealth of Massachusetts, at Their Semi-annual Meeting, June 12, 1804. Boston: Printed by Hosea Sprague, 1804.

Humphrey, Heman. The Promised Land. A Sermon, Delivered at Goshen (Conn.) at the Ordination of the Rev. Messrs. Hiram Bingham & Asa Thurston, as Missionaries to the Sandwich Islands, September 29, 1819. Boston: Samuel T. Armstrong, 1819.

Huntington, Daniel. The Duty of Christians to the Jews. A Sermon, Delivered at the Annual Meeting of the Palatine Missionary Society, in Halifax, June 18, 1823. Boston: Crocker and Brewster, 1823.

Johns, Evan. A Sermon Preached at Northampton, Before the Foreign Missionary Society of Northampton and the Neighboring Towns, at Their First Meeting, March 31, 1812. Northampton, Mass.: Printed by William Butler, 1812.

Keep, John. Motives for Well Doing. A Sermon, Delivered in Northampton, August 21, 1815, Before the Hampshire Missionary Society, at Their Annual Meeting. Northampton: W. W. Clapp, 1815.

_____. Nature and Operations of Christian Benevolence. A Sermon Delivered October 21, 1818, Before the Directors of the Domestic Missionary Society, of Massachusetts Proper, at their First Meeting in Northampton. Northampton: Thomas W. Shepard & Co., 1818.

Kendall, James. A Sermon Delivered Before the Society for Propagating the Gospel Among the Indians and Others in North America at Their Anniversary, November 7, 1811. Boston: John Eliot Jr., 1811.

Kimball, David T. The Obligation and Disposition of Females to Promote Christianity, an Address, Delivered June 15, 1819, Before the Female Education and Charitable Societies, in the First Parish in Ipswich. Newburyport: Ephrain W. Allen, 1819.

_____. A Sermon, Preached in Boston Before the Massachusetts Society for Promoting Christian Knowledge, May 30, 1821. Cambridge: Hilliard and Metcalf, 1821.

Knapp, Isaac. The Zeal of Jehovah for the Kingdom of Christ. A Sermon, Preached at Northampton, Before the Hampshire Missionary Society at Their Annual Meeting, August 27, 1812. Northampson: William Butler, Printer, 1812.

Kollock, Henry. Christ Must Increase. A Sermon Preached Before the General Assembly of the Presbyterian Church in the United States of America; by Appointment of Their Standing Committee of Missions, May 23, 1803. Philadelphia: Jane Aitken, 1803.

Lathrop, John. A Discourse Before the Society for Propagating the Gospel Among the Indians, and Others, in North America. Delivered on the 19th of January, 1804. Boston: Manning and Loring, n.d.

Lathrop, Joseph. A Sermon Preached to the Hampshire Missionary Society at Their Annual Meeting the Fourth Tuesday in August, 1802, in Northampton. Northampton, Mass.: William Butler, 1802.

_____. A Sermon, Preached in Springfield, Before the Bible Society, and the Foreign Missionary Society, in the County of Hampden, at Their Annual Meeting, August 31, 1814. Springfield (Mass.): Thomas Dickman, 1814.

Leland, John. "Substance of a Sermon Delivered April 17, 1814 Before the Convening of a Baptist Convention." The Writings of the Late Elder John Leland. Edited by L. E. Greene. New York: Printed by G. W. Wood, 1845.

Linn, William. A Discourse Delivered April 1, 1800, in the Brick Presbyterian Church, Before the New York Missionary Society, at Their Annual Meeting. New York: Isaac Collins, 1800.

_____. Discourses on the Signs of the Times. New York: Printed by Thomas Greenleaf, 1794.

Livingston, John H. A Sermon Delivered Before the New York Missionary Society, at Their Annual Meeting, April 3, 1804. To Which are Added an Appendix, and Other Papers Relating to American Missions. New York: T. & J. Swords, 1804.

_____, and M'Knight, John. Two Sermons Delivered Before the New York Missionary Society, the First on April 23d, in the Scots Presbyterian Chur ch by Rev. Dr. Livingston, the Second on April 24, in the North Dutch Church, by Rev. Dr. M'Knight. To Which is Added, a Charge Given to the First Missionary, by the Rev. Dr. Rodgers; Together With the Instructions to Missionaries, and the Report of the Directors. New York: Isaac Collins, 1799.

Lowell, Charles. A Discourse Before the Society for Propagating the Gospel Among the Indians and Others in North America. Delivered November 9, 1820. Boston: Sewell Phelps, 1820.

Lyon, Asa. The Depravity and Misery of Man. A Sermon Delivered Before the Vermont Missionary Society at Their Annual Meeting at Woodstock, September 15, 1814. Middleburg, Vt.: Printed by Timothy C. Strong, 1815.

Lyman, Joseph. A Sermon, Preached at Boston, Before the American Board of Commissioners for Foreign Missions, at Their Tenth Annual Meeting, September 16, 1819. Boston: Samuel T. Armstrong, 1819.

_____. A Sermon, Preached at Northampton, Before an Ecclesiastical Convention, Assembled for the Purpose of Forming a Missionary Society, for the Propagation of the Gospel Upon the Last Tuesday in September, A.D. 1801. With an Appendix, Containing the Doings of the Convention. Northampton, William Butler, 1801.

M'Chord, James. Two Sermons on the Divine Forgiveness, Prepared Originally for the Church at Nicholasville, and Now Published (by Request) for the Benefit of the Lexington Bible Society. Lexington: Thomas T. Skillman, 1812.

M'Clelland, Alexander. A Sermon in Vindication of the Religious Spirit of the Age: Preached April 9, 1820, in the Middle Dutch Church, New York, on the Anniversary of the New York Missionary Society. New York: D. Fanshaw, 1820.

M'Ewen, Abel. "A Sermon, Delivered at the North Presbyterian Church in Hartford, on the Evening of May 16, 1815; by Appointment of the Trustees of the Missionary Society of Connecticut," in Connecticut Evangelical Magazine VIII (June, 1815).

M'Farland, John. The Signs of the Times, Being the Substance of a Discourse Delivered in Chillicothe, Ohio, in May Last: and also in Paris, Ky. on the Last Tuesday of August, 1820. Paris, Ky.: Printed by Joel R. Lyle, 1821.

Mason, John M. Hope for the Heathen: A Sermon Preached in the Old Presbyterian Church, Before the New York Missionary Society, at Their Annual Meeting, November 7, 1797. New York: T. & J. Swords, 1797.

_____. Messiah's Throne. A Sermon Preached Before the London Missionary Society at Their Eighth Annual Meeting, in Tottenham Court Chapel, on the Evening of Thursday, the 13th of May, 1802. New York: American Tract Society, n.d.

Milledoler, Philip. A Discourse, Delivered in the Presbyterian Church in Wall Street, March 23, 1806, for a Society of Ladies Instituted for the Relief of Poor Widows with Small Children, and Published at Their Request. New York: T. & J. Swords, 1806.

Miller, Samuel. A Sermon Delivered Before the New York Missionary Society, at Their Annual Meeting, April 6, 1802. New York: T. & J. Swords, 1802.

_____. A Sermon Delivered in the Middle Church, New Haven, Conn., September 12, 1822, at the Ordination of the Rev. Messrs. William Goodell, William Richards, and Artemas Bishop, as Evangelists and Missionaries to the Heathen. Boston: Crocker and Brewster, 1822.

Miller, William W. An Address, Delivered Before the Auxiliary Missionary Society of Morris at Their Meeting Held at Morristown, October 24, 1820. Morristown, N.J.: Printed by Jacob Mann, 1820.

Morse, Jedidiah. A Discourse Delivered at the African Meeting House, in Boston, July 14, 1808, in Grateful Celebration of the Abolition of the African Slave Trade, by the Government of the United States, Great Britain and Denmark. Boston: Printed by Lincoln & Edmands, 1808.

_____. The Gospel Harvest, Illustrated in a Sermon, Delivered at the Old South Church is Boston, Before the Society for Foreign Missions of Boston and the Vicinity, at Their Annual Meeting, January 2, 1815. Boston: Nathaniel Willis, 1815.

_____. A Sermon Delivered Before the American Board of Commissioners for Foreign Missions, at Their Annual Meeting in Springfield, Massachusetts, September 19, 1821. Boston: For the Board of Commissioners by George Clark, 1821.

_____. Signs of the Times. A Sermon, Preached Before the Society for Propagating the Gospel

Among the Indians and Others in North America, at Their Anniversary, November 1, 1810. Charlestown: Samuel T. Armstrong, 1810.

Niles, Samuel. A Sermon Delivered Before the Massachusetts Missionary Society at Their Annual Meeting in Boston, May 26, 1801. Cambridge: William Hilliard, 1801.

Norton, Jacob. Faith in the Son of God Necessary to Everlasting Life. A Sermon Delivered Before the Massachusetts Missionary Society, at their Eleventh Annual Meeting, in Boston, May 29, 1810. Boston: Lincoln & Edmands, 1810.

Nott, Eliphalet. A Sermon Preached Before the General Assembly of the Church in the United States of America by Appointment of Their Standing Committee of Missions, May 19, 1806. Newburyport, Mass.: Reprinted for Samuel Doel, 1808.

Palmer, Benjamin M. The Signs of the Times Discerned and Improved, in Two Sermons, Delivered in the Independent or Congregational Church, Charleston, S.C. Charleston, S.C.: Printed by J. Hoff, 1816.

Parish, Elijah. A Sermon Preached at Boston, November 3, 1814, Before the Society for Propagating the Gospel Among the Indians and Others in North America. Boston: Printed by Nathaniel Willis, 1814.

_____. A Sermon, Preached Before the Massachusetts Missionary Society, at Their Annual Meeting in Boston, May 26, 1807. Newburyport: E. W. Allen, 1807.

Parsons, Levi. The Dereliction and Restoration of the Jews. A Sermon, Preached in Park Street Church Boston, Sabbath, October 31, 1819, Just Before the Departure of the Palestine Mission. Boston: Samuel T. Armstrong, 1819.

Perry, David L. The Spiritual Temple. A Sermon, Delivered at the Annual Examination of the Foreign Mission School, in Cornwall, May 17, 1820. Hartford: Peter B. Gleason and Co., 1820.

Pomeroy, Jonathan L. Report of the Trustees of the Hampshire Missionary Society, Made at Their Annual Meeting in Northampton, the last Thursday in August, 1806. To Which is Annexed, a Sermon, Delivered Before the Society. Northampton: William Butler, 1806.

Porter, Ebenezer. "A Sermon Delivered at the New Brick Meeting House in Hartford, on the Evenine of May 15, 1810, at the Request of the Trustees of the Missionary Society of Connecticut." Connecticut Evangelical Magazine and Religious Intelligencer, III (July, 1810), 241-253.

_____. A Sermon, Delivered in Boston, on the Anniversary of the American Education Society October 4, 1820. Andover: Flagg and Gould, 1821.

Porter, Eliphalet. A Discourse Before the Society for Propagating the Gospel Among the Indians and Others in North America, Delivered November 5, 1807. Boston: Munroe, Francis & Parker, 1808.

_____. A Discourse, Delivered Before the Roxbury Charitable Society, at Their First Annual Meeting, September 15, 1794. Boston: Printed by Samuel Hall, 1795.

Proudfit, Alexander. A Sermon, Preached Before the Northern Missionary Society in the State of New York, at Their First Annual Meeting in Troy, February 8, and by Particular Request, in Albany, March 6, 1798, at a Special Meeting of the Society. Albany: Loring Andrews, 1798.

_____. The Universal Extension of Messiah's Kingdom. A Sermon, Delivered in the North Church, New Haven, Conn., September 12, 1822, Before the American Board of Commissioners for Foreign Missions, at Their Thirteenth Annual Meeting. Boston: Crocker and Brewster, 1822.

Pruden, Nehemiah. "A Missionary Sermon, Delivered at Hartford, by the Desire of the Trustees of the Missionary Society of Connecticut on the Evening of May 9, 1805"; Connecticut Evangelical Magazine and Religious Intelligencer, VI, (July, 1805), pp. 6-11.

Romeyn, John B. A Sermon Delivered in the Middle Dutch Church, on the Evening of the Lord's Day, March 21, 1819, for the Benefit of the New York Marine Missionary Society. New York: J. Seymour, 1819.

Sabine, James. Glorying in the Cross. A Sermon, Delivered Before the Associated Congregational Ministers of Salem and Vicinity, at Malden, Mass., on Tuesday, September 8, 1818. Boston: N. Willis, 1818.

_____. The Relation the Present State of Religion Bears to the Expected Millennium. A Sermon Delivered in the Old South Church, Boston, Before the Foreign Mission Society, of Boston and Vicinity, January 8, 1823. Boston: Crocker and Brewster, 1823.

Sanborn, Peter. The Extent and Perpetuity of the Abrahamic Covenant a Motive to Missionary Exertion. A Sermon Preached Before the Massachusetts Missionary Society, at Their Annual Meeting, May 30, 1815. Boston: Printed by Samuel T. Armstrong, 1815.

Sewall, Joseph. Christ Victorious Over the Power of Darkness, by the Light of His Preached Gospel. Boston: S. Kneeland, 1733.

Sharp, Daniel. Obligation of Christians to the Heathen. A Sermon, Preached Before the General Convention of the Baptist Denomination in the United States, in the Baptist Meeting House in Sansom Street in Philadelphia, April 29, 1829. Boston: Printed by Lincoln & Edmands, 1829.

Smith, John Blair. The Enlargement of Christ's Kingdom, the Object of a Christian's Prayers and Exertions. A Discourse, Delivered in the Dutch Church, in Albany, Before the Northern Missionary Society in the State of New York, at Their Organization, February 14, 1797. Schenectady: Printed by C. P. Wyckoff, 1797.

Sprague, William B. A Sermon, Preached In Springfield, August 28, 1823; At the Annual Meeting of the Bible Society, the Foreign Missionary Society, and the Education Society, of the County of Hampden. Springfield (Mass.): William H. Cooke, Printer, 1823.

Spring, Samuel. A Sermon, Delivered Before the Massachusetts Missionary Society, at Their Annual Meeting May 25, 1802. The Annual Report Also of the Trustees, and Several Interesting Things Relative to Missions. Newburyport: E. M. Blunt, 1802.

Staughton, William. Missionary Encouragement: A Discourse, Delivered on Wednesday Evening, the 16th of May, 1798, Before the Philadelphia Missionary Society and the Congregation of the Baptist Meeting House, Philadelphia. Philadelphia: Printed by Stephen C. Ustick, 1798.

Stillman, Samuel. A Discourse Preached in Boston Before the Massachusetts Baptist Missionary Society, May 25, 1803. Being Their First Anniversary. Boston: Printed by Manning and Loring, 1803.

Stoddard, Solomon. Question Whether God Is Not Angry With the Country for Doing So Little Towards the Conversion of the Indians. Boston: Printed by B. Green, 1723.

Stone, Micah. An Address, Delivered Before the Moral Society in Brookfield, April 15, 1817. Brookfield: E. Merriam & Co., 1817.

Strong, Jonathan. A Sermon Preached Before the Massachusetts Missionary Society, at Their Annual Meeting, in Boston, May 24, 1808. Boston: Joshua Cushing, 1808.

Taylor, James. A Sermon, Preached at Northampton, Before the Hampshire Missionary Society, at Their Annual Meeting, August 20, 1818. Northampton: Thomas W. Shepard & Co., 1818.

Thayer, Elihu. A Sermon, Preached at Hopkinton, at the Formation of New Hampshire Missionary Society, September 2, 1801. Concord (N.H.): George Hough, 1801.

Thurston, David. A Sermon Delivered in Saco, June 26, 1816, Before the Maine Missionary Society, at Their Ninth Annual Meeting. Hallowell (Me.): Printed by N. Cheever, 1816.

Waterman, Elijah. "Extract from a Sermon Delivered at Hartford, on the Evening of May 12, 1803," Connecticut Evangelical Magazine, IV (July, 1803), 27-31.

Wayland, Francis. The Moral Dignity of the Missionary Enterprise. A Sermon Delivered Before the Boston Baptist Foreign Mission Society on the Evening of October 26, and Before the Salem Bible Translation Society on the Evening of November 4, 1823. Third Edition. Boston: James Loring, 1824.

Webster, Josiah. Christ, on His Way to Enlarge His Kingdom, and to Judge the World. A Sermon Delivered Before the General Association of New Hampshire, at Their Meeting in Haverhill, September 21, 1819. Exeter (N.H.): J. J. Williams, 1819.

Wells, Rufus. A Sermon, Preached at Northampton, Before the Hampshire Missionary Society, August 29, 1811. Northampton, Mass.: William Butler, 1811.

Whitman, Samuel. Blessedness of Those Who Shall Attend to Glory Without Dying. A Sermon, Delivered Before the Hampshire Missionary Society, at Their Annual Meeting in Northampton, August 21, 1817. Northampton: Ephraim Whitman, 1817.

Williams, John. A Discourse Delivered April 5, 1803, in the Baptist Church, in the Good Street, Before the New York Missionary Society, at Their Annual Meeting. New York: Isaac Collins and Son, 1803.

Williams, Solomon. A Sermon Preached at Northampton, Before the Ecclesiastical Convention, Convened to Consider and Ratify the Constitution of a Missionary Society for Propagating the Gospel, on the Fifth Day of January, 1802. Northampton, Mass.: William Butler, 1802.

Winslow, Miron. A Sermon Delivered at the Old South Church, Boston, June 7, 1819, on the Evening Previous to the Sailing of the Rev. Miron Winslow, Levi Spaulding, and Henry Woodward, & Dr. John Scudder, as Missionaries to Ceylon. Andover: Flagg and Gould, Printers, 1819.

Woods, Leonard. A Sermon, Delivered at the Tabernacle in Salem, February 6, 1812, on Occasion of the Ordination of the Rev. Messrs. Samuel Newell, A.M.; and Luther Rice, A.B.; Missionaries to the Heathen in Asia. Boston: Samuel T. Armstrong, 1812.

_____. A Sermon, Preached at Haverhill, Mass., in Remembrance of Mrs. Harriet Newell, Wife of the Rev. Samuel Newell, Missionary to India to Which Are Added Memoirs of Her Life. Fourth Edition. Boston: Printed for Samuel T. Armstrong, 1814.

Worcester, Samuel. The Wisdom of God. A Sermon Delivered Before the Massachusetts Missionary Society at Their Tenth Annual Meeting in Boston, May 30, 1809. Boston: Joshua Cushing, 1809.

Collections

Bellamy, Joseph. The Works of the Rev. Joseph Bellamy, D.D. 3 vols. New York: Published by Stehen Dodge, 1811.

Brown, Alexander. The Genesis of the United States. 2 vols. Boston: Houghton, Mifflin and Company, 1891.

Calvin, John. Works of John Calvin. 51 vols. Edinburgh: The Calvin Translation Society, 1844-1856.

Davies, Samuel. Sermons on Important Subjects. 4 vols. 7th ed. London: Printed for W. Baynes, 1815.

Edwards, Jonathan. The Works of Jonathan Edwards, A.M. With an Essay on His Genius and Writing by Henry Rogers and a Memoir by Sereno E. Dwight. Revised and Corrected by Edward Hickman. 2 vols. 10th ed. London: Henry G. Bohn, 1865.

Emmons, Nathanael. The Works of Nathanael Emmons, D.D. Edited by Jacob Ide. With a Memoir of His Life by Edward A. Park. 6 vols. Boston Congregation Board of Publication, 1861.

Fox, George. A Collection of Many Select and Christian Epistles, Letters, and Testimonies. 2 vols. Philadelphia: Marcus T. C. Gould, 1831.

Handy, Robert T., Smith, H. Shelton, and Loetscher, Lefferts A., eds. American Christianity. 3 vols. New York: Charles Scribner's Sons, 1960.

Heimert, Alan and Miller, Perry, eds. The Great Awakening: Documents Illustrating the Crisis and Its Consequences. Indianapolis: The Bobbs-Merrill Company, Inc., 1967.

Hopkins, Samuel. The Works of Samuel Hopkins, D.D. Edited with A Memoir of His Life and Character by Edward A. Park. 3 vols. Boston: Doctrinal Tract and Book Society, 1854.

Ibbotson, Joseph D. Documentary History of Hamilton College. Clinton, N.Y.: Published by the College, 1922.

Kock, Adrienne and Peden, William, eds. The Life and Selected Writings of Thomas Jefferson. New York: Modern Library, 1944.

Leland, John. The Writings of the Late Elder John Leland. Edited by L. F. Green. New York: Printed by G. W. Wood, 1845.

Mason, John M. The Complete Works of John M. Mason, D.D. Edited by Ebenezer Mason. 4 vols. New York: Baker and Scribner, 1849.

Massachusetts Historical Society. Collections. 1792-1871.

Miller, Perry and Johnson, Thomas H. The Puritans. 2 vols. Revised edition. Harper Torch-
    books; Harper and Row, Publishers, 1963.

Morison, Samuel E., ed. Winthrop Papers. 5 vols. Boston: Massachusetts Historical Society.

O'Callaghan, E. E., ed. The Documentary History of the State of New York. 6 vols. Albany:
    Charles Van Benthuysen, Public Printer, 1849-1851.

Peek, George A., Jr., ed. The Political Writings of John Adams: Representative Selections.
    New York: The Liberal Arts Press, 1954.

Perkins, William. The Works of that Famovs and Worthy Minister of Christ, in the Univer-
    sity of Cambridge, M. W. Perkins. 3 vols. London: Printed by J. Legatt, 1609.

Rippon, John, ed. The Baptist Annual Register. 4 vols. London: n.p., 1793-1802.

Shepard, Thomas. The Works of Thomas Shepard. 3 vols. New York: AMS Press, Inc., 1967.

Van Der Weyde, William M., ed. The Life and Works of Thomas Paine, Patriots ed. 10 vols.
    New Rochelle, New York: Thomas Paine National Historical Association, 1925.

Whitfield, George. Seventy-Five Sermons on Various Important Subjects. 3 vols. London:
    Printed for W. Baynes, 1812.

Zwingli and Bullinger. Selected Translations With an Introduction and Notes by Geoffrey W.
    Bromily. Vol. XXIV of the Library of Christian Classics. Edited by John Baille,
    John T. McNeill, and Henry P. Van Dusen. 26 vols. Philadelphia: Westminster Press,
    1953-1969.

Other Works

An Account of the Rise, Constitution and Management of the Society in Scotland for Propa-
    gating Christian Knowledge. 2nd ed. Edinburgh: Printed for William Brown and Com-
    pany, 1720.

An Account of the Society in Scotland for Propagating Christian Knowledge, From Its Com-
    mencement, in 1709. In Which is Included, the Present State of the Highlands and
    Islands of Scotland With Regard to Religion. Edinburgh: Printed by A. Murray and
    J. Cochrane, 1774.

The Acts and Proceedings of the General Synod of the Reformed Protestant Dutch Church in
    North America. New York: Board of Publication of the Reformed Dutch Church, 1859.

American Baptist Foreign Missionary Society. Valley Forge, Pa. Archives. Judson Letter File.

American Baptist Foreign Missionary Society. Valley Forge, Pa. Archives. MSS Minutes of Baptist
    Board of Foreign Missions, 1814-1832.

The American Baptist Magazine and Missionary Intelligencer. Vols. 1-4. 1817-1824.

American Bible Society. Proceedings of a Meeting and Constitution of the American Bible Society,
    Formed by a Convention of Delegates, Held in the City of New York, May, 1816, Together
    With Their Address to the People of the United States; a Notice of Their Proceedings; and
    a List of Their Officers. New York: Printed for the American Bible Society by G. F. Hop-
    kins, 1816.

American Bible Society. Proceedings of a Meeting of the Citizens of New York and Others, Convened in the City Hall on the 13th day of May, 1816; at the Request of the Board of Managers of the American Bible Society. New York: Published by order of the Board of Managers, 1816.

Ames, William. An Analyticall Exposition of Both the Epistles of the Apostle Peter. London: Printed for E. G., 1641.

_____. The Marrow of Sacred Divinity. London: Printed by E. Griffen, 1638.

An Address of the Congregational Missionary Society, in the Counties of Berkshire, Columbia, and their Vicinities, to the Churches and Congregational. Also, a Report of the Trustees of the Congregational Missionary Society, Relative to Their Proceedings from September, 1804, to September, 1805. Stockbridge: H. Willard. n.d.

Avery, David. The Lord is to be Praised for the Triumphs of His Power. Norwich, Conn.: Printed by Green, 1778.

Babcock, Rufus, ed. Memoir of John Mason Peck, D.D. Introduction by Paul M. Harrison. Carbondale, Illinois: Southern Illinois University Press, 1965.

Backus, Isaac. Church History of New England From 1620 to 1804, Containing a View of the Principles and Practice, Declensions and Revivals, Oppression and Liberty of the Churches, and a Chronological Table. Philadelphia: American Baptist Publication Society, 1853.

_____. A History of New England. With Particular Reference to the Denomination of Christians Called Baptists. 2 vols. 2nd ed. Newton, Mass.: Published by the Backus Historical Society, 1871.

Baptist Board of Foreign Missions. Proceedings of the Baptist Convention for Missionary Purposes; Held in Philadelphia, in May, 1814. Philadelphia: Printed for the Convention by Ann Coles, 1814.

Baptist Board of Foreign Missions. Proceedings of the General Convention of the Baptist Denomination in the United States, at Their First Triennial Meeting, Held in Philadelphia, From the 7th to the 14th of May, 1817: Together with the Third Annual Report of the Baptist Board of Foreign Missions for the United States. Philadelphia: Printed by Order of the Convention, 1817.

The Baptist Memorial and Monthly Chronicle. Vols. 1-3. 1842-1844.

Beatty, Charles. Journals of Charles Beatty, 1762-1769. Edited with Introduction by Guy Soulliard Klett. University Park, Pa.: Pennsylvania State University Press, 1962.

Benedict, David. A General History of the Baptist Denomination in America and Other Parts of the World. 2 vols. Boston: Printed by Manning & Loring, 1813.

Board of National Missions of the United Presbyterian Church. New York, N. Y. Archives. MSS Minutes of the Standing Committee of Missions, 1802-1830.

The Boston Evening Post. July 30, 1764.

The Boston Gazette. July 2 and 9, 1764.

Brainerd, David. Mirabilia Dei Inter Indicos, Or the Rise and Progress of a Remarkable Work of Grace

Amongst a Number of the Indians in the Province of New Jersey and Pennsylvania and Divine Grace Displayed or the Continuance and Progress of a Remarkable Work of Grace Amongst Some of the Indians. Philadelphia: Printed by William Bradford, 1746.

Brainerd, John. John Brainerd's Journal (1761-1762). Transcriptions of Early Church Records of New Jersey. Newark, N.J.: Historical Records Survey, 1941.

Bradford, William. History of Plymouth Plantation. Edited with Introduction by William T. Davis. New York: Charles Scribner's Sons, 1908.

Calvin, John. The Institutes of the Christian Religion. Translated by Henry Beveridge. 2 vols. London: James Clarke and Co., Lmtd., n.d.

_____. Sermons of M. John Caluin on the Epistles of S. Paule to Thimothie and Titus. London: Imprinted for G. Biship and T. Woodcoke, 1579.

Carey, Richard. To the Members of the Society for Propagating the Gospel Among the Indians and Others In North America. Boston: Printed by S. Hall, 1789.

Carey, William. An Enquiry into the Obligations of Christians to Use Means for the Conversion of the Heathens. New Facsimile Edition with an Introduction by Ernest A. Payne. London: Carey Kingsgate Press Limited, 1961.

Channing, William Ellery. Discourses, Reviews, and Miscellanies. Boston: Carter and Hendee, 1830.

Classified Digest of the Records of the Society for the Propagation of the Gospel in Foreign Parts 1701-1892. London: Published at the Society's Office, 1893.

Coffin, Paul. "Journals." Maine Historical Society, Collections. Vol. IV (1836).

The Connecticut Evangelical Magazine. Vols. 1-7. 1800-1807. New Series. Vols. 1-8. 1808-1815.

Cotton, John. God's Mercie Mixed with His Ivstice, or, His Peoples Deliverance in Times of Danger, London: Printed by G. M., 1641.

_____. God's Promise to His Plantation. London: Printed by William Jones, 1630.

Danforth, Samuel. A Brief Recognition of New Englands Errand Into the Wilderness; Made in the Audience of the General Assembly of the Massachusetts Colony, at Boston in N.E. on the 11th of the Third Month, 1670, Being the Day of Election There. Cambridge: Printed by S. G. and M. F., 1671.

Dwight, E. W. Memoirs of Henry Obookiah, a Native of Owhyhee and a Member of the Foreign Mission School, Who Died at Cornwall, Conn., February 17, 1818, Aged 26 Years. New Haven: n.p., 1818.

Dwight, Timothy. A Discourse at the Present Crises. New Haven: Printed by George Bunce, 1798.

_____. The Duty of Americans at the Present Crises. New Haven: Printed by George Bunce, 1798.

_____. The Nature and Danger of Infidel Philosophy, Exhibited in Two Discourses. New Haven: Printed by George Bunce, 1798.

Eames, Wilberforce, ed. John Eliot and the Indians, 1652-1657. New York: Privately Printed, 1915.

Edwards, Jonathan. A Sermon Preached on the Day of the Funeral of the Rev. Mr. David Brainerd, Missionary to the Indians, From the Honorable Society in Scotland for the Propagation of the Christian Knowledge, and Pastor of a Church of Christian Indians in New Jersey; Who Died at Northampton in New England, October 9, 1747, in the 30th Year of His Age, and Was Interred on the 12th Following. Containing Some Account of His Character, and Manner of Life, and Remarkable Speaches and Behaviour at Death. Boston: Printed by Rogers and Fowle for D. Henchaman, 1747.

Eliot, John. A Brief Narrative of the Progress of the Gospel Amongst the Indians in New England, in the Year 1670, Given in by the Reverend Mr. John Eliot, Minister of the Gospel There, in a Letter Directed to the Right Worshipfull the Commissioners Under His Majesties Great Seal for Propagation of the Gospel Amongst the Poor Blind Natives in Those United Colonies. London: Printed for John Allen, 1771.

_____. The Christian Commonvvealth: Or, The Civil Policy of the Rising Kingdom of Jesus Christ. Written Before the Interruption of the Government. London: Printed for Livewell Chapman, 1661.

_____. Communion of Churches. Cambridge: Printed by Marmaduke Johnson, 1665.

_____. The Indian Grammar Begun: Or, an Essay to Bring the Indian Language into Rules, for the Help of Such as Desire to Learn the Same, for the Furthurance of the Gospel Among Them. Cambridge: Printed by Marmaduke Johnson, 1666.

_____. The Indian Primer; Or, the Way of Training Up of Our Indian Youth in the Good Knowledge of God. To Which Is Prefixed the Indian Covenanting Confession. With an Introduction by John Small. Edinburgh: Andrew Elliot, 1880.

_____. A Late and Further Manifestation of the Progress of the Gospel Amongst the Indians in New England. Declaring Their Constant Love and Zeal to the Truth: With a Readinesse to Give Accompt of Their Faith and Hope; As of Their Desires in Church Communion to be Partakers of the Ordinances of Christ. Being a Narrative of the Examinations of the Indians, About Their Knowledge in Religion, by the Elders of the Churches. London: Printed by M. S., 1655.

_____. The Logic Primer. Some Logical Notions to Initiate the Indians in the Knowledge of the Rules of Reason; and to Show How to Make Use Thereof, Especially for the Instruction of Such as are Teachers of Them. Cambridge: Printed by J. J., 1672.

_____. Tears of Repentance: Or, a Further Narrative of the Progresse of the Gospel Amongst the Indians in New England: Setting Forth, Not Only Their Present State and Condition, but Sundry Confessions of Sin by Diverse of the Said Indians, Wrought Upon by the Saving Power of the Gospel; Together With the Manifestation of Their Faith and Hope in Jesus Christ, and the Work of Grace Upon Their Hearts. Related by Mr. Eliot and Mr. Mayhew, Two Faithful Laborers in That Work of the Lord. London: Printed by Peter Cole, 1653.

Ely, Ezra Stiles. A Contrast Between Calvinism and Hopkinsianism. New York: Published by S. Whiting and Co., 1811.

Emmons, Nathanael. To All, Who Are Desirous of the Spread of the Gospel of Our Lord Jesus Christ. Boston: n.p., 1799.

Engles, William M., ed. Minutes of the General Assembly 1789-1820. Philadelphia: Presbyterian Board of Publication, 1847.

The Evangelical Magazine and Missionary Chronicle. Vols. 1-18. 1793-1810.

Ferguson, John. Memoir of the Life and Character of Rev. Samuel Hopkins, D.D. Formerly
        Pastor of the First Congregational Church in Newport, Rhode Island. With an Ap-
        pendix. Boston: Published by Leonard W. Kimball, 1830.

First Ten Annual Reports of the American Board of Commissioners for Foreign Missions With
        Other Documents of the Board. Boston: Printed by Crocker and Brewster, 1834.

The General Assembly's Missionary Magazine. Vols. 1-3. 1805-1807.

The Georgia Analytical Repository. Vol. 1. 1802-1803.

Gillette, A. D., ed. Minutes of the Philadelphia Baptist Association, from A.D. 1707, to A.D.
        1807: Being the First One Hundred Years of Its Existence. Philadelphia: American
        Baptist Publication Society, 1851.

Glad Tidings, Or an Account of the State of Religion, Within the Bounds of the General Assem-
        bly of the Presbyterian Church in the United States of America and Other Parts of the
        World. Philadelphia: Printed by Jane Aitken, 1804.

Good News From New England: With an Exact Relation of the First Planting That Countrey: A
        Description of the Profits Accruing by the Worke. Together with a Briefe, But True Dis-
        covery of Their Order Both in Church and Commonwealth, and Maintenance Allowed
        the Painful Labourers in That Vineyard of the Lord. With the Names of the Several
        Towns, and Who Be Preachers to Them. London: Printed by Matthew Simmons, 1648.

Gookin, Daniel, Historical Collections of the Indians in New England. Massachusetts Historical
        Society. Collections. Series One, Vol. 1, (1806), 141-232.

Hall, Gordon and Newell, Samuel. The Conversion of the World: Or the Claims of Six Hundred
        Millions of Heathen, and the Ability and Duty of the Churches Respecting Them. Lon-
        don: Reprinted for W. Simpkin and R. Marshall, 1819.

Harvard University. Houghton Library Archives. MSS Minutes of the New York Missionary Soci-
        ety, 1799-1817.

_____. MSS Records of the Board of Managers of the United Foreign Missionary Society,
        1817-1822.

Hawley, Gideon. "Biographical and Topographical Anecdotes." Massachusetts Historical Society.
        Collections. Series One, III (1794), 188-193.

_____. Letter. Massachusetts Historical Society. Collections. Series One, IV (1795), 50-67.

Heckewelder, John. A Narrative of the Mission of the United Brethren Among the Delaware and
        Mohegan Indians, From Its Commencement, in the Year 1740, to the Year 1808. Phila-
        delphia: Published by McCarty and Davis, 1820.

History of the Young Men's Missionary Society of New York and the Hopkinsian Question. New
        York: n.p., 1817.

Holmes, Elkanah. A Church Covenant; Including a Summary of the Fundamental Doctrines of the
        Gospel. Baltimore: Printed by William Warner, 1818.

Hooker, Thomas. The Vnbeleevers Preparing for Christ. London: Printed by Tho. Cotes, 1638.

Hopkins, Samuel (1693-1755). Historical Memoirs, Relating to the Housatonnuk Indians. An Account of the Methods Used, and Pains Taken, for the Propagation of the Gospel Among That Heathenish Tribe, and the Success Thereof, Under the Ministry of the Late Reverend Mr. John Sergeant. Boston: S. Kneeland, 1752.

_____ (1721-1803). The Life of the Late Reverend, Learned and Pious Mr. Jonathan Edwards. Boston: S. Kneeland, 1765.

_____. Sketches of the life of the Late Rev. Samuel Hopkins, D.D. Pastor of the First Congregational Church in Newport, Written by Himself. Edited With an Introduction by Stephen West. Hartford: Printed by Hudson and Goodwin, 1805.

Humphreys, David. An Historical Account of the Incorporated Society for the Propagation of the Gospel in Foreign Parts. London: Printed by Joseph Downing, 1730.

Johnson, Edward. Wonder Working Providence. Edited by J. F. Jameson. New York: Charles Scribner's Sons, 1910.

Jones, David. A Journal of Two Visits Made to Some Nations of Indians on the West Side of the River Ohio, in the Year 1772 and 1773. Sabin Reprint No. 2. New York: Reprinted for Joseph Sabin, 1865.

The latter Day Luminary. Vols. 1-6. 1818-1825.

Leland, John. The Virginia Chronicle. Norfolk, Va.: n.p., 1789.

Lord, E. A Compendious History of the Principal Protestant Missions to the Heathen, Selected and Compiled from the Best Authorities. 2 vols. Boston: Samuel T. Armstrong, 1813.

McClure, David and Parish, Elijah. Memoirs of the Rev. Eleazar Wheelock D.D. Newburyport: Printed by Edward Little, 1811.

McCoy, Isaac. History of Baptist Indian Missions: Embracing Remarks on the Former and Present Condition of the Aboriginal Tribes; Their Settlement Within the Indian Territory, and Their Future Prospects. Washington: William M. Morrison, 1840.

The Massachusetts Baptist Missionary Magazine. Vols. 1-4. 1803-1816.

The Massachusetts Missionary Magazine. Vols. 1-5. 1803-1808.

Mather, Cotton. Another Tongue Brought in to Confess the Great Saviour of the World. Boston: Printed by B. Green, 1707.

_____. Blessed Unions. An Union With the Son of God by Faith, and, an Union in the Church of God by Love, Importunately Pressed; in a Discourse Which Makes Divers Offers for These Unions. Boston: Printed by B. Green & J. Allen, 1692.

_____. Bonifacius: an Essay Upon the Good. Edited With an Introduction by David Levin. Cambridge: Harvard University Press, 1966.

_____. Brethren Dwelling Together in Unity. Boston: Printed for S. Gerrish, 1718.

_____. Diary of Cotton Mather. 2 vols. New York: Frederick Ungar Publishing Co., n.d.

_____. The Day, and the Work of the Day. A Brief Discourse on What Fears, We May Have at This Time to Quicken Us; What Hopes There Are For Us at This Time to Comfort Us: And

What Prayers Would be Likely to Turn Our Fears Into Hopes With Reflections Upon Time and State, Now Come Upon the Church of God, and Collections of Certain Prophesies Relating to the Present Circumstances of New England Uttered on a Fast, Kept in Boston, July 6, 1693. Boston: Printed and Sold by B. Harris, 1693.

_____. The Day Which the Lord Hath Made. Boston: N.E.: Reprinted by B. Green, 1707.

_____. Dust and Ashes. An Essay Upon Repentance to Last. Advising a Watchful Christian, Upon That Case; How to Keep Alive the Daily Exercise of Repentance, to the End of His Life? Boston in N.E.: Printed by B. Green for Timothy Green, 1710.

_____. Eleutheria: Or, an Idea of the Reformation in England. London: Printed by J.R., 1698.

_____. Epistle to the Christian Indians. Boston: Printed by Bartholomew Green and John Allen, 1700.

_____. Frontiers Well Defended. Boston: Printed by T. Green, 1707.

_____. Hatchets to Hew Down the Tree of Sin. Boston: Printed by B. Green, 1705.

_____. India Christiana. A Discourse, Delivered Unto the Commissioners, for the Propagation of the Gospel Among the American Indians Which Is Accompanied With Several Instruments Relating to the Glorious Design of Propagating Our Holy Religion in the Eastern and as Well as the Western, Indies. And Entertainment Which They That Are Wanting for the Kingdom of God Will Receive as Good News From a Far Country. Boston in New England: Printed by B. Green, 1721.

_____. Letter About the Present State of Christianity Among the Christianized Indians. Boston: Printed by Timothy Green, 1705.

_____. A Letter Concerning the Terrible Sufferings of Our Protestant Brethren, on Board the French Kings Galleyes. n.p., 1701.

_____. A Letter to Ungospellized Plantations. Boston: n.p., 1702.

_____. Magnalia Christi Americana; Or, the Ecclesiastical History of New England; From Its First Planting, in the Year 1620, Unto the Year of Our Lord 1697. 2 vols. 1852 Edition. New York: Russell and Russell, 1967.

_____. Malachi. Or the Everlasting Gospel, Preached Unto the Nations. And Those Maxims of Piety, Which Are to be the Glorious Rules of Behaviour, the Only Terms of Communion, and the Happy Stops to Controversy, Among All That Would Meet and Serve Those Advances Which the Kingdom of God Is Now Making on the World; And What the Distressed Nations, Must See Distresses Go on, Till They are Brought Unto. Boston: Printed by T. C. for Robert Starke, 1717.

_____. A Midnight Cry. An Essay For Our Awakening Out of That Sinful Sleep, to Which We Are at This Time Too Much Disposed; and Four Our Discovering of What Peculiar Things There Are This Time, That Are For Our Awakening. Boston: Printed by John Allen, 1692.

_____. The Negro Christianized. Boston: Printed by B. Green, 1706.

_____. Nuncia Bona e Terra Longinqua. A Brief Account of Some Good & Great Things a Doing for the Kingdom of God, in the Midst of Europe. Boston in New England: Printed by B. Green, 1715.

_____. Old Paths Restored. Boston: Printed and Sold by T. Green, 1711.

_____. Pia Desideria. Or, The Smoking Flax, Raised Unto a Sacred Flame: in a Short and Plain Essay Upon Those Pious Desires, Which Are the Introduction and Inchoation of All Piety. Boston: Printed by S. Kneeland, 1722.

_____. A Pillar of Gratitude. Or, a Brief Recapitulation, of the Matchless Favours, With Which the God of Heaven Hath Obliged the Hearty Praises, of His New England Israel . . . Whereto There is Appendised, an Extract of Some Accounts, Concerning the Wonderful Success of the Glorious Gospel, in the East Indies. Boston: Printed by B. Green & J. Allen, 1700.

_____. The Present State of New England. Considered in a Discourse on the Necessities and Advantages of a Public Spirit in Every Man; Especially, at Such a Time as This. Made at the Lecture in Boston 20 d. 1. m. 1690. Upon the News of an Invasion by Bloody Indians and Frenchmen, Begun Upon Us. Boston: Printed by Samuel Green, 1690.

_____. Shaking Dispensations. An Essay Upon the Mighty Shakes, Which the Hand of Heaven, Hath Given, and Is Giving to the World. With Some Useful Remarks on the Death of the French King. Boston: Printed by B. Green, 1715.

_____. Souldiers Counselled and Comforted. A Discourse Delivered Unto Some Part of the Forces Engaged in the Just War of New England Againse the Northern & Eastern Indians. September 1, 1689. Boston: Printed by Samuel Green, 1689.

_____. The Stone Cut Out of the Mountain. And the Kingdom of God, in Those Maxims of It, That Cannot be Shaken. Exhibited in the Year, Seventeen Hundred & Sixteen. Boston: n.p., 1716.

_____. Suspiria Vinctorum. Some Account of the Condition to Which the Protestant Interest in the World Is at This Day Reduced. Boston: Printed and Sold by T. Fleet, 1726.

_____. Theopolis Americana. Boston: Printed by B. Green, 1710.

_____. Things for a Distress'd People to Think Upon. Boston: Printed by B. Green and F. Allen, 1696.

_____. Things to be Look'd For. Discourses on the Glorious Characters, With Conjectures on the Speedy Approaches of that State Which Is Reserved For the Church of God in the Latter Dayes. Cambridge: Printed by Samuel Green & Barth. Green, 1691.

_____. Things to be More Thought Upon. A Brief Treatise on the Injuries Offered Unto the Glorious and Only Saviour of the World; In Many Instances, Where in the Guilty Are Seldome Aware of Their Being so Injurious to the Eternal Son of God. With a More Particular Conviction of the Jewish and Arian Infidelity. Boston: Printed by Thomas Fleet, 1713.

_____. Three Letters From New England, Relating to the Controversy of the Present Time. London: Printed for Eman Matthews, 1721.

_____. The Triumphs of the Reformed Religion, in America. Boston: Printed by Benjamin Harris, and John Allen, 1691.

_____. Une Grand Voix du Ciel a La France. N. p.: n.p., 1725.

_____. The Wonderful Works of God Commemorated. Praises Bespoke for the God of Heaven, in a Thanksgiving Sermon; Delivered on December 19, 1689. Boston: Printed by S. Green, 1690.

Mayhew, Johnathan. Observations on the Charter and Conduct of the Society For the Propagation of the Gospel in Foreign Parts. Boston: Richard and Samuel Draper, 1763.

Memoirs of the Life of Mrs. Harriet Newell, Wife of the Rev. Samuel Newell, to Which is An
nexed a Sermon. Lexington, Ky.: T. T. Skilman, 1815.

Miller, Samuel. Memoirs of the Rev. John Rodgers, D.D. New York: Published by Whiting and
Watson, 1813.

Minutes of the General Assembly of the Presbyterian Church in the United States of America
From Its Organization A.D. 1789 to A.D. 1820 Inclusive. Philadelphia: Presbyterian
Board of Publication, 1847.

Minutes of the General Convention of Delegates Appointed by the Synod of New York and
Philadelphia and the General Association of Connecticut 1766-1755. Philadelphia:
Presbyterian Board of Publication and Sabbath School Work, 1904.

Minutes of the New York Baptist Association. 1791-1813.

Morse, Jedidiah. The Present Situation of Other Nations of the World, Contrasted With Our Own.
A Sermon Delivered at Charlestown, in the Commonwealth of Massachusetts, February
19, 1795; Being the Day Recommended by George Washington, President of the United
States of America, for Publick Thanksgiving and Prayer. Boston: Printed by Samuel Hall,
1795.

_____. A Sermon, Preached at Charlestown, November 29, 1798, on the Anniversary Thanksgiv-
ing in Massachusetts. With an Appendix, Disigned to Illustrate Some Parts of the Discourse;
Exhibiting Proofs of the Early Existence, Progress, and Deleterious Effects of French Intrigue and Influence in the United States. Boston: Printed by Samuel Hall, 1798.

New England First Fruits. London: Printed by R. O. and G. D., 1643.

The New York Missionary Magazine and Repository of Religious Intelligence. Vols. 1-4, 1800-1803.

The Panoplist. Vols. 1-16. 1805-1820.

Parish, Elijah and McClure, David. Memoirs of the Rev. Eleazar Wheelock D.D. Newburyport: Printed
by Edward Little, 1811.

Pascoe, C. F. and Tucker, H. W., eds. Classified Digest of the Records of the Society for the Propagation of the Gospel in Foreign Parts, 1701-1892. 5th ed. London: Published at the Society's
Office, 1895.

Penny, Norman, ed. The Journal of George Fox. 2 vols. With an Introduction by T. Edmud Harvey.
Philadelphia: The John C. Winston Co., 1911.

Pilcher, George William, ed. The Reverend Samuel Davies Abroad: The Diary of a Journey to England and Scotland, 1753-55. Urbana, Illinois: University of Illinois Press, 1967.

The Piscataqua Evangelical Magazine. Vols. 1-4. 1805-1808.

Princeton Theological Seminary. Archives. Society for Inquirey in Mission Correspondence.

The Records of the General Association of Ye Colony of Connecticut, Begun June 20, 1738, Ending June 19, 1799. Hartford: Press of the Case, Lockwood & Brainard Coimpany, 1888.

Records of the Presbyterian Church in the United States of America, Embracing the Minutes of the General Presbytery and General Synod 1706-1788. Philadelphia: J. B. Lippincott & Co., 1877.

Report of Rev. Mr. Puffer, to the Corresponding Secretary of the Evangelical Missionary Society. Also, the Report of the Trustees of Said Society at Their Annual Meeting, October 5, 1808. Worcester, Mass.: Isaiah Thomas, June, 1808.

Reynolds, Edward. A Further Accoumpt of the Progresse of the Gospel Amongst the Indians in New England, and of the Means Used Effectually to Advance the Same. Set Forth in Certaine Letters Sent From Thence for the Purpose of Printing the Scriptures in the Indian Tongue Into Which They Are Already Translated. With Which Letters Are Likewise Sent an Epitome of Some Exhortations Delivered by the Indians at a Fast, as Testimonies of Their Obedience to the Gospel. As Also Some Helps Directing to the Indians How to Improve Naturall Reason Unto the Knowledge of the True God. London: Printed by M. Simmons, 1659.

Schermerhorn, J. F., and Mills, S. J. A Correct View of That Part of the United States Which Lies West of the Alleghany Mountains, With Regard to Religion and Morals. Hartford, Conn.: P. B. Gleason and Co., Printers, 1814.

Sergeant, John. A Letter From the Revd. Mr. Sergeant of Stockbridge to Dr. Coleman of Boston; Containing Mr. Sergeant's Proposal of a More Effectual Method for the Education of Indian Children. Boston: Rogers and Fowle, 1743.

Shepard, Thomas. The Clear Sunshine of the Gospel Breaking Forth Upon the Indians in New England. Or, an Historicall Narration of Gods Wonderfull Workings Upon Sundry of the Indians, Both Chief Governors and Common People, in Bringing Them to a Willing and Desired Submission to the Ordinances of the Gospel; and Framing Their Hearts to an Earnest Inquirie After the Knowledge of God the Father, and of Jesus Christ the Saviour of the World. London: Printed by R. Cotes, 1648.

_____. The Day Breaking, if Not the Sun Rising of the Gospel With the Indians in New England. London: Printed by Rich Cotes, For Fulk Clifton, 1647.

Sherwood, Samuel. The Church's Flight Into the Wilderness: An Address on the Times, Delivered on a Public Occasion, January 17, 1776. New York: Printed by S. Louden, 1776.

Smith, Daniel and Mills, Samuel, Jr. Report of a Missionary Tour Through That Part of the United States Which Lies West of the Alleghany Mountains, 1814-1815. Andover: Flagg and Gould, 1815.

Spencer, Philip Jacob. Pia Desideria. Trans. by Theodore G. Tappert. Philadelphia: Fortress Press, 1964.

Spring, Gardiner. An Explanation of the Origin and Design of the New York Evangelical Missionary Society for Young Men. New York: n.p., 1817.

_____. Memoirs of the Rev. Samuel J. Mills. London: Printed for Francis Westley, 1820.

_____. Personal Reminiscences of the Life and Times of Gardiner Spring. 2 vols. New York: Charles Scribner & Co., 1866.

Staughton, William. The Baptist Mission in India. Containing a Narative of Its Rise, Progress, and Present Condition. A Statement of the Physical and Moral Character of the Hindoos, Their Cruelties, Tortures and Burnings, With a Very Interesting Description of Bengal, Intended to Animate to Missionary Cooperation. Philadelphia: Published by Hellings and Aitken, 1811.

Stiles, Ezra. Extract From the Itineraries and Other Miscellanies 1775-1794. With a Selection From His Correspondence. Edited by Franklin B. Dexter. New Haven: Yale University Press, 1914.

_____. The Literary Diary. Edited by Franklin B. Dexter. 3 vols. New York: Charles Scribner's Sons, 1901.

Thacher, Peter. A Brief Account of the Present State, Income, Expenses &c. of the Society for Propagating the Gospel Among the Indians and Others in North America. Boston: n.p., 1795.

_____. A Brief Account of the Present State of the Society for Propagating the Gospel Among the Indians and Others in North America. Boston: Published by Order of the Society, 1790.

_____. A Brief Account of the Society for Propagating the Gospel Among the Indians and Others in North America. Boston: n.p., 1798.

Tucker, H. W. and Pascoe, C. F., eds. Classified Digest of the Records of the Society For the Propagation of the Gospel in Foreign Parts, 1701-1892. 5th ed. London: Published at the Society's Office, 1895.

The Vehicle or New York Northwestern Christian Magazine. Vol. 1. 1814-1816.

The Virginia Evangelical and Literary Magazine. Vols. 1-3. 1818-1820.

Ward, Nathaniel. The Simple Cobler of Aggawam in America. London: Printed by J. D. and R. I., 1647.

Wheelock, Eleazar. A Brief Narrative of the Indian Charity School, in Lebanon in Connecticut, New England. Founded and Carried on by That Faithful Servant of God the Rev. Mr. Eleazar Wheelock. London: Printed by J. and W. Oliver, 1766.

_____. A Brief Narrative of the Indian Charity School, in Lebanon in Connecticut, New England. Founded and Carried on by That Faithful Servant of God the Rev. Mr. Eleazar Wheelock. London: Printed by J. and W. Oliver, 1766.

_____. A Continuation of the Narrative of the Indian Charity School. London: Printed by J. and W. Oliver, 1769.

_____. A Continuation of the Narrative of the Indian Charity School. Hartford: n.p., 1773.

_____. A Continuation of the Narrative of the State &c. of the Indian Charity School, at Lebanon, in Connecticut; From November 27, 1762, to September 3, 1765. Boston: Printed by Richard and Samuel Draper, 1765.

_____. A Continuation of the Narrative of the Indian Charity School, Begun in Lebanon. Hartford: Printed by Ebenezer Watson, 1775.

_____. A Continuation of the Narrative of the Indian Charity School, in Lebanon, in Connecticut; From the Year 1768 to the Incorporation of It With Dartmouth College, and Removal and Settlement of It in Hanover, in the Province of New Hampshire, 1771.

_____. A Plain and Faithful Narrative of the Original Design, Rise and Progress and Present State of the Indian Charity School at Lebanon, in Connecticut. Boston: Printed by Richard and Samuel Draper, 1763.

White, John. The Planters Plea. London: Printed by William Jones, 1630.

Whitfield, George. Journals. London: The Banner of Truth Trust, 1960.

Whitfield, Henry. The Light Appearing More and More Towards the Perfect Day. London: Printed by R. R. and E. M., 1651.

Winslow, Edward. The Glorious Progress of the Gospel Amongst the Indians in New England. London: Printed for Hannah Allen, 1649.

Wood, Leonard. History of the Andover Theological Seminary. Boston: James R. Osgood and Company, 1885.

Secondary Works

Alexander, James W. The Life of Archibald Alexander, D.D., LL.D. Philadelphia: Presbyterian Board of Publication, 1857.

Allen, Joseph, History of Worcester Association of Ministers. Boston: Nichols and Noyes, 1868.

Anderson, Charles A., Lefferts, Loetscher A., and Armstrong, Maurice W., eds. The Presbyterian Enterprise. Philadelphia: The Westminster Press, 1956.

Bacon, Leonard, Dutton, S. W. S., and Robinson, E. W., eds. Contributions to the Ecclesiastical History of Connecticut; Prepared Under the Direction of the General Association. New Haven: Published by William L. Kingsley, 1861.

Baird, Robert. Religion in America: Or, an Account of the Origin, Relation to the State, and Present Condition of the Evangelical Churches in the United States With Notices of the Unevangelical Denominations. New York: Harper and Brothers, Publishers, 1856.

Baird, Samuel J. A History of the New School, and of the Questions Involved in the Disruption of the Presbyterian Church in 1838. Philadelphia: Claxton, Remsen & Haffelfinger, 1868.

Barclay, Wade Crawford. Early American Methodism, 1769-1844. Vol. I, History of Methodist Missions. 3 vols. New York: The Board of Missions and Church Extension of the Methodist Church, 1949.

Barnes, W. W. The Southern Baptist Convention, 1845-1953. Nashville: Broadman Press, 1954.

Beaver, R. Pierce. All Loves Excelling. Grand Rapids: William B. Eerdmans Publishing Co., 1968.

_____. Church, State, and the American Indians. St. Louis: Concordia Publishing House, 1966.

_____. "The Concert For Prayer For Foreign Missions, an Early Venture in Ecumenical Action." The Ecumenical Review (July, 1948), pp. 420-427.

_____. Ecumenical Beginnings in Protestant World Missions. New York: Thomas Nelson & Sons, 1962.

_____. "Missionary Motivation Through Three Centuries." Jerald C. Brauer, ed. Reinterpretation in American History. Vol. V: Essays in Divinity. Edited by Jerald C. Brauer. Chicago: University of Chicago Press, 1968.

_____, ed. Pioneers in Mission. Grand Rapids, Mich.: William B. Eerdmans Publishing Co., 1966.

Benz, Ernest. "Pietist and Puritan Sources of Early Protestant World Missions." Church History, XX (June, 1951), 28-55.

Blake, Mortimer. A Centurial History of the Mendon Association. Boston: Published for the Association by Sewall Harding, 1853.

Blodgett, Harold. Samson Occum. Hanover, N.H.: Dartmouth College Publications, 1935.

Boorstin, Daniel J. America and the Image of Europe. Meridian Books. New York: World Publishing Company, 1960.

_____. The Americans: The Colonial Experience. New York: Vintage Books, 1958.

_____. The Lost World of Thomas Jefferson. Boston: Beacon Press, 1960.

Bourne, Edward E. The History of Wells and Kennebunk. Portland, Me.: B. Thurston & Co., 1875.

Bost, George H. "Samuel Davies, Colonial Revivalists and Champion of Religious Toleration." Unpublished Ph.D. Dissertation. University of Chicago, 1942.

Bradford, Alden. Memoir of the Life and Writing of Rev. Jonathan Mayhew, D.D. Boston: C. C. Little & Co., 1838.

Brown, Arthur Judson. One Hundred Years. Second Edition. Book One. New York: Fleming H. Revell Company, 1936.

Burrange, Henry S. A History of the Baptists in New England. Philadelphia: American Baptist Publication Society, 1894.

Chalmers, Harvey. Joseph Brant: Mohawk. East Lansing, Mich.: Michigan State University Press, 1955.

Clark, Joseph S. A Historical Sketch of the Congregational Churches in Massachusetts from 1620 to 1858. Boston: Congregational Board of Publication, 1858.

Cleveland, Catherine C. The Great Revival in the West 1797-1805. Chicago: University of Chicago Press, 1916.

Contributions to the Ecclesiastical History of Essex County, Mass. Boston: Congregational Board of Publication, 1865.

Crocker, Henry. History of the Baptists in Vermont. Bellows Falls, Vt.: Ph. H. Gobie Press, 1913.

Cunningham, Charles E. Timothy Dwight 1752-1817. New York: The Macmillan Company, 1942.

Dangerfield, George. The Awakening of American Nationalism. Harper Torchbooks. New York: Harper & Row Publishers, 1957.

Danielou, Jean. The Lord of History. Meridan Books. Cleveland and New York: The World Publishing Company, 1968.

Drury, Clifford Merrill. Presbyterian Panorama. Philadelphia: Board of Christian Education, 1952.

Elsbree, Oliver Wendell. The Rise of the Missionary Spirit in America, 1790-1815. Williamsport, Pa.: The Williamsport Printing and Binding Co., 1928.

Foote, William H. Sketches of North Carolina, Historical and Biographical. New York: Robert Carter, 1846.

Foote, William Henry. Sketches of Virginia Historical and Biographical. First Series. Richmond, Virginia: John Knox Press, 1966.

_____. Sketches of Virginia, Historical and Biographical. Second Series. 2nd ed. rev. Philadelphia: J. B. Lippincott & Co., 1856.

Foster, Frank Hugh. A Genetic History of the New England Theology. New York: Russell and Russell, Inc., 1963.

Furman, Wood. A History of the Charleston Association of Baptist Churches in the State of South Carolina; With an Appendix Containing the Principle Circular to the Churches. Charleston, S.C.: Press of J. Hoff, 1811.

Gaustad, Edwin Scott. The Great Awakening in New England. New York: Harper and Brothers, Publishers, 1957.

Gewehr, Wesley M. The Great Awakening in Vir ginia, 1740-1790. Durham, N.C.: Duke University Press, 1930.

Gibson, L. T. "Luther Rice's Contribution to Baptist History." Unpublished Ph.D. Dissertation. Temple University, 1944.

Gilsdorf, Joy Bourne. "The Puritan Apocalypse: New England Eschatology in the Seventeenth Century." Unpublished Doctoral Dissertation. Yale University, 1964.

Goen, C. C. "Jonathan Edwards: A New Departure in Eschatology." Church History. XXVIII (March, 1959), 25-40.

_____. Revivalism and Separatism in New England, 1740-1800. New Haven: Yale University Press, 1962.

Goodykoontz, Golin Brummitt. Home Missions on the American Frontier. Caldwell, Idaho: The Caxton Printers, Ltd., 1939.

Gookin, Frederick William. Daniel Gookin 1612-1687. Chicago: Privately printed, 1912.

Guild, R. A. Chaplain Smith and the Baptists: Or, the Life, Journals, Letters, and Addresses of the Rev. Hezekiah Smith, D.D., of Haverhill, Massachusetts, 1737-1805. Philadelphia: American Baptist Publication Society, 1885.

Haller, William. Foxe's Book of Martyrs and the Elect Nation. London: Jonathan Cape, 1963.

_____. The Rise of Puritanism. Harper Torchbooks. New York: Harper & Brothers, Publishers, 1957.

Hamilton, Kenneth G. John Ettwein and the Moravian Church During the Revolutionary Period. Bethlehem, Pa.: Times Publishing Co., 1940.

Hare, Lloyd C. M. Thomas Mayhew, Patriarch to the Indians (1593-1682). New York: D. Appleton and Co., 1932.

Haroutonian, Joseph. Piety Versus Moralism. New York: Henry Hold and Company, 1932.

Hawkins, Ernest. Historical Notices of the Missions of the Church of England in the North American Colonies, Previous to the Independence of the United States. London: B. Fellows, 1845.

Hawks, Francis L. Contributions to the Ecclesiastical History of the United States of America. 2 vols. New York: Published by Harper and Brothers, 1836.

Heyden, Roger. "William Staughton: Baptist Educator, Missionary Advocate, and Pastor." American Baptist Historical Society, Rochester, N.Y., 1965.

Heimert, Alan. "Puritanism, the Wilderness, and the Frontier." The New England Quarterly, XXVI (September, 1953), 355-362.

_____. Religion and the American Mind. Cambridge, Mass.: Harvard University Press, 1966.

Holmes, Thomas James. Cotton Mather: A Bibliography of His Works. 3 vols. Cambridge, Mass.: Harvard University Press, 1940.

Horsman, Regional. The Cause of the War of 1812. Perpetua Books. New York: A. S. Barnes & Company, 1962.

Hovey, Alvah. A Memoir of the Life and Times of the Rev. Isaac Backus, A. M. Boston: Gould and Lincoln, 1859.

Hudson, Winthrop S. Religion in America. New York: Charles Scribner's Sons, 1965.

Hunnewell, James F. The Society for Propagating the Gospel Among the Indians and Others in North America, 1787-1857. Boston: Printed for the Society, 1887.

Hutton, J. E. A History of Moravian Missions. London: Moravian Publication Office, 1922.

Jensen, Merrill. The New Nation. New York: Vintage Books, 1965.

Jones, Rufus M. The Quakers in the American Colonies. New York: W. W. Norton & Company, 1966.

Kellaway, William. The New England Company 1649-1776. New York: Barnes & Noble, Inc., 1961.

Keller, Charles Roy. The Second Great Awakening in Connecticut. New Haven: The Yale University Press, 1942.

Kelsey, Rayner Wickersham. Friends and the Indians 1655-1917. Philadelphia: Associated Executive Committee of Friends on Indian Affairs, 1917.

Klingberg, Frank J. Anglican Humanitarianism in Colonial New York. Philadelphia: The Church Historical Society, 1940.

Knappen, M. M. Tudor Puritanism. Chicago: University of Chicago Press, 1939.

Koch, G. Adolf. Republican Religion: The American Revolution and the Cult of Reason. Studies in Religion and Culture. American Religion Series VII. New York: Henry Holt and Company, 1933.

Latourette, Kenneth Scott. A History of the Expansion of Christianity. 7 vols. New York: Harper and Row, Publishers, 1937-45.

Lennox, H. J. "Samuel Kirland's Mission to the Iroquois." Unpublished Ph.D. Dissertation. University of Chicago, 1932.

Loetscher, Lefferts A., Armstrong, Maurice W., and Anderson, Charles A., eds. The Presbyterian Enterprise. Philadelphia: The Westminister Press, 1956.

Lorett, Richard. The History of the London Missionary Society, 1795-1895. London: Henry Frowde, 1899.

Love, William Deloss. Samson Occum and the Christian Indians of New England. Boston: The Pilgrim Press, 1899.

Lumkin, William L. Baptist Foundations in the South. Nashville, Tennessee: Broadman Press, 1961.

Lynd, S. W. Memoir of the Rev. William Staughton, D.D. Boston: Lincoln, Edmonds & Co., 1834.

McCallum, James Dow, ed. The Letters of Eleazar Wheelock's Indians. Hanover, N.H.: Dartmouth College Publication, 1932.

McConnell, Francis J. John Wesley. Nashville: Abingdon Press, 1939.

McDonald, Forrest. The Formation of the American Republic: 1776-1790. A Pelican Book. Baltimore, Maryland: Penguin Books, Inc., 1965.

Maclean, John. History of the College of New Jersey. 3 vols. Philadelphia: J. B. Lippincott & Co., 1877.

McNeill, John T. Modern Christian Movements. Harper Torchbooks. Philadelphia: The Westminister Press, 1954.

Marty, Martin E. The Infidel. Living Age Books. New York: World Publishing Company, 1961.

Maxwell, William. A Memoir of the Rev. John H. Rice. D.D. Philadelphia: Published by J. Whetham, 1835.

Mead, Sidney E. The Lively Experiment. New York: Harper & Row, Publishers, 1963.

Memoir of Rev. Joseph Badger. Hudson, Ohio: Sawyer, Ingersoll and Co., 1851.

Mercer, Jesse. A History of the Georgia Baptist Association. Washington, Geo.: n.p., 1838.

Merk, Frederick. Manifest Destiny and Mission. New York: Vintage Books, 1966.

Miller, John C. The Federalist Era: 1789-1801. New American Nation Series. New York: Harper and Row, 1960.

Miller, Perry. Errand Into the Wilderness. Harper Torchbooks. New York: Harper and Row, Publishers, 1964.

_____. Jonathan Edwards. New York: Meridian Books, 1959.

_____. The New England Mind: From Colony to Province. Boston: Beacon Press, 1961.

_____. The New England Mind: The Seventeenth Century. Boston: Beacon Press, 1961.

_____. Orthodoxy in Massachusetts 1630-1650. Boston: Beacon Press, 1959.

Millett, Joshua. A History of the Baptist in Maine. Portland: Printed by Charles Day & Co., 1845.

Morison, Samuel Eliot. The Maritime History of Massachusetts. Boston: Houghton Mifflin Co., 1941.

Mosteller, James D. A History of the Kokee Baptist Church in Georgia. Ann Arbor, Michigan: Edwards Brothers, Inc., 1952.

Niebuhr, Richard. The Kingdom of God in America. Harper Torchbooks. New York: Harper and Brothers, 1959.

Parrington, Vernon L. Main Currents in American Thought. 2 vols. New York: Harcourt, Brace & World, Inc., 1927.

Pascoe, C. F. Two Hundred Years of the S. P. G. An Historical Account of the Society for the Propagation of the Gospel in Foreign Parts, 1701-1900. London: Published at the Society's Office, 1901.

Philbrick, Francis B. The Rise of the West: 1754-1830. Harper Torchbooks, the University Library. New York: Harper & Row, Publishers, 1965.

Punchard, George. History of Congregationalism From About A.D. 250 to the Present Time. 5 vols. Boston: Congregational Publishing Society, 1880.

Quistorp, Heinrich. Calvin's Doctrine of Last Things. Translated by Harold Knight. London: Lutterworth Press, 1955.

Richardson, Leon B. History of Dartmouth College. Hanover, N.H.: Dartmouth College Publications, 1932.

_____. An Indian Preacher in England. Hanover, N.H.: Dartmouth College Publications, 1933.

Rooy, Sidney H. The Theology of Missions in the Puritan Tradition. Grand Rapids: William B. Eerdmans Publishing Co., 1965.

Rossiter, Clinton. 1787: The Grand Convention. Mentor Book. New York: The New American Library, 1968.

Schaff, Philip, et al., eds. American Church History. 13 vols. New York: Charles Scribner's Sons, 1894-1923.

Schwarze, Edmund. History of the Moravian Missions Among Southern Indian Tribes in the United States. Bethlehem, Pennsylvania. Times Publishing Co., Printers, 1923.

Semple, Robert B. A History of the Rise and Progress of the Baptists in Virginia. Richmond: Published by the Author, 1810.

Shedd, Clarence P. Two Centuries of Student Christian Movements. New York: Association Press, 1934.

Smith, H. Shelton, Handy, Robert T., and Loetscher, Lefferts A., eds. American Christianity. 2 vols. New York: Charles Scribner's Sons, 1960-63.

Smith, James Ward, and Jamison, A. Leland, eds. Religion in American Life. Princeton Studies in American Civilization, No. 5. 4 vols. Princeton, N.J.: Princeton University Press, 1961.

Smith, Joseph. Old Redstone: Or, Historical Sketches of Western Presbyterianism: Its Early Ministers, Its Perilous Times, and Its First Records. Philadelphia: Lippincott, Granbo & Co., 1854.

Spalding, George. Historical Discourses Delivered on the Hundredth Anniversary of the Piscataqua Association of Ministers. Dover, N.H.: Morning Star Job Printing Office, 1882.

Sprague, William B., ed. Annals of the American Pulpit. 11 vols. New York: Robert Carter & Brothers, 1877.

_____. The Life of Jedidiah Morse, D.D. New York: Anson D. F. Randolph & Co., 1874.

Stauffer, Veron. New England and the Bavarian Illuminati. Vol. LXXXII: Studies in History, Economics and Public Law. Edited by the Faculty of Political Science of Columbia University. New York: The Columbia University Press, 1918.

Strong, William E. The Story of the American Board. Boston: The Pilgrim Press, 1910.

Sweet, William Warren. Makers of Christianity From John Cotten to Lyman Abbott. New York: Harper & Brothers, Publishers, 1942.

_____. Religion in the Development of American Culture 1765-1840. New York: Charles Scribner's Sons, 1952.

_____. Religion on the American Frontier. 4 vols. Vol. I. The Baptists. New York: Henry Holt & Co., 1931; Vol. II: The Presbyterians. New York: Harper & Brothers, Publishers, 1936; Vol. III: The Congregationalists. Chicago: University of Chicago Press, 1939; Vol. IV: The Methodists. Chicago: University of Chicago Press, 1941.

Tanis, James. Dutch Calvinistic Pietism in the Middle Colonies. The Hague: Martin Nijhoff, 1967.

Thompson, H. P. Into All Lands: The History of the Society for the Propagation of the Gospel in Foreign Parts, 1701-1950. London: Society for Promoting Christian Knowledge, 1951.

_____. Thomas Bray. London: S. P. C. K., 1954.

Thompson, Mack. Moses Brown, Reluctant Reformer, Chapel Hill, N.C.: University of North Carolina Press, 1962.

Tolles, Fredrick B. Meeting House and Counting House. New York: W. W. Norton & Company, 1955.

Torbet, Robert G. Venture of Faith. Philadelphia: Judson Press, 1955.

Torrance, T. F. "The Eschatology of the Reformation." Eschatology. Scottish Journal of Theology Occasional Papers No. 2. Edinburgh: Oliver and Boyd Ltd., n.d.

_____. Kingdom and Church. Edinburgh. Oliver and Boyd, 1956.

Trinterud, Leonard J. The Forming of an American Tradition. Philadelphia: The Westminster Press, 1949.

_____. "The Origins of Puritanism." Church History, XX (March, 1951), 37-79.

Tuveson, Ernest Lee. Redeemer Nation. Chicago: University of Chicago Press, 1968.

Vail, Albert L. The Morning Hour of American Baptist Missions. Philadelphia: American Baptist Publication Society, 1907.

Van Halzema, Dick Lucas. "Samuel Hopkins 1721-1803, New England Calvinist." Unpublished Doctoral Dissertation. Union Theological Seminary, New York, N.Y., 1956.

Van Vechten, Jacob. Memoirs of John M. Mason, D.D., S.T.P. New York: Robert Carter and Brothers, 1858.

Vaughan, Alden T. New England Frontier: Puritan and Indian, 1620-1675. Boston: Little, Brown and Company, 1965.

Walker, Williston. The Creeds and Platforms of Congregationalism. New York: Charles Scribner's Sons, 1893.

_____. A History of the Congregational Churches in the United States. 5th ed. New York: Charles Scribner's Sons, 1900.

_____. Ten New England Leaders. New York: Silver, Burdett and Company, 1901.

Ward, Harry M. The United Colonies of New England — 1643-1690. New York: The Vintage Press, 1961.

Wayland, Francis. A Memoir of the Life and Labors of the Rev. Adoniram Judson, D.D. 2 vols. Boston: Phillips, Sampson and Co., 1853.

Weinlick, John R. Count Zinzendorf. New York: Abingdon Press, 1956.

Weis, Frederick L. "The New England Company of 1649 and Its Missionary Enterprises." Colonial Society of Massachusetts Publications. XXXVIII (1906), 134-218.

Wendell, Barrett. Cotton Mather: The Puritan Priest. With an Introduction by Alan Heimert. A Harbinger Book. New York: Harcourt, Brace & World, Inc., 1963.

Whelpley, Samuel. The Triangle. A Series of Numbers Upon Three Theological Points, Enforced From Various Pulpits in the City of New York. New York: John Wiley, 1832.

Williamson, G. R. Memoir of the Rev. David Abeel, D.D. Late Missionary to China. New York: Robert Carter, 1848.

Williams, George H. Wilderness and Paradise in Christian Thought. New York: Harper and Brothers, Publishers, 1962.

Winslow, Ola Elizabeth. Jonathan Edwards 1703-1758. New York: Collier Books, 1961.

Woodson, Hortense. Giant in the Land. Nashville: Broadman Press, 1950.

Wright, Conrad. The Beginnings of Unitarianism in America. Boston: Starr King Press, 1955.

Wright, Stephen. History of the Shaftsburg Baptist Association. N. p.: n.p., n.d.

About the Author

Charles Leonard Chaney was born near Alexander, Texas, April 11, 1934, the son of T. C. Chaney and Frances Marie Mitchell Chaney. He was married to Fannie Estella Ingram on December 21, 1951, and their children are Carey, Bart and Gena. He is a graduate of Howard Payne College in Brownwood, Texas, and has earned two professional and two graduate degrees. These are the Bachelor of Divinity and Master of Theology from Southern Baptist Seminary in Louisville, Kentucky, and the Master of Arts and Doctor of Philosophy from the University of Chicago. His major field was the history of missions, and this book is based on his doctoral thesis, *God's Glorious Work: The Theological Foundations of the Early Missionary Societies in America, 1787-1817.* He taught at the Northern Baptist Seminary in Chicago for two semesters. He writes for denominational periodicals and scholarly journals, and is author of the book, *Take: Essential Principles of the Full and Meaningful Life.* He has served as the pastor of Baptist churches in Texas, Kentucky and Illinois. Since 1972, he has been director of the Church Extension Division of the Illinois Baptist State Association in Springfield, Illinois. This is the parent body for Southern Baptist congregations in the state.